ENCOUNTER WITH ENLIGHTENMENT

SUNY series in Modern Japanese Philosophy
Peter J. McCormick, editor

ENCOUNTER WITH ENLIGHTENMENT

A Study of Japanese Ethics

Robert E. Carter

Foreword
by
Yuasa Yasuo

STATE UNIVERSITY OF NEW YORK PRESS

Cover art: Ma Lin. *Sunset Landscape.* Courtesy of the Nezu Museum, Nezu Institute of Fine Arts, Tokyo.

Published by
State University of New York Press, Albany

For information, address State University of New York Press, 90 State Street, Suite 700, Albany, NY 12207

Production by Marilyn P. Semerad
Marketing by Fran Keneston

Library of Congress Cataloging-in-Publication Data

Carter, Robert Edgar, 1937–
    Encounter with enlightenment : a study of Japanese ethics / Robert E. Carter; foreword by Yuasa Yasuo.
        p. cm.
    Includes index.
    ISBN 0-7914-5017-1 (alk. paper) — ISBN 0-7914-5018-X (pbk. : alk. paper)
    1. Ethics, Japanese. 2. Enlightenment—Japan. I. Title.

BJ970.C37 2001
170'.952—dc21
                                                                                00-046356

10 9 8 7 6 5 4 3 2 1

For Deanie,

Who stood steadfastly beside me through the dark days of grief and illness, and with whom I rediscovered the lightness of love and joy once more.
For being there . . .

Contents

———

Foreword   xi

Acknowledgments   xxxi

Introduction: Contrasts and Ideals   1
   Many "Easts," Many "Wests"   5
   The Critical Path   6

1. The "Do Nothing" and the Pilgrim:
   Two Approaches to Ethics   11
      On the Nature of the Will   14
      The Transformation of the Everyday World   16
      The Will in Eastern Thought   18
      Wu-Wei and Non-doing   23
      Evil   24
      On Human-Heartedness   26
      A Radical Interdependence   27
      The Morality of Enlightenment   29
      Conclusion   31

2. The Significance of Shintōism for Japanese Ethics   35
      The Importance of the Shintō Perspective   36
      Shrine Shintō (Common Shintō)   39
      In the Beginning   40
      Kami and Evil   43
      Attitudes, Virtues, and Rituals   47
      The Connection to Ancestors   49
      The Way to the Future   50

Reflective Epilogue   53
The Ecological Dimension   56
Ethics and Nature   61
Shintō and Zen   62

3. Confucianism and Japanese Ethics   63
   The Confucian Self   65
   Original Human Goodness   67
   The Importance of Sincerity   69
   Self as Field   70
   Spontaneity   72
   Confucianism in Japan   73

4. Buddhism and Japanese Ethics   77
   Introduction   77
   The Beginnings   79
   Buddhism and Morality   80
   The Ground of Morality   86
   What Happened to Nirvāna?   88
   Ethics and Enlightenment   90
   The Bodhisattva   92
   The Path of the Bodhisattva   94

5. Zen Buddhism and Ethics   99
   Zen and Enlightenment   101
   Evil and Zen   105
   The Cat Again   108
   Seeing into One's Own Nature   109
   Why Should One Be Moral?   110
   Cats! Cats! Cats!   112
   Zen and Nature   115
   And If the Cat Were Not a Cat?   117

6. The Fundamentals: Modern Japanese Ethics   123
   Ningen   126
   The One and the Many   128
   Ethics   130
   Toward Nothingness   132
   Sincerity   135
   Ethics as Contextual   136
   The Importance of the Family   143
   The Complexity of Climate   144

7. An Ethics of Transformation: Nishida, Yuasa, and Dōgen   149
    The Need to Differentiate   158
    Why the One Differentiates   159
    The Nature of Good Conduct   163
    From Self to No-self   165
    On Self-cultivation   170
    Dōgen   174
    Dōgen on the "Now"   179

Conclusion: The Mutuality of Learning in a Global Village   183
    Social Ethics   188
    Final Reflections   194
    Ecological Ethics, East and West   198

Notes   203

Selected Bibliography   231

Index   245

Foreword

———

INTRODUCTION

It was a great honor for me to have received a request from Professor Robert E. Carter, the author of the present volume, who asked me to freely offer my comments on his book. A primary reason I felt thankful for this request is because this book deals with Japanese ethics. The cultural differences between the East and the West are not much of a problem in those fields of philosophy such as epistemology and logic where intellectual judgment is fundamental. Unlike these disciplines, ethical traditions are born out of the ēthos and mores that have been uniquely nurtured and accumulated in the long histories and cultures within the natural environments of East and West. The contemporary period is one in which East and West have deeply connected with each other on an equal footing. I don't think that there has ever been a more crucial period for them to understand one another correctly. It would be beyond my pleasure if my comments prove to be even a little useful to the Western reader.

Any present situation in history is given direction by, and is always delimited by, some power arising from the past. Ordinarily, we go so far as to feel this power only through the changing conditions of material culture, but what actually governs us internally over a long period of time is the psychological and intellectual power of the tradition. Today, however, we are placed in busy situations with an excess of information and are simply driven to live daily life. We are therefore incapable of becoming aware of the power of the tradition that is operative in history. The author's eyes are cast into the depths of the spiritual tradition of this "invisible" Japan. I was also greatly impressed by the author's

———

Translated by Shigenori Nagatomo and Pamela Winfield, Dept. of Religion, Temple University.

xi

concern for the intellectual confusion and moral decay that we are facing today, which goes beyond the distinctions between East and West. I have exactly the same concerns as those of the author. In spite of the enormous difference in cultural traditions between the United States and Japan, we are faced with the common task of dealing with the intellectual confusion and decadence of contemporary civilization.

THE *BOOK OF CHANGES* AND THE ENLIGHTENMENT OF PERSONALITY

What piqued my interest in chapter one was the author's description of the fundamental stance of Eastern ethics, which he deals with primarily in terms of Daoist "non-action" (無為, Chin., *wú wéi:* Jap., *mui*). In Eastern ethics, there is no dichotomy between good and evil. This distinction is always relative and in reality there is no absolute good or absolute evil, for such notions are nothing but the fabrication of our intellectual logic. The ground out of which the distinction arises in actuality lies in the depths of our own mind. This is what the idea of "non-action" teaches us. "Non-action" doesn't mean not to act, but rather means to reach an enlightened state of personality (人格: *jinkaku*) in the interior of one's heart and soul *(psyché)*. This, I think, is a fundamental point that differentiates Eastern ethics from the Western ethical tradition which emphasizes will and action directed to the external world. The Japanese word *"jinkaku"* [translated here as "personality"] signifies one whose psychological personality and moral character are fused together.

Where can we find the origin of the Asian tradition that denies the good-evil dichotomy? In order to respond to this question, here I feel it is necessary to tell the Western reader about the *Book of Changes* (易経; Chin., *Yìjīng;* Jap., *Ekikyō*). The historical origin of this book is believed to go as far back as the divination practices and customs of the Yān dynasty which perished in the fourteenth century B.C.E. It served as the philosophical origin for both Confucianism and Daoism and it was most respected as a classic by the Chinese philosophers until modern times. It is said that Confucius treated the *Book of Changes* with utter deference and that he always attempted divination in his later years. Confucius's deference toward the *Book of Changes* informs us that he regarded it as a book of ethics that teaches one how to live one's life. Many modern people, however, fail to understand the reason why the *Book of Changes* is a book dealing with ethics. For the purposes of comparison with a Western classic text, it would not be inappropriate, at least for now, to contrast it with the Old Testament. According to Exodus, Yahweh gave Moses the Ten Commandments on Mt. Sinai and

Moses pledged to observe them. Ethics, then, were established as a mutually binding contract between God and humanity, which presupposes a relationship between two personalities. Out of this relationship arose clear imperatives for prohibition and action. By contrast, there is no personality in the *Book of Changes* who gives imperatives. According to legend, a certain god of the mythological age invented the hexagrams, but it is not he who gives the answer to divination. As it is said that Confucius respected "Heaven" (天; Chin., *tiān;* Jap., *ten*), while Lǎozǐ respected "Dao" (道; Chin., *dào;* Jap., *dō*), that which gives an answer is probably a sacred power, commensurate with the "Heaven" or the "Dao," that envelops the cosmos. A cautionary remark, however, is in order here, for Lǎozǐ refers to the Dao as originally having no name; rather, it is like a mother who gives birth to everything. When one faces the *Book of Changes* then, one poses a question concerning what path one ought to take to the nameless activity that gives birth to, and nurtures, everything.

In my judgment, the best Western counterpart to the *Book of Changes* is the teaching of "know thyself" which Socrates received from Apollo. To one who poses a question to it, the *Book of Changes* describes the "situation" that one is placed in at the "present." A present situation means the existential situation one is facing, in which the inquirer is placed in his/her life "now," i.e., the time of issuing the question. What is important here is that the answer is given only once. Moreover, it is not issued as an imperative. Psychologically speaking, one receives the answer by intuition, not by intellectual judgment or by inference. Furthermore, the *Book of Changes* does not give specific instructions to the inquirer. One is left to decide freely as to how to interpret an answer and how to act. Socrates used oracles by appealing to his *Daimōn* to minister to his own soul *(psyché)* and placed this practice at the foundation for his action. Before his last trial, his *Daimōn* didn't give him any instruction. This is because the issue was for Socrates himself to decide. This attitude completely agrees with the spirit of the *Book of Changes.* Socrates related to Crito the day before his death that "it is not respectful just to live, but to live well is respectful." To live well means to die well. This is the way of human living and this is the foundation for philosophy.

As seen above, the *Book of Changes* is, first and foremost, a book of ethics in that it teaches "how one ought to live life in a given time." Here we need to take note of the fact that it is also a book of metaphysics. The Chinese and Japanese term "metaphysical" (形而上者; Chin., *xíng-ér-shàng-zhě;* Jap., *keijijōsha*) is derived from a commentary Confucius is said to have written (繋辞伝; Chin., *jìcífù;* Jap., *keijiden*). Although this term is used to translate *meta-physica,* it has a slightly different meaning. That which is metaphysical does not possess visible form but exists prior to all that is in the world and transcends it. At the same time, however, it is continually emanating into the world. It is an incessant life-activity that constantly transforms all that exists in the world. The *"ér"* that appears in the phrase *"xíng-ér-shǎng-zhě"* means both "and" and "yet," and connotes a relation of transcendence and immanence. Seen in this manner, the *Book of Changes* recognizes the essence of human nature as "being-in-nature" (自然内存在, *shizennai sonzai*).

In summation, then, the *Book of Changes* teaches how the human being ought to live his/her life in nature through one's own decisions at given times of life. We can find the fundamental spirit of the *Book of Changes* in the statement: "the *Book of Changes* is a noble[1] man's way for dealing with difficulty and distress." This means that one who is worthy of moral respect attempts divination when one is troubled at a turning point of life. The nobility of the inquirer's moral personality appears in the kind of decision he/she makes after performing the divination. There are many cases reported in history of people who experienced failure because they believed in the "answer" that the *Book of Changes* bestowed, but it is not its fault. What it seeks is for the self to become an enlightened personality who is in communication with "Heaven," i.e., the cosmic mind/heart.

SHINTŌISM AND THE JAPANESE COLLECTIVE UNCONSCIOUS

In chapter Two, the author reflects on the historical role which Shintōism played in the Japanese ethical tradition. He remarks that nature is *kami* (神). Many foreign people who visit Kyoto and Nara may be led to believe that Japan is only a Buddhist country. As Shintō shrines are surrounded by the trees in forests and are designed to be part of nature, they may not attract people's attention. The philosopher Watsuji Tetsurō (和辻哲郎, 1889–1960), who is often cited in this book, called the characteristics of Japanese culture "multi-layered" (重層的, *jūsōteki*). Although history continually undergoes change, all that is newly introduced to Japan does not obviate things of the old, but rather, places itself upon the latter. In other words, things of old, like the annual layers of a tree, continue to exist and work in the center. The author likens this process to a bamboo grove whose root system has taken deep root beneath the earth and which connects every tree with each other. It is a deep, flexible structure that can resiliently re-

spond to earthquakes and storms without facing the danger of destruction. The heart/mind of Shintōism has taken root deep in the
great earth, even now supporting the Japanese people's sentiment of
life. We might say that it is the deep structure of the Japan's ethnic
collective unconscious.

Among Western intellectuals, the British-born Lafcadio Hearn
(1850–1904) was probably the first to recognize the significance of
Shintōism when he visited Japan about one hundred years ago. His
Japanese name is Koizumi Yakumo (小泉 八雲). He lived in the city of
Matsue for a while, where Izumo Shrine is located. There he came to
know that Japanese spirituality was alive. He loved the Japanese legends
and folklore that contained spirituality and introduced them to the
West. We can also probably mention the more recent example of the
well-known French anthropologist, Lévi-Strauss. He observed and inves-
tigated the customs of mountain and fishing villages as well as craftsmen's
techniques in various parts of Japan, and remarked that Japan is an
extremely rare country among the highly industrialized nations in the
world where the ancient animism is still alive. One cannot comprehend
the tradition of Japanese people's mind/heart simply by observing the
surface of politics and economy.

Originally, Shintōism was a faith of the mythological age stretching back several thousand years. Its essence lies in the mind/heart prior
to faith based on intellectual dogmas. Myths are the womb out of which
many civilized religions of the world emerged. There, one discovers a
religiosity itself prior to religion. The term "religion" is derived from
the Latin word *relegere,* meaning "to reunite" or "to join." Religiosity
joins the self with the sacred and refers to the mind/heart that always
repeats this act. This is the characteristic of the people's mind/heart in
the mythological age, where there was no logic to distinguish "I" from
"others"(the making of distinctions which is integral to theorized, intellectual dogmas. In Shintōism we can find an unconditional tolerance
that accepts all that is sacred. Various peoples throughout the world
once lived with spiritualities of prehistoric periods no different from
this.

The *kami* of Shintōism have no form whatsoever. In this respect,
they do not differ from the *Book of Changes.* Ordinarily, the existence of
kami is symbolized by the placement of a mirror and twigs of a tree with
white strips of paper tied to them. If nature itself is kami in the inner
sanctuary of a shrine, this symbolic expression is an appropriate one
and must be taken as a matter of course. Shrines originally designate
a place where an earth-mind dwells; the so-called "spirit of the land"
(*genius loci*) or spirituality dwelling in a place is called *kami.* To contrast

it with a Western counterpart, it probably corresponds to the sacred regions of the ancient Celtic and German peoples or to the dolmens of the prehistoric period. In Japan, however, shrines are not historical sites, but continue to work even today in regional communities as psychological centers for people's everyday life. The author maintains that we can find in Shintō thought a principle for deep ecology necessary for the contemporary period. For the human is originally a "being-in-nature" and nature is the mother of all life. It is what Plato calls "the world soul" *(anima mundi)*. Consequently, we must say that the destruction of nature is tantamount to matricide. Might we not discern the original ground for morality there?

It is through the arts in particular that we can find in concrete form the way in which traditional Asian cultures understand the relationship between nature and humanity. Here I shall mention two examples: landscape painting and mountain-water painting associated with Zen. In the woodblock prints of Mt. Fuji by Katsushika Hokusai (葛飾北斎, 1760–1849), for example, it is sufficient for only the mountain to be depicted without the presence of man. Even if a man is painted, it is a mere point in the scenery. In the brush and ink style of mountain-water painting, the black color of the India ink and the empty space of the underlying blank paper or silk accomplish the same effect and purpose. Zòng Bǐng (宋 火丙, 375–443), a Chinese painter who wrote the first essay on landscape painting in human history, states in the beginning of his book, *A Prelude to Mountain-Water Paintings* (*Huàshānshuǐxù*, 画山水序): "although scenery has physical form, it tends towards the spiritual." The "spiritual" here, in keeping with the philosophy of the *Book of Changes* and Lǎozǐ, refers to the incessant activity of exchange between the *yīn* and the *yáng ki*-energy (氣; Chin., *qì*). *Ki*-energy designates the life activity that connects nature and humanity in a correlative micro/macro-cosmic relationship. The Eastern arts seek to form a personality that is able to apprehend this kind of spiritual *ki*-energy. Watsuji Testurō's theory of influence of climate in *Climate and Culture,* for example, expresses a philosophy which attempts to grasp the essence of the human as this kind of "being-in-nature."

The author brings to the reader's attention the important significance of the Shintō shrine, namely that it is surrounded by trees in a forest. Ancient people believed that trees in nature were sacred and spiritual. In the West, too, there existed the Germanic mythological tradition of worshipping trees that persisted until the medieval age.[2] Some Japanese Shintō shrines have origins that go back more than several thousand years, and there are many other shrines that were built anew in each period in history. Meiji Shrine, located in the heart of Tokyo and which used to have Emperor Meiji (明治天皇, 1852–1912) as its worshipping priest, is located in a large forest whose trees were gathered from all over Japan. When one examines the structures of old shrines with such historical origins, it is possible to recognize, in concrete form, ideas reflective of the mythological age. Ōmiwa Shrine in Nara for example, as the author mentions, is located in the foothills of Mt. Miwa, while the mountain itself is regarded as the body of the *kami*. The physical structure of the shrine is simply a building where people worship and pray to the *kami*. Moreover, the visible mountain which people can see with their physical eyes is not the *kami*. At the summit of this mountain, there is a ceremonial platform built of stone called the "innermost sanctuary" (奥宮, *okumiya*). The physical structure at the foothill is called the people-palace (里宮, *satomiya*) where people dwell. People can enter the innermost sanctuary only when conducting special ceremonies. At the time of a ceremony, the *kami*-spirit descends to the sacred region in response to people's prayer. There are many examples of this type of shrine. Okinoshima, for example, is an island bound by imposing cliffs on all sides that floats in isolation in the Korean Straights. There is no physical structure here for a shrine, and it is strictly forbidden to land on this island on ordinary days. For people who want to worship the *kami* of this island, there is Munakata Shrine on the coast of Kyūshū, which is fifty kilometers away from Okinoshima Island. Kutakashima Island is another *kami* island that is also worshipped from afar, namely, from a sacred region on Okinawa Island.

Here I must touch on the destiny of Shintōism since the modern period. In the middle of the nineteenth century, Japan's doors were forced open by the powerful pressures of the great Western nations. The Meiji government that was inaugurated at that time separated Buddhism and Shintōism, and established state authority over the shrines by directly controlling and managing them. Minakata Kumakusu (南方熊楠, 1867–1941), a prominent natural historian in Japan who was also known to Europe and the United States, opposed the institutionalization of this policy and went so far as to appeal directly to the Emperor. He believed that such a policy was an act of destroying the mind/heart of the great earth. He was probably the world's first pioneer in the movement to protect the environment. The reason that the new government forcefully executed this policy of state over nature despite the objection raised by the people was because there was no psychological symbol greater than the Emperor who could ideologically unite Japan as a modern nation. The Emperor was considered the descendant of a *kami* of the mythological age (i.e., the Sun Goddess

Amaterasu, 天照大神). The seed for modern Japanese nationalism was sown at this time.

Robert Bellah makes the following observation at the end of his essay on Watsuji Tetsurō's cultural nationalism. Japan is almost the only nation in the world in which the once ubiquitous monarchies of the Bronze Age persisted until modern times. Bellah distinguishes the various nations of history between the ancient type and the historical type. The latter historical type of nation refers to empires that subjugate other ethnic peoples under its dominion, such as the ancient Mesopotamian, Egyptian, Roman, and Maurian dynasties of India as well as the various dynasties in China. The modern Empire of Great Britain as well belongs to this category. The entire history of humankind has been shaped by these empires. As the giant empires bulldozed smaller nations in the historical process, the smaller nations disappeared from history. Considering this fact, I feel that it is a miracle, born out of human history, that Japanese Shintōism is still alive and active today.

CONFUCIAN ETHICS AND JAPAN

In chapter three the author deals with Confucianism. Although Confucianism is the characteristic Asian ethic, it was difficult for Japan to accept it without modification since Confucianism developed in connection with the historical characteristics of Chinese society. I think this requires a historical comment for the sake of the Western reader.

Ancient Confucianism in China had two pillars: political ethics and family ethics. In the former, "loyalty" to the emperor (忠; Chin., *zhōng*; Jap., *chū*) was considered to be the cardinal virtue—the emperor who followed the "Mandate of Heaven" (天命; Chin., *tiānmìng*; Jap., *tenmei*) governed the country therewith. In the latter pillar of family ethics, the fundamental virtue was considered to be "filial piety" (孝; Chin., *xiào*; Jap., *kō*) with its psychological nucleus of ancestor worship. Japan was introduced to Confucianism along with Buddhism during the period of national unification (around the seventeenth century C.E.), but Confucianism was not linked to the family system. The Japanese family system at the time took, in principle, the form of equal matriarchy and patriarchy, and unlike China, did not regard patriarchy as possessing singular importance. In politics, too, Confucianism didn't take root in Japanese soil, since Japan did not incorporate the Chinese civil examination system (科挙; Chin., *kējǔ*; Jap., *kakyo*).

It is probably accurate to say that Japanese Confucianism is primarily a new Confucianism that was developed after the Sòng dynasty (tenth–thirteenth century), i.e., the so-called Neo-Confucianism, or alternatively *riki* philosophy[3] (理気哲学; Chin., *lǐqì*). Neo-Confucianism is represented by Zhūzǐ (朱子, 1130–1200; Jap., Shushi) and Wáng Yángmíng (王陽明, 1472–1536; Jap., Ōyōmei). The fundamental contention of this philosophy is found in the idea that "Sagehood can be achieved through learning" (i.e., anyone can become a sage through one's efforts). The characteristic of Neo-Confucianism then, is the emphasis on efforts to nurture an ethical personality as an individual. That is, to use the author's terminology, its goal is to establish an enlightened personality. In this connection, it needs to be noted that Neo-Confucian ethics incorporated meditation methods as a result of Buddhist and Daoist influence. They called this method "quiet sitting" (静坐; Chin., *jìngzuò*; Jap., *seiza*) and its content is similar to Zen meditation. In this meditation method, the Confucian system of ethical virtues is linked to the psychology of personality.

Riki philosophy was introduced into Japan around the fourteenth century by Zen monks, and in the Edo period (after the seventeenth century), it exercised extensive influence among the samurai-warrior class of people known as *bushi* (武士). The foundations for the system of virtues in *riki* philosophy were laid by incorporating the Four Beginnings of Měngzǐ (孟子, 372–289 B.C.E) and the Eight Items of the *Great Learning* (大学; Chin., *dàixué*; Jap., *daigaku*). The author interprets the Four Beginnings as an ethic which places importance on the mind/heart relation with others. We Easterners are often not conscious of this fact. It comes only from the author who emphasizes the importance of East-West comparisons. The Eight Items are eight virtues that are collected together to connect the process of personality formation with the influence it has on the community. The first half of these eight items are the four virtues of: (1) "investigation of things" (格物; Chin., *géwù*; Jap., *kakubutsu*), (2) "reaching knowledge" (知致; Chin, *zhīzhì*; Jap., *chichi*), (3) "right mind" (正心; Chin., *zhèngxīn*; Jap., *seishin*), (4) "sincerity" (誠意; Chin., *chéngyì*; Jap., *seii*), or nurturing a pure mind/heart. When the first and the second are taken together, i.e., "coming to know things through investigation of them," it means becoming one with the truth of the cosmos. This presupposes the experience of meditation; all four of these virtues are predicated on the practice of meditation. Although "the investigation of things" and "reaching knowledge" were interpreted as a kind of epistemology after Western philosophy was introduced, they were originally the ethics that were concerned with personality formation. (Zhūzǐ, for example, states: "although I naturally do not disregard physics, ethics are more impending problems for the human being.") The latter half of the Eight Items are the four ethical ideals of: (5) "self-cultivation" (修身; Chin., *xiūshēn;* Jap., *shūshin*), i.e., establishing an ethical personality as an individual, (6) "to make a good family" (斉家; Chin., *qíjiā;* Jap., *seika*), (7) "to govern a regional community" (治国; Chin., *zhìguó;* Jap., *chikoku*), and (8) "to establish peace under heaven" (平天下; Chin., *píngtiāxià;* Jap., *heitenka*), i.e., realizing these ethical ideals. To summarize then, these ideals are designed to help one achieve an enlightened personality such that the influential power of such a personality gradually extends beyond the confines of the individual to the country. The sage is the ideal enlightened, ethical personality who supports the whole system of these virtues.

Western ethics that are commensurate with these Neo-Confucian ones are probably those of Aristotle. His ethics probe into various virtues necessary for the citizen of the *polis,* and the fundamental ideal of the personality that would correspond to the Neo-Confucian sage can be sought in the virtue of wisdom *(phronesis)* that provides the means to achieves an end. Moreover, we may mention the mean *(mesotēs)* as an ideal according to which Aristotle systematized various virtues. In this respect, there is a complete agreement between Aristotle's and Confucianism's idea of the mean.

Incidentally, while the main bearer of Chinese Confucianism was the literati and not the military aristocracy, Japanese Confucianism took hold in the class of *bushi*. This was due to the fact that during the Edo period (1603–1867), the *bushi* assumed the aristocratic role of the controlling class. In Japan, however, the political aspect of Confucianism was not stressed so much as the issue of personality formation. We may mention Yamaga Sokō (山鹿素行, 1622–685) as the representative person who insisted on *bushi* Confucianism. He used the term *shidō* (士道), or "the way of the *bushi*." This term represents the ideal image of a personality who embodies a gentle and accommodating power on the exterior, but who also conceals strength and dignity on the interior. He enumerates ten items for this image: (1) "nurturing *ki*-energy" through the practice of meditation (養気, *yōki*), (2) "intentionally directed ki-energy" (志気, *shiki*), i.e., clear consciousness of purpose, (3) "caliber" (度量, *doryō*), i.e., the power of accommodation, (4) "generosity" (温籍, *onsha*), (5) "the manner of carrying oneself" (風度, *doryō*), i.e., gallantry (6) "discretionary power" (分別, *bunbetsu*), i.e., the power of judgment, (7) "resting on one's destiny" (安命, *anmei*), being loyal to one's task, (8) "being upright" (清廉, *seiren*), i.e., of pure mind/heat without personal desire, (9) "honesty" (正直, *shōjiki*), i.e., sincerity, and (10) "the virtue of a strong and persistent will power" (剛操, *gōsō*). In short, the ideal of his ethics was to build up a moral personality who is capable of guiding others spiritually. Herein we can find the origin of the so-called the way of *bushi* (武士道, *bushidō*).

    In addition, I would like to bring the reader's attention to the fact that Wáng Yángmíng's philosophy also exercised influence on the bushi at the time of the Meiji Restoration (1868). We can mention Saigō Takamori (西郷 隆盛, 1827–77) and Yoshida Shōin (吉田松陰, 1830–1859) as the two representative leaders of this period who were influenced by Wáng Yángmíng's philosophy. Saigoᵀ's motto, "respect heaven and love people" (敬天愛人, *keiten aijin*), borrowed the words of Wáng Yángmíng. Yoshida, insisted on realizing justice by means of action without calculation of interest, which was no doubt influenced by Wáng Yángmíng's theory of conscience.

    Since Japanese Confucianism was developed in connection with the feudal class system controlled by the *bushi*, its ideological influence gradually waned as the Meiji Restoration abolished class distinctions. However, various Confucian virtues were retained in the system of "national ethics" (国民道徳, *kokumin dōtoku*) as late as World War II. Those who were influenced by the *bushi* way in modern Japanese history, were, for example, the military men of the Meiji period (1868–1912). It is also noteworthy that there were many people who were of the *bushi* class, who converted to Christianity (particularly Protestantism) in the beginning part of the Meiji period. As examples of people who belong to the former group, we may mention Nogi Maresuke (乃木希典, 1849–1912). As examples belonging to the latter group, we may mention Uchimura Kannzō (内村鑑三, 1861–1930) and Nitobe Inazō (新渡戸稲造, 1862–1933). Nogi is well known as the general who attacked the base of the Russian fleet at Port Lǔshùn. He was influenced by Yamaga Sokō, and upon the death of Emperor Meiji, Nogi terminated his own life. Shocked by hearing the news, Natsume Sōseki wrote the novel *Kokoro*. The main character of the novel, who commits suicide, is named Sensei and is modeled after Sōseki himself. It is rumored that a friend to whom Sensei writes a letter is modeled after Watsuji Tetsurō. Martyrdom was a unique custom that emerged in the beginning part of the Edo period. Nitobe and other students, who were then studying in the United States, felt a psychological affinity between Puritan asceticism and the moralism nurtured by *bushi* Confucianism.

    However, after the Japanese defeat in the Pacific War, the system of national morality was attacked by progressive Marxist intellectuals as war ideology. The fundamental framework for national morality was built upon two pillars of ancient Chinese Confucianism; namely, loyalty to the nation and filial piety i.e., the morality of the family premised on ancestor worship. This framework incorporated various virtues pertaining to the parent-child relationship, the brother-sister relationship, the relationship among relatives, the relationship among friends, and other relationships pertaining to education and the social order. While modifying it to meet the eye of the modern period, Watsuji Tetsurō placed great importance upon this national morality and secured it at the foundation of his ethical theory of virtues. Progressive Marxist intellectuals attacked and criticized his ethics as being nationalistic, but they never proposed another ethics in place of his. As a result, people's trust in the nation altogether plummeted in Japan after the war. In family relations, the authority of older people and fathers has been lost, while the psychological ties between mother and children have been strengthened. In recent years, the degradation of education has become prominently noticeable, and crimes committed by youth have dramatically increased. Today, movements are springing up among people who are concerned by the present situation.

THE SETTLEMENT OF BUDDHISM IN JAPAN

In chapter four, the author seeks the foundations of Buddhist morality in the oneness of psychological and ontological perspectives. Japanese researchers of Buddhism tend to be interested in the details, and many are indifferent to the fundamental paradigm of Buddhist philosophy. Taking note of the noble Eightfold Path, the author focuses especially on the fundamental process of self-cultivation aiming at the experience of *nirvāna*. When we compare this process with the tradition of Western philosophy, a fundamental difference emerges. In the tradition of Western philosophy, *theōria* takes precedence over *prāxis* and logic takes priority over ethics; in the case of the East, the tradition upholds personality formation as the most fundamental problem in philosophy.

For the sake of the Western reader, I would like to give a brief explanation of the historical process through which Buddhism settled in Japan. One of the important points that needs to be noted here is the relationship between Shintōism and Buddhism. They are now considered to be separate religions, but this separation, as noted in the foregoing, only emerged out of the policy that the new Meiji government adopted. Prior to that period, there was no consciousness of clearly distinguishing them on the part of the people. Shrines that are today considered to be Shintō were oftentimes originally Buddhist temples. (For example, Yasaka Shrine in Kyoto was originally a temple which worshipped the guardian *kami* of Jetavana.[4] Tsukubasan Shrine in the Kantō area was also a Buddhist temple before the Meiji period.) In addition, many old shrines with historical origins in the mythological age were absorbed into Buddhist temples after the introduction of Buddhism in Japan. This phenomenon is called *"shinbutsu shūgō"* (神仏習合), or the syncretism between Buddhism and Shintōism. This historical tradition explains the Japanese people's religious consciousness which psychologically overlaps Buddhas and *kamis*.

The historical origin of this syncretism goes back primarily to Kūkai's (習合, 774–835) Esoteric Buddhism (密教, *mikkyō*). After repeatedly undergoing self-cultivation experiences in the mountains of various parts of Japan, Kūkai sailed to China where he learned Esoteric Buddhism. In the world of Buddhism in which he lived, self-cultivation practice in the mountains flourished widely. In the faith of the mythological age as well, the mountains were considered to be dwelling places of *kami*. Since Esoteric Buddhism is a "pantheistic" religion that worships many tathāgatas, bodhisattvas, and heavenly beings, it was commensurate with the Shintō world-view which recognizes numerous *kamis*. As a result of Kūkai's philosophy founded on the process of self-cultivation experiences, ancient Buddhism up until the twelfth century ended up being Esoteric Buddhism, in which *kamis* and Buddhas were grasped inseparably together. After the twelfth century, the teachings of Zen and Pure Land Buddhism arose, in part, in reaction to Mikkyō's close ties to state politics.

ZEN AND JAPANESE CULTURE

In chapter five, the author delves into the details of Zen Buddhism. As there is not much more to add to his treatment, I would like to limit myself to offering some comments from a historical and cultural perspective.

Zen is a school of Buddhism which flourished during the Sòng dynasty (eleventh–thirteenth century) in China. This period in Chinese intellectual history is referred to as the period of exchange among the three teachings. It was an extraordinary period in which Confucianism, Daoism, and Buddhism mutually influenced each other. Furthermore, all three placed a common emphasis on methods of self-cultivation and meditation. Zhūzǐ and Wáng Yángmíng incorporated meditation into their philosophies, which they learned from the cultivation methods of Daoism and Buddhism. Such mind-body techniques of self-cultivation through meditation are unrelated to theoretical doctrines, and from the contemporary point of view, are deeply connected with the psychology of the unconscious, the martial arts, and medical *techné*. Herein one can find the characteristic Zen openness to experience over and above intellectual understanding.

Even though Zen Buddhism disappeared early on in China, it continues to thrive even today in Japan. This is because it is still deeply connected with the Japanese cultural tradition. In various parts of the book, the author refers to the spirituality of aesthetic consciousness which appears in Japanese arts. At the beginning of chapter six, for example, the stone garden of Ryōanji Temple is introduced. Zen gardens are usually composed by condensing natural scenery such as mountains, rocks, rivers, stones, trees, moss, and grass, and show a marked contrast with the Western gardens which emphasize symmetrical and artificial compositions. Chinese gardens incorporate strong architectural elements of geometrical artificiality, and favor rocks of peculiar shape which lend a particularly "heavy" sensation. Elements of Japanese gardens, however, all assume non-linear compositions, so that the garden attempts to express symbolically the essence of the natural world. What one experiences there is a motherly environment with a fundamental tone of stillness and gentleness. Musō Soseki (夢窓疎石, 1275–1351) created the form and design of the Japanese garden with these characteristics. He is famous for designing the Tenryūji and Saihōji Temples in Kyoto, where the mind/heart of the participating observer can feel a certain poetic sympathy with nature that is commensurate with the sensibility of *waka* and *haiku* poetry.

Musō advocated that Japanese Zen should not follow Chinese Zen, which he criticized as being dominated by, and becoming subservient to, political powers. Musō lived in a period of wars and turmoil when the Muromachi government (1338–1573) was established in Kyoto after the collapse of the Kamakura government (1192–1333). He endeavored to establish peace and harmony by preaching the senselessness of war to the leaders in Kamakura and Kyoto. In his *Dream Dialogues* (夢中問答, *muchū mondō*) and other didactic sermons and letters, he instructed leaders to know that wars, regardless of victory or defeat, leave longstanding hatreds and deep enmities in the hearts of both parties. Even though a retainer's family may celebrate victory, they will still harbor enmity towards the political power-brokers as they think of all those who died in war. He emphasized that those who assume the seat of political authority have the responsibility of comforting the departed spirits of the dead, regardless of whether or not the dead are enemies or allies. Tenryūji Temple was erected through Musō's recommendation to General Ashikaga Takauji (足利尊氏, 1305–1358) for the purpose of putting the spirit of Emperor Godaigo (後醍醐天皇, 1288–

1339) to rest since he was defeated by the Muromachi government and died in indignation.

Japanese Zen developed by the support of the *bushi* class. Although the stillness and gentleness of the Japanese garden may appear incongruent with the image of the *bushi* warrior, it seems there is a paradoxical psychological relation. The *bushi*, as a being-toward-death (*Sein zum Tōde*) of which Heidegger speaks, must train himself in daily life to resolve the issue of his own death. Meditation was that training. The stillness of the Japanese garden and of meditation designates a mind/heart commensurate with eternity beyond life and death, and their gentleness designates a mind/heart that sympathizes with all that is endowed with life. Naturally, these alone are not sufficient for the *bushi*, for he must also nurture strong will power that enables him to participate in war. Let me cite an episode here. When the Mogolian army attacked Japan twice in the latter half of the thirteenth century, there was one Chinese Zen monk residing in Kamakura. His name was Mugaku Sogen (無学祖元, 1226–86). He was a teacher of Hōjō Tokimume (北条時宗, 1251–84) who was then Regent to the Shogun. While Mugaku was still in China, a Mongolian platoon intruded into his temple and engaged in plundering and killing. He was captured. He said the following with calm composure: "What a splendid Mongolian sword! It cuts the Spring wind like lightning!" It is reported that Mongolian soldiers were overpowered by his personality and fled in fear.

Zen places its fundamental teaching on "no dependence on word" (不立文字, *furyūmonji*). That is, its teaching does not depend upon linguistic expression. In spite of this, Zen places extreme importance on dialogue (問答, *mondo*)[5] between master and disciple, and has left an inordinate amount of dialogue records. Zen ignores this sort of contradiction altogether, because in Zen dialogue, one must speak what is originally unspeakable. In the history of Western philosophy, Socrates emphasized dialogue. Can we find something in common between them? Socrates' dialogues are accompanied by a kind of funny sentiment which is created by irony. It indicates the simultaneous emergence of mental activity in both parties that is difficult to communicate when intellectual logic is about to be activated between two people. There is a psychological field that is established prior to linguistic expression. At times we feel a mood commensurate with it in Zen dialogue. An unenlightened disciple asks: "What is the meaning of Bodhidharma's coming to China?" The enlightened master responds: "An oak tree in the garden!" These sentiments disclose that a logic of equal standing cannot be established between an enlightened personality and an unenlightened personality. Generally speaking, this would mean that psychological fields are formed in human beings' lives based on the ethical relationships that control the "betweenness" (間柄, *aidagara*) of the two people prior to intellectual logic. However, by the time Aristotle appeared, the Platonic dialectic had disappeared, and instead logic became dominant. Modern dialectics like those of Hegel, for example, are erected on logic, where the problem concerning ethics and personality have disappeared.

THE VIEW OF THE HUMAN BASED ON BETWEENNESS

Chapter six primarily discusses Watsuji Tetsurō. He is a philosopher who represents the modern Japanese ethics. He maintained that the stance of modern philosophy since Descartes is erroneous, since it attempted to grasp the essence of the human being by using ego-consciousness as its point of departure. His fundamental view is that people originally exist in "betweenness" (間柄, *aidagara*), that is, in a relationship between person and person.

At the foundation of his contention, I think, is his insight into the mind-body relationship. When reflecting upon the human being, it is possible to approach it by the following three perspectives: by looking at it in the first person, in the second person, and in the third person. The third person perspective may be seen in cases such as calculating the population of a given country, investigating the number of casualties in a traffic accident or in a disaster. In such cases, the human is treated as an objective number only by virtue of having a body. Because the human is grasped as being what Descartes called an "extended thing" (*res extensa*), that is, as a material object occupying volume in space, the individual's psychological condition is ignored. In this respect, the standpoint of science assumes the third person perspective. By contrast, in the first person perspective, (that is, when one's own self is fundamental), the essence of the human is placed in ego-consciousness and is understood only as a subject of cognition and action directed to the environment. As the human is taken here only as a thinking being (*res cogitans*), the somaticity of the human is excluded from the essence of the human. The somaticity of the human is not considered essential for the modern rationalistic ethics and epistemology. However, Watsuji's "betweenness" is thought out in terms of the fundamental second person relationship. This view, based on the relationship in which people mutually know each other in both body and mind, attempts to understand the human being at its very foundation through relationships between parent-child, husband-wife, friends, relatives, etc. Watsuji actually maintains that the first person perspective (which accommodates the standpoint of ego-consciousness) and the third person perspective (which regards the human only as a physiological body) are merely derivatives of the second person perspective. In this sense he contends that modern philosophy and science assume the way of thinking that is based on the secondary, derivative mode which is grounded in the view of humanity in betweenness.[6]

The theoretical point of departure for various human communities, according to Watsuji, lies in the "two-person community" (二人共同, *futari kyōdōtai*). The two-person community designates a husband-wife relationship, or a relation that is tied together by means of love and trust between a male and a female. Since a human being comes into the world through the relationship between two genders, he/she is a being who originally starts life in betweenness. Although Watsuji does not delve into this issue, it seems that he has inherited at the background of his stance the traditional Eastern view of the human being. When his stance is examined from a contemporary point of view, this issue will be related to the problem of how to philosophically think of the relationship between physiology and psychology, between sexuality and gender, between the masculine principle and the feminine principle.

Here I want to briefly offer my opinion on this issue by comparing the philosophical traditions of East and West. As the tradition of Western philosophy has logic at its foundation, rarely does philosophy concern itself with the problems of physiology and psychology. Ever since Plato insisted on the distinction between eidos and hylé, between the soul and the body, and ever since Aristotle took logic as the principle of intellectual thinking, the problem of eros has never become a central theme in the history of Western philosophy. It was psychologists such as Freud and Jung who brought this issue back to the world of contemporary thought. They thought that the base of the unconscious held psychological structures of myths like the Oedipus complex. Based on his research on Eastern religions, Jung attempted to take a fresh look at the religious tradition of the West. By psychoanalyzing Yahweh (see for example, his *Answer to Job*), Jung observed that this God lacked femininity. Although God's femininity later appeared in the wisdom literature of the Old Testament, it sank into the collective unconscious of popular belief in the form of the worship of Virgin Mary once Christianity was established. Jung contended that it was necessary to rethink God's femininity in order for Christianity to be alive in the contemporary period. He actually learned this when he researched the

meditation methods of Daoism and Tibetan Buddhism. These meditation methods train one to become closer to a perfect personality by
synthesizing masculine and feminine virtues in which the unconscious
libido is transformed into a spiritually pure quality. (In the case of
Daoist meditation, it is taught that "the conception of a true person"
[真人受胎, *shinnjin jutai*] occurs through the synthesis of the masculine and the feminine; a notion that is based on the *yīn-yáng* principle
as explained in the *Book of Changes*.) Jung says that this kind of view of
the human being can be found in the West in the prayers and medita-
tions of ancient Egyptian mythology, Gnosticism, and medieval alchemy.
I think that the issue concerning God's femininity will become an extremely important task for philosophy not only in view of comparing
the East-West thought, but also in view of future feminist thought.

Self-Identity of Absolute Contradiction

In chapter seven, which is a long chapter occupying the last portion of
the present book, the author focuses mainly on the philosophy of Nishida
Kitarō (西田幾多郎, 1870–1945). Nishida and D. T. Suzuki were friends
since their youth, and Nishida practiced Zen meditation for a long time
and thus was intimately familiar with it. His meditation experience lies
at the background of his maiden work, *An Inquiry into the Good*. His
ethics investigate the problem of personality formation and are flavored
with a sense of religiosity. They lay a foundation for will that attempts
to realize true self, distinct from the self-realization grounded in ego-
consciousness.

Nishida calls the condition of the human being-in-the-world "self-
identity of absolute contradiction" (絶対矛盾の自己同一, *zettaimujun
no jikodōitsu*). This is a view that emerged through his criticism of modern
Western epistemology. It will become understandable, I think, once we
take note of the problem of the body. In Western epistemology, ego-
consciousness as an epistemological subject grasps the world as an object.
In spite of the fact that this stance artificially situates the self outside of
the world, it finds itself in the world vis-à-vis the body; hence, it exists
in a state of contradiction. That is to say, it is a contradiction that the
human, to use Heidegger-like terminology, is both a "being-in-the-world"
and a "being-outside-of-the-world." Nishida calls this the fundamental
identity of the human being. The human and the world are rendered
separate only through intellectual logic, as if they somehow stand opposed to each other as the epistemological subject and the epistemological object. This mode of thinking was established by Kant who

logically grounded modern science. In opposition to this stance, however, Nishida proposes *basho* (場所; *topos* or place) as a base out of which the subject-object separation and opposition arises in epistemology. *Basho* connects the subject and the object, the self and the world at its synthetic base. It is a pure experience in the flowing movement of each and every time, where an invisible unifying power is operative. Following this sort of reasoning, the author analyzes Nishida's basho in detail from the perspective of enlightenment through meditation experience. Meditation abolishes the egoistic self. It is a path towards the height of personality; it is found in Zen's *satori* (悟り) or in Buddhist *nirvāna* that is the ideal of personality. The author interprets this path to mean the endeavor to investigate the sacred will that controls the cosmos. God cannot be discovered unless one looks into the interior of one's self. According to Nishida, it means that God itself will become self-aware. The sacred power becomes expressed when infused into our mind/heart *(psyché)*. In his essay of later years, Nishida called it "inverse correspondence" (逆対応, *gyakutaiō*). Behind the ego-consciousness which tends towards the external world, God becomes aware of itself, from behind the springing source of purity. There, the enlightened personality (人格, *jinnkaku*) which the author thematizes, is being formed.

CONFUSION OF THE CONTEMPORARY WORLD AND THE DISINTEGRATION OF MORALITY

Professor Robert. E. Carter has studied Japanese culture for a long time and has published a book, *Becoming Bamboo: Western and Eastern Explorations of the Meaning of Life*. He is an earnest, enthused researcher of Japanese artistry, martial arts, and tea ceremony. I hope interested readers in the English sphere will read his book.

However, the thoughts expressed by the author in this book do not stop simply at the limits of cultural studies. He scrutinizes the intellectual confusions that are being witnessed in the contemporary world, and expresses his concerns over its moral decay. They are grave issues that confront both the United States and Japan. In the 1970s when the anti–Vietnam War movement drew both the United States and Japan into a whirlpool of confusion, the novelist Mishima Yukio (三島由紀夫, 1925–70) warned the extremist students at the University of Tokyo: "If Japan continues to move in the way it has been moving, it will perish, and only an economic giant will remain."[7] Shortly after making this speech, he terminated his life. The writer's outcry thirty years ago clearly predicted today's situation. Japan has indeed become an economic giant next to the United States. For this reason, mammonism, or the desire for gold, has scattered around the world and there seems to be no end to economic crimes. This is a consequence of capitalism, which has developed by leaps and bounds in the latter half of the twentieth century, and which has been the major player in the destruction of the environment. Towards the end of *Protestant Ethic and the Spirit of Capitalism*, Max Weber wrote about the future of capitalism while keeping the United States in mind. He said that there would emerge "Epicureans without love" and "professionals without spirit" and that they would start taking pride in having climbed up to the highest stage in human history. Today, the "Epicureans without love" are symbolized by the inundation of sexual materials in both the United States and Japan. The Puritanism that originally constituted the spiritual foundation of the United States can no longer be found anywhere in America. The "professionals without spirit" are the groups of engineers working at giant corporations. The masses are dazzled and thrown into the vortex of material wealth, while seeking the sensual pleasures presented before their eyes. By virtue of this, their souls are damaged and they slip into thoughtless violence.

I think we need to separate ourselves from the hustle and bustle of contemporary life to reflect on history now and then. What was the destiny of *Pax Romana*? It was not destroyed by external forces. The gigantic empire collapsed from within; it imploded spiritually out of its own cultural decadence vis-à-vis the emergence of stern Christian asceticism which didn't flinch even from martyrdom. "Spiritual poverty in the midst of material affluence" destroyed "the eternal Rome." This collapse occurred from within the soul. However, this lesson of human history also teaches us that a reverse flow of culture can only start from within that country spearheading the age.

YUASA YASUO

Acknowledgments

There are many people and supporting institutions to thank for their generous support in aid of the completion of this book. It has taken six years; the project has been interwoven with both tragedy and illness, as well as happiness and fulfillment. The Japan Foundation provided generous support in the form of a Professional Fellowship; the Social Sciences and Humanities Research Council of Canada provided generous support in the form of a Research Fellowship; and the Trent University Research Committee has also supported this endeavor over several years. Kansai Gaidai University has also come to my aid in the form of housing assistance. To all of these institutions I wish to express my deepest thanks, and hope that the results in some small way will serve to justify your faith in me, and your patience.

My wife, Deanie LaChance, has been by my side through grief and illness, and has aided enormously in the final editing of the manuscript. Professor Yuasa Yasuo, Professor Emeritus of Obirin University, in Tokyo, not only agreed to write the Foreword, but with care and patience commented on each chapter of my manuscript, providing detailed background and analysis which only one thoroughly steeped in the arts and sciences of the cultures of the East could have made available. My deep appreciation to you for this magnificent contribution, and to your colleague, Professor Nagatomo Shigenori, and to Pamela Winfield, of Temple University, who translated the Foreword from the Japanese.

Many others have provided energy, skill, and considerable amounts of time along the way. Kelly Liberty and Professor Sean Kane helped to make the manuscript a book; Tara Mitchell not only helped with research and typing, but also with the bibliography; Allen and Cathy Reid of the University of Ottawa made suggestions for improvement, and

Allen helped immeasurably with the index; Kana Ueda of Kansai Gaidai University helped with the footnotes, bibliography, and copyright requests; the Reverend Dominic Lloyd of the Edmonton Buddhist Meditation Group read and constructively critiqued the chapter on Zen; Pal Dosaj has made valuable suggestions as well. Bradley Park of the University of Hawaii has made helpful suggestions for improvement. In Japan, Professors Jeff Shore, Thomas Kirchner, and Morimoto Satoshi, all of Hanazono University, read sections of the manuscript with great care, providing considerable help; Professor Yamada Kunio, of Osaka Prefectural University, and a Zen Buddhist Priest, met with me numerous times to discuss Zen and Nishida. Professor Yamamoto Seisaku, my friend and colleague at Kansai Gaidai University, helped with the Nishida chapter, and another friend and colleague at Kansai Gaidai, Professor David Young helped with the chapter on Zen. Professors Oshima Shin, and Enomoto Yasuhiro helped with language issues, and with procuring permission to make use of the painting which appears on the cover of the book, from the Nezu Museum in Tokyo. Julie Fine helped with the final editing. Professor Jan Van Bragt, now retired from Nanzan University, served as advisor during my Japan Foundation Fellowship sojourn in Japan. Many others have helped in untold ways, and to all of you I offer my heartfelt thanks for your intelligent and caring suggestions, and for your support throughout. I, of course, am responsible for the final misunderstandings and factual and theoretical errors, but just imagine the condition the manuscript might now be in had you not helped!

Permission to reprint passages from the following sources is gratefully acknowledged. Copyright © Damien Keown, from *The Nature of Buddhist Ethics,* by Damien Keown, reprinted with permission of St. Martin's Press, LLC, and with permission of Macmillan Press, Ltd.

The International Shintō Foundation, for permission to quote from Carmen Blacker, "Shintō and the Sacred Dimension of Nature," *International Symposium: Shintō and Japanese Culture,* June 1995; Mark Teeuwen, "Western Understanding and Misunderstanding of Shinto—Progress of Studies on Shinto in the West and Some Remarks," *International Symposium Commemorating the Founding of the International Shintō Foundation: Shintō—Its Universality,* July 1996; Yanairu Tetsuo, "Special Characteristics of the Japanese kami—A Symbol for the Future," *Third International Symposium of the International Shintō Foundation—Shape of Religion in the Twenty-first Century: In Search of World Co-existence,* October 1997.

The University of Hawai'i Press, for permission to quote from Douglas A. Fox, "Zen and Ethics: Dōgen's Synthesis," *Philosophy East and West* 21, no. 1 (1971).

Yale University Press and Iwanami Shoten, Publishers (Tokyo), for permission to quote from Nishida Kitarō *An Inquiry into the Good,* translated by Masao Abe and Christoper Ives (New Haven and London: Yale University Press, 1987). Originally written by Nishida Kitarō in Japanese under the title *Zen No Kenkyu* (1911), and republished in *Nishida Kitarō zenshū* [*The Complete Works of Nishida Kitarō*], ed. Shimomura Toratarō et al., (Tokyo: Iwanami Shoten, Publishers, 1965–1966).

Finally, my thanks to Hamada Hiroshi, Chairman of Ricoh Company, Ltd., Tokyo, for permission to quote from his book, *Achieving "CS Number One: 'Oyakudachi,'"* translated by Simon Partner and published by Ricoh Company, Ltd., Tokyo, 1995.

Introduction:
Contrasts and Ideals

———

I am writing this introduction at my desk, in Japan. While I have visited Japan for varying lengths of time on six previous occasions, this will be my longest stay. The ideas and ideals which I describe in this exploration of Japanese ethics are not always evident in modern Japan, just as brotherly love and the patience of turning the other cheek are not always evident in countries under a decidedly Christian influence. Here in Japan, our apartment is overshadowed by the daunting electrical transfer towers that pass overhead—a situation that I have always insisted other people ought not to tolerate because of the possible health consequences. Now it is my turn. My journey to and from the university is often characterized by dreadfully overcrowded buses, carrying overworked people to or from work, since the Japanese work unusually and, from my Western perspective, unhealthily long hours. The food we buy is woefully overpackaged, with Styrofoam trays as plentiful as leaves on a tree in summer.

I do not wish to idolize Japan, but to pay attention to those influences and high points in Japanese culture that have shaped the character of the people, forged their instinctive attitudinal stance towards the world, and encouraged them to see harmonious and cordial relationships as the most important achievement of our short time on this earth. Japan is still comparatively exemplary in terms of the quality of life that prevails, and the sensitivity to others that can be discerned. It may well be true that this caring for others is less heartfelt and more an uneasiness about being seen not to care, yet it remains true, nonetheless, that it is still a culture that encourages a remarkable degree of other-directedness. The ideal continues to remain that of wholehearted

1

concern for others, including a respectfulness which extends from one's ancestors to one's neighbors.

Another ideal is that of the expression of beauty in all of life's dimensions, and while it again loses something in its translation into reality, it is nonetheless one of those foundational attitudinal stances that has contributed greatly to the cultural difference that constitutes Japan. Charles A. Moore remarks that the aesthetic may well be "the essentially unique expression of spirituality in Japan."[1] In reality, it may be more accurate to describe Japan as a land of incredible contrasts, rather than one of exquisite beauty: beautiful gardens rest next to ugly, sprawling industry; sensitive, extraordinarily polite and remarkably non-violent people are still plagued by high teen-suicide rates; a deep love for nature remains in the Japanese breast together with a drive for more and more capitalistic growth. On weekends we visit magnificent temples, shrines, and gardens with our Japanese neighbors, but at cherry blossom time, or in the autumn when the leaves have turned their marvelous colors, the beauty-seeking crowds are so thick that one is swept along without having time to decide whether this might be a place to linger and admire.

Nor are such contrasts strictly contemporary. Sallie B. King, in a study of a twentieth-century Japanese woman, Satomi Myōdō (1896–1978), observes that "Mahāyāna Buddhism and Shintō both have egalitarian, nonsexist, optimistic philosophies concerning human nature and spiritual potential. Both, nevertheless, are embedded in obviously sexist institutions."[2] Once again the contrast between the ideal and the existential, the theory and the practice, is unmistakably present. King goes on to ask whether the institutionalization of ideas in everyday life is not, in fact, the only operative reality, with the ideals themselves being of little or no importance in the actual sociopolitical world. Are ideals, theories, and ideologies of little or no practical significance? King's response is honest, in that she admits that, "It is disturbing to realize that a tradition can profess the 'right' kind of ideas (from a feminist perspective) and still maintain sexist institutions."[3] My concern about ideals in Japan is echoed by King's conclusions. I too am disturbed by the realization that a tradition rich in the "right" sorts of ideals, and in possession of both an aesthetic and a spiritual awareness of its relation to the greater whole of nature, continues to move towards destructive, insensitive, and unharmonious actions, given that the Japanese culture abounds in potentially creative solutions, as I hope the pages which follow will indicate in detail.

If culture is thought of as the wellspring of survival, enrichment, and creative adaptation, then Japan is amongst the luckiest of nations, for its culture goes very deep and is very old. For example, even though most Japanese will understate their "spiritual" interests, surveys done for the current New Year's shrine and temple visitations totaled almost eighty-nine million. Shintō shrines and Buddhist temples continue to have an influence on the Japanese. The various cultural and aesthetic "ways" are alive and well, although their influence may well be decreasing. The tea ceremony is still practiced, poetry is still an important part of the school curriculum, the martial arts, including the specifically Japanese *kendo* and *aikido,* are alive and well. Calligraphy is thought of as an art, not just a basic skill learned by everyone, and one can improve, and is encouraged to improve, one's artistic ability over an entire lifetime. Respect for educators is remarkably present, as is respect for the elderly (although now one often sees young people sitting in the seats for the elderly and impaired on trains and buses; they seem quite oblivious to any responsibility to relinquish their comfort for those for whom the seats were designated). Generally, there is an atmosphere of good will, of happiness, of respect, of caring for others, of reluctance to show anger or ill temper, of the nurture of interpersonal relationships that can make one feel very much at home without being able to speak a word of the language and with little understanding of the Japanese culture.

This deep and nourishing water continues to bubble to the surface of human relationships, allowing more than a glimpse of what might be possible if lives were more spring-fed, rather than surface-water focused. What these springs still deliver to the surface of everyday life is an abiding quest for interpersonal harmony and authentic relationships; a living spirituality; a thirst for beauty; a deep respect for learning and for the elderly; a deep pride in one's work; the taking of difficulties as opportunities for personal growth, rather than as cause for lament; an ability to focus, and to work steadfastly at a task; and a universally widespread courtesy, gentility, and civility.

Japan's historical ability to borrow and learn from many cultures without relinquishing its own is an illustration of the depth of the culture. Japan has adopted many non-Japanese traditions, but it has always done so by adapting them, and making them its own. Confucianism, Buddhism, Neo-Confucianism, and modern and contemporary Western influences have all become "Japanese" in one way or another. Ezra Vogel makes this point in a variety of ways in his book *Japan as Number One.*[4] Whether in business management, the writing of a constitution, or the practice of a government style brought from the West, the Japanese have borrowed, copied, and then improved on what they have taken, often making it significantly better or more efficient in the process of trimming and shaping it to fit the contours of Japanese sensibilities. The cultural depths of Japan have been sufficient to allow the adoption of foreign ideas, without a resultant loss in Japaneseness. Instead, foreign ideas have been "Japanized," or reshaped to fit comfortably within the cultural understanding already in place. The Japanese have taken in Confucianism, Buddhism, and a variety of ideas from the West, but all of these have taken on a specifically Japanese flavor, as will be seen in the chapters that follow.

We are as a world, without a doubt, coming upon difficult times. Choose your environmental poison. There is significant trouble ahead environmentally, socially, and politically. We will need to draw on our reserves if we are to be able to recover from what it is that we have done and are doing to nature, and to ourselves. Deep cultures that harbor reserves of humane interpersonal relationships and ecological concern may provide the springs of strength and adaptation to lead us out of a troubled world, and into a better world, a world of humanity and not just technology and relentless economic and consumer growth. My experiences in Japan, my study of the Japanese and their influences, and my hopes and fears for our future have all led me to suggest an approach to the understanding of Japanese attitudes and ethics which might be of service as we enter the twenty-first century. Deep springs continue to run, even in arid times, and they continue to replenish and to heal long after optimism has vanished. Sallie King adopts a similar stance when she concludes her study of Satomi-san, mentioned earlier, by remarking on the very strong impact that Shintō and Zen religious philosophy had on her life:

> While the example of Satomi-san's life by no means resolves the complexity of the conflict between sexist and egalitarian tendencies in these traditions—nor does it negate the frustration of living and practicing within a religious context which is self-contradictory—it does indicate that the power of philosophy to affect the course of a human life is not to be overlooked, even when that philosophy is embedded in an institution that sets up obstacles for the practitioner.[5]

Ideals continue to inspire, and to give hope. They must not, of course, be allowed to cover over the veritable chasms that often exist between what the teachings profess and the reality presents. Things will not somehow work out unless we are active in seeing to it that they do: following an ideal, or "doing the will of God[,] necessarily includes a response to what is going on around us."[6] It is necessary both to lament the shortcomings of an institution or a nation, and to be active in narrowing the gap between the ideal and the actual. In my book, I attempt to narrow that gap.

Many "Easts," Many "Wests"

I write as a Western scholar. At times I write "we" in an attempt to identify and distinguish Western ways of thinking in general from Eastern ways of thinking in general. West vs. East is always too simplistic to be left unqualified. Contemporary China, to take a single but important example, is not only as different from Japan as is Canada, at least in many ways, but it is also now radically separated from its own classical past. The Temple of Confucius, in Beijing, is in terrible disrepair, no doubt in part because of the militant rejection of Confucian (and Taoist) "counterrevolutionary" thinking during the Cultural Revolution. China's past is now virtually a "foreign" influence, and is stamped out wherever it appears. The East is certainly not a uniform and single tradition. Still, it was the American jurist, Roscoe Pound, who supposedly said, "the art of teaching is the art of lying, and then qualifying that lie," and I hope that by the end of this study the lies will be at least less glaring than they seemed at first. When I irritate you by including "you" in my perhaps too easy characterization of East and West, please keep in mind that I do understand that there are many Easts, and many Wests, and many sorts of Japanese. Many who are not Japanese, or who are from the various Easts, may read this book only to find themselves more in tune with the ideals of Japan than they might have guessed. Such people, wherever they are from, simply cannot be corralled by my depiction of Western or Eastern values, or attitudes, or moral stances, or religious understanding. I do not intend to speak for you, but I do try to identify some of the tendencies and inclinations. In the West, reason is emphasized, and often at the expense of the emotions. Reason is used to conquer something rather than to befriend it or simply to understand it; or to analyze something rather than merging with it in some quasi-mystical direct experience; or Westerners instinctively stress objectivity rather than the subjective element in experience as important—all of these seem to me to be more prevalent in the West than in the East.

To speak of cultural, philosophical, or religious characteristics as being more or less "present" or "absent" is already to assume, as I do, that what is to be found in ample measure in the one cultural tradition is not altogether absent in the other cultural tradition. Rather, a majoritarian emphasis in the one merely survives as a minoritarian trace in the other, but, nonetheless, it is far from being altogether absent. This is the strategy of the book as it unfolds—if it is not too bold to so dignify it—for it does seem that everything in the East is in some way echoed in the West, and that everything in the West is in some way echoed in the East. The great and allegedly "inscrutable" difference has been largely one of emphasis: that the East is more intuitive, group oriented, and holistic in its approach, and the West the opposite, although all of the ingredients in the mix, East and West, may be found in each of these two imaginary single cultural traditions. By setting up the contrasts, I try to establish where the differences seem to lie. I do not wish to suggest that I am dealing with anything so monolithically exclusive that the characteristics of the "other" are unimaginable and utterly alien. Rather, I want to suggest that they are all too familiar, but either largely forgotten, or noticeably under-emphasized. This mutuality is what makes learning from one another possible, and it is what makes comparative philosophy both rewarding and important.

THE CRITICAL PATH

This study is an attempt to lay out some of the main influences in the development of the peculiarities of Japanese ethical sensitivity. The Japanese take pride in their openness to outside influences, for it demonstrates psychological flexibility, and a willingness to take in the best in cultural, intellectual, religious, scientific, and technological achievements from any source. They have not, for the most part, taken pride in keeping out "foreign" influences—although this seems an odd claim given the periods of enforced and total isolation that also mark Japanese history. But while it has seemed necessary to protect Japan from undue outside influence at least periodically, the array of such cultural influences in Japan include their own "kami-cults" (which became Shintōism at a much later date), Confucianism, Taoism, Buddhism, Ch'an Buddhism (which became Zen Buddhism), and, of course, more recent Western influences. Japan's cultural history is not a simple fabric, for it is woven of numerous colors and strands. Nevertheless, in spite of the variety and inherent differences of these influences, there are a surprising number of similarities, and these similarities, taken together, have taken on an unmistakable Japanese texture.

One thing I attempt to do at the outset is to establish the enterprise of cross-cultural understanding in ethics as of some possible use to Western readers. Can those of us with a decidedly "Western" take on morality and ethics hope to learn anything of significance from the

East in general, and from Japan in particular? It is the assumption of the comparativist that lessons may be taken from a serious study of other cultural perspectives. It is with this assumption that I begin. Nonetheless, this assumption is challenged by no less a figure than the contemporary American philosopher Arthur Danto, who contends that the factual differences in perspective, East and West, make it impossible for Westerners to live the moral life of the East, and that the West has nothing to learn from the East, ethically speaking at least. He writes that "the civilizations of the East are defined through sets of factual and moral propositions pragmatically connected in the minds of their members," and since these factual beliefs are "too alien to our representation of the world to be grafted onto it," it follows that their moral perspective is "unavailable to us."[7] It is not just that I disagree with Danto's assessment of Eastern thought being "too alien to our representation of the world," but I also reject his image of rigid and static world-views which are unable to undergo modification in the light of encounters with "alien representations." I shall argue that world-views are, in fact, open to change, even radical change, if people can find the humility to put their most basic and foundational views "at risk." Socratic humility demanded that one examine especially those views which seemed truest, and most obvious. Only then, when one doubted what one thought one knew, could one be said to be open to learning and discovery. Each of the Platonic dialogues is a textbook demonstration of openness to change, especially world-view change, but it is achievable only when one no longer assumes that one knows the way things really are. Even Plato's own views are critiqued in the dialogues, presumably in order to demonstrate that the "Socratic humility" demanded applies to all perspectives and viewpoints, all habits and seeming truths. My hope is that I have been able to put my cultural inheritance sufficiently "at risk" and for long enough to have begun to comprehend the moral world-view from at least something of a Japanese perspective and to have communicated that understanding.

Danto's assertion of the extreme alienness of Oriental views forces matters to be too black and white, too either/or. I see no reason why I can't temper my own world-view with a healthy dose of otherness. Indeed, it seems imperative to me that I do so, and doubly so at a time when both the natural and the human worlds are in such disarray, and at such risk. I wish to rethink, and to rethink fundamentally, in order to breathe new life and new health into my way of being in the world. Yet, it is not just because we live in critical times that I think it is incumbent upon us to explore alternative ways of being in the world. Even if we lived in the best of times I would argue that our well-being demanded that we look at and seriously consider alternative lifestyles and world-views, in order to avoid the stagnation of complacency and habitual smugness. It seems to me that a healthy way of life must be self-corrective: it must be open to feedback from many sources, distilling from them some sense of what is still working elsewhere, and what is working less well, in order that we might make changes that will improve our understanding and our application.

At times such changes are paradigmatic: they are so major that a shift occurs, a radical tranformation as major as that which made our perspective heliocentric rather than earth-centered. We live at a time when boundaries are breaking down of necessity, as the cities of the West are increasingly populated with incredible racial diversity, as the information highways link us ever closer together, and as travel makes the image of global community a virtual reality, if you will pardon the pun. We are no longer strangers to each other, by and large, and as a result we ought to be less "alien" as well. The world-views of a nearby tomorrow will inevitably display a "fusion of horizons," rather than a stand-off of one alien perspective from another. Take a recent and popular example: while it may be true that to apply the Japanese business management system to the West without modification would be to alienate most workers and managers in North America, it is also true that we have learned a great deal from the Japanese about business management, customer service, and bottom-up as well as top-down suggestions for improvement and change. We have learned just how important it is to put customer service at the forefront, if customer satisfaction and repeat sales are to result; we have learned the importance of involving employees in decision making and in dealing with financial crises, and we have learned how to elicit quality suggestions from assembly-line workers, as well as from management. We have learned a great deal from the Japanese, and to a remarkable extent our new management systems are "horizonal fusions" of North American and Japanese styles. Why should we not be similarly open to cross-cultural fusions morally, spiritually, and practically in the living of our lives?

Change is a characteristic of life, and death is the absence of (most) change. It would seem to follow that it is important to be open to, and to actually seek out, changes in order to expedite growth and maturation, and to thwart developmental sterility and boredom. The renowned brain physiologist, J. Z. Young, writes that suppleness of mind is to be found in some people well into their old age and even beyond, while mental rigidity can overcome one at any age, even in one's youth.[8] He concludes that the important influences contributing to longstanding suppleness of mind are new and refreshing circumstances. Really interesting brains, he quaintly tells us, are those that continue to seek out fresh and enlivening circumstances: those that approach senility, which can overcome one at any age, seem to do so as a result of living in a habitual rut of familiar circumstances, and drab sameness. Openness to new ideas, new circumstances, new cultural, philosophical and religious circumstances may not only be demanded intellectually, they may be essential physiologically if we are to remain creatively alive, and available to the newness of seeing each morning as though it were the first, one's lover afresh, and one's neighbor as himself or herself, rather than as oneself. Openness not only expedites growth and maturation, suppleness and youthful zest for life, but also thwarts developmental sterility and real life boredom. The Japanese have often altered their lifeways, and the concern raised here is whether there are things to learn from the Japanese, and from those Eastern influences on the Japanese, at least in the field of ethics, which might enhance or partially reshape some of our Western ways of being in, caring for, and acting in the world.

1

The "Do Nothing" and the Pilgrim: Two Approaches to Ethics

It may be that human civilization is in decline. At least in the West, there is a decided increase in violent crime, in the frequency and intensity of terrorist attacks, in air, water, soil and noise pollution, and in environmental destruction generally. The nuclear threat is still with us, wars continue to break out, cloning and genetic and biological engineering is outdistancing our laws and our moral sense, and "adult" crimes are being committed by children of a shockingly young age. The quality of life on Earth seems to be slipping away. The resulting angst seems to be propelling us to embrace yet again those "old-fashioned" values, emphasizing family, and whatever virtues we have come to associate with a more "golden" era from the past. But the romance of an imaginatively remembered past which did not include violence, dishonesty, and unfaithfulness is neither true to those eras, nor particularly applicable to our own day and age—except as it causes us to re-think who we are, what we are doing as individuals and as nations, and where we are and ought to be heading. The past can never be an answer unless we bring it into the present after incredible amounts of thinking and adaptation. It needs to be reappropriated, and that is hard work. We may yearn for the "good old days," but we can never simply go back to those days from the here and now. The here and now is a different window in history, with its own outlook and its own complexities which yield a view on the world that is both distinctive and requires never-before-tried potential solutions. It requires both a memory of the past, an assessment of the present, and a vision of the future. It is not clear that the West has such a vision, and so there is an aimlessness—except for economic pursuits and the incessant drive of consumerism—an apparent boredom, and a rising anger resulting from racial inequality, homelessness, economic stratification, a rising crime rate, and chronic unemployment. These are not the worst of times, but neither are they the best of times. For the first time in human history, we have the potential to destroy all life on this planet, and perhaps even the planet itself: "we have never before been in the position of potential 'uncreators' of life, of being able to prohibit birth, but it is precisely imagining the extent of this power and feeling deeply what it means to live in a world where this is possible"[1] that is causing many of us to rethink our theologies, philosophies, and our way of being in the world. This is not a situation that breeds hope and contentment.

As a comparativist, I find I turn instinctively to other cultural traditions for insight which comes from distance, encountering insights and ideals that might enhance and cleanse those of my own. It is not that I think other cultures do not pollute and exploit, and are without their own share of problems and stresses. No culture lives up to its ideals, and increasingly few seem concerned by that fact. Yet it remains within the hopeful depictions of the ideal that any real guidance is to be found. We need to listen to the wisdom of peoples of other cultural perspectives, as well as to our own cultural past and present, if we are to find effective ways of salvaging this sick young planet.

Indeed, it is somewhat in this spirit that Arthur Danto, in a book of quality entitled *Mysticism and Morality: Oriental Thought and Moral Philosophy*, concludes, at the beginning rather than at the end, that

> There are times when the moral fabric of our lives appears so rent that one must look with sympathy upon anyone who in desperation turns to other civilizations for guidance. The East has always held the promise of a deeply alternative existence, satisfying and pacific and exalting. . . . It is nevertheless an aim of this book to discourage the hope that a way through our moral perplexities may be found in the Orient.[2]

One should take seriously a warning of such unconditional clarity from as eminent a scholar as Danto. Therefore, before I begin my inquiry into Oriental thought, I want to address his concerns.

Making the journey from one of the world's distinctive cultural traditions to another is, at best, daunting, and at worst, impossible. The

reasons have much to do with the inability, and sometimes unwillingness, to put one's own cultural assumptions "at risk"; it is not simply a
matter of linguistic and cultural differences. Not that Danto and others
would not be willing to put at risk their own positions, but that, as
Gadamer and his teacher and colleague Heidegger observe, it is never
clear and distinct that one's "translation" of an idea from another culture into the ideational language of one's own culture has not ripped
that idea or conceptual cluster out of its own bed of assumptions, and
rendered it safe and unthreatening by making it "one of our own."
Indeed, Danto warns of this very possibility, except that he *only* speaks
the language of *assimilation*, and never the language of risk-taking. To
assimilate a tradition to one's own always already presupposes that one's
own "house" of language and being is the ruling one, and that whatever
is learned must be fitted into this house, or left outside to rust harmlessly on the lawn. There is no thought of *foundational renovation*. Danto
writes,

> . . . we cannot take over the moral beliefs of the East without accepting
> a certain number of factual beliefs—beliefs about the world—that such
> a system of moral beliefs presupposes. But the relevant factual beliefs
> cannot easily be assimilated to the system of beliefs that define the world
> for us. The fantastic architectures of Oriental thought . . . are open to our
> study and certainly our admiration, but they are not for us to inhabit.[3]

But why not? Yes, there are difficulties, evident even in the fact that
there are few in the world who can straddle two cultural traditions
intellectually, with half a brain and half a heart in each, who have
facility in both languages, or language groups. Yet it is also evident that
some do break through the barriers of inscrutability and mystery, and
successfully begin the arduous and demanding business of the *fusing of
horizons*. Of course, a fusion of horizons leaves neither horizon of understanding intact. The one alters the other, else there would be no
fusion but only harmless juxtaposition. Not only does fusion demand
the placing of key and fundamental assumptions at risk, but it puts at
risk one's way of life as well. Even more to the point, whenever ethics
enters into the picture, our defences go up and we become doubly
protective for fear of losing the slight hold on civilization that we have.
The yawning gap of nihilism and scepticism is usually enough to keep
us at home. Indeed, it is the fear of that yawning gap that has already
caused many of us to turn backwards in time, towards the days of our
grandparents and great grandparents, when we imagine things to have
been better and more moral. Perhaps they were, but they were not

without their own problems and, in any case, you simply can't get there from here.

ON THE NATURE OF THE WILL

Insofar as we may be willing to risk it all (ethically speaking), at least for the purposes of reading further in this book, let us push on, inquiring of Danto what it is that forces him to reject the entire Orient as a source of moral renewal and critical reassessment. Writing as an analytic philosopher, he argues that moral beliefs and factual beliefs are connected: moral beliefs presuppose factual ones. *Karma*, the relationship between *samsara* and *nirvāna*, and the Taoist sense of flowing with the heavenly Way are all factual claims about how things really are, and are quite foreign to our own way of perceiving ourselves in the world. Danto thinks it too much to expect that we convert philosophically to perspectives on the world which are, in so many respects, radically exotic and bizarre when compared to our own. And, of course, he is right, if what is demanded of us is that we take over lock, stock, and barrel the various world-views of the East. Yet the goal of comparative philosophy is not conversion. Rather than advocating an alternative world-view, one inquires into that world-view to discern whether there is anything there which might help us to understand where our own is deficient, or whether there is another way of walking in the world that would enhance our personal and cultural understanding. The risks on both sides are of excess: if we take too much, then we may abandon our own homeground, and convert to another understanding; if we take too little, we distort that alternative perspective by making it comfortable and applicable, leaving our own homeground only slightly altered by our utterly safe mining in foreign fields of thought. Yet surely there is a range of middle positions in which we may significantly alter our own understanding, and our own homeground as well, by taking seriously an aspect of another tradition, without distorting its force and integrity, and thereby coming to see the world in a different light.

Nevertheless, even if I am right that one can glean insight from other traditions without seriously distorting that tradition, and while modifying and fundamentally reinterpreting one's own, Danto argues that the Achilles heel of Oriental thought in general (with the possible exception of Confucianism) is its conception of the will. Why is the East's teachings on the will so inimical to the very possibility of ethics? His answer is crisp and to the point: in the East, "the will is not anything like the important moral concept . . . that it is in the West. Equally, there is none of the agony over freedom of the will, which is, after all, the paradigmatic philosophical concern in the Western tradition."[4] The focal issue is the place of the will, and as I will suggest one of the nature of the will in different cultural traditions. Danto is quite right in observing that in the Western traditions, the world that we live in demands that we struggle along the path of righteousness, and that we enlist in the noble battle against evil along the way. Comparing the Japanese *haiku* poet Basho, to Dante, Danto writes,

> He [Basho] is no Dante, puffing up an arduous path through a hierarchical universe to a permanent lodging in Paradise. The Way has no vector. One cannot get lost. The way is everywhere. . . . So the wanderer does not follow an itinerary, like a pilgrim thirsting for the final beatitudes. Happiness is the way one goes, not something luminous at the end. Of course there is no rest there: we are always moving . . . but we can move without effort, and that is what following the Way is.[5]

By now the reader may already have inklings about how one might reinterpret the sense and place of the will in the East in order to find a way through this rather sharp dividing of the moral West from the amoral East. For example, one might contend that it is not that the Taoists, the Buddhists, and the Zen Buddhists are amoral, but that their vision of morality is always already an implicit critique of precisely the sort of morality and conception of will which we in the West have taken to be the only genuine and true willful morality. Indeed, the Zen Buddhist philosopher Abe Masao makes this abundantly clear when he formulates a Buddhist perspective on the human will as it is understood in the West:

> . . . in Buddhism, human free will is grasped as an endlessly self-determining, self-attaching, and self-binding power—which is the ultimate source of human suffering and which inevitably leads us to the final dilemma— that is, death in the absolute sense. However, when this endlessly self-binding blind power (karma) is realized as it is, through the practice of *dhyana*, meditation, one can be emancipated from it and awaken to boundless openness, [ś]ūnyatā [emptiness, nothingness]. . . . In this awakening to [ś]ūnyatā, human free will is realized entirely anew in its pure form by eradicating its self-attaching and self-binding character. Instead of producing a chain of causation and transmigration, free will, which is now based on the awakening to [ś]ūnyatā, freely works in this phenomenal world without attachment, delusion, or bondage.[6]

No wonder the temptation is not to invite the culturally "different" into our houses: to allow them to enter may result in things at least being significantly altered, and possibly left in tatters. In the above passage by Abe, a rather different conception of the will is being advanced, one of a will that is not fettered by anguish, intellectual sweat, and intense and focused persistence. Rather, the emancipated will now appears to operate effortlessly, apart from our cravings and selfish desires, and in tune with some sense of the whole of things which makes us a vital part of the universe itself.

THE TRANSFORMATION OF THE EVERYDAY WORLD

It is sometimes alleged that Oriental thought is unable to make legitimate moral distinctions because it sanctifies this world, making all of it good, or as the Buddhists say, *nirvāna*. All action, all existence is religiously drenched. Danto asserts "this is a teaching it is difficult not to respect. But I do not believe it will do as a moral philosophy."[7] If everything and every action in the everyday world (*samsara*) is good (*nirvāna*), then the distinction between good and bad breaks down, since there can be no evil, "and some way has to be found for rationalizing evil."[8] Good and evil, we often hear in Eastern thought, are distinctions made in the state of delusion and ignorance. They are relative, not absolute distinctions, and what they are relative to is the way of thinking that we habitually take to be the absolutely correct and reasonable way(s) of thinking. "Good and evil," writes Abe, "are completely dependent on one another. They always co-arise and co-cease so that one cannot exist without the other." There is no "supreme good which is self-subsistent apart from evil."[9] Abe concludes that the surface impact of all of this makes it "understandable why . . . Christians find an indifference to ethics in Buddhism."[10] By contrast, what is typical, particularly in the Far East, is to focus on the ideal state of mind/heart, in which one is transformed to such an extent that one spontaneously does "the right thing." Doing of any kind "still comes about within the world-nexus through being related to other things," but now doing "possesses the character of non-doing or *play* in its elemental sense."[11] Abe adds that this playfulness is at the same time an earnestness, and that earnestness results from our infinite task of saving, or releasing from suffering all sentient beings, human and non-human.[12] One is infinitely concerned, in this way, because from the standpoint of *śūnyatā*, one's vision is now a

> selfless self-centredness in which the self and other are completely non-dual within the nexus of reciprocal interpenetration, and thus the self-centredness and other-centredness are dynamically one. This is possible

only through the completed negation of any kind of self-centredness including the religious self-centredness, and the awakening to śūnyatā free from the will itself."[13]

Language is being stretched beyond its normal elasticity, and hence, no phrasing seems quite right: "selfless self-centeredness," or the expanded self, or selfless compassion, or non–self-centeredness—all of these phrases reach beyond the dualistic thinking which separates self and the other.

From the standpoint of śūnyatā, one no longer follows the moral imperative like a novice learning to paint by number, for now one's capacity to empathetically identify with others is an effortless and unthinking compassion. The ideal, enlightened state of mind is pre-reflective, "without-thinking,"[14] a state of awareness prior to all distinctions and conscious differentiation. And it is a rather constant opinion in the Far East that this pre-reflective state, in particular because it is also pre-ego, is a compassionate state of awareness which seeks to preserve or maintain what is, that it is evenhanded in its compassionate identification with whatever is, and that it is intuitively active, rather than calculative. Pre-reflective change is real and continual, but it is spontaneously and effortlessly active, slipping between the paths of greatest resistance and opposition. Thus, it is not that the will is ignored or depreciated in value, but that it is no longer tied to calculative reasoning. " 'To do good, not commit evil' is an ethical imperative common to the Easterner and the Westerner."[15] But having abandoned the duality of good and evil, how is this imperative to be understood?

In Buddhism, the non-dualistic state of awareness which transcends the good/evil distinction, you will recall, is called śūnyatā. In fact, it is probably more accurate to say that śūnyatā is the root source from which all dualistic distinctions are carved or discriminated; it is the original nothingness (or no-thing-ness), or radical emptiness. It is the formless prior to the coming into existence of all distinctions. The technical phrase that Nishitani borrows from Takeuchi Yoshinori to refer to a point before the opposition of the polarities is initially developed is "trandescendence." What results from taking the standpoint of śūnyatā is a clearer realization of the relative discriminations which come to be carved from the undifferentiated, allowing a fresh trans-valuation of values to occur, but now against the background of valuational relativity, and the compassion which results from seeing that conventional values are delusory and arbitrary. Abe quotes a Zen story in which the master answers a student's question about where the master will go after death, by saying that he will go straight to hell! The student is shocked, but the master responds to the student's expressed disbelief by adding, "If I will not go to hell, who will save you at the bottom of hell?"[16] As is so often the case in the parables of Jesus, ordinary values are turned over, and what seemed sinful is now revalued as moral, and what was thought to be moral, is now taken to be immoral. If anything, we have come face to face with a "higher wisdom," one that transcends ordinary morality and puts "at risk" that which one heretofore held dear and sacrosanct. Yet this does not mean that one now acts in an unprincipled manner. New principles will take the place of the old, but now set on a more deeply rooted foundation. One's capacity for moral judgment is now more discerning, and one knows that it may be a better thing to dine with sinners than with the smug and habitually unfeeling holy of society. One now looks beneath the surface, and rethinks what it means to be holy, open to the "good will" of a prostitute and sinner, to the desperate and suffering. At the same time, one is now less open to the hypocrite, to the habituated smugness of one who assumes the good, like Plato's Euthyphro. One is open to the other, and as such one must first have become transparent to oneself: because one is more aware than one was previously, listening is now more possible, and so is the mustering of helpful advice.

THE WILL IN EASTERN THOUGHT

What should emerge from the discussion that follows is an awareness of a distinctive "Eastern" point of view, which assumes that it is the aggressive will that is the problem, rather than the ingredient without which there can be no ethical or moral solution. Morality is not a matter of willing the flesh and the mind into a steadfast obedience and renunciation, but of abandoning willfulness altogether in favor of a spontaneity, compassion, and human heartedness which arises from our "truer" nature, if not overlaid with egoistic and individualistic desires. D. T. Suzuki argues that the will in the Zen tradition is prior to the self as discursive deliberator, or as motivator of an ego separate from its objects of awareness:

> The will in its primary sense . . . is more basic than the intellect because it is the principle that lies at the root of all existences and unites them all in the oneness of being. The rocks are where they are—this is their will. The rivers flow—this is their will. The plants grow—this is their will. The birds fly—this is their will. Human beings talk—this is their will. The seasons change, heaven sends down rain or snow, the earth occasionally shakes, the waves roll, the stars shine—each of them follows its own will.

To be is to will and so is to become. There is absolutely nothing in this world that has not its will. The one great will from which all these wills, infinitely varied, flow is what I call the 'Cosmic (or ontological) Unconscious,' which is the zero-reservoir of infinite possibilities. The 'Mu!' thus is linked to the unconscious by working on the conative plane of consciousness. The koan that looks intellectual or dialectical, too, finally leads one psychologically to the conative center of consciousness and then to the Source itself.[17]

In a way, "will" is being defined equivocally in what I have suggested thus far: on the one hand, from the point of view of *śūnyatā*, one is beyond will; and yet, as Suzuki argues, there is a "primal will," a will which wills without willing. What accounts for this ambiguity, I think, is the attempt to deconstruct the old notion in such a way as to speak of willing as non-willing, free of all the baggage that "will" carries with it. But there is more to say here. *Śūnyatā* is a state of awareness that is beyond most people in its fullest sense, and yet in East Asia it is accessible culturally in literature, scripture, art, and in the various "ways" such as the tea ceremony, flower arranging, haiku poetry, the martial arts, etc. Few people attain *śūnyatā*, but most are acquainted with the literature and the tradition of enlightenment, and perhaps with those engaged in practices engaged in by those who attained the perspective of *śūnyatā.* What one learns is at least something about how to will without willing, while recognizing the radical relativity of good and evil. One comes to see the things of the world a little differently, from a broader/wider perspective (as though *sub specie eternitatis*), and in a state of peace and tranquility. The result is likely to be a more compassionate interaction with others, with other living things, and with the world of nature generally—with which one now senses a genuine identification. While few experience the state of *śūnyatā*, most are affected by its reported contours, and are engaged in the practices which slowly move one somewhat in the direction of those characteristics preparatory to its realization. In this sense, *nirvāna* is always already underfoot, once it is more clear what it is that *nirvāna* is all about.

Danto's criticism of Eastern "morality"—and he takes Taoism as "the more typically Oriental attitude"[18]—is that it "aims at the stunning of the will," and this stunning of the will appears necessary because "the will is considered the enemy of ultimate happiness throughout the East."[19] The picture that he gives is of effortless, undisturbed, strictly unwillful flowing—a "monotonous flowing away"[20]—of being at one with the stream of life such that morality as we understand it becomes literally impossible. One no longer possesses the ability to act against the stream of things, or to set out to change the world in some small way, for happiness demands that one flow in conformity with the world. "Exactly that space that Taoism intends to collapse is what makes morality possible at all."[21]

Where Danto goes wrong, I think, is in assuming that the will is turned off, allowed to atrophy, and abandoned. Rather, the will is understood in a different light, is nurtured differently in the cultural gardens of the East, and yields both quite different methods of application and distinctively different results. To begin, let me focus the discussion by quoting from Danto once more, this time on the concept of *wu wei* (or *wei wu wei*) in Taoist thought. I will analyze the meaning of the term shortly. For now, let me dwell on Danto's rendering of the meaning of this Chinese phrase, for he explicitly defines *wu wei* as "to do nothing," emphasizing that "*wu wei*, non-doing, celebrates the power of immobility."[22] In fact, it means nothing of the sort! Rather than implying inaction, it is that which makes all doing, of whatever kind, possible, including moral doing. Chapter forty-eight of the *Tao Te Ching* tells us that we must stop acting altogether, and that once we do so, then there will be nothing that we do not do. "The Tao never acts, yet there is nothing it does not do" (chapter thirty-seven). The Tao is "universal spontaneity."[23] When all is well, one digests one's food without willing it done or checking it step by step through its process. An even better example is pregnancy. The less aggressive and less dominating female is the heroine of Taoist thought, and not because she can bear children, but because the effortless and spontaneous *doing* over nine months is more frequently evident in the way women live their lives generally. Women are more likely to have come to terms with nurturing, and with the importance of gentle interaction and persuasion. One does not force a pregnancy, normally, deciding at seven months that one has had enough. Nor does one force physical and mental development of the fetus. The more aggressive male, in China and here, is more likely to force things, to advocate a "war" on drugs, a "war" on poverty, to discipline quite severely because of a breach of good conduct, to become impatient quickly, and to see to it that injustice does not go unanswered.

By contrast, the Taoist sage intervenes minimally, with others and with the natural world, letting each thing develop in accordance with its own nature. Deliberate intervention, particularly forced intervention, sooner or later results in failure, or in strikingly bad consequences. As Holmes Welch puts it, "in human relations force defeats itself. Every action produces a reaction, every challenge a response." The combination of humility and compassion "work like gravity between man and man," accomplishing effortlessly, and by attraction rather than by force, what might otherwise not be accomplished, or if forced, accomplished with severe penalties flowing from it in the future.[24] Rather than fighting evil, the Taoist realizes that "good creates evil . . . [N]ever [try] . . . to do good, because this requires having a concept of good, which leads to having a concept of evil, which leads to combatting evil, which only makes evil stronger."[25] Welch summarizes his account of *wu wei*:

> *Wu wei* does not mean to avoid all action, but rather all hostile, aggressive action. Many kinds of action are innocent. Eating and drinking, making love, ploughing a wheat-field, running a lathe—these *may* be aggressive acts, but generally they are not. Conversely, acts which are generally aggressive, like the use of military force, may be committed with such an attitude that they perfectly exemplify *wu wei*. The Taoist understands the Law of Aggression and the indirect ways that it can operate. He knows that virtuousness or non-conformity can be as aggressive as insults or silence. He knows that even to be non-aggressive can be aggression, if by one's non-aggressiveness one makes others feel inferior. It is to make another person feel inferior that is the essence of aggression.[26]

Rather than "do nothing," then, *wu wei* means not doing anything that is not done naturally, i.e. spontaneously, and from the heart as well as from the mind. One's doing must be an expression of one's whole character, and must in some way embody an empathetic awareness of the situation of the other. One may stop someone from doing harm, and in so doing harm that person. But one's intent is not to do harm, but to avoid as much of it as one can. The Chinese character for mind, *hsin*, is also the character for heart. Similarly, the Japanese term *kokoro* means both mind and heart, or mind/heart, and underscores that a "heartfelt" gesture is also a "mindful" *and* a *spontaneous* act. It arises naturally and spontaneously from the depths of one's self, from deeper than one's surface will; it is not mere acting but an authentic expression of one's whole person as "knower," "feeler," and "willer." Such acts are not acts of calculation, not because they are mindless—for indeed they are allegedly mind-full—but because calculation implies being at an objective remove from the situation. Acts of calculation are more like running down the list of debits and credits on a cluttered sheet in order to decipher what would be best in this case. Calculation can result in the ignoring or setting aside of one's feelings and one's sense of how to act in this circumstance here and now. Instead an abstract principle or law is applied to an instance that is rarely ever exactly like what the law envisioned or what is set out in the manual as a test case. T. P. Kasulis articulates the case and the place for the "Eastern" outlook and contribution to moral thought when he concludes:

Even if Western philosophers continue to maintain that consciousness should always remain primarily rational and conceptually oriented, the *capacity* to respond prereflectively should still be nourished. Otherwise, we will lose, along with that capacity, the possibility of being truly compassionate, selfless, and spontaneously moral.[27]

But deeper still is the observation that ordinary morality arises only from the surface of egos already in social conflict. Morality is a web of prohibitions and prescriptions for people who might otherwise do each other great harm. By contrast, if we saw each other as brothers and sisters, we would identify with each other's gains and losses, pleasures and pains, aspirations and fears. This is not to say that morality requires nothing more—at least it need not mean this—but that whatever rules of morality do arise, should arise out of this foundation of human-hearted capacity for empathetic identification. David Loy makes this point in some detail:

The nondualist traditions make the same point [that the problem of morality is not evil, but delusion] as part of their critique of dualistic categories. The tendency to evaluate all acts as good or bad, pure or impure is a classic example of the delusive *vikalpa* [discrimination or the bifurcation of experience] that needs to be eliminated. To eliminate all delusion therefore means to eliminate all moral codes as well. But this does not excuse selfishness, for a true elimination of delusion will also eliminate all those self-centered ways of thinking that motivate selfish behavior. Deeper than the imperfectly flexible strictures of any moral code (which may still have value as "rules of thumb") is the concern for others that springs up spontaneously within those who have realized their true nature. This is the heart of the Taoist critique of Confucianism, which sees Confucian emphasis on such doctrines as righteousness and propriety as an attempt to close the barn door after the horse of natural feeling has already run away.[28]

The will, in the dualistic state of awareness, attempts to manipulate the numerous separate and emotionally unattached entities of the world in order to reconstruct some sense of interconnection, by means of laws, regulations, prohibitions, and intellectual prescriptions and requirements. But, "nondual action does not imply wanton, merely spontaneous activity like that of a spoiled child. The point is more subtle . . . [A]cculturation introduces ethical factors (e.g., a superego) that condition our instinctive selfishness, but nonduality, in denying an ego-self, eliminated the basis of selfishness."[29] Action which emanates from a willful ego simply serves to increasingly dualize us, i.e. separates us from others, and from the natural environment. Action which ema-

nates from a peaceful, meditative, empathetically enfolding state of awareness is already selflessly acting so as to preserve and to protect all that this
embrasive state embraces. It is not that such action is necessarily done
without thinking, but that the thinking is a heartfelt and spontaneous
thinking from the depths of one's integrated being, and that this state is
a state of compassion and love. This point is emphasized again and again
in Far Eastern philosophy: "When the cursed barrier of egoism is broken
down, there remains nothing that can prevent us from loving others as
ourselves."[30] Or, "It is apparent that the ethical application of the doctrine of [n]irvāna is naught else than the Golden Rule, so called. The
Golden Rule, however, does not give any reason why we should so act, it
is a mere command whose authority is ascribed to a certain superhuman
being."[31] The reason which Suzuki gives in support of acting in accordance with the Golden Rule, on behalf of Buddhism, is the finding of
"the oneness of things . . . from which flows the eternal stream of love
and sympathy."[32] The emphasis on the "enlightenment state," is an emphasis on "the spiritual expansion of the ego, or, negatively, the ideal
annihilation of the ego," which then produces a "never-drying stream of
sympathy and love."[33] David Loy states the case this way:

> Insofar as I realize my true nature, perhaps love becomes, not something
> that I have, but something that I participate in. Such love would neces-
> sarily be non-discriminatory. In moving from the sense of myself as an
> alienated consciousness to an awareness that all phenomena are a mani-
> festation of the same nondual ground, love and compassion would spon-
> taneously arise for all beings. Understanding myself as a facet of the
> Whole, I would naturally identify with all other facets of the Whole.[34]

If the self is not thought of as an independent, self-existing, substantial entity, we are less likely to have a disposition towards self-love and
self-attachment, the Buddhists maintain. "Self-centeredness is simply an
outcome of this reification or substantialization of the self." Indeed, this
reification and substantialization of the self, "and its resultant self-
centeredness are the root-source of evil and human suffering. Accordingly, as a way of salvation, Buddhism teaches the necessity of realizing
the nonsubstantiality of the self, that is, of realizing no-self or *anatman*."[35]

WU-WEI AND NON-DOING

For the most part, evil is conceived of quite differently in the East and
West. In much of the East, evil arises when one covers over one's
natural inclinations towards goodness. Evil is, more often than not,

associated with willfullness and selfishness. In the West, it is willfullness that is the solution, and willfullness is inescapably an individual matter. To be an individual in no way requires that one be selfish, but it is not always a simple matter to keep the two separate. From the perspective of much of the East, it is necessary to get the will out of the way if one wishes to move from egoism to a wider vision of things, and in order to grow from selfishness to selflessness. In any case, Danto's assertion that "[w]u [w]ei, nondoing, celebrates the power of immobility,"[36] reads the ironic surface of Taoist and Oriental thought in general, while missing completely its deeper insights. The Tao is able to do without doing not by being immobile, but by acting powerfully and decisively in the least aggressive, least damaging, and the least disempowering way possible with respect to others. The water that finds the path of least resistance as it meanders down a hillside still finds its way to the stream-bed at its base. It may take longer, but it does less harm along the way. Humans would do well to follow the example of the stream, for human ways tend to be forcing ways, violent ways, and the wounds acquired in war and in courts of justice often take whole lifetimes—or longer—to scar over. Long before that, the stream of gentle persuasion and patient example will have reached the bottom of the hillside, having achieved what it set out to achieve without the negative fallout that besets the other model. We may well ask ourselves which approach is more likely to achieve its ends. Force is not ruled out, but is a far distant last resort. We in the West, by contrast, are often of the opinion that if we are courageous and principled, we ought to be able to bring about the desired results right now, at whatever cost. There is something about steadfastly standing for one's beliefs and values without waver-ing that brings with it a sort of bonus moral credit. The Taoist quietly urges non-violent, non-aggressive action, which will in all likelihood achieve its goal before any aggressive action—at least long before the aggressor has been able to heal the scars of conquest and the suffer-ing and indignity of violence done. It is anything but a do-nothing model.

EVIL

There is much more to say about nonaggressive action, or creative quietude, or active inaction, or not-forcing, but I want to say something more about how evil arises in this Taoistic-Buddhist scheme of things. If the Confucian Mencius distilled the focus of the Chinese assumption that human beings are by nature good, then Lao Tzu was able to throw out the bath water while saving the baby by maintaining that our natural state is prior to the distinction between good and evil. As babies, we come into the world as "uncarved blocks" (*p'u*), free from hostility and aggressiveness, but also free of a vast array of distinctions that divide the world up into the useful and the useless, the good and the bad, the progressive and the regressive. It is the mark of civilization that distinctions arise, and when there is recognition of goodness, there is, necessarily and axiomatically the recognition of evil, for otherwise "goodness" would be unable to identify what it is that it is not. Benjamin Schwartz beautifully describes the fall from the Taoist "garden of Eden":

> But why does civilization arise? Here our focus shifts to the mysterious emergence within the human *hsin* (mind) of an unprecedented new kind of consciousness that seems to exist nowhere else in nature. Somehow within the Eden of the *tao*, there arises the deliberative, analytic mind which has the fatal capacity to isolate the various forms, constituents, and forces of nature from their places in the whole in which they abide, to become fixated on them, and to make them the objects of newly invented desires and aspiration. The human mind itself becomes, through this new consciousness, isolated from the flow of the tao and finds its meaning in asserting its separate existence against the whole.[37]

The Taoists were fully aware of the evils that were perpetrated in the name of the good, of the goods of yesterday that have since been "seen" to have been evil, and of the evils of yesterday that are now considered to be socially acceptable, or encouraged. But perhaps the point of Taoism can be best understood by us as an ancient form of ecological living. As with the Far East generally, in overwhelming proportion, human nature is seen to be an extension of the nature of the universe itself. To follow nature is to be in accordance with one's own nature, and to follow one's own nature is to be in accordance with the rhythms of nature, the world, and the cosmos as a whole. As Schwartz observed, it is the analytic mind which isolates by distinguishing, and then sets about to encourage what it values positively, and to eliminate what it values negatively. And while some of this is inevitable, even for the Taoist, it is the excessiveness with which we reform nature, with which we carve out a place for civilization, by which we harness and exercise our dominion over nature, and with which we so quickly attack evil and then aggressively extract the good-for-our-purposes that leads to the personal, social, and ecological downfall of the present day. We have lost the sense of flowing, and we no longer are content with dwelling in a world which is our neighborhood. But what we have lost that is most precious is our sense of the whole of things, our sense of the supportiveness of this great evolutionary flow of adventure that is this human and non-human existence. It is not that we have simply lost our sense of wonder, but that we have lost our sense of the whole. And while the curse is evident, both East and West, it might be argued that it is worse in the West because we are the home of the analytic mind, where the word "mind" does not mean "heart" or "spontaneous arising." Nor does this analytic mind synthesize nearly as well as it takes apart. For us there is no recent loss, just the inexorable working out of what we have already put in motion as our manner of being-in-the-world.

ON HUMAN HEARTEDNESS

An Eastern perspective switches focus from the tension from the will and the keeping under control of those inevitable evil inclinations, to the spontaneous arising of our natural sense of compassion and feelings of human heartedness. It is a move from the will to the heart. Focus on the "letter of the law," on rules and regulations, can take us away from what is the center of ethical thinking, for Confucians, Taoists, and Buddhists: that central ethical ideal is human heartedness (*jen* in Confucianism; *tz'u* in Taoism; *kokoro* in Zen Buddhism; *mettā* and *karunā* in Buddhism). One can do the right thing without either wanting to, or without a feeling of caring, or with no human heartedness. One can go through the motions, one can act correctly, but for the Oriental mind, the great characters in their tradition all act as they do out of the spontaneous arising of human heartedness which they express in whatever ways are appropriate to the situation at hand. This is an agent-oriented criterion of ethical action, rather than an act-oriented criterion. Whereas Kant would have us act in accordance with maxims and principles, and would praise us for acting against the grain of our natural inclinations, the Far East stresses doing what we do, not out of duty alone, but out of a sense of respect, reverence, righteousness, or caring. It must arise spontaneously, effortlessly and uncalculatedly, and for no ulterior reasons. It arises from our deeper "will," which is more like an expression of innate goodness, rather than from the more surface will of obligation and calculation. Ideally, as Confucius remarks, when one matures, then one's inclinations, one's moral duty, will always and spontaneously coincide. To quote David Loy once more, "the only way to transcend the dualism between the self and the other is to act without intention—that is, without attachment to some projected goal to be obtained from the action—in which case the agent can simply be the act."[38]

The dualistic state of consciousness emphasizes separation from the world, and it is this sense of separation that is itself the root cause of both evil and suffering. The non-dualistic state leads one to recognize that the entire course of history has led to the existence of things existing here and now, just as they are. While we necessarily interfere and intervene in order to live, and to eat and to act, we are likely to interfere and to intervene less, and certainly less aggressively, when we both see and feel the world in this way. We will act non-actively, we will live from a sense of peaceful coexistence, and we will take joy from the manifoldness of the flux which is the world, and of which we are not only a part, but which, at our depths, we actually are.

A Radical Interdependence

While Danto's image of Western ethics is one of arduous striving to keep negative impulses in check, the East emphasizes the spontaneous and seemingly effortless arising of feelings of human heartedness and compassion. It is not that effort is not required to achieve such a state of spontaneity, but that the goal is an effortless "willing," a spontaneous expression of an already existing inclination from deep within one's whole being. In the Far East, spontaneity comes at the end of training and discipline, and not early on. As with ballet, one has to practice for years before one can break loose and interpret in an individualistic way, perhaps breaking new ground. Ethically, too, one is brought up within a civilizing tradition, and even the Taoists broke away from Confucian training and did not grow up in a cultural vacuum. Ordinary people continue to march more or less in step with the rules and regulations of their culture (*li*), but the enlightened, wise, and sage-like few go beyond the rules and regulations to that state before moral distinctions were carved out of the heretofore undifferentiated whole of existence. Chuang Tzu in particular refers to this undifferentiated state as *chaos*, presumably because *cosmos* already implies order and classification, whereas chaos is to be taken as referring to everything that is a part of the undifferentiated flow. He engages us in a process which one writer has termed "chaotification,"[39] which means that all boundaries and distinctions will appear and disappear, move, shuffle from one place to another, and reappear in a different place, as in a dream. So, whether Chuang Tzu dreamt that he was a butterfly, or the other way around, the fluidity which this image presents is that of "the transmutation of things." Reality is something quite different from what it appears to be to reason. Thus, what we are given is two quite different points of reference: that of ordinary consciousness, where things are civilized and distinct, and where good and evil are in their place however much they shift from age to age, and that of the chaotic vision which apprehends things as they might be seen by one who had not yet distinguished them, classified them, and made judgments about them morally and valuationally. Everything is a manifestation of one and the same reality, and while there is *b* and *c*, phenomenally, *b* and *c* are both *a*, at this deeper level of metaphysical understanding.

Similar images apply to many of the other Far Eastern traditions, as well. In Buddhist thought, the Jewel Net of Indra is a powerful image of cosmic interconnection and interdependence which reappears again and again. Each jewel in this great net reflects every other jewel, and each of them, in turn, reflect it. Francis H. Cook has observed that in the West, the science of ecology has only recently begun to show that the environment is an interrelated and interdependent web of existence. He notes as well that "the traditional methods of analysis, classification, and isolation [have] tended to erect boundaries around things, setting them apart in groups. . . ."[40] What Hua-yen Buddhism has pictured from earliest times is not just a world, but a cosmos, a universe which is so interrelated that any one thing reflects everything else, and everything else is reflected in any one thing. Let me quote Cook's paraphrasing of this image:

> Far away in the heavenly abode of the great god Indra, there is a wonderful net which has been hung by some cunning artificer in such a manner that it stretches out infinitely in all directions. In accordance with the extravagant tastes of deities, the artificer has hung a single glittering jewel in each "eye" [or section] of the net, and since the net itself is infinite in dimension, the jewels are infinite in number. There hang the jewels, glittering like stars of the first magnitude, a wonderful sight to behold. If we now arbitrarily select one of these jewels for inspection and look closely at it, we will discover that in its polished surface there are reflected all the other jewels in the net, infinite in number. Not only that, but each of the jewels reflected in this one jewel is also reflecting all the other jewels, so that there is an infinite reflecting process occurring.[41]

The result is that there is a mutual identity to be grasped such that what happens to any one jewel happens to all of the others as well. To destroy a single jewel will not cause the net to fall, or even to flutter noticeably, but the loss will be recorded infinitely, in each of the other jewels, and in the reflections of each of the jewels in each of the other jewels. To "understand" any one jewel is to understand them all. Each is inextricably connected to the other.

In Mahāyāna Buddhism, the doctrine of "dependent origination," or of "interdependent origination" as it is sometimes termed, the interrelatedness of all phenomena, is again emphasized. Causally, everything causes everything else, and rather than there being a first cause, everything simultaneously arises, or simultaneously is. Everything is empty in that everything is interdependent, or dependent, and nothing whatsoever is self-sufficient. At the same time, each individual thing is, if properly understood, a mirror of the entire universe, since its coming to exist is inseparable from the causal net of the whole cosmos. Nakamura Hajime draws the appropriate moral conclusion when he writes that ordinary consciousness pays "too much attention to the aspect of difference and to the confrontation between individual human beings. We are not separate beings who are absolutely irrelevant to each other, and have nothing to do with each other."[42] Thus, the all-encompassing ultimate reality is one, or chaos, or nothingness, or emptiness, and it is in this that each person, and every atom moves, and understands.

THE MORALITY OF ENLIGHTENMENT

The state of enlightenment is a non-dual state, a direct awareness of the interconnection that is discernable at the base of all things. At one's deepest level of understanding, one is identified with others, and with everything, as clearly as one is identified with one's own body and mind. If one is the whole world, then one cares about it all as though it were one's self—because it is oneself. One is indistinguishable from it. Evil is delusion, therefore. It is the mistaking of the surface of things as their depth, a confusing of figure and ground, a confusion of one perspective with another—a valuational transposition. The great delusion is that of selfishness, of self-centered action. In avoiding selfish behavior one must eliminate all distinctions that divide one person or one group from another, and this includes moral distinctions. Only selfless thinking, "willing" and feeling, can take us beyond the vagaries of moral codes, and the ultimate in selfless thinking is thinking that eliminates the self altogether, that empties it, and grasps it as a mirror of, or a manifestation of, the whole of things. Delusion is failing to see that one is a manifestation of the whole, and as such, actually re-presents the macrocosm in the microcosm. Rather than speaking of "evil," the Buddhist speaks of "suffering." Suffering is the result of ignorance, and ignorance is the result of delusion, namely, the sense of separation, individualization without a sense of the whole of things. The result is one's alienation from the world and from the cosmos, and eventually from other people as well, and finally from oneself. Evil is separation, willful aggression, selfish separation, painful isolation. "Someone who manipulates the world merely for his own advantage increasingly dualizes himself from it. Those who live in this way cannot help expecting the same from others, leading to a life based on fear and the need to control situations."[43] So, if the entire causal history of the world exists just to bring me into the world, it also exists to bring you into the world, and to bring the single flower to bloom.

> For the nondualist, life is nothing but a series of such timeless sunya experiences: a sip of coffee, a few words with a friend, a walk down a path. Someone who cannot trust his world enough to 'forget himself' and *become* these situations is condemned—or condemns himself—to watch his life ooze away.[44]

In my own work on Nishida Kitarō, I wrote that one may live, act, and understand in such a way as to move away from interdependence, and towards independence. Estrangement from the whole, or centrifugal movement, is the root cause of evil, and identification with the whole, or centripetal movement, is good.[45] But if one has had the nondual experience of interconnectedness, then one spontaneously and effortlessly flows with the whole of things of which he or she is now fixedly conscious. It is not that one cannot pick out the good and evil paths or ways when one applies the analytic mind to the subject matter, but that one can simply live and act in accordance with things such that one respects them as being of the same worth and of the same stuff as one's own self, and one's own beloved, and one's own family, and it might never arise, therefore, that you would wish to harm or destroy another. It is no longer a matter of refraining from harming others, for there is no reason not to be inclined to maintain the whole. No law is needed to protect others, for one *is* others, and to become willful about it by trying to get clear about when and when not to do something will only destroy this original spontaneity and lead to a contrived series of regulations which will never be detailed enough to handle all possible circumstances and situations in a constantly changing world such as ours. Compassion is the natural way, and for one who glimpses the interconnectedness of things it is inevitable. To act compassionately is to act in accordance with the "suchness" of the cosmos. To Buddhists, the cosmos is "radiant" with infinite compassion. Great compassion and a great pitying heart is termed "Buddha-nature," and is seen to be natural to us. What we call "good" actions spring naturally as expressions of who one really is, without calculation, for no reason, for no gain, as expressions of our suchness. Freedom is to do spontaneously what it is one's nature to do. As always, from most Eastern perspectives, such spontaneity arises only after intensive discipline and training, and certainly not automatically as we grow in years. Spontaneity comes after discipline, not before, and it is in our nature only in that it is what we are capable of expressing and experiencing as masters in the art of living and acting. The necessity of freedom is an internal necessity, and expresses a truly good nature. It is true that this inherently good nature must be "cultivated," and can be warped and diseased by an unhealthy environment. Yet if you and I are still lost in discrimination, rather than in the emptiness of things, then we must be taught the traditional Buddhist virtues. But if, as Nakamura writes, "we allow the virtue of compassion to grow in us, it will not occur to us to harm anyone else, any more than we would willingly harm ourselves."[46] We can access this outlook, this way of being in the world, through meditation. Now meditation is not a firm aspect of Western cultural traditions, although it is far from unknown, but it is ubiquitous in the East. The effects of meditation are, writes Nakamura,

> ...to abolish our deep-rooted egoism in our own existence: it aims at cherishing compassion and love towards others. By dissolving our human existence into component parts, we can get rid of the notion of ego, and through that meditation we are led to a limitless expansion of the self in a practical sense, because one identifies oneself with more and more living beings.[47]

CONCLUSION

Have we enough here for a full-blown theory of ethics? I think not, although I am willing to listen to one who thinks we might. Everyone is not enlightened, and so walking within a world which is dualistically perceived, it remains necessary to carve out a system of distinctions, rules and regulations, political and social conventions, etc., in order for us to coexist reasonably well. Yet it is possible to view these as empty necessary conveniences and delusions that allow us to coexist with less harm than might otherwise be the case, the Taoists notwithstanding. Moral rules are empty because we now know that they are but rules of thumb, rough and ready approximations at best, which miss the mark far more often than we would like to admit—and when they do hit the mark, they often do so for the wrong calculated reasons, and can do so without compassion. But for those who do not know that they are empty, they are useful guidelines, and may lead to eventual recognition of their inherent inadequacy. Yet, I am unwilling to abandon rules and regulations in a cultural tradition that does not even recognize the possibility of non-dualistic enlightenment, and that is unaccustomed to meditative peace and quiet. Far Eastern thought, and feminist thought as well, do much to transform our hyperaggressive and hyperactive meddlesome ways into life-patterns which are considerably more interrelational and adaptive. Nell Noddings, in her provocative book *Caring: A Feminine Approach to Ethics and Moral Education,* defends an understanding of human nature as characterized by relatedness rather than separation or isolation in the world. She describes the "ethical ideal" as arising from two sentiments: "the natural sympathy human beings feel for each other, and the longing to maintain, recapture, or enhance our most caring and tender moments."[48] What is distinctive about the Far Eastern perspective on ethics, and is echoed, although no doubt for quite different reasons, in the feminist West of today, is the fundamental assumption that we are from the beginning *in relation,* and only secondarily and dependently individuals. We are individuals, and yet we are individuals only insofar as we are individuals-as-foregrounded expressions of the background whole, which is the family, the social group, society at large, humankind, or the entire cosmos. It makes no sense to speak of an individual except as the individual stands out from the whole of which s/he is a part. Of course, to speak of the whole is to be an individual who stands out from it and reflects back on it, as well. We are individuals only as we recognize that we are individuals related to the social whole, and there is the social whole only as there are individuals who both constitute it and stand apart from it, in reflection, in order to assess its worth, and to direct it. What results is a relational unity of opposites, for we conclude that we are not only part of the social whole, and not just individually distinct, but we are also related to the other person because we are one in communal existence. The group is more than the sum of the individuals who make it up. We are always already related, as well as individual, and this double structure, or double aperture, or stereoscopic vision, is needed in order for us to be able both to account for human individuality and for human relatedness.

Speaking as a comparativist, I think it can now be stated that Danto sees with one lens only. He understands relatedness as an atomistic activity among individuals who must set about to control their wills, lest selfishness prevail. But relatedness can also be glimpsed as the sense of interconnection from the family to the cosmic expanse, which sidesteps the willful need to establish and maintain morality and civilization by instead knowing, feeling, and spontaneously willing that the magnificent whole with which we identify, even to the point of selflessness, be left more or less as it is to wander on in its own seemingly spontaneous and timeless way. The dualistic calculating mind has not brought us a healthy environment, an altogether healthy soul, or nearly as much agreement in the world as one might have thought after several thousand years. I am far too Western to want to abandon the good it has wrought, but too Eastern to ignore the bad. I think it would do us a world of good to breathe feeling back into our ethical theory, and to rekindle the sense of relatedness both to each other, and to the natural environment. The East does not give us "the answer," but I think it does provide us with a part of it. Danto condemns Taoism for recommending that the individual not allow himself to be disturbed by the state of happiness, or its lack, in others. He adds, "no man could be counted moral who did not have that minimal concern for others that permits his own felicity to vary as theirs does."[49] Here he is right, but it is Taoism, and Zen Buddhism, and Buddhism that teach us that we are intrinsically interrelated, and the ground of ethics and the foundation of ethical sentiment is the selfless recognition that we are each other's hopes and aspirations, sufferings and disappointments. The Taoist and the other stances from the Far East can answer why we do and ought to care about the universe, but can Danto answer why we ought to be moral? I think he can do so only by expanding the circle of caring concern (and not just bare intellectual seeing) from smaller group to large, and then to larger still. But that is exactly where the Far Eastern vision of being-in-the-world *begins*. Shintōism, Confucianism, and Buddhism all emphasize the centrality of human heartedness, or compassion as the foundation of ethical theory and practice. An analysis of these ways of thinking and feeling is requisite for a proper understanding of ethics in Japan, where all three of these traditions continue to contribute to that subtle weave which is Japanese cultural consciousness.

2

The Significance of
Shintōism for Japanese Ethics

Eastern thought as a rule offers much more than serious consideration of how we ought to behave with respect to others. It includes the spiritual and the secular, a sensitivity to beauty and to behavior, and attention to dying well and not just living well. Much of this stands in sharp contrast with modern and contemporary Western thought, which has been concerned with theories of truth and the criteria of knowledge and its justification; the "meta" discussion of the standards of correct and defensible action, and the creation of distinct methodologies and quite separate content for each of the "disciplines." Ethics in Eastern thought is intended to point towards an entire way of life, a way of being in the world. It includes guidance with respect to our interpersonal and societal relationships and requirements, as well as our ideal relationship with nature, and it also moves us towards a deeper understanding of our own happiness, developmental transformation, and spiritual growth. Eastern philosophic and religious traditions regularly instruct in the cultivation of appropriate attitudes and states of consciousness that will enhance the quality of one's life, and the lives of those with whom one interacts. Yet in Western traditions, at least in modern times, it would not be considered an ethical imperative that one be cheerful, or even sincere. From the Shintō perspective cheerfulness is ethically relevant, for how one greets and treats others is a part of what it means to be in social relationships. To be sincere is not only an affirmation of one's integrity, but it fosters trust between people, and announces at least a partial willingness to reveal something of one's self beneath the surface presentation of self. Cheerfulness and sincerity are basic expressions of one's attitudes towards others, towards the world and one's place in it. They express who we are, and for the Japanese mind, such expression is ethically drenched in significance. We are not born alone, nor do we die alone from the Japanese perspective: we are always already in relationship, from the mother's womb, through the various relationships of living, to one's eventual death. Even if one should be unlucky enough to die in a remote place, with no one else around, one nonetheless dies in relationship to others: one's clothes and shoes, food and medicine, and memories are either the products of others, or an affirmation of one's inextricable ties to others. Interconnection with others is an inescapable aspect of being in the world.

THE IMPORTANCE OF THE SHINTŌ PERSPECTIVE

Until quite recently I had assumed that Confucianism and Buddhism were the ethical springs of Japan. Now, along with some others, I am convinced it is Shintō that continues to serve as the most significant source of Japanese ethics. Robert J. J. Wargo remarks that Japan is not a Buddhist culture like Thailand, nor is it a Confucian culture as China clearly was and may well still be, nor is it a Western culture in spite of the many Western elements that Japan has adopted: "Rather, the basic *Weltanschauung* is, for want of a better term, Shintōist. Not the codified set of regulations and dogmas propounded in the nineteenth century under the title of State Shintō; but rather the basic attitudes toward the world that underlay the agriculturally oriented religious practices . . . which continue down to this day."[1] It must also be admitted, however, that modern scholarship is divided over whether in ancient times there was any such thing as "Shintō," not only because it was not until the fifteenth century that the term was used to refer to Japan's indigenous religion, but also because it is now clear that what we now term "Shintō" was anything but a homogeneous collection of practitioners of the same rituals and rites, let alone beliefs. Summarizing the work of Kuroda Toshio, Mark Teeuwen writes that so-called "Ancient Shintō" was nothing more than "an unorganised set of beliefs which owed much to Taoism; that Shintō in the Nara and Heian periods 'occupied a subordinate position and role within the broader scheme of Buddhism'; and that in medieval times, the term was 'not used to distinguish popular beliefs from Buddhism but rather to signify the form in which the

Buddha converts and saves human beings.'"[2] The transformation and reinterpretation of the "*kami*-cults," as some scholars prefer to call them, continued into the Meiji period when an ideology of national identity and imperial fervor was appended. What is most at issue is the extent to which it can legitimately be claimed that Shintō is a continuous and more or less homogeneous indigenous spirituality. As Teeuwen suggests, "the closer we look at Shintō, or, for that matter, at indigenous religion as a whole, the more variety we see. The conventional use of the word Shintō hides a baffling variety of rituals, beliefs, and community structures."[3]

However one stands on this issue, it must be admitted that there is not just one sense of Japanese culture, let alone one sense of Shintō, but that whatever comes to be taken as Japanese is a confluence of many sources, indigenous and imported, in varying measures forming distinct differences. That is why this book considers several basic strands of influence, even before moving to the modern period. Nonetheless, while all generalizations are lies, they do seem to be necessary in coming to understand how one thing is—more or less—the same as or different from something else. Thus, keeping the warning in mind, surely there are common characteristics to be discerned in the attitudes of the Japanese people. While the origins of Shintō (or the *kami*-cults) is, and may remain obscure, the mere fact that Confucianism, Taoism (in Zen, amongst other places), Buddhism and Ch'an Buddhism all underwent metamorphosis upon entering the Japanese environment makes it abundantly clear that there was a cultural/religious/philosophical environment that was powerful enough to both withstand and reshape all that entered. Whatever that amalgam of qualities was, for the purposes of this study, it will be referred to as Shintō.

Utilizing a tree metaphor, Wargo writes the

> Shintōist orientation is like the root system of a tree that has been subjected to massive pruning and shaping by external forces. It is the shape and interlacing network of branches that excite one's interest and admiration; but it is the *roots*—which store and send back up vital nutrients—that underlie the dynamism of growth and revitalize the cultural tree, which otherwise would die from injury to its above-ground parts.[4]

It is an unusual tree, because even what is visible aboveground is intentionally shrouded. As Jean Herbert observes, while the traditional schools of Shintō teach their initiates precise "metaphysical concepts" about the world, these teachings are "kept secret from the uninitiated, whether laymen or scholars and priests, who have not submitted to the appropriate disciplines." Indeed, he adds, "Shintōists view with a considerable amount of disfavour all intellectual cogitation on religious matters, and are content with a metaphysics which is both fragmentary and vague."[5] Shintō is an instinctive stance, an attitudinal predisposition, unconsciously or non-consciously ingested in much the same way that language, and so many subtle forms of social behavior simply appear, without seemingly having been taught at all. One's relationship "to the *kami* was a communal rather than an individual affair, since the local objects of worship were most likely non-personified powers that protected the village or the forces of nature essential to the agricultural cycle."[6] Furthermore, it is predictably the case that the best way to come to comprehend the power and the essence of the Shintō experience is through participation in a communal ritual or festival. Stuart Picken writes that "the strength of Shintō lies in its survival in ritual. Ritual has the power to keep thought alive. . . . Shintō has been preserved most effectively not through doctrines but rituals and attitudes."[7] More often than not, religion in the West is doctrinal or creedal—what is important to know, for example, is whether or not one believes in God—whereas in much of Eastern religiosity emphasis is placed on experience, or perhaps on the rituals that one performs in an attempt to bring on the spiritual experiences sought. As Picken observes, "Japanese religion tends to be based on feelings rather than ideas, on experiences rather than doctrines." Religion is to be found at the subconscious level, rather than at the conscious level of verbal affirmation or theological distinction making.[8]

Sustaining the image, the Shintō tree has no founder (whose life can be scrutinized for guidance and understanding); no scripture (except for a few creation myths about the creation of Japan, and the lineage of the Emperor from the creator *kami* or gods); no revelation to study (including the fact that there are no moral directives from above to be obeyed on pain of punishment); no systematic moral code; no codified teachings; no sin to overcome; and therefore no thirst for salvation. And what little there is that is taught, is taught only to those who are initiated into the priesthood, and whose meditative advancement warrants their being told (in full, to a greater or lesser extent, depending on the degree of their advancement and spiritual awareness), thereby assuring its proper use. For the rest of us, at least at first glance, there are simply festivals, festivals, and more festivals.

To repeat, the climate of Shintō is so unconsciously derived, that is to say, it reaches back so far into the wellsprings of Japanese cultural tradition, that it is difficult to notice or recognize, let alone articulate.

Picken notes that even Shintō priests are more often than not unable to provide either coherent or consistent accounts of their tradition, if for no other reason than that "there is indeed a notable lack of interest in formal consistency of beliefs or ideas."[9] Intellectual debate, precisely formulated doctrines, the fine shaving of an intellectual nuance or two, are all utterly beside the point. Shintō is about directly experiencing one's kinship with the world around one, with purifying oneself in order to experience once more the divinity of one's own inner depths.

Shrine Shintō (Common Shintō)

Misunderstandings arise as well because of the ambiguity and hostility created by the relatively recent appearance (nineteenth to twentieth centuries) of State Shintō, which served the cause of ultra-nationalism with such dedication before and during the Second World War.[10] The many acts of magic and fortune-telling which seem to cluster around popular Shintō also create misunderstandings. Of course, Western religions are not without their popular magic, either. Be this as it may, what continues to emerge from the serious study of Shintō is something quite admirable, and philosophically and religiously significant. It begins, much as did Confucianism, with the view that human beings (and in Shintō, the world of Nature itself) are basically good.[11] Mason opts for a different position, maintaining that humankind "is neither naturally sinful nor naturally good, but is divine spirit on earth seeking self-development and creative action in new ways, and in the course of this evolution, experience and inexperience lead to good results as well as bad results. In this sense Shintō is pragmatic."[12] Either way, there is certainly no sense in which humankind is thought to be basically sinful, or intrinsically corrupted in some way. Rather, our genuine purpose is divine purpose. We have divine parentage. Moreover, to speak of evil is to miss the point of active and aware living in the first place: it is not that there is evil to contend with, but that the incessant flow of things brings with it things to deal with, natural circumstances to overcome or to learn from. Having to deal with things is an integral part of the human condition: it is not that we have fallen, but that the world issues challenges, and demands experimentation and personal growth if we are to flourish. Apparent evil, therefore, may bring about much good, and what was once thought to be evil, like speaking one's mind in a society that previously prohibited it, may come to be thought of as good. As Wargo aptly summarizes, "what was counted as good or evil depended very much on the specific conditions obtaining as well as on the nature of the community to which one belonged. This is not to say that all moral evaluations were merely conventional or totally relative, but simply that any attempt to spell out the distinctions in a tightly reasoned system would fail."[13] Wargo goes on to say that what counted more than anything else were sincerity and courtesy, or a clear indication of purity of heart and good will. These attitudes would do much to overcome whatever circumstances there were to deal with, thereby maintaining harmony in, and the good will of, the community.

The key notion for understanding the standpoint of Shintō is *kami*, which we often translate as "god." Such an attempt at translation misses the mark in almost every way, and is more an overlay of Western assumptions (and theological requirements) on a very different tradition. *Kami* means something more like the mystery, superior quality, and the awesome, whether in what the West might call the "supernatural," or in men and women of special achievement, or even in rocks, and trees, and magnificent waterfalls and high mountains. Divinity, the awesome, the mysterious, the *mysterium tremendum* is immanent in the world, rather than transcendent and separate from the world except for specific interventions in its history. Nature is not something to be tamed, overcome, and subdued; Nature is divine, to be learned from, to be thankful for, and to be immersed in. Throughout its history Shintō has refused to express the nature of *kami* in any sort of image. Kadowaki Kakichi contends that this is due to the fact that *kami* is not grasped as a substance, but as an infinite activity, a process, "and an infinite activity cannot be expressed as any kind of image."[14] Furthermore, we apprehend this process, or life force, or awesome power, with our hearts, rather than with our minds. Therefore, "because the recipient of the kami-experience is the sentient, guileless [sincere] heart, innocent of any reasoning process, when the content of the experience is translated into words, the constructive imagination and not the intellect is at the center and controls the process; thus it cannot escape using the form of myths."[15]

In the Beginning

Metaphysically speaking, in the beginning there was subjectivity as the unseen and not yet objectified, or "divine spirit"—creative spirit. Then, subjectivity objectified, that is to say, the invisible became visible, the unseeable became seeable, the non-material materialized. It did this as something which we might refer to as self-expression, as a "seeking [after] self-creative growth, with freedom of choice."[16] This account of the divine spirit expressing itself implies that everything that exists is, therefore, divine. There is no dualism of good and bad, divine and satanic, heaven and hell. There simply is what there is, and it is all the divine as manifest. Human beings are divine. Human beings "share one and the same divine blood which flows through animals, plants, minerals and all other things in Nature."[17] It is not that we are *kami*-like, for that implies a difference, and therefore a separation, and a dualism. There is no sense, however, of a supreme deity, separate from that which is created, creating the human and material world, and guarding and guiding it in some omniscient and omnipotent way. *Kami* literally refers to that which is superior, and thereby occasions a sense of awe, and elicits respect. "Whenever an object or a place inspired a sense of awe in man because of its power or beauty, it was said to be a *kami*— or a place where a *kami* resided. Anything which had this cosmic charisma was a *kami*, whether it was a rock, a mountain, a man, or a phenomenon of nature. Hence there is an essential oneness about the universe."[18] But even beyond this sense of the "special," or the "extraordinary," in a real sense everybody and everything is *kami*, that is, everybody and everything has a heavenly origin, and therefore everybody and everything is essentially good.

However, goodness is not simply a relabeling of everything that might be termed "bad" or "evil" as "good." For *kami* has both a heavenly and an earthly sense or meaning. There is not a dualism of valuation, however, with the heavenly being higher, and the earthly less worthy. The earthly is the heavenly objectified, as material. We are not *kami*-like, then, for we are *kami* in the full sense. Nor is our body the source of corruption, and our soul divine. Body is the materialization of *kami*, and what we might call "soul" is the immaterial aspect of *kami*. Again, there is no dualism. There is a higher and a lower nature, but both are divine spirit. Herbert analyses this double sense in some detail, beginning with the word *hito*, a word for "human being" that means "a place where the spirit is."[19] A fuller account of human being may be derived from two phrases that include *hito: ame-no-masu-hito* and *ao-hito-gusa*. *Ame-no-masu-hito* displays the double meaning with considerable precision: it means "heavenly-increasing-man" or "sacred human being increasing infinity." *Ao-hito-gusa* literally means "green-man-grass," which compares humankind to grass as thriving and filled with vital force, and thereby "it clearly stresses his [humankind's] earthly nature."[20] We are of the earth, and we are spirit. While there is little or no reference to the issue of human immortality in ancient Shintō, it is generally agreed by scholars that there is something akin to a soul which survives the death of the body, and which continues to live on, as is recognized in

Japan by the practice of showing respect for dead and distant ancestors. This show of reverence, or "worship" as it is often mislabled, is even today everywhere in evidence in Japan. That which lives on is *tama* or *mitama*, and is related to *tamashii*, which means "the spirit bestowed by the *Kami* . . . probably the higher part or aspect of the *tama*."[21] *Tamashii* may be that part of the *tama* which can become *kami*, whereas *mono*, the so-called lower part, cannot. This would seem to imply that everything is not *kami*, but Herbert reports that the lower may be that "which governs the unconscious movements of the body, [and] appear at conception; the other . . . is really the soul of the parents. . . ."[22] The lower is lower in that it is more or less equivalent, it would seem, to the autonomic nervous system, and is tied to the body, and is therefore perishable, as is the body. It is not that it is not divine, but that it is not eternal. The "higher part," as divine spirit, and, therefore, as subjectively immaterial, is eternal and the essential aspect of a human being. But it *is not lower because it is material:* "It is . . . believed that many— perhaps most, perhaps even all—entities of the animal, vegetable and even mineral kingdoms have *tama* of their own."[23]

Furthermore, it is the case that *kami* themselves have a dual nature. While it is true that anything and everything may be *kami,* there is another sense in which the *kami* are personifications of divine spirit enshrined in a sacred building, or located at a sacred place. At least so they appear to us, or are represented by us in this personified way. At the same time, this personification is held lightly, for as one writer has put it, "the *Kami* have no form, but only function."[24] It is generally maintained that *kami* may be classified into two groups, the heavenly *kami* and the earthly *kami*, and it is less than clear how they interact with one another. Perhaps that need not concern us here, for the more important point for ethics is that each and every *kami* has both a "Rough Divine Spirit" (*Ara-Mitama*), or the spirit of creative activity, and a "Gentle Divine Spirit" (*Nigi-Mitama*), which Mason refers to as "the balancing counterpart."[25] It is not that some *kami* are of one type, and others are of the other: all *kami* are both, for these are but different aspects or manifestations of the same spirit. Why the two? Jean Herbert explains this by means of the focal Shintō word, *musubi. Musubi* means "the spirit of birth and becoming; also birth, accomplishment, combination; the creating and harmonizing powers." It comes from *musu*, which means "to beget," and from which the Japanese words for son (*musuko*) and daughter (*musume*) also derive, and *bi*, which applies "to whatever is wonderful, miraculous and ineffably worthy of honour, and to the Sun *par excellence*." *Musubi* is a dynamic, creative, evolutionary power in things which produces, fecundates, brews, and ferments. This creative fertility includes the positive, male energy, which is "the forward, expansive, swelling, exhaling, diversifying" energy of spring and summer, and the female energy which is "contractive, absorbing, inhaling, unifying or reintegrating," as in autumn and winter.[26] This female energy is particularly pertinent to our continuing tree analogy, for it is in the autumn and winter when the tree's vital energy is focused on the growth of the root system underground. *Musubi* also means completion or conclusion, and the power of synthesis, which makes of male and female, summer and winter, a harmonizing cycle of creative regeneration and growth. Thus, "Divine spirit in human beings has its two natures. Divinity does not mean, in Shintō, absolute purity, for if it did, the impure would not be divine spirit and a dualistic conception would result which is not contained in Shintō mythology. Virtue and vice both characterize divine spirit."[27]

KAMI AND EVIL

By now it should be apparent that *kami* does not refer to an omnipotent deity, or a perfect deity of the kind that St. Anselm and Descartes, among others, took to be utterly self-evident. Divine spirit is adventurous, ever seeking out new avenues of experience, of development, of growth. "So divine spirit can take the wrong road as well as the right, and can sacrifice itself to its own eventual progress. Whatever the result, good or bad, *kami* is always *kami:* divine spirit can never lose its divinity."[28] Divine spirit is expansive, seeking out new ways of advancement, seeking "to expand in absolutely new ways not known in advance."[29] An omnipotent and omniscient God cannot be thought of as expanding, or seeking out the unknown, or making mistakes in order to learn from them. But creativity in Shintō means producing the spontaneously new, the unforeseen and unforeseeable, without end. As Mason writes, "in self-creating limitless reality of objective action, divine spirit encounters obstacles due to lack of experience, and these obstacles we call 'evil.' "[30] How different this account is from the more typical Western account which puzzles over why an all-powerful and all-good God would allow evil. Even the escape, which emphasizes human freedom, suffers from the fact that God "the Father" certainly could have given us more information, more direct contact, more counseling than He did, even with Moses, Christ, Mohammed, etc. considered. I do not mean to say that these traditions are unable to cope with the problem of evil, but only that they must struggle with it in ways that are different from the ways in which Shintō must struggle with evil. And that difference may be instructive in our own attempts to understand our nature as human beings, as embodied, as part of nature, and even as divine.

The whole world, then, is sacred, and the mistakes that are made by the divine spirit incarnate *as us*, are but learning experiences. Ah, but surely the Holocaust cannot be so easily dealt with, nor can the rape of women in Bosnia/Hersagovena, nor the brutal slaughter of aboriginals in the rainforests of the Amazon. And however much one may have succumbed to the "difference" which is so characteristically Japanese, it is simply impossible to think so glibly of the willful cause of suffering, indignity, pain, and the loss of life as a "mistake."

Before attempting a Shintōist answer to such questions, it might be helpful to explore the nature and origins of Shintō. While Shintō is perhaps the heart of Japanese spirituality, Ian Reader maintains that it is a mistake to overlook "the influence of the religious traditions that entered Japan from the sixth century C.E. onwards, an era in which Japan received enormous cultural infusions from the Asian mainland, including the Chinese writing system, but most notably the cultural and religious traditions of Buddhism, Confucianism and Taoism."[31] Shintō, then, is likely a blend of indigenous and adopted influences, sharing a common emphasis on ritual and an animistic sense of the sacred in natural objects. Given this awareness of the sacred all around and even within, the aim is to walk in accord with this sense of the divine. A Shintōist then, is one who follows "the Way of the *kami*," *kannagara-no-michi*. In Herbert's words, human beings "should conform to what they understand to be the will of the Heavenly *kami* and should emulate the lives of those earthly men [and women] who themselves became great *kami*."[32] One is not given a catechism of morality, but one comes to absorb the right attitudes and stances in the world from one's family, community, nation, and shrine. *Michi* means something like the sacred blood or energy or spirit of the cosmos, and is the cosmic vitalizing force or energy, "and may be taken to be the present biological link between individual man [and woman] and the cosmos, including the *Kami*."[33] Hirai Naofusa explains this divine interconnectedness; "That which is in the universe is called *Kami;* that which is in all things is called spirit (*tama*); and that which is in man is called heart (*kokoro*, [the spontaneous welling-up of human heartedness, or fellow-feeling which seeks no rewards or recognition, and is totally uncalculated or planned])."[34] Herbert claims that *michi* "is probably the most expressive term in the Japanese vocabulary of ethics and religion."[35] In its common use, it means a way, path or road, and is akin to the Chinese Tao. A person of *michi* is a person "of character, of justice, of principle, of conviction, obedient to the nature of his [her] humanity." *Michi* is the path of the ideal, and it links "the subject in some awe-inspiring way with the height and the depth of the great All. It implies the essence of human life linked with the life superhuman."[36] Picken captures this nicely by means of a clever "table" of comparison: "Shintō is indeed a religion that is 'caught' rather than 'taught,' its insights 'perceived' before they are 'believed,' its basic concepts 'felt' rather than 'thought.'"[37]

Teaching by emulation is common in the Far East. (Think of the many campaigns launched in Communist China that, by means of huge billboards and countless flyers, tell the story of comrade X, who gave up his summer vacation in order to voluntarily work on a farm, thereby selflessly contributing to the greater good of the entire nation. Confucius, too, encouraged us to emulate the wise men of old, who displayed their virtue and honor in their lives.) By modeling oneself after another, one does not need to memorize rules and regulations, but to make one's own those attitudes and motives which characterize a "hero" or "heroine." Jesus summarized the "law" by reminding his followers that all that was necessary was to love God with all of one's heart, and to love one's neighbor as thyself. For the law was substituted a fundamental attitudinal stance towards the universe, and towards other people. Reading the New Testament, one is inspired by a man/God who was filled with the divine spirit, and who was fully expressive of love for all people, of whatever kind. The Buddha was an enlightened being, i.e., one who was fully aware of his own divinity or divine-filledness, and whose heart-felt empathetic identification for all earthly suffering and pain made him an utterly compassionate being. Gandhi was a model of the steadfast, truthful, and selfless human being who acted without regard for his own physical safety. Mohammed was a God-intoxicated human being who sought to bring his people back to righteousness, and to remind them of their intrinsic closeness to the divine spirit. These are but a few examples of the conveying of ethical and religious attitudes by means of an emulatory approach to the great religious leaders, past and present, rather than a legalistic attempt to identify the specific ethical decisions made in order to generalize or even universalize their intent. Of course, while it is easy to say that one wishes to love one's neighbor as oneself, it is often extremely difficult to know in practice what to do, given that one's neighbor's children continually break down the fence surrounding your house, or break the branches from the trees that you have newly planted. Attitudes require specific implementation, and not only is it difficult to know how to resolve difficulties of this sort, it is not always plain whether the rough or the gentle *kami* ought to be in charge. Still, it would be easier to deal with one's neighbor if that neighbor were also emulatory of the spirit of Jesus, or Buddha, or Mohammad, or the Heavenly *kami,* if for no other reason than its implying a spirit of good will, and an eagerness to work things out in a positive and creative way. Such negotiations would take as their background a sense of the relational interconnections between those involved and their mutual desire to realize their desire to act with integrity, and in the sight of the deity.

Coupled with this sense of being linked with one's neighbor and with the "All," is the sense of flowing with the All. *Michi* describes a Way which is effortless, and which expresses itself in a spontaneous ethical correctness. One now acts with the flow of nature itself, flowing as effortlessly as a trickle of water flows down a slight incline. The natural is right. Well, perhaps, but there are many meanings of "natural," and in one sense there was nothing unnatural about the Holocaust, or about vicious rape. Such acts are done by natural beings, to natural beings, in a natural world, at least in some sense. "Nature" must be qualified somehow.

We use the term "inhuman" to describe an action that is despicable. It is an attempt not to sully our conception of human being, either in the ideal, or in the rather wide sense of "ordinary" or "normal" or "healthy." But literally, of course, any and all actions performed by human beings, are "human" acts, nonetheless. It is the deviation from the norm, from what is considered to be normal, or healthy, or ordinary, that distinguishes such acts as abnormal, evil, or inhuman. Similarly, in Shintō, a "non-Shintō"[38] act, or an "undivine" act is, nonetheless, a divine act, i.e. an act performed by one who is divine, whatever he or she has done, and however little he or she realizes that divinity, seemingly covered over with the grime and ugliness of everyday living. Such a person has deviated so far from her/his primal, innate, endowed, intuitive awareness of self-divinity and other-divinity, that he or she is no longer worthy of being dignified by the term "divine," or as a follower of the Shintō way. In what has been said, however, a standard of goodness, or right action has been implied. But it cannot be expressed as laws, rules, regulations, etc., because of the ever-changing circumstances, and of the drive for moral and spiritual improvement. Instead, the right way may simply be identified as a way-of-being-in-the-world, or as a *cluster of attitudes* that make possible personal happiness, harmony of self-integration, growth, and creative development and expression (transformation), as well as familial, communal and the wider social happiness, harmony or integration, growth, and creative development.

While goodness is characterized by these qualities, Shintō teaches as well that growth sometimes requires upsetting things, leaving the complacency of happiness and harmony and self-integration behind, and following the unknown and untraveled roads of the rough side or aspect of divinity. Just as the water-bound prehistoric fish had to struggle, and no doubt often die in order to develop the lungs necessary to survive on land, and just as the child places itself in real danger in learning how to stand and then to walk, so people and families, and communities, and groups, and nations, too, need to move on, to adjust to change, to try something new, to strive to improve and to cope with the changing times. The goal of Shintō is not homeostasis, but the readiness and willingness to adapt to new demands while at the same time staying centered, balanced, and agile. Like a Taoist Tai Chi master, one must be rooted while at the same time remaining flexible and ready for anything. Knees and elbows bent, able to go on the offensive or to become defensive from the same initial stance, one's center of gravity is so focused that it is almost impossible to knock the adept off his chosen spot. He is utterly maneuverable, yet grounded. Shintō is the center, the balance, the rootedness which affords flexibility and adaptability, the power to withstand. Like a bamboo tree, with its exceptionally deep roots, it can lean over right to the ground in a storm, and not be uprooted, overturned, or blown over. Shintō is the way of rootedness in a tradition that provides the power to withstand and to overcome, and for the most part, to find happiness in the midst of it all.

ATTITUDES, VIRTUES, AND RITUALS

What does this rootedness consist of? A variety of attitudinal virtues and ritual. I have already mentioned *michi*, or character and integrity. Buddhism is the *michi* of Buddha, Christianity the *michi* of Christ, and so on. *Michi* is one's sense of connection with the All, and the sense of flowing in accordance with its development and progress. There is also purity (*harai*), which is achieved symbolically by washing out the mouth, and scrubbing one's hands before entering the shrine or its grounds, and by salt, which is sprinkled on doorsteps, and thrust into the Sumo ring by its wrestlers. But it is an inward purity of the heart that is sought, and this is achieved by acting in accordance with several virtues, including *michi*. In this sense, absolute purity is never attained, but as an ideal, it is always at best to be approximated, and is ever in process.[39]

If purity is to be achieved by means of several virtues, and *michi* is but one of these, then another and extremely important additional virtue is *makoto*, or sincerity. Whether one reads Chinese texts or Japanese texts, Confucianism, Taoism, Chinese Buddhism, or any of the Japanese traditions, sincerity is always front and center. In the West, however, sincerity is not a major virtue, nor at the present does it play a significant role in ethical theorizing. Sincerity means that one's words will become deeds, that one is intrinsically trustworthy, or has genuine integrity of character, and so on. The twentieth-century Japanese philosopher Watsuji Tetsurō writes of *makoto* as being the root of truthfulness, honesty, and trustworthiness, all of which qualities are necessary for anything resembling dependable and worthwhile social interactions.[40] Sallie King also unpacks a cluster of meanings in *makoto*, namely "honesty, genuineness, spiritual purity, and the completion and perfection of the individual."[41] By serving the *kami* with sincerity, one is able to "conform to the will of the Kami."[42] Sincerity demands one's entire commitment, a putting of one's heart, mind, soul, and body into one's commitment to whatever it is that one does. It includes the awareness of the workings of the *kami*, our assurance that they exist, and that we share their divine spirit. *Makoto* is manifested as genuine piety, which results from the sense of the divine, real benevolence towards children and those one loves, faithfulness towards friends, loyalty towards those to whom one owes or is expected to show loyalty, and love towards one's neighbors.[43] Sincerity is the careful avoidance of error in word or deed, and the fastidiousness to keep one's soul unsullied by the grime of selfish desire, hatred, ill will, or materialism. It is *makoto* which leads to *wa*, or group harmony. It implies solidarity, a solidarity of community feeling which manifests itself as peacefulness, good will, and happiness. *Akaki* means cheerfulness of heart, and is another virtue, and evidence of the presence of *makoto* and *wa*. *Kansha* is a spirit of thankfulness, which should be directed to the *kami*, the nation, the society, and the family, and should be manifested by sincere effort, hard work, steadfastness, etc.[44] *Kenshin* means to offer one's person, in the sense of surrender in worship. It is a total offering of what one is, and what one has. But it is not duty, for duty is a recognition of a rational requirement, notes Herbert, whereas the sense of surrender and offering in *kenshin* is a matter of the heart. It is akin to the devotion of *agape* in Greek thought, which is deeper and purer than ordinary love, and it is unconditional. It is perfectly spontaneous, arising from the heart for no extrinsic or calculated reasons. It has been referred to as "devotion to the common interest."[45] Between human beings, the appropriate relationship is that of benevolence *(itsu-kushi-mi)*. This implies *uyamau*, or showing proper respect, courtesy, displaying the correct etiquette. *Tsutsushimi* is reverence, and so on.

The bite in all of this is that if one falls significantly short of any of these virtuous attitudes, or ways of walking with others in the world, one brings dishonor to oneself and to one's family and to the groups with which one is associated. A statement attributed to Nitobe concludes that "honour is the only tie that binds the Japanese to the ethical world,"[46] and is a powerful alternative to the more traditional Western goad of sin. Whereas awareness of one's sinfulness is recognition both of our intrinsically corrupted nature and of our being watched and judged by God, shame rests more on our own shoulders, calling attention to our being less than we could be. The responsibility for change, and even "salvation" is our own, and we are capable of knowing what is needed because our nature is originally and intrinsically good. Any wrongs committed are not to be attributed to an "original" incapacity or corruption of our nature, but to accumulated impurity or lack of responsibility. The solution is in our hands, and our hands and minds must be washed pure, both literally and metaphorically. One brings shame upon oneself and upon others if one misses the mark and is dishonored. In a shame culture, one bears the responsibility for being less than one could be, or could be expected to be, and given the collectivist orientation of Eastern cultures generally, everyone shares in the disappointment and the failure, at least to some degree. People are not thought of as sinners, who inevitably show human weakness and imperfection; they are thought of as capable and responsible beings who can and should achieve much more than might have been imagined. The shame is that one is less than one might be; that one has not taken on the responsibility, for oneself or for another, of greater achievement and purity of character.

THE CONNECTION TO ANCESTORS

We are tied to the past through our ancestors and our traditions, and to the family and the various groups with which we are connected in the present. We need to be aware of our debt to the past, as well as to those involved with us in the present. A contemporary writer, Yanairu Tetsuo, suggests that *kami* die, and become *kami* spirits, as humans become spirits at death, or may actually rise to the level of *kami* themselves. Thus, "humans and *kami* spirits are bound together by the concept of the 'ancestors.' The ancestral cult, which is at the root of the religion of the Japanese people, is what links the cults of the *kami* and the human."[47] But we are also tied to nature, or rather we are part of nature. We, and nature itself, are aspects of the materialization of divinity. No doubt this attitude explains in part the Japanese sensitivity to natural objects: ". . . the Japanese are . . . capable of feeling vividly a consanguineous kinship with plants and animals."[48] The famous eighteenth-century Shintō scholar Motoori Norinaga (1730–1801) popularized the phrase, *mono no aware*, which refers to our natural sympathy with and for all of nature's richness. Nature is not for our privileged use, any more than our neighbor, or spouse, or children are for our use, or for that matter, any more than our own bodies are material at hand, to be carelessly dealt with as though cheap and altogether unimportant. We do not come in parts, body and mind, nor are we in nature, like being in a foreign land. The trees around a Shintō shrine are considered to be "sacred," not in the sense that they are different from other trees, or are specially deified, but simply as a visible, continuous reminder that the entire universe is divine spirit.[49] Trees are particularly revered if they are unusually old, or of abnormal size, or give evidence of hardiness and life (as do evergreens which keep their greenery throughout the year), or have unusual shapes, for any and all of these characteristics are taken to signify vigor and the flow of divine energy. We *are* nature, and nature is us, and we are all divine, and none of this divinity is to be thought of simply as material at hand. How we work out how to be in nature, whether to eat meat, whether to kill viruses, cannot be known in advance, by anyone. These are problems to be worked out, partly by experiment, partly by consulting our inner sense of what we ought to do, and how we ought to treat other aspects of existence. It is we, as individuals and as members of our groups, who must take responsibility for our actions—but we certainly do not have dominion over nature, nor are we its shepherds or caretakers. Such thinking is already dualistic, we and it, and the Shintō sense of monistic deity, or dualistic–non-dualism is considerably stronger than this. Nature is awesome, mysterious, and divine, just as we are. Therefore, how we live and act in the midst of our natural surroundings likely says a great deal about how we are with others, and how we are with ourselves. We are, of course, all of us, still trying to work this out. But carelessness, brutishness, and exploitation are clearly not the *kami* way.

THE WAY TO THE FUTURE

Shintōism remains optimistic, in the midst of much present stupidity, for our carelessness and our atrocities do not condemn us as intrinsically unworthy. It may well be that the viruses and bacteria will take over, if we are stupid enough to despoil our "home," or more accurately, "ourselves" to such an extent that our survival is rendered impossible. Individuals may commit suicide, and so may species! It is *not* foreknown or foreordained one way or the other. But, then, neither is it inevitable, and if we can catch even a faint glimpse of the divine possibilities ahead, then we will right ourselves before it is too late.

Already it is clear that there will be suffering as a result of what we have done to our environment, but we can learn. We can take the experiment of dualistic conceptualization and materialistic-mechanical views of human nature to heart, and leave them behind for something better, as soon as we possibly can. We have outgrown, and hopefully we will outlive, views which, while once helpful and a clear step towards progress and human advancement, are now holding us back, destroying our sense of belonging in the world, and even to each other. We are estranged, living in the midst of an "existential vacuum," not knowing why meaning has drained from our world, from our political lives, and even from our family life. We must now learn from the experiment, and take up another model, another way that draws upon divinity, a non-dualistic sense of things, and a reverential solidarity with all that exists—as utterly wonderful, miraculous, mysterious, awesome: as *kami*. But the present and the future, as with the present and the past, are never spiritually separated, and it is from the past, as well as from the experiences of the present and the anticipations of the future, that solutions to the problem of life and death will be found. Shintō is passed on in an unbroken line, from the unknown to the unknown, from the beginningless to the endless, not through texts or creeds, but as "racial memory and is imbibed from infancy by training in ways of life that have become traditional without being analyzed. The most characteristic traits of any race are the traditional ones that are seldom self-consciously expressed and can rarely be described by the individuals, themselves."[50] What is passed on, with the very milk of infancy, are the attitudes, the living virtues which are not systematically intellectualized, but which are learned within the family, the schools, in those unusually sacred places where there is a concentration of divine presence or energy known as shrines, through the various rituals, the writing of *haiku* poetry, or *sumie* painting, or the martial arts, or the tea ceremony, or in any of the other ways which non-intellectually and non-discursively pass on the proper manner of being in the world, and with others. One learns of the divinity of all that exists, of one's connectedness with the past, and one's responsibility for the future,[51] of the sacredness of creative vitality and sustained effort, of sincerity, integrity, spontaneity, peacefulness, cheerfulness, of the importance of purity, of the importance of reverence, benevolence, loyalty, love, steadfastness, and the ability to offer oneself unconditionally and spontaneously to whatever is supportive of any of the above. This list would provide a magnificent moral education curriculum, except that it cannot be taught in any straightforward sense. To teach the outer shell is to miss the inner spirit, to teach the laws is to miss the life, to codify is to rigidify, and to intellectualize may well be to kill the intuitive capacity to live and to love with the heart, instead of with the head. The Japanese language is a language of great emotional nuance, and the emotionality of the people makes evident that a great deal more emphasis is placed on feeling than in many other cultures. The unsaid, the hinted at, the empty space of Japanese architecture, painting and poetry, and, yes, even the nothingness of philosophy and religion, pull one into that realm of the indefinite, where one is aware of something, or catches a glimpse of something, or has a feeling that is difficult to put into words. One finds oneself uncomfortable in the presence of another person because what is said is not what is meant, and what is promised is not what is intended. One reads character, one feels, and one sees more than one can put into crisp words and sentences. Can such attitudes be systematically, logically and discursively taught? Can any attitude be so directly taught, or are attitudes learned indirectly, absorbed from one's culture, through all of its expressions? If the latter, then each of us might ask, what is *our total cultural environment* telling our children about the proper way to be with others, to be with oneself, and to be in the world? The moral education curriculum, our main defence against future evil, may well be the way we see ourselves interacting with our fellow citizens, our TV programs, perhaps especially news broadcasts, our newspapers, magazines, books, sporting events, the violence in our movies, music, dance, and all the other festivals of our age. Not wanting to prejudge your own reflections on such environmental influences, perhaps I might begin by asking how many of these teach the divinity of men and women, trees and dogs, rivers and rocks? And would it make a difference if they did?

Mason offers an illustration of the Shintō understanding of evil in the telling of the story of the *kami,* Susano-no-Mikoto, in ancient mythology.[52] Susano's father was Izanagi, the *kami* from whose spear drops of water fell into the ocean, coagulating to form the islands of Japan. His mother was Izanami, who bore Susano and Amaterasu, Susano's sister. Amaterasu-mikami is the Sun-Goddess, with a soft and gentle character, who rules over the Plain of High Heaven. Susano rules the earth. After Susano's mother Izanagi died, Susano angered his father by wishing to visit his dead mother's spirit, "in the Land of Yomi," in order to bid her farewell before he took up his earthly responsibilities. It became necessary to discover Susano's sincere intentions in this act of visiting his mother, and it was agreed that the matter should be settled by brother and sister engaging in a divine childbirth contest. If Susano produced sons, he was to be declared innocent, and if he produced daughters, guilty. For reasons that are not important, the five sons produced by Susano were claimed by Amaterasu as really hers, and her five daughters, she said, were really Susano's. This "trial by birth" caused Susano to cry that he had won, but the decision went against him. He was angered, and as "the storm-*kami*," he damaged rice fields, and became a boisterous and ill-tempered *kami*. Susano was expelled by Heaven, which cannot but remind Western readers of the expulsion of Lucifer from Heaven. Instead of dedicating himself to an eternity of revenge, however, and a struggle to overthrow the sources of apparent injustice as the embittered arch-enemy of the divine, Susano settled down, and began to create "harmony on earth." Indeed, he did not become a devil, but remained a *kami* or divine spirit, and today the shrine dedicated to him, the Yasaka Shrine, is one of the most honored of Shintō shrines. Rather than being dishonored, his spirit continues to be honored, and bearing no lasting resentment, he became a helpful and harmonizing *kami*. "Susano can serve as a personification of human nature, impetuous, angry at being misunderstood but not vindictive, having strong family affections, generous, brave and individualistic but helping co-ordination."[53] He is the best representative of both the Rough Divine and the Gentle Divine spirit of *kami*, in one personification. Susano's son, Omagatsumi, was called the "Great Evil Doer," as "a warning that impetuosity in the father may have evil effects on the offspring."[54] To offset her brother, Susano's daughter Suseri-bime, married Okuninushi, who, with Susano's *direct help*, pacified the earth. They overcame the evil forces, and made it ready for "co-ordinated government." Mason concludes that the Susano myth, representing the struggle between good and evil, the Rough and the Gentle aspects of divinity, is all part of the working out of the coordinating of creativity itself, in order to achieve an evolutionary advance, the divine spirit's own self-development, and, therefore, each person's as well. "The struggle to adjust each to the other is divine spirit's own struggle, which self-consciousness will understand when it gains competence to attune itself to the subconscious depths of man's inalienable divinity as intuitively known to primaeval Shintō."[55]

REFLECTIVE EPILOGUE

A remarkable characteristic of the Japanese people is their acceptance of the phenomenal, everyday world as the "absolute," which is to say that "heaven" is underfoot, or in Buddhist terms, that *nirvāna* is *samsara*, and *samsara nirvāna*. But this cultural insight existed long before the introduction of Buddhism into Japan. Nakamura Hajime locates this predisposition in the "religious view of the ancient Japanese." It gradually gave shape to Shintōism, and runs "through the subsequent history of Shintōism down to the present day." Such a perspective is distinctively Japanese, for it defines "enlightenment" as the understanding of things within the phenomenal world, rather than an "ultimate comprehension of what is beyond the phenomenal world." Nakamura goes on to suggest that this recognition of the absolute significance and worth of the phenomenal world "seems to be culturally associated with the Japanese traditional love of nature. The Japanese in general love mountains, rivers, flowers, birds, grass, and trees, and represent them in the patterns of their *kimono*, and they are fond of the delicacies of the season, keeping their edibles in natural forms as much as possible in cooking."[56] Nakamura insightfully contrasts the pessimistic tendencies of the Japanese and the West, by noting that "Western pessimism means to become wearied of existence in this world," whereas for the Japanese it is "to be wearied only of complicated social fetters and restrictions from which they wish to be delivered. Consequently, the sense of pessimism is dispelled as soon as one comes to live close to the beauties of nature, far apart from human society."[57] As in classical Taoism, there is a nostalgic desire to return to the simplicity of natural living, and to leave bureaucratic complexity behind. There is no general world weariness, but only a despair arising out of social complexity and desolation. J. W. T. Mason offers an example of Japanese this-worldliness and their love of nature, which at least suggests what primal cultural anticipation may have led to this difference in response (in the interests of gender neutrality, please read "human being" or "human kind" for "man"):

> In Southern Kii, one of the centres of creative action in the primitive era of Japan, the Nachi Waterfall descends from a great height amid graceful, bowing foliage. The spray softly strokes the rocks and disappears into invisibility while the trees stand guard against pollution. The water follows its narrow downward way gently, with swift, smooth unconscious accuracy seeking its spreading goal beneath. The white threads of the falling current seem like ethereal coverings of purity, enveloping an inner spiritual power emerging from lofty Heaven into the universe beyond. Primitive Shintō regarded the falling Nachi stream in its cathedral setting of Nature's design, as an inspired spot, and called it Hiryu Shrine—the Shrine of the Flying

Waterfall. No sacred building is there. Nature has given sanctity to the place; the universal spirit of Nature consecrated the Flying Waterfall for primitive man's spiritual refreshment. To-day, still, the Shrine of the Flying Waterfall is part of Shintō with white-robed priests in attendance, for the Falls are Kami or divine spirit. . . . Has modern man so lost his understanding of the universality of divine spirit that the power of Nachi Falls to hold primitive man in devotional attitude of mind must be dismissed as a superstition of the past? Does modern man so neglect to pay proper respect to his ancestors who first saw spiritual values in life that he can regard the Flying Waterfall only as an aesthetic aspect of Nature? If so, modern man is spiritually the loser and moves away from the divine personality of the universe toward a debasing concept of materialism. . . .

Shintō regards the universe as Heavenly divine spirit coming forth into material form for the purpose of self-developing creative progress. Before man appeared on the planet, Heavenly divine spirit, according to Shintō, began its forward movement of objection action through the power of Nature. In this original impetus of the spirit of creative action, Heavenly divinity displayed its intent to evolve as the material universe for its own advancement in newly externalized fields of space. Nachi Falls, moving from quiet heights to its new level, far below, releases its energy for active effort. This ceaseless, sudden power, as it is viewed by Shintō, is spiritual in its source and form; and it inspires man to move from the still altitudes of inaction into the current of accomplishment, creating progress by self-effort as an obligation to the creative purpose of universal life. The Flying Waterfall priests of Shintō could say to man: here is Heavenly spirit's early effort at earthly activity; and the source of this divine energy is the same Heavenly source that is man's. The Flying Waterfall, itself, however does not think and does not speak. Man is the more progressive development of divine self-creative spirit, the more expansive attainment of the Shintō *Kami*. Yet, the further man advances in mental development, the more ought he to understand that the heights he climbs must not be allowed to separate him from the universality of divine spirit of which he is the fortunate earthly pinnacle. Without the base of universal spirit there would be no pinnacle.[58]

Nachi Falls represent a confluence of attitudinal givens: the phenomenal, everyday world is everywhere divine; and yet, where we encounter the divine is in the everyday. The everyday world is beautiful, aesthetically rich beyond words; yet the aesthetic is not merely the locus of the beautiful, it is also the place where divinity is to be found, where *kami* reside and express themselves. It is an animistic, and at the same time a pantheistic perspective: the whole world is alive with spirit, i.e. is everywhere divine, and everything is divine. It is not merely filled with divine spirits, it is divinity itself. The universe is not dual—material and spiritual, human and divine, human and non-human, animate and inanimate, etc. Mason even hints at an ecological thrust in Shintō, for that "enduring intuition of reality that caused primaeval Shintō to bow in acknowledgment of the divine co-ordination between humanity and the material manifestations of Nature,"[59] might well infuse modern day science and technology with a new vision of and respect for the phenomenal "data" of its endeavors.

THE ECOLOGICAL DIMENSION

Nature is itself *kami*. The divine spirit is everywhere manifest in material form as this very world. It is not that the universal spirit creates a world, but that it takes form *as* the world. The world of nature is itself the incarnation of the divine. It is the divine materialized, given form, made visible and tangible. A somewhat similar conception has recently been expressed by a contemporary theologian from the Christian West, Sallie McFague. She underscores the importance of allowing a metaphor such as the world as God's body in order to re-sacralize the world of nature.[60] Her writings have inspired many Christians to take seriously the sacredness of the earth, the divinity of the world of nature. Religion demands an ecological consciousness and an ecological conscience, if we are to save nature and ourselves from destruction. To borrow a phrase from Heidegger, we have become settled in our insensitivity to nature by thinking of it as mere material at hand for our use. It is easy to dispose of it, to consume it even on a whim of gourmet fancy, and even to reconstruct it in the hope that a short-term economic gain will not result in very long-term pain for ourselves and all other sentient creatures. Nature is simply there for our use we have somehow come to think, and has no value of its own. It is this attitude that McFague tries to unsettle by offering us a metaphor through which the value-less as habitually perceived takes on the values of the divine and the sacred. The world *is* God's own body.[61]

Shintō has understood this from the beginning, and its metaphors have been both profound and striking. Mason gives us three such examples, beginning with the Nachi Waterfall in Southern Kii, in Japan, which I have already cited above. Mason's "theological" gloss on this divine incarnation is that "Shinto regards the universe as Heavenly divine spirit coming forth into material form for the purpose of self-developing creative progress. Before man appeared on the planet, Heavenly divine spirit . . . began its forward movement of objective action through the power of Nature."[62] Mason understands Shintō to be a monism, a universally spiritual expression in material form of the divine. Picken, too, speaks of a Shintō monism, which unlike Western religion does not see the world as either dualistically good and evil, or as a battle ground for the forces of God and Satan, Heaven *vs.* Hell. The world is divine, and both good and evil are aspects of divine nature itself expressing itself through innumerable instances of differentiation, in a cosmos of unending richness and inevitable surprises. Evil is real, often deadly, a genuine cause of suffering in the world, but not a separate force. The source of evil is within, and its form is impurity.

The world is, in this sense, God's body; nature is *kami* made manifest, the subjective has become objective as the form of the formless, the materialization of the immaterial, the invisible become visible. While nature is not all that the creative spirit of the universe is, all of the universe is an expression of the divine. The seen is not all that there is, for there is the source as unseen, but all that is seeable is itself divine. David Shaner refers to "a 'seamless' web of divine presence," a term which he borrows from Joseph Kitagawa. Shaner argues that the Shintō sense of this seamless web of divinity is a non-symbolic grasp of nature as symbol. He writes: "The experience of intimacy with nature requires the cultivation of a non-symbolic attitude wherein one does not search for any hidden symbolic meanings or evidence of realities 'beyond' or 'after' (Gk. *meta*) the physically apparent."[63] No doubt this acceptance of the things of this world as themselves divine is what Nakamura Hajime meant when he affirmed that the Japanese may be characterized as a people who have come to accept the phenomenal world as absolute.[64] Shaner adds that this love of nature as divine includes a mutuality, an "interpenetration," such that one becomes filled with *kami*, with the divinity of the moment and the place. To worship is not to stand separate from that which is divinely present, but to become filled with it, to experience it directly inside oneself, or perhaps to expand one's sense of self—to lose one's limited ego-self—and to merge with one's surroundings and even beyond. Stuart Picken, taking the waterfall example as a contemporary real-life opportunity to experience the mystery of spirit which Shintō preserves, challenges the serious inquirer to make the journey to a mountain shrine to plunge into an ice cold waterfall at midnight with crisp, frozen snow on the ground. In *misogi shuhō*, purification under a free-standing waterfall, the cosmic, the mysterious, and the energizing life of the waterfall meet and explain more eloquently than any number of words why Shintō, with neither scriptures nor saints, has survived as the basis of Japanese religion and culture and why it will continue to remain the living spiritual roots of Japanese culture."[75]

Furthermore, such purification is one step towards the restoration of our original innate "ability to live in harmony with the divine and with nature . . . because of the various forms of impurity that overtake life, purification becomes necessary."[66] Just as we are born by nature good, rather than sinful, so we are instinctually capable of living in harmony with our environment. It is not necessary to inculcate, as though for the first time, a sense of oneness with nature and a vision of our interconnectedness with the environment: it is already there, needing only to be uncovered, swept clean of the impurities of civilization and petty ego-desires which have accumulated over the cultural and personal years of living. We are always already ecologically sensitive, at least at the subconscious or "deeper" levels of our existence. Rather than loud shouting designed to bring us to an ecological consciousness, quiet meditation or participation in a ritual of purification might serve us better. We need less teaching and more self-realization, less consciousness raising and more (sub)consciousness deepening. The discovery is that the waterfall is *kami*, and we are united with it as *kami*.

Mason's second example is the Omiwa Shrine, near Nara, Japan, which has taken a mountain to be the divine spirit as manifest. Mason comments that as the Nachi Waterfall symbolizes "Heavenly divine spirit coming down to earth," the "Mountain Shrine of Omiwa represents divine spirit on earth reaching upward toward the Heavenly source of life—the inseparable union of Heaven and earth in universal divinity."[67] One does not need to enclose the divine or to create great cathedrals to draw our attention to the divine presence. Indeed, "Shinto, making a mountain into a primaeval cathedral, took the living spirit of Nature, and saw the cathedral not as an inert pile of matter but as creative divinity, itself come forth into objectivity from Heaven."[68] There can be little doubt that the heavily industrialized and materialistic West has all but completely lost its sense of the divinity of nature, and has exchanged a spiritual monism for an inert dualism of matter and behavioristically conceived mind. What was once an enchanted and precious mystery has become a system of highways with a paved parking lot at every corner. Japan, too, is in the midst of the suffering and the joy of twentieth-century industrialized living. Nonetheless, "to this day, one can visit the urban centers of Japan and notice a conspicuous absence of buildings on surrounding hilltops."[69] The mountains are still considered to be holy places, natural shrines where *kami*-energy is to be found in abundance. Blacker summarizes such a perspective:

> Shintō can remind us that the natural world is not a machine put there for our sole enjoyment. It does contain a dimension which induces reverence, respect and the intuition that we are part of this subtle fabric, not its exploiter. Shintō can help us look again with new eyes at the world about us, and see that what our grandfathers may have dismissed as superstition, and the missionaries sought to deride as idolatry, is in fact a fundamental if hidden truth which we have neglected for too long.[70]

The ease with which Western thinkers have been able to dismiss so-called "pagan" or "primitive" rituals, fortune-telling, folk customs and animistic, polytheistic, and monistic awareness of the interconnectedness of the divine, the natural, and the human world may better be understood as the uneasy protests of "people who live in a totally demythologized universe."[71] What is needed to restore a sense of connectedness may well be traditions that "can remind us that there is a holy dimension in natural objets and that space is not homogeneous, that there are indeed places imbued with the presence of something 'wholly other.'"[72]

Mason's third example is the Iishi Shrine, in Izumo, Japan, where a large rock is enclosed by a picket fence. People bow before the rock, seeing it as a manifestation of the divine creative spirit, "not symbolically but in full reality," providing another instance of divine self-expression materializing as rock, or mountain, or waterfall, and, of course, as flowers, bees, birds, beasts, and human beings. Ono Sokyo reminds his readers that Shintō has long held that the qualities of *kami* as manifest include the qualities of growth, fertility and production, and such natural objects "as the sun, mountains, rivers, trees and rocks; some animals; and ancestral spirits."[73] The universe itself is "the objective self-creativeness of Kami or divine spirit."[74] Mason is utterly clear in reminding us that the "the Falls, the Mountain and the Rock are themselves *Kami*, self-creative divine spirit emerging from spacelessness and self-developing as the material universe; and man is the same in origin."[75]

Metaphor or fact, even if one assumes these two to be radically different, Shintō has found a way to keep alive the wonder that is nature, and
the mystery and magnificence that is existence itself.

More often than not, Shintō shrines are simple and natural affairs, usually wooden, and they may be thought to mark the natural
rather than to replace or confine it. The beautiful *torii,* or entrance
gateway to a shrine, are perhaps to be thought of as noticeable excla-
mation points: Here! Here! Here is divinity, which is all around you,
but since you do not seem to recognize it, then here it is harder to miss,
to overlook. Can you feel it now? That remarkable sense of awe, of
incredible fascination, the hair standing up on the back of your neck,
together with a weakness in the knees or an increase in heart rate. Any
or all of these alert you to the fact that you are in the presence of
mysterious divinity. Now, as you leave the shrine, can you take away with
you, and sense as though for the first time, the incredible beauty of the
falling snow, of the mist, of a great blue heron lumbering slowly overhead, of the chattering squirrel? If the world is now alive with spirit,
with divinity, then Shintō has done its work, and you have been re-
opened, in a way born again to the astonishing wonder of being in its
many forms. The simplicity and naturalness of shrine architecture serves
to remind us that "the primaeval intuition of universal spirituality must
remain simple and direct to escape theological complications and mis-
conceptions."[76] Once again we catch a glimpse of the unwillingness to
enter into theological speculation and intellectual conceptual clarifi-
cation. It is all beside the point, for the aim is to return to a more pre-
reflective and experiential immersion into the sense of the throbbing
and evolving experiment of which we ourselves are an integral part. It
is not a matter of reflection, of mediated musing, but of immediate
experiential involvement. If you feel any of this, then *kami* is present,
and if you do not, then *kami* is still present but you have become
opaque, encrusted by rational overactivity and societal tension. *Kami*
and nature, *kami* and human beings, *kami* and creative expression are
not two but one.[77]

At Ise, a new shrine is built every twenty years. A special supply of
the best Japanese cedar is grown and cared for just for this important
shrine replacement, and since no nails are used in its construction,
only the best joiners are commissioned to undertake this sacred labor
of love. The original purity is renewed, the honor of building a great
temple is repeated, and the symbolism of a never complete and ever in
process conception of human and divine activity is symbolized.
". . . Shintō never completes its enshrinements. New Shrines come into

existence as posterity recognizes leaders who have guided the people in the quest for greater attainments. They are enshrined to perpetuate their influence and to emphasize that human effort is also divine effort having its originating impetus in Heaven."[78] Indeed, any place may come to be regarded as a *kami* energy center, a place where the divine energy is particularly concentrated, and where those of us who have lost our transparency and have become opaque may encounter the divine energies once again, however tired and secular we may have become.

ETHICS AND NATURE

Ethics is not just a matter of the rightness and wrongness of human relationships, but also concerns our relationship with nature and with the cosmos at large. Shintō offers an authentically ecological spirituality that could well contribute to overcoming the modern mistreatment of the environment as mere material at hand to be used and abused. At present, as is the case the world over, it has not proven to be sufficient in Japan to have kept the Japanese from polluting, and paving, from pirating the oceans, or from exploiting the underdeveloped and wasting the diminishing resources of the earth. But it may well have preserved the love of nature which seems not far below the surface of every Japanese, and which has preserved trees and park land, and even now compels the rank and file in Japan to create beauty through the growing of flowers and trees (including an array of flower pots in spaces so tiny as to make those of us from less populated continents look in amazement at what can be accomplished in a space no greater than a few square inches or feet). The residual and still robust Japanese love of nature may come to serve as a spiritual and cultural resource for eventual ecological reformation. As humankind moves closer and closer to the brink of disaster on several ecological fronts—water, noise, air, and soil pollution; farming by chemical and genetic means; germ and explosive warfare; over-population—it may well be the latent and implicit cultural and spiritual depth of a people that will bring about the energy for reform, and the insight for radical transformation of outlook and expectation the world over. If this is so, then Shintō remains one of those cultural treasures which remains alive and well, awaiting its time to spring forth healthy and vibrant, residing in the hearts of the Japanese people, and biding its time even in the midst of the modern and postmodern worlds of asphalt, stainless steel, and glass.

SHINTŌ AND ZEN

Yet, while the influence of Shintō on the Japanese psyche seems both strong and everywhere present, it is little recognized, in part because it is unwritten, and in part because it is Zen that has more often than not claimed the credit. It is true that Zen and Shintō share a considerable amount as stances-towards-the-world, and yet it is Zen that has been the focus of insight into the Japanese character and its development. D. T. Suzuki, for example, wrote that "to understand the cultural life of the Japanese people in all its different aspects, including their intensive love of Nature . . . it is essential . . . to delve into the secrets of Zen Buddhism."[79] While this is certainly true, it is but a part of the whole story. Much of this sensitivity to and love of nature arises out of Shintō, reaching far back into the dark prehistory of the Japanese *kami*-cults. Similarly, to assert (with Charles Eliot) that "Zen is the expression of the Japanese character,"[80] is to take the part for the whole. The Japanese character is formed by several strands of influence, not the least of which is Shintōism. Furthermore, it was Shintō, long before Zen had arrived on the scene, that had understood nature as divine. Suzuki again attributes only an "innate aesthetic sense for things beautiful" to the "primitive" Japanese animists, praising Zen for providing the Japanese love for nature with "a metaphysical and religious background."[81] The kind of "metaphysical and religious background" which Zen provides is undoubtedly unique, but it is its difference that should be stressed, and not its exclusive rights or originary claims. Undoubtedly, Zen added to Shintō's monistic outlook a non-dualist metaphysics and epistemology. Yet, it is simply wrong to regard the former as somehow "primitive," and to assume the latter to be the undisputed epistemological and metaphysical winner in some undeclared contest of philosophical sophistication and ultimate theoretical correctness. Both traditions are alive and well in Japan, and each contributes to the diverse cultural weave. But it is Shintō that has taught the Japanese to experience directly, and without theological niceties, that "there is no place in which a god does not reside, even in the wild waves' eight hundred folds or in the wild mountain's bosom."[82]

3

Confucianism and
Japanese Ethics

Surveying the broad strokes of Shintō thought first may prove helpful in understanding how effortlessly Confucian thought and Buddhist thought were taken in by the Japanese, as by and large complementary to those ways of thinking and acting which had already been established in Japan. The general compatibility of these new traditions with Shintō arose both from the fact that they shared many attitudes and thought patterns, and because the Japanese were willing to take from foreign traditions those ideas and practices which enhance their own quality of life and understanding. Genuine dialogue between traditions demands that each side put genuinely "at risk" their own fundamental beliefs and assumptions, and the Japanese show a remarkable ability to do just that, while at the same time remaining steadfast to those ideas and traditions, assumptions and beliefs which continue to serve them well. No hermeneutic encounter successfully puts at risk all, or even most, of one's basic lenses of understanding, but to the extent that a flexibility and an adaptability of mind, belief, and attitude are present, some significant transformation as a result of such encounters will occur. The Japanese were and are able to open themselves to encounters from the outside, in spite of the fact that their nation is known for its self-imposed isolation over an incredibly long period of time. And in the short century and a quarter that they have been opened to foreigners again, they have moved from a feudal isolationism to the direct center of the financial and industrial world of the contemporary West. Their flexibility appears to derive from their willingness to take what is best from their encounters with new cultures, remaining open to new ideas and influences, while keeping the traditions and beliefs that have served them well.

For such a long time, the West was convinced that the Japanese were copiers, not inventors and creators. That they copy as well as any nation is evident from earliest times, but that copying is all they do is a serious misjudgment based on a serious misunderstanding. In the seventh century Prince Shōtoku, the Vice-Regent of the Empress Suiko, decided to build a great capital city for a recently unified Japan. He sent his brightest and best young men to China, to study architecture, town planning, civic management, water and sewer construction and maintenance, etc. Several years after the new city was completed, at Nara, the Chinese themselves journeyed to Japan to view it. They were impressed by the faithfulness of the copy that had been created, but even more impressed by the changes that were brought about by the Japanese to make the city far better.

In 1868 when the Meiji restoration had been effected, the ablest young men were sent to Europe and North America to study the state of the art achievements in various fields of study: law (France and England), commerce (the United States), philosophy (Germany), etc. The goal was not to copy, but to move their people to the top level of achievement in each of these fields of inquiry by going to those places known for their excellence and even superiority. Then, having quickly amassed the best in the field, one could adapt and improve what was learned to the Japanese situation. In the Far East, creativity does not come at the beginning of a process or an activity, but at the end, after an incredibly arduous period of discipline, study, and training. Genuine creative improvisation comes at the end of hard work and deep understanding, as with a musician or a ballerina. The sounds and graceful moves are built on tradition and discipline, hard work and diligent practice, and are not the expressions of the dilettante or the novice.

Exactly what is it in the Japanese character that has allowed them to adopt, and adapt without losing the original force of their indigenous outlook on the world? There is, of course, no way of actually answering such a complex question in anything like a definitive manner. Nevertheless, it is possible to identify ingredients contributed by Confucianism which have no doubt strengthened qualities that were already present in early Japanese culture. Confucian thought viewed the self as an "open system," open to the society and world around it, as well as to the entire cosmos at large. Furthermore, this Confucian "self" was conceived of as always in process: always open to self-improvement, self-transformation, and educational growth en route to sagehood. Wherever the virtues of Heaven are manifested on earth, there one can find guidance and wisdom in one's journey towards personal and social betterment.

THE CONFUCIAN SELF

Tu Wei-Ming, in attempting to describe the Confucian "self," maintains that in Confucian thought the self is "a dynamic, holistic, open system, just the opposite of the privatized ego."[1] Additionally, "the Chinese conceive of the cosmos, as well as the self, as an open system. 'As there is no temporal beginning to specify, no closure is ever contemplated. The cosmos is forever expanding; the great transformation is unceasing.'"[2] And while the notion of the self does include the person as individual, the sense of self which is central to East Asian thought in general, and to Confucian thought in particular, is one "which is rooted in the reality of a shared life together with other human beings and inseparable from the truth of transcendence."[3] As with Shintō, communality and a sense of one's connectedness with the divine flow are essential aspects of selfhood, and not just one's individual difference. To be an individual is not to lose sight of one's social and cosmic connectedness, but to engage in a process of self-transformation, or improvement, open to change in the same way that the cosmos itself is an expression of ceaseless change. The Confucian ideal is that of sagehood, and the way—again, a way—to sagehood is via the "true self." Knowledge of one's true self is the result of an "inner intuition," which confirms both that a human being is a microcosm of the transcendent macrocosm of the whole of existence, called heaven, and that one should live in such a way that one's daily activities are a "manifestation of one's real nature."[4] Recognition of our relatedness with others is, in fact, our point of departure on our quest for awareness of our own deeper dimensions, and the goal of our attempts to live a life of personal self-cultivation, in relationship with others, is to "make our gathering together worthwhile."[5]

What makes "intellectual intuition" possible is the lack of an impassable gulf between heaven and earth, a creator and that which is created. Instead, what is assumed to make intellectual intuition possible is the oneness of humanity with heaven, earth, and all things.[6] One can look within, and in the immediacy of one's own introspective experience, discover the very laws that permeate the entire universe. The microcosm of human life perfectly reiterates the macrocosm of heaven.

There is sageliness in every one of us already, yet becoming a sage is a never-ending practice, a development without closure. As well, the goal of sagehood for all would, if realized, lead to a society in perfect harmony. Yet this would be achieved in a specifically Confucian manner, for the sage would, by transforming him/herself, transform "others as well as himself."[7] And s/he would do so by means of a moral charisma, whereby others would be inspired to search their own depths and natures for the same springs of goodness and virtue. Such a "holistic vision of humanity which transcends not only self-centeredness, nepotism, ethnocentrism, nationalism, and culturalism but also anthropocentrism," is a kind of "anthropocosmic"-ism in the sense that the complete realization of the self, which is tantamount to the full actualization of humanity, entails the unity of humankind with heaven.[8]

At its best, then, the ideal of Confucian sagehood, whereby one would be sagely or wise within, and kingly or exemplary and quietly charismatic in one's external relations with others, is founded on *jen,* i.e., human heartedness, fellow-feeling, or love. It is *jen* which enlivens, or makes authentically heartfelt the obedience to *li,* or the rules of social relationship, rituals, rites, propriety, decorum, good form, etiquette, proper ceremony, and appropriate protocol when dealing with officialdom.[9] A lesser number of Confucian scholars suggest that *li* is the superior element in Confucian virtue, in the sense that *li* prescribes the proper living of life in terms of ritual practice, and in the eyes of heaven, human beings become sacred vessels for the enacting of such appropriate life-practice. This is not the place to enter into that debate, except to note that whichever is the foundational notion, the *li* of moral practice is to be enlivened and rendered heartfelt by *jen.* Whether moral education consists of the teaching of a *jen*fulness of spirit by means of the practice of appropriate behavior (in Aristotelian terms, by means of the development of the right *habits* of behavior), or the development of *li*-like habits by emphasizing the importance of empathetic identification (*jen*) with the aspirations and suffering of others, both *jen* and *li* must be appropriately present and in proper form and proportion. And one must be *jen*-filled, and aware of the duties and obligations of *li* in a steadfast and willing way—this is *yi* (sometimes *i*) meaning "righteousness," which arises from the sense of shame at not having lived up to the ideals of one's tradition, at not being as cultivated or civilized or morally advanced as one thinks one ought to be. After all, we all have the inner capacity to identify what is the right thing to do (*hsin*), even in unique circumstances, for we all have what Donald Munro terms the "discriminating mind."[10] It is within us and available from birth, wrote Mencius, as are the seeds or buds of the other elements of virtue within the Confucian vision of the human self as intrinsically good:

> When I say that all men have the mind which cannot bear to see the suffering of others, my meaning may be illustrated thus: Now, when men suddenly see a child about to fall into a well, they all have a feeling of alarm and distress, not to gain friendship with the child's parents, nor to seek the praise of their neighbours and friends, nor because they dislike the reputation [of lack of humanity if they did not rescue the child]. From such a case, we see that a man without the feeling of commiseration is not a man; a man without the feeling of shame and dislike is not a man; a man without the feeling of deference and compliance is not a man; and a man without the feeling of right and wrong is not a man. The feeling of commiseration is the beginning of humanity; the feeling of shame and dislike is the beginning of righteousness; the feeling of deference and compliance is the beginning of propriety; and the feeling of right and wrong is the beginning of wisdom. Men have these Four Beginnings just as they have their four limbs. Having these Four Beginnings, but saying that they cannot develop them is to destroy themselves. When they say that their ruler cannot develop them, they are destroying their ruler. If anyone with these Four Beginnings in him knows how to give them the fullest extension and development, the result will be like fire beginning to burn or a spring beginning to shoot forth. When they are fully developed, they will be sufficient to protect all people within the four seas [the world]. If they are not developed, they will not be sufficient even to serve one's parents.[11]

ORIGINAL HUMAN GOODNESS

Of the Four Beginnings, perhaps the most controversial is the claim of original human goodness. However, it is not one on which to get bogged down. Indeed, it is less than clear from his writings whether Confucius held that human nature (*hsing*) was by nature good, or both good and bad, or neither good nor bad but capable of becoming either. The debates with Kao Tzu, which are recorded by both Hsun Tzu and the Taoist mystic Chuang Tzu, attribute to Kao Tzu the position that human nature is neither good nor bad. Hsun Tzu, who also was a Confucian, held that human nature was evil, and desperately needed the *li* of social and political coercion in order to rise above the dictates of desire and become socialized. It is society (encoded in the *li*) which propels us towards the good, not our own nature. Taoism rejects this highly abstract discussion about human nature, and in the *Tao Te Ching*, Lao Tzu does not mention the issue of human nature even once. Nevertheless, in all of these thinkers, Confucian and Taoist alike, there is an evident optimism about what human beings are capable of becoming if they follow the right path or way. Human beings must work hard and long at cultivating themselves, with sincerity and integrity, in order to achieve the state of the moral ideal sage and the realization of their primordial identification with the supreme mystical ultimate, the universal force behind all that is as manifest. The selfless-self (*tz'u*) of Taoism, while to be achieved outside of the corrupting influences of (Confucian) society, is nonetheless an optimistic view of what diligent meditative introspective awareness can yield—a human being acting in harmony with the lawfulness and the changeability of the universe, in a state of peaceful non-aggressive flow (*wu wei*).

Yet, as important as hard work and diligent practice are in moving one along a path towards sagehood, it is the interior transformation of the person that is sought. Tu Wei-Ming concludes that "*li* as ritualism and *chih* as cleverness [or intelligence] . . . without *jen*, easily degenerates into formalism or insensitivity."[12] While the details of *li* are quite remarkable in complexity and demand over the course of Confucian history, initially they comprised the Five Relationships, plus instructions concerning the lengthy three-year mourning period after the death of one's father, and instructions for the proper conducting of ritual and ceremony. The Five Relationships are described in Confucius' *Doctrine of the Mean*: "The duties are those between sovereign and minister, between father and son, between husband and wife, between elder brother and younger, and those belonging to the intercourse of friends. These five are the duties of universal obligation."[13] With these five were associated the three virtues of wisdom, compassion, and courage. Throughout, these rules and rituals had as their purpose the creation of a social environment in which human beings could interact with a high degree of comfort, encouraging self-development and the peaceful social relationships needed for the creation and maintenance of a harmonious society. Emphasis was placed on the spirit of respect, reverence, loyalty, sincerity or integrity, and honesty and truthfulness as the virtues of a developed Confucian.

The importance of the *li* of filial piety cannot be overstated. The actions of truly filial sons represent those attitudes and virtues that ought to typify the ideal society: "Ceremonial acts in this connection symbolize desirable behavioural patterns. To respect the old and to honour the dead is to show special concern for the common origin of all." Moreover, respect for one's ancestors "brings forth communal identity and social solidarity. Society so conceived is not an adversary system consisting of pressure groups but a fiduciary community based on mutual trust."[14] Mutual trust, social solidarity, the sense of being a member of one large family—extending from the humblest peasant to the emperor on the one hand, and from generations yet to be born through generations of ancestors who have come before, and whose path we follow as we stride forth to try our own hand at life—is the ground of that relatedness which comprehends the importance of the interconnectedness of lives. This connectedness extends beyond the human, as well, to heaven, or the divine spirit, or to absolute nothingness as that primary and indescribable source of creative origination from which all things come, and to which, in some sense or other, they return. The web of cosmic interconnectedness is both immanent and transcendent, transcendent and immanent, or, as the Buddhists will say, *nirvāna* is *samsara*, and *samsara* is *nirvāna*: the divine is manifest in the everyday, and the everyday manifests in the divine. One of the most noticeable qualities of the divine, both in heaven and on earth, is that of *sincerity*.

The Importance of Sincerity

The virtue of "sincerity" is perhaps the most difficult to comprehend in much of East Asian morality, for it has an evidently central role that the English "sincerity" simply is unable to carry. *Ch'eng,* or "sincerity," we read in the *Chung-yung* (*Doctrine of the Mean*), is "the way of heaven" itself, and that "to think how to be sincere is the way of man. He who is sincere is one who hits upon what is right without effort. . . ."[15] Sincerity is not just a personal quality, but has cosmic implications as well. While it does refer to one's own integrity or truthfulness with oneself,[16] it also points to Heaven as sincere, and sincerity becomes something like the natural reality of heaven, and of human beings who give expression to their heavenly qualities.[17] Such a person is the "profound person" who has discovered his or her own authentic humanity. No doubt the power to charismatically transform others stems from this authenticity of self, for it causes others to "wake up" to their own deep stirrings within. We are all potentially profound, but we become distracted by the details of living, and by the power of our unbridled desires and egoistic yearnings. An encounter with a sage, however, is irresistible, for it awakens us to what we ought to be like: "its brilliance radiates. As a result, the person who possesses *ch'eng* moves, changes, and transforms others."[18] But *ch'eng* also means creativity. It is ceaseless, ever manifesting, in the same way that heaven is ceaseless, and continuously manifests itself in the procession of the ten thousand things of this world. In its primal state, reality is a ceaseless process of creation, a "magnificent display of fecundity in heaven, earth, mountains, and oceans,"[19] and is reminiscent of the ever-manifesting divine spirit of Shintōism. Again, it is not difficult to imagine the ease with which Confucianism was grafted onto the already sturdy, but implicitly indistinct, Shintō tree.

Paul Reasoner argues that the Japanese word for "sincerity," *makoto*, is inextricably associated with Confucianism. He identifies three features of sincerity, all of which are to be found in both Confucian and Japanese thought. The first element is the correspondence between an outward or external activity or behavior, and an inner mental or emotional state. Indeed, "the inner state of sincerity is a necessary condition of the outward activity. . . ."[20] The second element concerns being sincere with oneself. It, too, is a necessary condition of genuine sincerity, and requires an understanding of what is good. To be sincere with oneself, one needs to be aware of whatever standard of goodness reigns, in order to judge whether or not one is truly trying to live up to it. The third element is significantly Confucian, and has no straightforward equivalent in the West: "this third sense of sincerity identifies sincerity with the Way of Heaven."[21] So conceived, sincerity is a force that actively transforms whatever it encounters. Reasoner quotes *The Doctrine of the Mean*, which asserts that "sincerity is the beginning and end of things. Without sincerity there would be nothing."[22] Sincerity is "a Way" that draws Heaven and earth together, human and nature together, families together, and nations together. *Makoto* results from seeing things as they are, both oneself, and one's interconnection with others and with the world of nature, and with the ontological course of the cosmos itself. *Makoto*, or sincerity, is a metaphysical or ontological principle, and as such is "presumed to be part of the framework of reality."[23] A sincere person, then, is one who both comprehends and nourishes his/her connections with heaven, the world of nature, the extended relational family, and with the various communities with which s/he feels, or ought to feel, some kinship and some obligation. The Confucian self is anything but a closed and isolated self. Rather, it is an expansive self which reaches all the way to heaven itself.

SELF AS FIELD

The trajectory of Confucian ritual and practice takes sagehood as its eventual target, with the "self" of sagehood anything but an isolated entity. Borrowing an insight from George Herbert Mead, Hall and Ames argue that the concept of self that is operative in Confucianism is the self as a field of social relationships. Unlike the more typical Western understanding of the self as individualistically separate and autonomous, the Confucian sense of self is "irreducibly social," and is constituted by its many social roles and relationships. The more or less unquestioned Western assumption that the self is a "separate, distinct, individual in its various forms is anathema to the Chinese."[24] This is so because this sense of self tends to be heedless of the well-being of the greater communal whole with which it is inextricably connected. The Western concept is a formula for selfishness, social isolation, alienation, and the total abrogation of one's social interconnectedness, and with it, one's sense of social responsibility. Moreover, it is actually to be without a self, for in Confucian thought the self is defined in terms of its social contexts: "the self is contextual." The self is a societal happening, at least in part, and is "a shared consciousness of one's roles and relationships."[25] Hall and Ames describe self-consciousness in the Chinese sense not as the consciousness of myself as isolated and objectified, as boundaried and distinct, but rather as a "me" in society, and not as an "I" in abstract isolation: "this involves an image of self determined by the esteem with which one is regarded in community, an image that is captured in the language of face and shame."[26] To be fully a self is to be involved in the various contexts of the social (the relational), and to be able to function well and appropriately in such contexts one needs to know the "forms" of effective social interaction. Not to be able to function effectively socially is to be stunted, or even warped as a self. For the Confucian, as for the Japanese, communal harmony is a social and personal ideal, and this is to be most effectively achieved "through ritually defined relationships."[27] The ideal result is a society in which each person is attuned to the needs and expectations of others, and where social interaction is regulated by each person's desire to preserve and protect his or her social interactions with others through accepted ways of behaving and responding. This is not to imply that one gives up one's autonomy, but that one's so-called autonomy must never be flaunted in opposition to, or thought of as separate from, the various contexts which define the self. To so act would not be to assert one's true independent self, but to demonstrate that one was less than a self, a truncated self, a rudimentary self, a primitive self. For the Confucian, the achievement of true selfhood "is measurable in terms of the quality of the relationships that one is able to effect. It is 'ritualizing,' taken in its broadest sense, that enables persons to assume roles which define their appropriate relationships with others."[28] Ritualized sociality serves as the ground of shared values and meaning, and allows one to effectively interact with others, and through such activity to further enhance the well-being of the social whole of which one is an esteemed part. Yet such ritualized practice must be "personalized" by the agent, and expressed in ways that are unique to him or her, appropriate as to time and place, and transparently expressive of the feelings and concerns of the agent. No doubt the "heart" could go out of ritualized expression in the same way that it does in the West, with such formalities as "How are you today?" and even "I love you." On the other hand, no one who has loved would trade in the expression "I love you" for "I have an increased heart rate in your presence." The goal should not be to find an alternative to this time-worn expression, but to breathe new life into it, to express transparently how one feels, and to project one's intensity through these very words. It is not clever variation that will win the heart of one's beloved, but the authenticity and sincerity of one's spirit as expressed.

Yet it remains to be seen, both in Confucian China and in Japan, how ritualized behavior can be continuously re-infused with authentic, living, and heart-felt emotion. How can one remain "spontaneous" in the midst of the demands and the relentless habits of the everyday?

SPONTANEITY

One is most fully human when one acts in society out of a spirit of human heartedness (*jen*), expressing one's fellow feeling spontaneously and wholeheartedly. It is to authentically express one's concern for the well-being of the greater communal context and to act on one's sense of community. If one is able to do this with great effectiveness and with transparent authenticity "to the right person, to the right extent, at the right time, with the right motive, and in the right way,"[29] then one is a moral artist, an exemplary human being, one who approaches the ideal as a sage, and the sage is always one who approaches the *moral* ideal. The quotation above is from Aristotle, not Confucius, but I think it captures the difficulty of enacting social ritual in a way that is both appropriate in all of its senses and performed in a way that elicits from the recipient the same human hearted transparency. The ideal is to engage in authentic and full-hearted interaction with others. Given this ideal, it is little wonder that the adversarial, antagonistic struggle of individual against individual, of the appeal to individual rights, and the spectacle of rugged individualism seems relentlessly selfish, morally impaired, and socially immature to the Confucian Far East. Social harmony is not to be achieved "out of an *agon*, a struggle of one agent against another. The sort of interactions that are likely to take place among selves characterized by the dominance of volition would be truly counter productive in a society grounded in communal forms of ritual practice."[30] Rather than forced and individualistic willing and a striving to make a mark in the world and to achieve some sort of notoriety, the Confucian equivalent of will is *zhi*, which carries the meaning of both heart and mind, and the strong motivation of setting one's heart on something. Rather than an active willing, it is more a disposition, and points to "what one has in (heart) mind."[31] In other words, for the Confucian, to will is to act as a whole person out of respect for human ideals, which includes the interests of all concerned, as a spontaneous expression of what one has in one's heart and mind. It is not calculation, nor can it be the covert expression of a hidden agenda—although such is possible—but is instead an outpouring of human heartedness by a self that understands it is a social being, acting in socially acceptable ways in order to enhance the harmony and well-being of all of those involved. The Confucian self is more a field in which social relationships happen, than a focus against which other selves contest for space and respect. The self is a field in which human encounter is possible, and the primary task is to prepare the ground of that field for relatively effortless and fruitfully harmonious interactions. The moral sage is one who is able to accomplish this with seeming ease, and with a deftness that is to be emulated by others who are in the earlier stages of tilling their own field-selves in anticipation of future social interaction.

CONFUCIANISM IN JAPAN

When Confucianism came to Japan from Korea, about 404 A.D., it was welcomed, rather than resisted. In significant respects, it provided precisely what Shintō lacked: specificity of behavioral pattern in an organized and written form. It was not thought of as a new religion to be taken in, replacing the indigenous religiosity of Japan, but rather was understood to be a systematic account, and perhaps a deepening of what was already actively Japanese: a profound belief in the importance of paying continued respect to one's ancestors, a sense of the importance of filial piety, an existing practice of various rituals and ceremonies, and a codification of an acute ethical sensitivity.[32] In its characteristic way, Japan both adopted and adapted Confucianism to fit the Japanese context, which was already richly endowed with its own cultural identity. As Nakamura Hajime writes,

> The Japanese, owing to the tolerant and more open side of their nature, assimilated the heterogeneous cultures of foreign countries without much repercussion. They try to recognize the value of each of these different

cultural elements, and at the same time they endeavour to preserve the values inherited from their own past. They seek national unity while permitting the co-existence of heterogeneous elements. . . . They are extremely sensitive to adopting and absorbing foreign cultures. But, in fact, a foreign culture is adopted as a constituent element of the Japanese culture. Whatever the intension and outcry of the men in charge of its adoption might be, as a social and cultural fact, foreign culture is accepted insofar as its value is recognized as a helpful means to Japan's progress. Such an attitude in the past gave rise to the conception of "the Japanese spirit and Chinese learning." Such a traditional standpoint of the Japanese is the key to understanding their cultural multiplicity.[33]

Confucianism, and later Buddhism, were considered as useful vehicles for advancing Japanese understanding and practice. While the Five Relationships were clearly a part of what was gleaned from Confucian writings, loyalty and respect were the two virtues taken to be of the utmost importance in the Japanese context.

Initially, Confucianism in Japan was limited to the aristocratic classes, unlike China "where it was theoretically available to all." In fact, it became the exclusive specialty of a collective of hereditary scholars, primarily attached to the Imperial Court. Because of this monopolization, the influence of Confucianism was severely limited, and by the tenth and eleventh centuries, "the appeal of Confucianism, whether among scholars, military men, or the common people, had been nearly entirely replaced by Buddhism."[34] Ironically, it was the Buddhist priests in Japan, who continued studying Confucianism, who kept alive the Confucian legacy of learning, and it was they who were most responsible for the spread and popularization of Sung dynasty Neo-Confucianism, beginning in the twelfth century. Still, as Smith observes, "it was not until 1600 that it began to gain an independent position, separate from that of the Buddhists or the hereditary scholars of Confucianism supported by the Imperial Court."[35] It was the Neo-Confucianism of Chu Hsi, a Confucianism liberally improved by Taoist and Buddhist teachings, that eventually became the "official" Confucianism of Japan, by Imperial command, in 1647.[36] By this time the widespread study of Confucianism was recommended, and already in 1632 a Confucian temple and school were constructed. The school became the active center for the training of Tokugawa officials, along Confucian lines. The school and the temple became "the mainstays of the government's control over educational and intellectual activities all over Japan, for they set the pace for most of the other clan schools and established a common Confucian basis for the consideration of all social problems."[37] Smith quotes the regulations of a guild that existed during Tokugawa times, which expresses well the specifically Japanese adaptation of Confucian ethical expectation:

> We shall require children to respect their parents, servants to obey their masters, husbands and wives, brothers and sisters, to live in harmony, and the young to revere and cherish their elders, in short, we will endeavor to lead the people to walk righteously. Whoever fails to do so shall without fail incur your punishment. . . .
>
> On the other hand, if any person is distinguished by obedience to parents, diligence in duties, or praiseworthy conduct in any other matters, he shall be reported by us and rewarded by you.[38]

In the twentieth century, Japanese Confucianism was tied to the aims and aspirations of the ultra-nationalists. It was a time when Japan was reacting against the materialistic individualism of the West, and extolling the unique superiority of the Japanese people and their ways. Ōkawa Shūmei, for example, in his history of Japan (published in 1940), maintained that Japan was the only country in the world where Confucian doctrines were still alive. He wrote,

> We Japanese first had contact with Chinese thought and culture, and we made it our own; and then we had contact with Indian thought and culture which we also made our own. These fields of thought and culture, which may be termed the two extremes of Asian mentality, due to having been given direction by the Japanese spirit, have continued to exist and develop up to the present. . . . And isn't the quintessence of Chinese thought and the basis of Chinese civilization the teachings of Confucius and Mencius? These teachings remain alive in Japan, but have died in China. . . . Confucianism has raised the level of virtue of the Japanese people.[39]

The school ethics textbooks of the time (morals courses were compulsory), were replete with Confucian admonitions. Writes Smith, "loyalty and filial piety were constantly extolled as basic to family life, harmony in society, and the carrying out of one's duties to the Emperor."[40] One ethics textbook described the type of citizen to be admired:

> In our homes, our parents are always devoting their strength to family occupations, the education of their children, and the prosperity of their homes and country. We their children must obey our parents' instructions, be filial to them, and, by keeping harmony among our brothers and sister, set our parents mind at ease.
>
> We must be sincere in everything we do. Our personal conduct will then naturally become just and we shall become men of virtue.[41]

Smith additionally notes that these textbooks did not list "these types of Confucian virtues merely abstractly or theoretically. Stirring examples of loyalty, filial piety, and sincere devotion to duty were taken from Japanese history."[42] Smith provides numerous examples from the morals textbooks of the time, such as "we have splendid traditions in our family," and "filial piety in our country has its true characteristics in its perfect conformity with our national entity by heightening still further the relationship between morality and nature." The latter example continues by stating that Japan is "a great family nation, and the Imperial Household is the head family of the subjects and the nucleus of national life," and concludes with the quintessential Japanese Confucian insight that "in our country there is no filial piety apart from loyalty, and filial piety has loyalty for its basis."[43]

The quip that in Japan, one is born and married as a Shintōist, dies a Buddhist, but lives one's daily life as a Confucian, is not without its point. However much ethics in Japan has been influenced by Shintō and by Buddhism, which we will inquire into next, it is ever colored by Confucian structures, social forms, and the basic attitudes of loyalty to emperor and to others, and the sense of respect and politeness which comes from emphasis on filial piety. As well, the Confucian, Shintō, and pre-Shintō emphasis on ancestor worship is ever present in Japan, extending the sense of history and historical connectedness into the distant past of the nation. It is a continuity of respect and appreciation, kept very much alive through the practice of active remembrance at the Buddhist cemeteries, community and national commemorations and ritual festivals, and at home shrines. The social connectedness, which is so central to the attitudes of the Japanese, is a complex historical web that extends backwards to the prehistory, and to the creation myths of the nation.

4

———

Buddhism and Japanese Ethics

INTRODUCTION

Sometime during the fifth century A.D., both Confucianism and Buddhism made their way to Japan. The impact of Buddhism (originally of Indian origin although for the Japanese it was predigested and already altered by its prior encounter with Chinese Confucianism and Taoism) was truly enormous. Even though it is often said that the major responsibility of Buddhism in Japanese culture is for the rituals of death and dying, it is evident after even a cursory study of Buddhism that ethics in Japan is significantly influenced by Buddhist ideas, practices, and attitudes. The intellectual subtlety and complexity of Buddhist metaphysics and epistemology seemed perfect as an overlay which, when placed over Shintōism and other indigenous ways of being, feeling, and epressing, provided a much needed explanatory and descriptive power— the power of theory—to Japanese ways of comprehending their world and the nature of the self. As well, within Buddhism there are numerous conceptual similarities to Shintōism, making it difficult to be sure what has been borrowed or altered through cultural transmission, and what was shared in common from the beginning. Be that as it may, it was Confucianism, not Buddhism which provided the ethical norms for human interaction: "when Buddhism entered the region, it tended to function within, rather than without, that system of Confucian relations."[1] Thus, Buddhism did not replace Confucianism (or Shintōism either), but rather enriched and added to the already existing moral and spiritual mix. Buddhism supplied the Japanese with a sophisticated

77

philosophical and intellectual account of things. It is that account that this chapter sets out to explore.

Gunapala Dharmasiri, who writes as systematically as anyone on the subject, suggests that the Buddhist outlook on the world may be summarized in terms of three metaphysical truths, and that the suffering in the world is the direct result of our ignorance (*moha*) of these truths.[2] It is not just that we are ignorant of the truth, but that we have developed assumptions which seem so real, so evident, even so perceivable that we have no reason or cause to doubt their truth. We are so mesmerized by our own way of seeing the world that there is, by and large, not a single doubt about our life-pattern, our actions, or our assumptions. We take them all as fact, as "givens." It is as though the sense of the world were simply handed to us on a platter, fully formed and cooked. The first metaphysical "given" or "truth" is (1) the assumption that there are real, fixed, stable, and even unchanging objects in the world, including ourselves and other people. The truth, for the Buddhist, is that there are no unchanging objects in the world, for the world is in "ever changing flux."[3] However, rather than apprehending this flux, the truth of impermanence, we project a conceptual fixity and stability onto things, which renders us incapable of seeing the flux, but only the generated fixity and stability which we ourselves have superimposed on the reality of the flux. The truth of impermanence (*anicca*), could we but comprehend it, would release us from the expectation that anything is lasting, and prepare us for the continual stream of change, disappearance, and death which is the reality of our lives. This awareness already embraces the second truth, (2) that of *non-substantiality (anattā)*, "that nothing has a soul or a substance."[4] The self, as an independent and substantial entity, is an illusion. All that exists does so as a result of the confluence of causal events and influences. Take these away, and the effect ceases to be. Take away water and/or wind, and a wave vanishes back into the sea. It had existed only as long as the conditions were in force which brought it into existence in the first place. Take away those conditions, and the wave simply is no more.

The third basic truth about the world (3) is that life is filled with suffering (*dukkha*), a notion that includes more than just physical suffering, but also the transitoriness of relationships, achievements, wealth, etc., as well as mental discomfort and restlessness, and the sense of the unsatisfactoriness of life. We do achieve short-term or temporary happiness, but in reality this happiness is always edged with the realization that nothing lasts, that even this is precarious, and that sooner or later everything perishes or comes undone. The illusion is that we can expand these temporary happinesses, and stitch enough of them together to create a lifelong quilt of comfort and stable happiness. This is our folly! No one is exempt from change, from disease and old age, from disappointment and eventual death of oneself or of loved ones. It is not that there is no joy or happiness, or peace and contentment to be found in living, but that it is a cause of suffering to take such states as being somehow permanent, rather than precariously open to decay and change. In other words, a major cause of suffering is clinging to what presently is the case, as though doing so will make it last, rather than accepting the inevitability of change, and being prepared for it. Indeed, such acceptance makes the transitory happinesses all the more precious, like Japanese cherry blossoms which may last but for a few hours, and certainly no longer than a few days (depending on the vagaries of the weather). All the more important it is to glory in the cherry blossoms while they are out—to expect them to last is futile, and to put off viewing them may be to have lost the opportunity altogether.

This third metaphysical "truth," as stated above, is actually the first of the Buddha's Four Noble Truths, viz. *dukkha*. These truths are (1) that all life is filled with *dukkha* (suffering), (2) the cause of suffering is craving, (3) we can be released from suffering by eliminating its cause, and (4) this can be achieved by following the Eightfold Path. Walpola Rahula leaves "*dukkha*" untranslated, because while it does mean " 'suffering,' 'pain,' 'sorrow' or 'misery' . . . it also includes deeper ideas such as 'imperfection,' 'impermanence,' 'emptiness,' 'insubstantiality.' "[5] In any case, we suffer because we seek after a permanence and an unchangeability which is simply unavailable. This craving and other thirsts bring about the Second Noble Truth: the cause of suffering is such craving, such desiring. The Third Noble Truth informs us that there is a way out of this state of craving that yields suffering. And the fourth and final Noble Truth describes the "Middle Way" out, and it is divided into eight subcategories, called the Eightfold Path, which forms the heart of Buddhist ethics.

In summary, suffering (the unsatisfactoriness of life) is the result of three false ways of looking at things: "[1] . . . that there are really existing non-changing objects in the world (*nicca*) . . . , [2] that persons and objects exist as independent substances (*atta*) . . . , [3] that we can achieve lasting happiness in this worldly life (*sukha*)."[6] Truth, for the Buddhist is exactly the opposite of these three falsehoods.

THE BEGINNINGS

Gotama, the Buddha, was born in the sixth century B.C. in India. He began his spiritual quest when he saw that all of life, as it is ordinarily lived, is unsatisfactory. Neither a life of sensual and material enjoyment nor of austerity will yield happiness, but rather some middle path between these and all other extremes must be sought. By following such a path, he thought he had gained insight into the true nature of things— things as they really are—and thereby became enlightened, awakened. Such enlightenment was not just epistemological, but self-transformative and ethically significant as well. Indeed, "in this enlightenment, he realized that *morality* [*sīla*] and *wisdom* [*paññā*] were the two main paths for attaining the ultimate happiness or salvation."[7] Two seeming paradoxes might be thought to emerge from the separate demands of morality and wisdom. First, enlightenment, and the resultant wisdom, represent a transformation of the individual, yet that self-alteration results in a concern for others which is anything but self-oriented. Second, the emphasis on truth and the correct view of things seems to dominate ethical and social concerns, and yet, it is morality and compassionate concern for all beings that is inviolably required if true happiness and one's own salvation is to be achieved. To be sure, the ultimate goal for the Buddhist is the attainment of *nirvāna*, but *nirvāna* (ultimate release, but from exactly what will be discussed later) requires both proper understanding, and proper behavior. The two are inextricably linked in such a way as to make personal salvation quite unattainable apart from a selflessly compassionate desire to assist others towards their own happiness and salvation. Buddhist social ethics cannot, and does not, exist apart from the transformation of the individual, but such self-transformation is neither genuine nor complete *unless* it is ethically drenched with other-concern.

Yet there is a path, a spiritual path, which leads to a permanent state of well-being, the path to *nirvāna*. To reach *nirvāna*, or ultimate reality, or "nothingness" as it is often termed, is not to leave this existence in favor of another, as is sometimes thought by critics of Buddhism, but to be in this world in a radically different way, having broken one's attachments to the ordinary perceptions of the world and our place in it, and the grip of a fanciful view of who it is that we ourselves are. The wisdom of enlightenment breaks our attachment to the old world-view, and our clinging to it. It is only through ignorance *(moha)* that we clung to that perspective in the first place. Such wisdom demands that one act morally.

BUDDHISM AND MORALITY

The prevailing impression of Buddhism is often of people drawing into themselves, meditating in the quiet peacefulness of a forest retreat. It is considered a self-centered search for personal salvation at the expense of others, who, for one reason or another, cannot or choose not to withdraw from social obligations. Yet such a view is not in accord with the Buddha's teachings. Dharmasiri argues that Buddhist asceticism and withdrawal from society, if properly understood, recommends "forests and lonely places only as ideal sites for training in meditation, but never for living, and he [the Buddha] always advised monks that they 'should travel around for the benefit and happiness of the multitude of human beings' *(Caratha bhikkhave cārikam bahu jana hitāya bahujana sukhāya)*."[8] Meditation and retreat is a preparation, not an end in itself. The goal of *nirvāna* itself cannot be reached independently of helping others through fully compassionate acts.

Damien Keown defines the Pali word "*sīla*" as denoting "the sphere of moral excellence . . . [it] may be translated by a range of more or less interchangeable English words such as 'morality,' 'virtue,' 'ethics,' and 'good conduct'. . . ."[9] Keown begins his account of Buddhist ethics, or *sīla*, with the first of the thirteen *suttas* constituting the *Collection of Moral Practices* (*Sīlakkhandhavagga*) from the longer *Long Discourses* (*Dīgha Nikā ya*), one of the oldest portions of the Pali canon. This first *sutta* is entitled *Discourse on Brahma's Net* (*Brahmajālasutta*), "listing various observances or *sīlas* for which it is said the Enlightened One (*Tathāgata*) might be praised by a worldly person."[10] This emphasis on the "worldly person" is significant, for it serves to make clear that the sort of morality being referred to is conventional Buddhist morality and not the moral awareness reached by enlightened people, who, it is often said, no longer have need of a list of abstentions and rules for proper behavior. The list includes many prohibitions which are common to virtually all moral systems, with a few that accent distinctively Buddhist non-violence, or which speak specifically to the times when the text was composed. I will list only some of the prohibitions: taking life, stealing, unchastity (sexual misconduct), lying, slanderous and/or harsh speech, frivolous talk, causing injury to seeds and plants, accepting women or girls (as gifts or payment, temporary or otherwise), accepting men or women in bondage (as gifts or payment), cheating, bribery, maiming or murdering, putting anyone in bonds, and robbery or violence.[11] Throughout there are various prohibitions against excessive luxury, or elevated social status. Add to these three additional moral precepts (from *The Ten Good Paths of Action* [*dasakusalakammapatha*]), and the result is an insight into what Buddhist ethics expects of Buddhist adherents: non-covetousness, non-malevolence, and the holding of right views.[12] There are numerous other prohibitions against taking intoxicants, dancing, singing, watching shows and using garlands, etc., but most would take them today as being of lesser importance, if not outdated, with the possible exception of the prohibition of intoxicants. To live in accordance with this list is to model oneself on the morally exemplary life of the Buddha himself. As is well known, the simplest summary of this list is found in the Eightfold Path, the fourth and last of the noble truths, described as the path leading to *nirvāna* and away from suffering. The path insists on Right Views, Right Resolve, Right Speech, Right Action, Right Livelihood, Right Effort, Right Mindfulness, and Right Meditation. The emphasis on ethical action here constitutes, according to some authors, a revolution in Indian religious thought. It is not that metaphysical knowledge is absent, for "Right Meditation" is the direct path to enlightenment and the various realizations such as non-substantiality, no-self, emptiness, etc. Nevertheless, whereas Hinduism taught that the paths of wisdom and action were alternative paths to enlightenment, ". . . in Buddhism they are both essential facets of the path towards, and the experience of, enlightenment itself."[13] As usual the Buddha taught a middle path between excessive emphasis on wisdom and knowledge, and excessive emphasis on ethics and virtue. One-sided emphasis on "moral development" at the expense of "intellectual development" will result in "a tendency to become obsessed with external forms of conduct such as rules, rituals and rites."[14] The result could be an attachment to the rules and rituals themselves, as ends in themselves, thereby losing sight completely of the original spirit of such formulations. If there is a one-sided emphasis on the intellect, on speculation and the details of Buddhist doctrine at the expense of moral development, there will be a clinging to theory and a relative indifference to love, compassion, and the well-being of others. In other words, either way one will in fact be less than mindful. The Buddha taught that the Path requires both alternatives: his middle way "was to steer between both extremes and pursue the even-handed cultivation of morality and insight."[15] Indeed, if morality and wisdom "are cultivated asymmetrically, a psychological imbalance will emerge in the form of intellectual or legalistic fixation instead of insightful knowledge and compassionate moral concern."[16]

The most remarkable difference between ethics, East and West (of course, this is a broad generalization), is that the former encourages heartfelt feeling as the central core of ethical behavior, and the latter precise formulation of a code of behavior, and the identification of some universal criterion of what is good (or right). What I have in mind is the difference in emphasis between the encouragement to develop human heartedness (Confucian *jen*), of feeling primordially "one" with all things (Taoist *tz'u*), or compassionately embracing and identifying with all beings (Buddhist *metta* and *karunā*) on the one hand, vs. the Ten Commandments, or the stringent codes of behavior in some

Islamic traditions, or the criterion of the greatest happiness for the greatest number, or acting strictly in accordance with the dictates of duty on the other hand.[17] Not that you can't find the one in the other, but that there is a readily identifiable difference in emphasis—and of course, in the supporting context, as well.

Buddhism is a wonderful example of the sort of emphasis found in the traditions of the East. What student of religion has not compared the Eightfold Path of Buddhism to the Ten Commandments of the Judeo-Christian tradition? After all, on the surface of things there is only a difference of "two." I won't perform the tedious task of a one-by-one comparison here, but it is important to note that the Buddhist "eight" are positive prescriptions, whereas the "ten" are negative prohibitions—"thou shalt not." Not surprisingly, as a result, the "ten" are very specific—"do not kill," "do not lie" ("or bear false witness"), "do not steal," etc., whereas the "eight" are astonishingly vague—"right understanding," "right speech," "right action," "right effort." And this "vagueness" is actually the point. To teach someone not to steal is not necessarily to make him an honest person. Indeed, as Lawrence Kohlberg discovered, it may simply be to have taught that person not to get caught, or not to steal in specific circumstances, e.g. do not steal in Miss Johnson's class, but steal from the department store if you think you can get away with it.[18] Not that this is in Judeo-Christian teaching, but that it is easier to appear to "fulfil the letter of the law" without recourse to more generalized interpretations, or without a feeling of identification with the shopkeeper and his or her aspirations, or without grasping the context of the tradition and its teachings when the moral requirement is crisply articulated, isolated, and apparently simplistically clear. Furthermore, there is no need for any self-transformation, any raising of consciousness whereby one internalizes a behavioral prescription. One can do what is required of one, yet all the while be cursing the fact that one is made to do so. In a sense, the prohibitions are *imposed*, as though coming from outside rather than from within, orders from a higher authority, rather than impulses or feelings from within one's own nature, consciousness, or sensitivity. By contrast, notice how the Buddhist "eight" draw you into the evident need to interpret, and into the supportive context of the entire tradition in order to make any sense at all of what is being ethically prescribed. How might one learn to refrain from stealing, as a Buddhist? Of course, for the child, the path might be superficially similar: parental disfavor, punishment, being "grounded," or actually being expelled from an institution. Yet, as sophistication becomes more evident, the meaning of "right action" might be sought. Rahula tells us that it means "promoting moral, honourable and peaceful conduct. It admonishes us that we should abstain from destroying life, from stealing, from dishonest dealings, from illegitimate sexual intercourse, and that we should also help others to lead a peaceful and honourable life in the right way."[19] How many "commandments" are included here, and how much is said and implied about the sort of person we are to strive to become; about the sorts of attitudes we ought to display in our interaction with others, and what sort of self-image are we encouraged to embody as we walk the path? But there is more still. For, to greater or lesser extent, each of the "eight" implies all of the others. Thus, the absence of right action is already to imply the lack of "right effort," for instance.

> Right Effort is the energetic will (1) to prevent evil and unwholesome states of mind from arising, and (2) to get rid of such evil and unwholesome states that have already arisen within a [person]..., and also (3) to produce, to cause to arise, good and wholesome states of mind not yet arisen, and (4) to develop and bring to perfection the good and wholesome states of mind already present in a [person]....[20]

A genuine and extensive change in consciousness is demanded, and not simply a more or less strict adherence to the letter of a prohibition. Still, a Christian could reply that the ethical component of the new law introduced by Jesus, "love thy neighbor as thyself," is remarkably akin to the Buddhist approach to consciousness transformation. He reduced the ten to two. However, the tradition of interpretation of that teaching has, more often than not, returned to the ten as that which is both more teachable and more enforceable. Recall, however, that my claim is not that such an approach is wrongheaded, but that it is different from the Buddhist emphasis. It is more than likely that the ideal world will require both approaches.

Buddhism emphasizes the heartfelt, and eventually spontaneous impulse towards compassionate identification with the joy and the suffering of the other, with the resultant desire to do him or her good, and the concomitant absence of any desire, reason or motive to do any harm or evil. It is not that evil is prohibited (at least not in the long run), but that there is simply no place within one from which it could arise. There is no cause remaining to generate evil, whereas the causes of compassionate goodness are now effortlessly strong and (ideally) exceptionless. It is no longer necessary to prohibit, for the causes of wrong action have been eliminated, or are being eliminated. Either way, the central feature of Buddhist ethics is not prohibition, but transformation resulting in an incredibly strong compassionate identification with all other beings, and an intense desire to eliminate their suffering and to rejoice in their happiness. It is ethical behavior occasioned from the inside of a person, rather than the result of external attempts at prohibition and enforcement. Psychological health, or "purity," is the result of having eliminated greed, hatred, and delusion. Buddhist scholasticism (the *Abidharma* tradition) teaches that *dharmas* "are the basic constituents or elements of reality; they are ultimate reals or ontologically grounded existents which cannot be further subdivided or analysed."[21] *Dharmas* are no more permanent than anything else from the Buddhist perspective, but they constitute, in their impermanence as ultimate simples, the rock-bottom structure of reality in its most basic as-it-is-ness. Keown cites Winston King, a major interpreter of the Abidharmic tradition, who concludes that its views on ethics would be "almost completely foreign and meaningless to the Western mind."[22] Keown counters King, however, by demonstrating that the Aristotelian conception of virtues is an equivalent and parallel Western understanding of what the *Abidharma* teaches, namely how to eliminate "those factors which impede enlightenment, namely the defilements (*kles/a*)."[23] It describes fifty-two mental states which form the ultimate foundation of ethics.

"Ethics" itself is a general term which gathers together various kinds of virtuous mental states (*caitta*). "Mind" (*citta*) includes both "mental and emotional operations and [is] the centre around which the constellation of psychic events (*caitta*) revolves."[24] Mind "includes an arsenal of dispositional properties which take the form of mental predispositions, proclivities, tendencies and dormant and latent forces which activate themselves at the subliminal level of consciousness."[25] There have been numerous translations of *citta*, including mind, thought, heart, conception, consciousness, mood, emotion, spirit, idea, and attitude,[26] making it abundantly clear that here "mind" includes many more states of consciousness (and unconsciousness) than does the modern Western conception of "mind" as primarily the seat of thought processes.

Keown reduces the list of *dharmas* that are ethically significant, as listed in the *Abidharma*, to ten good qualities, and eighteen bad.[27] The good *dharmas* include faith, zeal, equanimity, liberality, benevolence, and understanding, and the bad *dharmas* include ignorance, heedlessness, and torpor. Keown further points out that Buddhist ethics is naturalistic in kind, because the *dharmas* are not mental or social constructions, but are ontologically grounded in and by the structure of reality itself. In essence, the *dharmas* are ingredients in human nature, and as such are descriptive of how we come into the world. Keown draws this and other implications with force and clarity:

... Buddhist ethics is naturalistic: good and bad are not abstractions to be apprehended by observers according to their various intuitions and sensibilities. Nor can morals be reduced to questions of taste or personal preference as suggested by Emotivism. A final implication of this objectivisation of ethics is that relativism is ruled out: what is to count ultimately as good and bad is not determined by accidental factors but grounded in the reality of human nature. Since human nature is everywhere the same the moral teachings of Buddhism are of universal extent and will hold good at all times and in all places.[28]

Vice and virtue may be either intellectual error (and therefore cognitive), or inappropriate emotional tendencies or responses (and therefore non-cognitive). Intellect and feeling are both involved in ethics, and are inextricably intertwined. Both craving and ignorance are involved in suffering and evil. Indeed, "false views could quickly be replaced by right views through a process of reasoning and analysis were it not for the stubborn emotional attachments (*lobha*) to the wrong view and fear of and aversion (*dosa*) to the right view."[29]

THE GROUND OF MORALITY

The ground of morality in Buddhism is, both from an ontological and psychological perspective, love or compassion. Nothing exists in this world independently, for everything arises and exists in relation to and interconnected with everything else. There is only a web of interconnectedness in which things arise and exist as a result of mutual interaction. Nothing exists in isolation. It is we who isolate things in our minds, imagining them to arise and exist in and by themselves. Conception isolates and grants substance and independence to things. In reality, for anything to arise or to be, everything else has to be more or less as it is. As things change, some things are no longer mutually supported and cease, and other new things arise.

Ethically speaking, what we have in place here is a "declaration of interdependence." We simply are connected to others, and to our environment, for we exist co-dependently from a metaphysical perspective: "Nothing can be independent in a world where everything is interrelated."[30] Our very existence is dependent on the support of this wider web of interconnection.

Psychologically, this translates into a feeling something like *kinship* with other human beings, and with our environment as well. If I am not, in fact, an independent, rigidly bounded center of consciousness, but an aggregate of forces which persist only so long as the greater context of forces keep me afloat in a sea of non-substantial energy, then this so-called "I" actually has no boundary, but extends out into the aggregate energies of others, and even into the wider animate and inanimate forcefield of nature. "I" am an energy center, distinct from other things but inextricably connected with and related to them. In this sense, other things are a part of me, and I am a part of them. We are each other, and it is only rational that I should treat others as I would be treated, because they are me! As Dharmasiri observes, "because my existence is dependent on the rest of the universe, I naturally owe a debt and an obligation to the rest of the universe. Therefore, my attitude to others and other objects should be one of respect and gratitude. Thus Buddhism advocates a sense of awe and respect towards living beings and nature."[31] It is the person of ordinary awareness who sharply divides the world into self and other, my good and the good of others. The person who understands that s/he is not separate grasps what it means that my good is your good, and yours mine. The distinction, again usually sharply drawn, between egoism and altruism simply breaks down. The illusion of a separate self gives way to an awareness of an extended web of interconnection in which there are centers of awareness, each of which is responsible for others, and in need of support from others.

Metaphysically, what we have is a field-like vision of the mutual interconnectedness of all non-substantial "things" or seemingly independent centers of awareness, whereby each center is but a focus of awareness or consciousness in a seamless field of becoming. Psychologically, such awareness is grounded in *sympathetic* awareness. Aronson notes that "etymologically, 'sympathy' (*anukampā*) can be understood as the condition of 'being moved' (*kampa*) 'in accordance with [others],' or 'in response to [others]' (*anu*)."[32] But Buddhist sympathy does not simply rest on the awareness that I see myself in the other, for it goes beyond even anthropocentrism to an affirmation of the intrinsic value of all living beings (Zen Buddhism interprets the extent of such sympathy to include all beings, animate and inanimate). Dharmasiri compares the teachings of the Buddha to the philosophy of Immanuel Kant, whose Categorical Imperative includes the admonition never to treat persons as means, but only as ends in themselves: "But the Buddha goes much further when he advocates the treatment *of all beings* as ends in themselves. The Buddha maintains that life is the only ultimate, intrinsic and sacred value in this universe."[33] Furthermore, Kant's position is a rational deduction, whereas the Buddha's is a metaphysical insight based on rational and empirical analysis of phenomena given in experience, and reveals a psychological disposition resulting from the recognition of our interconnectedness and our kinship. As a mother's caring for her child is (at least ideally) an extension of the same protectiveness, caring, and desire to live and to flourish which she feels for herself, so the Buddhist (ideally) extends his or her awareness of concern, sympathy, and empathetic identification to all living beings. Dharmasiri quotes from the *Karanīya Mettā Sutta*, where the Buddha rhapsodizes on this sense of reverence for all life: "Whatever living beings there may be: feeble or strong, long (or tall), stout, or medium, short, small, or large, seen or unseen, those dwelling far or near, those who are born and those who are yet to be born: may all beings, without exception, be happy-minded."[34] The Buddha even prohibited monks from injuring plants or trees, or from digging in the soil in order not to harm the worms and other small creatures that reside there. *Ahimsā* (non-injuring) is a Buddhist ideal which creates in us, even when not perfectly observed, a tendency or disposition to respect and revere life, to see it as sacred and of fundamental value in the same way that we instinctively feel about our own life and inherent worth. This ultimate ethical awareness is made possible, metaphysically, by un-deluding ourselves about the substantiality and separateness of our own individual ego-self. It is made possible psychologically by allowing our instinctive sense of our own ultimate worth to expand in such a way as to apply it to all living things, and possibly even to all existing things in this mysterious and ultimately supportive universe.

WHAT HAPPENED TO NIRVĀNA?

The Buddhist, in emulating the Buddha, seeks *nirvāna*. *Nirvāna* is a solitary achievement, not a communal or societal one. Yet the only way to reach this ultimate state is to come to see the emptiness of self, and the interconnection of one's awareness with all other living beings. Such insight, as has been argued above, results in an extended love, or all-life-embracing compassion. *Nirvāna* is not just the result of metaphysical insight, nor is it a selfish, individual act. Rather, it is the cultivation of an ethical life, a life of compassionate and sympathetic identification; it is part of what enlightenment is all about. "The Buddha emphasises that morality and wisdom are interrelated and interactive: "From morality comes wisdom and from wisdom morality . . . like washing one hand with another . . . so is morality washed round with wisdom and wisdom with morality!"[35] *Nirvāna* is the *summum bonum* of Buddhist ethics, but the path to it is inescapably one of moral concern for, identification with, and responsibility for all other living beings.

There simply is no other road to it. The very wisdom that prepares one for *nirvāna* is the same wisdom that paves the way for extended compassion; and extended compassion is part of true wisdom, and, therefore, preparation for *nirvāna*. Wisdom, you will recall, is the realization that the true nature of all things is that they are impermanent, without substantial selves, and intrinsically unsatisfying. Wisdom, however, is not mere conceptual knowledge. Ordinary conceptual, discursive, rational knowledge (*ñāna*) is itself a dogma which covers over reality, yielding only a constructed and largely false overlay. *Paññā*, or wisdom, takes us beyond *ñāna*, which is actually an obstruction we must get rid of, in order for a *direct experience* of reality to be possible. Wisdom also demands a harmonization of the conscious and unconscious aspects of our minds, achieved through meditation, in order to fully mobilize our entire and integrated consciousness. It is such wholeness that wisdom demands, and is equally required in order for there to be direct insight into reality.[36]

Ethical living, and the hoped for achievement of *nirvāna* are inseparable. Rhys Davies went so far as to affirm that "*nibbāna* [*nirvāna*] is purely and solely an *ethical* state, to be reached in this birth by ethical practices, contemplation and insight."[37] Similarly, Keown, too, argues against the forced separation of achieving *nirvāna* and living ethically. He repudiates "the claim that the attainment of perfection necessitates the transcendence or rejection of ethical values and marks the entry to a state beyond good and evil."[38] Final *nirvāna* (ultimate escape from the cycle of births) is, of course, completely beyond this life and this world, but for the Mahāyānist the life of Buddhism is an ethical life, as it is for the bodhisattva as well, who continues to serve and to exemplify goodness—ethical goodness—in this very life, here and now. Keown examines in some detail the Parable of the Raft, which is generally taken as scriptural evidence that once one has achieved *nirvāna*, ethics as a mere instrument may be jettisoned, and one is then truly beyond good and evil: "You, monks, by understanding the Parable of the Raft, should get rid even of (right) mental objects, all the more of wrong ones."[39] Even Dharmasiri, whom I have cited often, interprets the raft parable as clearly going beyond good and evil: one who has reached the far shore by means of the raft "has transcended ordinary morality."[40] Yet Keown argues that the parable has been understood out of context, and he sets out to develop an interpretation that is more in keeping with the Buddhist path in general, and with the wider text in which the raft parable is but a small part, in particular.

To begin, the teaching of the raft parable, if we understand it in the sense of leaving ethics behind, is not repeated elsewhere in the wider teachings, whereas the Eightfold Path and its clear ethical implications are repeated over and over again. Further, the Mahāyāna tradition itself seems not to have interpreted the passage as one of ethical exemption, nor one in which the boddhisattva is somehow beyond ordinary morality. In fact, in the numerous other instances of "crossing over" by means of a raft, it is the Eightfold Path itself which is spoken of as the raft, and it is *nirvāna* which is the further shore. In only one instance is the raft left behind, whereas in most of the other instances it is emphasized that the further shore includes moral perfection as originally taught and understood, viz. the Eightfold Path is explicitly cited, as are the Ten Good Paths of Action.[41] Keown concludes that "it is . . . clear . . . that *sīla* along with *samadhi* and *Paññā* are part of the further shore and are not left behind on the near side of enlightenment." The purpose of the raft parable is to warn "that one should not become slavishly attached to a view *even when that view is true.*"[42] Clinging always corrupts, and in this case is an instance of missing the point. After all, excessive emotional attachment or craving is a root cause of suffering.[43] The raft is itself good, and is indispensable in order for us to reach the other shore and live ethically thereafter, but it can become a noose around our moral necks if we focus on it and its requirements, rather than on the purity of knowing and feeling which yields spontaneous and heartfelt love and compassion, without a trace of anger, hatred, or greed.

ETHICS AND ENLIGHTENMENT

Sīla (ethics) is an indispensable ingredient in the journey to enlightenment. There can be no achievement of *nirvāna* without such action. Acting ethically "is precious, valuable and pleasant in itself, and at the same time is the necessary foundation for the entire spiritual project envisaged by Buddhism."[44]

Keown identifies the Eightfold Path as the "cornerstone" of Buddhism, which insists on the cultivation and eventual perfection of both moral and intellectual virtues, leading to selflessness. In the *Incremental Discourses*, the Buddha emphasizes this connection, concluding: "so you see, Ananda, good moral conduct leads gradually up to the summit." Ethics remains "a central enduring feature of the conduct of the enlightened," Keown concludes.[45] He offers striking evidence for this conclusion: the nature of the Buddha's own ethical life.

> We can see that the Path and Nirvāna lie in the same continuum if we shift our attention briefly from those who are still travelling to those who

have arrived. The difference between the Buddha's perfection and that of someone still following the Path—profound though it may appear—is only one of degree. The attainment of nirvāna-in-this-life marks the fulfilment of human potential, not its transcendence. . . . [The Buddha] had not transcended goodness but fulfilled it. What he had "gone beyond" was the possibility of evil.[46]

The Buddha represents the perfection of ethical living motivated by his total benevolence towards all beings. What is distinctive about the Buddha's ethical behavior is its spontaneity, and its utter steadfastness. Having eliminated all evil from his own dispositional makeup, there is no reason to do any harm, and a complete inclination to do what is good out of a benevolence grounded in both wisdom and compassion. It is an uncluttered, unfettered, unified, and whole-person empathetic disposition towards the good, towards the removal of suffering and the teaching to others of the Path. "In such a person the desire for the good is instinctive and the choice of right means can be made immediately without the distorting influence of egotistical considerations." The result of such a dispositional clarity and unity is not the elimination of all desire, but the elimination of the desire for that which is not good: the "aim is not to exterminate feeling (*vedanā*) but to liberate it from it attachment to false values (*vipallāsa*)."[47] Reason, together with right desire, that is to say desire that no longer seeks the inappropriate out of ignorance and/or greed (or other negative dispositions), but rather finds joy in the good, are the necessary requirements of genuine cultivation. At its highest, such joy is intense but neither overwhelming nor an instance of craving; it is spontaneous, and yet dependably present.

Negative reactions to Buddhism early on in our scholarly reception of it in the West took literally the Buddhist description of *nirvāna* as "extinction" (*nirodha*). But Dharmasiri makes clear that "extinction" refers to "the extinction of the thought processes as well as the extinction of the attachment to Samsara and therefore the end of the process of rebirth." Dharmasiri adds that the enlightenment that is *nirvāna* "is by nature, a high moral state."[48] As well, since it is a timeless state, not tied to spatial location, "because both time and space are derivatives of consciousness, it is best described as 'just being in the present moment'. . . ."[49] To this extent, it is clear that *nirvāna* is *samsara*, and *samsara* is *nirvāna*, although such positive depictions were absent in early Buddhism. By the time we get to Nāgārjuna, the doctrine is that *nirvāna* is this worldly, in the sense that when grasped from within *wisdom*, heaven is underfoot, and is a transformed way of being in this world. As Nāgārjuna put it, "there is absolutely no difference between

[s]amsara and [n]irvāna, and there is absolutely no difference between [n]irvāna and [s]amsara."[50] *Nirvāna* is everywhere underfoot, available to each and every one of us. That is what makes enlightenment so available to each and every one of us, and yet, it is also what makes it so difficult to discern. The temptation is to look beyond, or transcendentally above, rather than at the near at hand, or at that which has been underfoot all along, but unrecognizable as what it is.

THE BODHISATTVA

Christina Feldman, in an essay entitled "Nurturing Compassion," writes that "the Buddha was once asked by a leading disciple, 'would it be true to say that a part of our training is for the development of love and compassion?' The Buddha replied, 'No, it would not be true to say this. It would be true to say that the whole of our training is for the development of love and compassion.'"[51] This is echoed by Rahula, who comments that for Buddhism, "ethical conduct (*Sīla*) is built on the vast conception of universal love and compassion for all living beings, on which the Buddha's teaching is based."[52] Buddhism's ethical foundation is a passionate compassion, an intense feeling of empathetic identification with all that is, and an awareness that we are all inextricably interconnected.

Plato's ethically committed philosopher voluntarily returned to the cave in order to educate and enlighten those who remained behind, chained by habit and unwilling to leave shadowy illusion behind; Jesus entered the world to teach a new salvation, and willingly gave up his life out of love for all humankind; the bodhisattva, the ultimate ethical ideal in Buddhism, is an enlightened one who refuses to get off the wheel of rebirth in order to continue to work on behalf of the bulk of humankind with whose suffering he identifies, and tirelessly seeks to eliminate. Dharmasiri suggests that the vow of the bodhisattva, as popularly conceived, is to be rendered as follows: "that I attain enlightenment for the sake of all beings, and may I not enter final [n]irvāna until I have helped the last blade of grass to attain [n]irvāna."[53] The bodhisattva ideal is a Mahāyānist, rather than a Theravādin notion. For the Theravādin, there has been one, and only one, bodhisattva—the Buddha, and that we should aspire to become an enlightened disciple (*arahant*), rather than a full-fledged bodhisattva. Contemporary as well as earlier interpreters of Buddhism have concluded that "the normative ethic of Theravāda Buddhism is one of withdrawal from society and abstention from social involvement."[54] It seems a selfish ideal, a desire for personal salvation without further regard for the suffering of the multitudes. The Mahāyānists argue that such a view is one of wisdom without compassion, and therefore is only part way to enlightenment, at best. The bodhisattva ideal of Mahāyāna "represents an extremely subtle and sophisticated combination of wisdom and compassion."[55] Yet Aronson's account of Theravāda makes amply clear that while it is without the bodhisattva emphasis, a careful reading of the Pali texts makes it incontrovertibly clear that love and compassion are focal concerns in Theravāda, as well as in Mahāyāna, Buddhism. Theravāda is not at all a selfish tradition, but is exemplary in its compassionate other-directedness. To provide an instance, the Buddha in his discourses praises his disciple Mahākasappa

> because he teaches others out of simple compassion, tender care, and sympathy. The commentary indicates that these three fraternal attitudes are similar in that:
>
> > *Tender care* is the condition of protecting another.
> > *Sympathy* is the state of having a tender mind.
> > Both are the same as simple compassion. (SA.ii.169)[56]

It is Mahāyāna Buddhism in which the bodhisattva ideal is an open ideal for each and every one of us. Self-regard and other-regard merge into one since ". . . a [b]odhisattva must be always on the alert for any possible avenue to reach out and help all beings, because that is the only way to help himself. This is the essence of the doctrine of 'the transformation of oneself into others' *(parāmaparivartana).*"[57]

Buddhist scripture reminds us that the Buddha teaches others not from a sense of duty or obligation, but out of compassion and sympathy.[58] This thoroughgoing concern for the well-being of others is, ultimately, based on the complete elimination of selfishness. Interestingly, Anagarika Dharmapala actually summarizes the second Noble Truth not as desire being the cause of suffering, but rather "selfish desires" being the fundamental cause.[59] In any event, this "non-self-referential concern for the well-being of others" is a sentiment, a feeling or affective state which is "a non-cognitive state as distinct from the intellectual understanding or acceptance of the validity or rationality of a set of moral rules or principles. It is this sentiment which animates moral life and its absence which reduces morality to prudentialism or self-interest."[60] It is this "natural affection" or "natural sympathy" which is the true and singular motive for moral action. So it is, Keown concludes, "that the fundamental inspiration for the Buddhist moral life is concern for others."[61] Such sympathy, love or compassion is not the result of reasoning, nor does it result from acting in accordance with duty. Rather, it must be there at the beginning, as that which generates the desire to act dutifully, to follow a moral path. Concern for others "*precedes* the formulation of moral objectives." It is absolutely central, utterly foundational, and because of this "morality is not a means to enlightenment but a *part* of enlightenment. It cannot be chosen as a means to anything because it is impossible to *choose* to care or not to care about others."[62] Still, sympathy can be cultivated. The path to perfection, which includes moral perfection, is a path which reduces self-focus, and thereby engenders fraternal concern: it reduces the hold of such negative emotions as greed, anger and hatred, and increases the strength and focus of love, compassion, sympathetic joy, and equanimity. When the latter qualities have completely taken hold of one's psyche, then one is truly liberated. All of this is possible when and if the original seed of love and compassion is cultivated diligently, and allowed to grow into the deep-rooted tree of enlightenment.

The central or sublime attitudes or virtues in Buddhism are four in number: love (*mettā*), compassion (*karunā*), sympathetic joy (*muditā*) and equanimity (*upekkhā*). Aronson reports that in the Buddhist texts, *love* "has the characteristic of devotion (*pavatti*) to the aspect of [others'] welfare." *Compassion* "has the characteristic [of] devotion to removing [others'] suffering." *Sympathetic joy* refers to rejoicing in other's well-being and success, and being non-envious. *Equanimity* refers to "seeing being[s] equally," or being even-minded in one's apprehension of, and, I take it, involvement with, sentient beings.[63] These attitudes not only represent the best way of living, but each of them "is an antidote to an unwholesome reaction"[64] or attitude. Love counteracts anger, compassion counteracts harmfulness, sympathetic joy displaces displeasure and envy, and equanimity counteracts lust.[65]

THE PATH OF THE BODHISATTVA

The path of the bodhisattva is a practice, a putting into practice of the wisdom and compassion which one sees clearly, and feels deeply, but may not have enacted. In any event, it is this oneness of knowing, feeling, and willing, and actually willing without willing, i.e. spontaneously expressing in each of the minute aspects of one's interaction with other beings. It is a path to *perfection* (*pāramitā*), and Mahāyāna Buddhists recount several such perfections. First, there is the Perfection of Charity (*dā na*). Dharmasiri quotes from a sutra preserved in Chinese translation which identifies numerous charitable acts such as "feeding the hungry, giving drink to the thirsty," warming the cold and cooling those distraught by the heat, etc. But the "perfection" in such seemingly ordinary acts of charity is "to show that absolute non-attachment to worldly things," including things most dear to oneself.[66]

Even in sacrificing oneself what is shown is not mere courage, but a final overcoming of the illusion of one's own self, one's own ego, to the extent that there is no longer any distinction between one's own suffering and the suffering of others.[67] Yet there is more to practice than securing the physical and material well-being of others. What they need most is to grasp why they are unhappy, why they suffer, and what is the remedy. The practice of perfection is the practice of teaching others, of presenting to them a better way, a way beyond suffering.

Whether the gift is material, or the protection of another's physical well-being, or the gift of teaching about the path to enlightenment and release from suffering, the way of the bodhisattva involves a giving which is very different from ordinary gift giving:

> How should a [b]odhisattva give? "He should always be very courteous to the suppliants, and receive them with every mark of respect and deference. He should also be happy and joyful, when he gives away anything. This condition is important and essential. The donor should be even happier than the recipient of the gift. A [b]odhisattva should not repent of his generosity after bestowing gifts on others. He should not talk of his charitable deeds. He should give quickly (*tvaritam*) and with a humble heart. He should make no distinction between friends and enemies, but should give to all alike. He should give to the deserving and the undeserving, the wicked and the righteous, everywhere and at all times. But he should not lose the sense of proportion in his charity.[68]

Indeed, at the approach to some semblance of the "perfection" of charity, the individual loses any sense of his/her individuality, or that of the individual to whom the gift is given. The perfection of charity, like all other perfections of virtue, takes us to an awareness that is non-dualistic, where all is absorbed in a sea of indistinction, and yet in another sense and from a more ordinary perspective, distinctions exist with a new clarity and vividness. As the Japanese philosopher Nishida Kitarō was to describe this seeming paradox, what is evident is an identity of self-contradiction.[69] It is true *both* that all distinctions disappear in this non-dual awareness, *and* that all distinctions continue to appear in an even more intense manner than before. Perhaps this brief contemporary gloss will make the following quotation from an ancient text more accessible: ". . . a [b]odhisattva gives a gift, and he does not apprehend a self, not a recipient, nor a gift; also no reward of his giving. He surrenders that gift to all beings, but he apprehends neither being, nor self. He dedicates that gift to supreme enlightenment, but he does not apprehend any enlightenment."[70]

The second perfection is the Perfection of Precepts (SīlaPā ramitā). What is intended here is the practice of the Eightfold Path, the sublime attitudes, and all other precepts of conduct which the Buddha had prescribed, to the point of the perfection of all such virtues. The warning is, however, "that the practitioner should not think that 'he' is becoming virtuous because of this practice and therefore should vigilantly avoid any egoistic feelings of superiority."[71] This is yet another dimension of what it means to be selfless.

The third perfection, the Perfection of Patience (KsāntiPā ramitā), has to do with developing full-blown equanimity, "a feature of Nirvanic experience." Dharmasiri expands on the complexity of the meaning of the term "patience," including "not only patience and forbearance, the literal meanings of the term [Ksānti], but also love, humility, endurance, and absence of anger and of desire for retaliation and revenge."[72] Patience includes the ability to withstand pain, and even torture as is evidenced by the story of the Buddha, who (in a previous life) had angered the King of Kalinga. The king ordered physical mutilation as a punishment, and the Buddha recounts that as the king "cut my flesh from every limb, at that time I had no notion of a self, or of a being, or of a soul, or of a person, nor had I any notion of non-notion. Why? If, Subhuti, at that time I had had a notion of self, I would also have had a notion of ill-will at that time."[73] He has transcended completely the ordinary belief in the existence of a self, of things, of pain, and even that his suffering is caused by a real being. Patience thus perfected is far beyond forbearance, for it completely transcends the awareness that there is anything at all to forbear. Short of this nirvānic transcendence from ordinary awareness, one must learn to be indifferent to pains and to pleasures, although this extreme abandonment of "this world" is not so easily found in Chinese Chan, or especially Japanese Zen Buddhism, where the stoical acceptance of pain and suffering is in great contrast to the heightening of sensitivity to the pleasures and joys of this world.

The fourth perfection is vigor (Vīrya), or strength and effort. Avoid sloth, despair, and the inaction which persists in the wake of a poor self-image. The fifth perfection is meditation: Becoming technically proficient in one or more of the various meditative arts and diligent practice yielding higher degrees of awareness is the path of meditational perfection.

The sixth perfection is wisdom, viz the attainment of *nirāna*, or enlightenment. But it is a sense of enlightenment that leaves this world to become utterly delusory, and as such, neither bothersome nor controlling. On the other hand, to the extent to which nirvanic awareness brings us back to *samsara*, or this world once more, the new non-delusory world is itself bright, vibrant, worthy, and ultimately valuable to the point of being sacred as manifestation of the Divine. The nothingness of *nirvāna* in its austere voidness, allows the world of others and things to advance anew, just as they actually are, in a voidness which serves as a backdrop enhancement to each foreground sacred particularity. This Far Eastern Mahāyānist interpretation enthusiastically renders *nirvāna*, and Buddhism in general, as a positive, ultimately this-worldly, yea-saying tradition. Enlightenment is jubilantly in this very world, and is before you here and now.

It is through these perfections that the bodhisattva continues to improve and develop in his/her saintliness, becoming ever more adept at teaching and leading others out of their state of limited and opaque awareness, soothing them in their suffering, coming to their physical, material, psychological, and spiritual aid in a world which is labelled a place of suffering and unsatisfactoriness. By the time the Chinese and later the Japanese added their own interpretive layers to the Indian texts, Buddhism had become a stridently this-worldly approach to a deeper sensual way of experiencing and anticipating the joys of this world, and of accepting the disappointments and the suffering of this world. The Japanese are zealously appreciative of this life and this world; but they are realistic and steadfast in their resolve to accept obstacles, setbacks, and tragedies as part of life, as well. Life is, by and large, an opportunity to grow in the very midst of difficulties and suffering.

5

Zen Buddhism and Ethics

Two fundamental questions need to be addressed before we proceed. First, is Zen Buddhism really Buddhist? And second, is there anything like a basis for ethics in Zen Buddhism? The answer to the first question is at best ambiguous. But, then, Zen is a specifically Japanese form of Buddhism (arising out of Ch'an Buddhism, the peculiarly Chinese adaptation of Buddhism), and as such, it serves as the fountainhead of paradoxicality. Abe Masao answers the former question about whether Zen is a form of Buddhism as follows: "the answer . . . would have to be in both the affirmative and the negative at the same time." Affirmatively, Zen developed from Bodhidharma's introduction of Buddhism to China in the sixth century, when Zen acquired "the trappings of a religious order," and so may be properly seen as one among several forms or schools of Buddhism. Negatively, Abe contends that Zen is not just another form of Buddhism "but rather, in a fundamental sense, [Zen is] the basic source of all forms of Buddhism."[1] Such a claim is startling, because it contends not that Zen does not genuinely qualify as a species of the genus "Buddhism," but that it is the ground and originary insight of all Buddhisms. What is the basis for such a claim?

Within Mahāyāna Buddhism, the Buddha is not the only human being to have become enlightened, to awaken to the *dharma* (the truth, the teachings), but merely the first. The truth, the *dharma*, persisted before its realization by the Buddha, and it persists afterwards. Thus, in Abe's words, "the fact [is] that the realization of the [d]harma is nothing but *the self-awakening of the [d]harma itself.* Your awakening is, of course, *your own;* it is your awakening to the [d]harma in its complete universality."[2] It is little wonder that Buddhism encourages each person to look within to find the truth; to rely upon themselves to establish the truth of the *dharma* and to become enlightened. Thus it is that Zen does not base itself on the sutras or scriptures of Buddhism, but understands its position as being outside of the scriptural teachings, but not outside of the insights which are, to greater or lesser degree, recorded in those sutras. Whereas the written teachings are an imperfect and flawed attempt to capture the *dharma*, Zen maintains that the true *dharma* can only be passed on from person to person directly, and not through the mediation of words. Words, scriptures, teachings, and traditions are at best fingers pointing to the moon, catalysts for triggering inner realization. Zen teaching is often silent, wordless teaching. Abe collects four "classic formulations" of Zen difference: ". . . not relying on words or letters; and independent transmission apart from the scriptural doctrine or any teaching; directly pointing to the human mind; and awakening to one's Original Nature, thereby actualizing one's own Buddhahood."[3] Zen is beyond words, and is a direct pointing to and realization of one's own divinity, one's own Buddhahood. Zen points within, not without to scripture or tradition or anything else. The answer to the question "What is Zen?" is the same as the answer to the question "What is Buddha?"[4] It is in this sense that Zen is the inner core of Buddhism. Zen's preoccupation and focus is a direct pointing to and transmission of the same enlightenment that was the Buddha's.

The development of the Zen *kōan* was no doubt an attempt to demonstrate that the heart or essence of Zen cannot be captured in words or by logical, discursive, and rational analysis. The well-known "What is the sound of one hand clapping?" defies rational solution. Similarly, Zen masters often put off rational thinking and intellectual solutions by answering questions such as "What is Buddha?" with "Three pounds of flax," or "The oak tree in the front garden!" Any speakable answer is distortive, while authentic answers are beyond words and intrinsically non-verbal. Is it perhaps the case that just as this direct awareness is the core of all Buddhism, that the Zen approach to ethics is also the essence of Buddhist ethics?

Alas, many interpreters have concluded that Zen "appears divorced from or perhaps even contrary to ethics."[5] While Zen does transform individual character, it is less clear that its introspective stance generates a social ethic of any real significance. Indeed, even "friendly interpreters of Zen have been reluctant to propose that there is, could, or should be a distinctive, coherent, and consistent moral standpoint integral to Zen theory and practice." Whitehill adds that unsympathetic interpreters see Zen as morally iconoclastic, and even indifferent. Nonetheless, Zen does have a "moral content" since Zen has for centuries relied "on general Buddhist and Confucian precepts, codes, virtues, and exemplars. . . ."[6] Zen Buddhists have lived moral, even exemplary, lives, but not due to a philosophically consistent and developed moral position arising out of the Zen tradition specifically. According to the cliché, Confucianism, not Buddhism or Zen, has provided the ethical core of Japanese society and personal morality: the Japanese are born into Shintō, live ethical lives as Confucians and Neo-Confucians, and die Buddhists. Yet it seems both impossible and implausible to strictly separate and isolate influences in this tidy and precise way. For starters, Neo-Confucianism is an amalgam of Confucian, Buddhist, and Taoist teachings and practices. Add to that the re-reading of anything entering Japan through Shintō eyes, and it becomes easier to say what is "Japanese" than it is to say what is "pure" Confucianism or Buddhism. What is clear is that the "flavor" of Confucianism or Buddhism is present, although it is sometimes possible to find influences that have been taken in by the Japanese with little or no change. Then, add Zen to the mix as a distinctively Japanese take on Buddhism (with strong Chinese influences, of course), and the result is a way of looking at the world and each other which is both unique and complex. It is unique because of Zen's unswerving emphasis on the enlightenment experience that is at the heart of Buddhism. Neither scripture nor tradition nor organizational structure can serve as substitute. It is complex in that its language, its history, and its practices are all of them calls to a kind of non-verbal immediacy, making the task of the interpreter very difficult indeed. How to describe the moon when all you have are fingers pointing to the moon?

ZEN AND ENLIGHTENMENT

It would not be incorrect to conclude that, for the most part, the ethics of Zen is the ethics of Buddhism and Confucianism.[7] Thus, to claim that a Zen master has gone beyond morality by having attained a non-dual and distinctionless awareness, is to assume that such awakening is already well grounded in the ethical teachings of the Buddhist and Confucian traditions, with all of the "civilizing" depth of those cultural traditions. On the other hand, as one Zen teacher told me, in his years of teaching and practice, no Zen Buddhist has ever made such a claim. That is, Zen does not teach that the precepts and moral teachings of Buddhism are breakable, but rather that they are to be strictly obeyed. "Zen monks are also Buddhists,"[8] remarks Philip Kapleau. Kapleau compares the precepts to the scaffolding used when a tall building is erected, which seems to imply the ethical teachings are tools that are indispensable in the building process, but that are no longer needed once the building is completed. So we have a kind of *kōan* in effect, at the very beginning of our discussion of Zen and ethics: the precepts and moral teachings of Buddhism are to be strictly followed, and yet they are sometimes broken by Zen Buddhists who are exemplary in their practice and insight. *Kōans*, of course, are intrinsically unsolvable: one cannot intellectually resolve what the sound of one hand clapping might be. The purpose of the *kōan* is, at least in part, to lead the student away from intellectualizing, and towards direct experience. Unresolvable puzzles leave conceptualization and rationalization behind, unmasking their inadequacy in dealing with that which is beyond words, concepts, and rational deduction.

As the Taoist *Tao Te Ching* says, the Tao that can be spoken is not the real Tao, and similarly, the Zen that can be spoken is not Zen. Zen is practice, and practice is itself morality, and practice is the way to eliminate evil, and the way to confront one's own karma, and for Dōgen and Sōtō Zen, practice *is* enlightenment. Therefore, what I set about to do here is simply not possible. To intellectualize and attempt to conceptualize Zen is not only to miss the point of Zen, it is to continue doing precisely what it is that actually blocks the way to Zen. Zen is the direct encounter with one's own self, and with reality, and the way to this encounter with authenticity is to be found along a path which leads in the opposite direction: from mediated rationalization and conceptualization to direct and immediate experience. We should, rather, meditate together, over many months and years, and not try to speak the unspeakable in abstract, wordy phrases. But, then, there would be no book, no pointing to Zen. Nor would Lao Tzu have written his *Tao Te Ching*. To speak the unspeakable is itself a *kōan*. You simply cannot speak the unspeakable, and, as Lao Tzu warned, those who do try to speak the unspeakable brand themselves as not knowing, else they would not try, and those who know simply don't attempt to speak the unspeakable. So here goes . . .

At the time of the flowering of classical Taoism in China, Lao Tzu advocated the unlearning of Confucian rules and regulations, and the undoing of habitual and unthinking ritualism and artificial restraint, and urged replacing these with an open-ended and spontaneously "natural" flowing with the Tao (without) and the Te (within). Cries of "anarchy" or "lawlessness" are misconceived and for the most part miss the point, for the Taoist hermit has likely been brought up a Confucian, and now, in the midst of Taoist self-cultivation and awakening, seeks to go beyond the artificiality and rigidity of rules and rituals to a deeper expression of spontaneous, pre-reflective action based on a primordial identification with the source of all things. It is not that an uncivilized, untutored, and unaware cave dweller is told to do as he or she pleases, thereby giving free reign to as many basic and momentary desires as possible. Rather, Taoism flourished *because* Confucianism flourished. It was the *yīn* to the highly structured Confucian *yáng*. Taoism broke through the bureaucratic rigidity and the rule-bound "hardening of the arteries" of Confucian orthodoxy, but it presupposed the existence of the civilizing outlook of the Confucian cultural tradition.

Similarly, Zen Buddhism continues to flourish in a culture that is second to none in the industrialized world in its low crime rate (murder, assault, rape, burglary),[9] and in its emphasis on the quality of interpersonal relationships, social harmony, and proper behavior. Zen Buddhists in Japan, therefore, are already well "bedded down" in the civilizing influences of the Japanese culture. This is not to imply that evil is well under control. Evil abounds in Japan as elsewhere. One's karmic inheritance, the inability to comprehend one's deeper nature, the prevailing socioeconomic conditions, lust, envy, greed, anger, and hatred all contribute to this. All cultures are far from their ideals, and it is the message of Zen that this will continue to be so unless and until people actively practice the precepts and meditation, in order to deal with their own karma, their own psychic distortions, and their own emotions. Still, we survive, the world over, because of the veneer of civility and morality which prevents evil overcoming all else, and in Japan that veneer is given through Shintō, Confucian, and Buddhist teaching and experience. The cultural veneers of the world only stem the tide of negative forces: a transformation, either personal or social, requires diligent, steadfast, and wholehearted practice, including meditation, the task of dealing with *kōans*, and no doubt washing dishes and toilets mindfully.

Zen has long sought to shatter unthinking habit and complacency. Like Nietzsche striking with a psychological "hammer" precisely at the emotional reflex point (as when shouting via Zarathustra that "God is dead," or claiming to have gone beyond good and evil altogether), the Zen Buddhist predictably shocks the highly controlled, role-conscious, and approval-seeking Japanese. Admonitions to kill the Buddha if you see him, or comparing the Buddha to a "shit-stick," or grizzly tales such as that of the Zen master cutting a cat in two in order to make a teaching point, are but a few examples. To take any of these literally, however, is to miss the point. Killing the Buddha is a metaphor for not mistaking the ideal of Buddhism, which is the cultivation of one's own enlightenment experience itself, for the external shell of creed, ritual, or the precise following of some list of moral rules. It is also a metaphor for one's own opinions. The point of Zen is a personal and direct encounter with enlightenment, the same realization or awakening attained by the Buddha. Even one's understanding of the Buddha's enlightenment experience and its import is ever changing, and the same is true of one's own understanding: the Buddha is impermanence, and no enlightenment experience is ever final, or complete in the sense of a final and ultimate closure. And yet, at one and the same time, there is a permanent reality beneath or behind this flux, a reality which manifests itself, or takes or shows form as impermanence. The absolute is flux, and yet, while the flux is therefore absolute, it points towards that unfathomable potentiality which is not form, and which is permanently the ground of all that is. The "shock" of Zen moves us away from a ceaseless search for the correct form or conceptualization of that which is by its nature without form, and towards an experience of that which is both without and within each existing being. Thus, a shit- stick (a Zen example), or even shit itself is as much Buddha as is anything else. Awakening, as an immediate and profound awareness of the interconnection and divinity of all things, completely overturns one's valuational awareness. Bad smells, mosquitoes, snakes, and even earthquakes are all manifestations of the glory that is the ongoing creative flux of divine manifestation. It is all thoroughly divine!

Well, at least that is what we might imagine the view to be from the point of view of the absolute. One Zen teacher chided me for this overly poetic and romanticized view of the cosmos, reminding me that for Zen all that there is is "a vast emptiness and nothing holy." Furthermore, to only emphasize the goodness of human nature is to forget the karmic inheritance which each of us brings into the world, and which each of us must deal with in depth. Get rid of the words, the concepts, the philosophical thirst to speak meaningfully of the unspeakable, and the seemingly insatiable urge to render it dualistically good and bad, holy and unholy, clean and dirty. There is only emptiness, and it is vast, and must be drained of its supposed holiness. The eternal does not watch over each and every individual being, but rather dynamically expresses itself as immanent creation, and so things are neither good nor evil in themselves. They just are the way they are. Still, from the human valuational perspective, earthquakes and cancer are evil, for they cause suffering, pain, death, and grief. It is not that the Zen Buddhist is unaware, or unsympathetic, but rather that he or she knows that from another perspective, that of the ultimate and formless, it is the complexity of forces and events, motivations and decisions, that have brought about the events of the day and hour. It is things working out as they are working out, and not some evil cosmic intent, or a willful indifference to human suffering.

EVIL AND ZEN

Why, then, is there evil? Part of the answer has to do with individual human causes: we ourselves are responsible for some of the evil that occurs. The law of karma applies without exception: for every action there is a reaction. Deeds performed bring about results, and if the deeds are our own, then it is we who are responsible for the results. Then there is so-called "natural" evil. Why are there mountains, or trees, or viruses? Why is there anything at all? If one does not assume that there is a perfect and omniscient God whose function it is to look after us, and to lead us to a perfect afterlife in heaven, then the universe simply works itself out causally, for it is abundantly clear that our universe is causally ordered. Yet it is divine, magnificent, incredibly beautiful by and large as an array of forms and motion where there might have been none. To be alive is an extraordinary opportunity, for most of us, most of the time. The other times simply go with the good times. To be human means that we have to deal with life as it is presented. Rather than saying "if only things had been different," or "why has this happened to me," it is more appropriate to say "now that this has happened, how shall I best deal with it?" It is not resignation so much as it is realism. Without a doubt there is evil in the world, and much of it is perpetrated by people. Meditation, and the other daily practices of the Zen monasteries are major factors in bringing about an inner harmony and tranquility, and in quenching the fires of anger, hatred, lust, and aggressive behavior. They are not always successful.

As for the killing of the cat—a scandal for any Buddhist, given that not killing is the first and the foremost of ethical prescriptions— there is good reason to wonder whether it ever happened, and there is absolutely no reason to conclude that it is somehow a Zen ethical teaching. But, then, here I go again trying to resolve the difficulty, making the story rational and understandable. But it, too, is a *kōan*, and to try to resolve it is to pluck it out of its living environment, only to have it wilt before one's eyes. The precepts are to be kept, yet human conditions must be taken into account. What must one do? That is the *kōan*.

Nevertheless, I trudge on in my attempt to speak the unspeakable. The story is about Nan-ch'uan, or Nansen (748–834), a Zen priest, whose monks were quarreling over a cat. Why this dispute arose is not

indicated, but as Sekida Katsuki indicates, "at the bottom of all disputes, egocentric thinking is invariably present."[10] Wishing to put a
quick end to this squabbling, Nansen held up the cat, saying that if
anyone could say something he would spare the cat, but if no one could
say anything he would cut the cat in two. Quick! Quick! The assembled
monks were tongue-tied, and the priest cut the cat in two. The story
continues that the same evening, a monk named Jōshū returned to the
monastery, and Nansen told him of the earlier incident. "Jōshū took off
his sandal, placed it on his head, and walked out. 'If you had been
there, you would have saved the cat,' Nansen remarked."[11]

Roshi Robert Aitken deals with this example in his book *The Mind
of Clover:*

> Like all *kōans,* this is a folk story, expressive of essential nature
> as it shows up in a particular setting. The people who object to
> its violence are those who refuse to read fairy tales to their
> children. Fairy tales have an inner teaching that children grasp
> intuitively, and *kōans* are windows onto spiritual knowledge.
> Fairy tales do not teach people to grind up bones of English-
> men to make bread, and *kōans* do not instruct us to go around
> killing pets.[12]

Sekida Katsuki takes us in a quite different direction with his interpretation: "What is the cat? It is your own ego. If you get rid of your ego's
demands, there is no dread, no anger, no fear of death. 'Cut the cat in
two' implies a decisive, determined action."[13] Jōshū performed such a
decisive and determined action, by simply placing his sandal upon his
head. His action completes the *kōan* by pointing us in the proper direction, i.e. away from intellectual solutions, away from the sensible thing
to have done, and towards a direct affirmation of one's own being-in-
the-world. It is not the only thing to have done, but it is a clear indication of the sort of direct expression that makes evident the depth of
one's grasp of the situation. It is a direct movement away from intellec-
tualization and the search for a universally correct answer.

What is distinctive about Zen is not its radical separation from
Buddhist ethics, which is simply not the case, but its unyielding emphasis on what it takes to reveal the originary experience or foundational
starting-point of ethics itself: namely, the enlightenment experience,
the non-duality of pure experience prior to all distinctions and in which
all later things are seen to be utterly interconnected. However, in order
to bring oneself to this prized awareness, one must diligently practice
meditation, trying to be fully present and mindful in the moment and

living a moral life in accordance with the teachings of Buddhism and the societal demands of Japanese Confucianism. Self-cultivation is not a quick fix, but a lifelong journey: "the purpose of Zen practice is the perfection of character."[14] (Although there is a problem in mentioning "purpose" here at all. To have a purpose is, for the most part, probably quite un-Zen in that the purpose of meditation is not to have a purpose. One meditates because one has decided to meditate. It is done for no other reason, with no goal or intense overriding desire of whatever sort. It is a sort of *kōan*, puzzle, or paradox: one meditates in order to meditate. *Zen practice is itself the perfection of character.*)

In interpreting this statement by Roshi Yamada Kōun, Robert Aitken writes that "morality in classical Buddhism is the observance of the precepts, not killing, not stealing, not misusing sex, not lying, not clouding the mind, and so on. Precepts are useful for the Zen student, who seeks to internalize them, to find their source in the mind, and to make morality altogether familiar." He adds, "Moral behavior that is altogether familiar is the mark of the truly mature person. Everyone else needs guidelines."[15] The precepts are but guidelines, and the goal—although it is dangerous to codify this as a goal—is to "find their source in the mind," which I take to mean in one's own direct experience, so that one comes to see for oneself that the guidelines are expressions of the foundational experience of awakening to the nondual wonder of the divinity, emptiness, no-thingness, and utter interconnectedness of things.

Kapleau expresses this clearly in seeing that

> those advanced in their practice are not attached to the precepts, nor do they break them to prove how liberated they are. . . . The precepts are not moral commandments handed down by an omniscient or divine being. Rather they reveal how someone thoroughly familiar with Self and other behaves. Such an individual doesn't imitate the precepts; they imitate him. Until you reach that point, however, you would do well to observe the precepts.[16]

Nor does one ever reach total perfection, and so the precepts are always there as guides: "Shakayamuni Buddha is only half-way there," is a startling reminder that all systems, theologies, philosophies, ethical guidelines, and enlightenment experiences are but partial truths, and we are all always on the way, and even the Buddha is always becoming Buddha. The expressing of any and all reports of the awakening experience, and even the rational attempt to understand, is but a dualistic mapping in language of a non-dual and ineffable experience. The map is simply not the territory, and indeed, as helpful as it sometimes proves to be, we should remember Heidegger's warning that all revealing is at the same time a concealing, a distorting of what is simply too rich to be adequately contained by any mapping and any attempt at speaking.[17] The map, the words, the moral rules are but fingers pointing at the moon of experience. Understand the finger for what it is, and look beyond it to the source and meaning of it all. (A Zen teacher suggested that it would be wise to look beyond even this moon of experience as well, "just to be on the safe side.") In this sense, awakening is "the *starting point* of a truly ethical life."[18] It is also the ever-developing end point of Zen ethics, for awakening is itself transformative, and as such it enlivens one's practice, and one's understanding of the precepts and moral insights of tradition. To know the good, in this foundationally transformative sense, is at least to take away most of what stands in the way of doing the good. It makes practice and achievement more possible, for the "poisons" of selfishness, greed, hatred, and unwarranted anger have been watered down, if not altogether eliminated. The blocking of goodness is removed, as have the causes of evil.

THE CAT AGAIN

But the cat! The fable of the cat is like a slap in the face, a kick in the shin, a fierce shout! Shift your focus, give up trying to reason your way to ethics and to real understanding. Be present; experience others as extensions of yourself, and as manifestations of the divine energy; grasp all things as empty, temporary, fleeting, and impermanent moments in the flux of existence. Experience, don't just think; love, don't think about rules; be here now—*nikon*—don't be regretting the past or planning the future. Quick, quick, or the cat will be sliced in two! Grab the master, shout, take the sword from him, or scratch the cat's chin. Disable the master, show him that you are present and that you understand the importance of the moment, that you are right now, right here in the midst of direct experience. Even just scratching the cat's chin would be enough. Just scratch, and listen to the purring. Or howl like a cat in danger!

Of course, there is nothing un-Buddhist or unique in acknowledging the importance of the enlightenment experience. Awakening is, after all, the beginning of Buddhism itself. Within Rinzai Zen, what is unique is the almost exclusive emphasis on that experience, and on obtaining that experience for oneself. Without *satori* (the Zen term for the enlightenment experience), there is no Zen, D. T. Suzuki proclaimed.[19] This may seem like good Rinzai Zen but bad Sōtō Zen—Dōgen, the founder of Sōtō Zen, was abundantly clear that *satori* was not only overrated, it was often a hindrance to the Zen life, and that the substance of Zen is practice. But this is not to say that Dōgen denied experience—since for Dōgen, to decide to practice was already to be enlightened. This sense of enlightenment is not that of the "big bang" of *satori*, but the gradual, patient, everydayness of meditating. Training, not *satori*, is the lifeblood of Sōtō Zen. Dōgen tried to bring practice and enlightenment together, as being one and the same in essence. Nonetheless, he did not disregard enlightenment; he was dissatisfied with his own training until he had experienced the "falling off of body and mind" which he steadfastly sought with "total exertion." What he opposed was a halfhearted practice geared only to the achieving of a one-time experience somewhere down the path of practice. Practice, when done with total exertion and concentration, is itself enlightenment.

SEEING INTO ONE'S OWN NATURE

Sōtō or Rinzai, it is the genius of Zen that all other doctrinal, ecclesiastical, scriptural, and ethical systematizations fall by the wayside due to the single-minded emphasis on meditation and/or awakening. Whereas the Buddhist might well take the Buddha's teachings (the *dharma*) as central, and in particular the Four Noble Truths, the Eightfold Path, and the precepts, the Zen Buddhist sees all of these as only partially successful attempts at unpacking and giving expression to what was included in the vastly richer originary insight. It is the direct transmission of enlightenment itself that propels Zen practice, and for each and every person, that is the justification and substance of Zen.

To place the Four Noble Truths at the center would be akin to thinking that God himself had composed and delivered the Ten Commandments, and that they, along with the rest of the Bible were to be taken as the word of God. This, of course, is precisely the position taken by many Jews and Christians, in whole or in part, but it is far from the Zen perspective. What is important about the teachings of the Buddha is not their infallibility or divine origin, for they are fallible and very human, nor is it their universality, for they are but guides to thought and action, to be seen to be effective (or not) in one's own experience.

Furthermore, to place full emphasis on the rules and the texts is to forget how they came to be in the first place. Rules and teachings are nothing more than attempts to give expression to an extraordinary originary experience which itself is unlike any ordinary experience. It is a return to that formlessness which begat all form. It is an experience of non-duality, prior to the distinction between right and wrong, good and bad, or any other distinction. It is an experience of creativity itself, of the interconnectedness from which all things and all distinctions are derived. It is the reservoir of all things, and yet it itself is no-thing, is utterly without distinctions. It is an experience of profound compassion in that in it one comes to grasp that all is divine, and thus one is one's brother and sister, one is all animals, all living and all existing things, because all of these are but manifestations of the primal, the divine, and it is this seamless affinity and kinship that is recognized in awakening. One sees into one's own nature, and one finds there the pulse of the creative force of the universe itself. It is, therefore, the ground of all ethics.

WHY SHOULD ONE BE MORAL?

Why should one be moral? Because everything is a manifestation of nothingness, of the divine, of God. And just as one should not and would not cut off one's own foot unnecessarily, so one should not and would not harm another (which now translates as 'oneself') unnecessarily. Unnecessarily? This is not a dodge. To be ultimately compassionate simply means that one would never willingly harm another living or existing thing. One would not unthinkingly rape the earth, or eat animals for food, or get involved in a fight or in a war except as a last resort, or because of extraordinary circumstances. One might well use antibiotics to survive, eat meat to heal (as did Albert Schweitzer when he deemed that an extremely ill patient could not be expected to get better without the protein found in meat; and yet, a strict vegetarian himself, he would snap at visitors slapping mosquitoes on their foreheads, exclaiming that "it was my mosquito that you have just killed!"), or actually use violence as a last-ditch effort to protect the defenseless. But the breaking of a rule such as "do not kill" is an act of the utmost seriousness, and it should never be considered unless and until one finds oneself in a situation where all other alternatives have been exhausted. One might argue similarly as a utilitarian, which again points out the similarities that often emerge when comparing East and West. The significant difference is that the Zen Buddhist turns to the enlightenment figure as

the moral agent who points the way beyond the rigidity of rules while
steadfastly honoring them for the most part. In the West it is the rational moral agent who leads the way.

Furthermore, while the West more often than not emphasizes the
unbreakable nature of moral rules (deontology, divine command theo-
rists), the Zen Buddhist emphasizes the relative and circumstantial nature
of all rules, pointing beyond them to their source, the sense of genuine
compassion which arises from the wisdom of seeing the emptiness of
things, the interconnectedness of things, and the divine kinship of things.
A. D. Brear describes the nature and significance of the emptiness of
all moral and valuational distinctions, and contrasts the nature of moral
discernment before and after enlightenment. "Before enlightenment,
behavior is seen as good or bad, interpreted absolutely; after enlightenment, behavior is seen to be neither good nor bad absolutely, but still
so relatively. 'Good' actions, rather than 'bad' continue to be performed,
but their nature is truly seen—they are merely 'actions,' without qualities of goodness or badness."[20] To see "beyond" good and evil is not a
warrant for the abandoning of good in favor of evil, nor for the equal-
ization or neutralization of ethical and value distinctions in the everyday world of practice and engagement. It is an insight "into the true
nature of the relative, and, as such, totally inappropriate" as a basis "on
which to build more, merely relative, courses of action."[21] All existence
is empty, and yet we are to treat all beings with compassion; all moral
actions are empty, and yet we are bound by moral law and duty precisely because these are expressions of our own true nature, and thus
of the nature of the ultimately real as well. "To act compassionately is
to act in accordance with the suchness of the cosmos, for the cosmos
is 'radiant with infinite compassion.'"[22] To recognize one's own divinity
is the cause of acting divinely, and to act divinely is to express wisdom
and compassion in one's every move. Still, even if one is enlightened,
and spontaneously breaks a moral precept or law, one "still gets the
karma" (as a Zen teacher commented after reading this section). Whatever you choose to do will come back to you to deal with, one way or
the other. In *kōan* fashion, one has had to keep the precepts by not
keeping them: one has acted morally by acting immorally. The karmic
results will reflect this paradox, leaving the enlightened moralist with
karma to work off for having strayed from the preceptual path, however
caring the act might have been. To stray from the path in unusual
circumstances may well be the path a master would choose: but he still
gets the karma to deal with. He is not exempt from this universal
causality, and to stray means to have to pay the price. Of course, not to
stray means to have to pay a price as well. Which alternative is best

cannot be decided by rational means in advance, nor is one let off the hook by appealing to compassion, or the interconnectedness of all things in the cosmos. Life is like that. One must decide. Neither living, nor living morally, may be said to be easy.

CATS! CATS! CATS!

Oh, but the cat! Surely the non-violence of Zen is severely compromised by the incident with the cat. Cut it in two just to make a point? What is the point? Is it not that any rule is flawed, relative, appropriate in some contexts and not in others? Do not commit violence, but kill carrots to eat,[23] and use antibiotics to kill invaders to one's own body; do not steal, but take away and hide a weapon which is likely to be used to harm another; tell the truth unless it will cause unnecessary suffering. Kill a cat to bring another to awareness? Well, not really, because any of these exceptions could themselves be turned into rules of thumb (or something stronger): kill when it aids one's teaching; steal when it will be of help; use force to keep the peace; tell lies, but we like to think that we do so for good reasons. Such rationalizations would undermine any form of ethical system, and as such they must be rejected. On the other hand, to treat rules as absolutes simply does not work either, for we are always called upon to consider exceptions, and to consider new circumstances. The Eightfold Path, the precepts, the Ten Commandments—these are all important guides to moral living, but they are all based on an originary experience which is their ground and foundation. Through diligent practice one has become good-willed, open to compromise, compassionate and desirous of helping all things achieve their own originary experience or awakening, and doing what one can to help preserve others. The bodhisattva wishes all beings to awaken, and will not cease helping others until that is achieved. This is compassion, and an ultimate expression of an ethics of cosmic or radicalized caring.

Zen relentlessly pushes us towards *satori*. Alas, most of us will never experience enlightenment. Most of us will cling to the teachings, rules, and commandments as though they were   well, the word of God. We will try to apply them without exception, for fear of being in error, or we will treat them as rules of thumb without having had the originary experience which grounds both the rules and the exceptions. Inevitably, we will fall far short of the teachings, hampered as we are by our own shortcomings and blindness. Either way, we will be applying only the husk of enlightenment out of ignorance of the inner enlivening kernel itself. Zen is uncompromising in demanding that we take it upon ourselves to self-cultivate in order to become a Buddha, from which status each of us will be our own lawgiver, our own moral source simply because we will directly grasp that we are the source, and that it/we is/are divine, precious, remarkable, mysterious, and utterly beyond words, rules, regulations, precepts, and form. It also signals, at least ideally, the elimination of all of the negative poisons or emotions, leaving evil no place from which to spring or to develop within us. To give verbal expression or doctrinal shape to this insight is already to distort, limit, pervert, and misunderstand the originary experience itself, by conceptualizing it and thereby rendering it a mediated event. To speak or give shape to the ineffable is to distort it; not to do so is to be unable to act, to teach, or to do good and show compassion. That is the paradox of Zen, and its greatest contribution. Thus, to speak of the ineffable as "three pounds of flax" is to distort the ineffable, and yet this Zen response gives shape to the ineffable by not giving it conceptual, rationally graspable shape. Perhaps it points to the divine underfoot, or perhaps it points to the ridiculousness of saying anything at all. Again we confront a *kōan* of human existence and understanding. Any expression about the ineffable is deconstructable, and yet words can turn us away from themselves and towards an experience of immediacy, where the ineffable is a shit-stick, or the sound of a ripe fruit hitting a metal roof, the sound of a frog splashing into an isolated pond, or the hot grinding of a cicada in summer.

Still, what if the cat was actually sliced in two, that it was not just a fable? Or, what if some Zen teacher used his position and power to seduce a student for the purpose of his own sexual gratification? Or what if a Zen master, overtired and financially troubled, lashed out and assaulted a creditor, causing severe personal injury? Impossible? Surely Zen masters make mistakes. In all of us there does remain the possibility of moral error, corruption by power, and the existence of a variety of conditions resulting in psychological disharmony. Whitehill grasps the resulting dilemma with both hands:

> Perhaps the moral acts of the enlightened, accomplished without ethical pause for reflecting, weighing pros and cons, consulting others, wrestling with calculations of consequences, and other tossings and turnings, are moral simply because the Buddha-mind is acting through them. But, is this true of all their moral acts? Is it possible that some of their acts may not flow freely and directly from Buddha-mind, but be distorted by ego-clinging and psychic distortions to a degree that the acts

must be declared unworthy? Of course, they can—and that is why ethical judgment has a place here.[24]

It would be to perpetuate a shortcoming to ignore the rich ethical traditions, East and West, that represent both the highest ideals and the best attempts at systematic moral guidance, by focusing only on *satori* and spontaneous compassion. The heart of ethics for Zen is practice, and through practice the grasping of the essential divine kinship and interconnectedness of all things, and the resultant peeling away of ignorance and the negative emotions. But in order to reach this height, one has to practice diligently, to meditate, to become mindful in everything that one does,[25] and lead a conventionally moral life based on the ideals of Buddhism (and any other traditions which inform it). Practice (as self-cultivation), both morally and spiritually, is the only route open to us if we are seeking to act in accordance with the enlightenment teachings of the Buddhas who have gone before. D. T. Suzuki succinctly captures Buddhism's essence, and Zen Buddhism's insistence on experiencing directly this essence as the gateway to and foundation for a truly human ethic:

> Without Enlightenment Buddhism would have no meaning whatever, and when Zen claims to transmit the essential experience of Buddha we have to go up to the plane of that Enlightenment. When this is understood Zen will be understood.
>
> To be a good Zen Buddhist it is not enough to follow the teaching of its founder; we have to experience the Buddha's experience. When we just follow the teaching, that teaching, however noble and exalted it may be, does not become our own. Buddha did not want his followers to follow his teachings blindly. He wanted his disciples to experience what he himself experienced, and to have his teachings proved by each follower's personal experience. Experience, therefore, counts much more in Buddhism than its teaching. In other religions the founder expects his teachings to be followed by his devotees, who do not necessarily repeat the experience of the founder. The founder gives instructions, and the followers follow those instructions; they do not necessarily experience the same experience. In some religions the repetition of such experience is even considered to be impossible because the founder's experience is divine, and we humans cannot have the same divine experience.[26]

The originating experience of ethics itself is to be made our own, making ethics itself familiar. Anything less is to resort to memory rather than to act from realization, and to count on legalistic enforcement and coercion rather than the spontaneous expression of who it is that we now are, as cultivated, practiced, and awakened beings. To be "beyond good and evil" is to see them for what they are, but it is not to abandon them. Seen in this light, it is not Zen that has a moral scandal to grapple with, but most other traditions. Zen is remarkably clear about the importance and the emptiness of moral codes, whereas other traditions must face the scandal of not being able to comprehend morality's authority and origin. Not that Zen is simply to be assumed to be right, for that is a complex matter about which no final judgment is possible. It is simply that a scandal from an outside perspective may well disappear altogether when viewed in greater depth from within. In the process of this deepening of understanding, difficulties presented by other traditions may come to light which now need to be dealt with. The process of dialogue, and a resultant horizonal fusion can continue without letup, indefinitely. The virtue of comparative philosophy is that it can point out scandals within each tradition, and seek out yet higher understandings by means of which genuine moral advancement may arise. Fresh perspectives are the goads both to discovery and to humility.

ZEN AND NATURE

Certainly the Japanese "love of nature" is closely tied to Zen. As was the case with Shintō, Zen ethics extends beyond strictly human relational concerns, to appreciation of and responsibility for the natural world. What Zen brings to this salient characteristic of Japanese sensibility is its unyielding insistence on non-dual awareness. More will be said about the characteristics of such awareness when we come to consider the philosophy of Nishida Kitarō, but by way of anticipation it might be helpful to return to D. T. Suzuki's characterization of the Zen way with respect to nature.

Suzuki retells a dialogue that occurred between the Zen master Ummon (died 949) and a disciple. It is a curious, and typically cryptic Zen encounter which begins with the disciple asking, "What is the Pure Body of the [d]harma?" The question has to do with the nature of ultimate reality, and the true nature of the Buddha and his teachings. Ummon's response is "the hedgerow." The divinely ultimate is an object of nature, the hedgerow which separates the monastery grounds from its neighboring farms. The answer is not too surprising, for it affirms the ordinary as is done so often in Zen. The disciple next asks how one with such an understanding is to behave in the world, and Ummon responds with "he is a golden-haired lion," referring to a traditional understanding of the Buddha's natural color, and presumably, way-of-being-in-the-world. Suzuki's interpretation of this response is that the golden-haired lion "is not a manifestation of anything else, he is supreme, he is autonomous, he is king of the beasts, he is complete as he is. No idea is suggested here of the manifestation of anything in any form."[27] One who lives like a lion holds nothing in reserve, but is precisely as he appears, is spontaneous and without hesitation in action, reacts immediately rather than as a result of calculation, and thrusts forward into whatever situation wholeheartedly, sincerely, and with the gusto of total vigor. Such a one "is not a manifestation but Reality itself, for he has nothing behind him, he is 'the whole truth,' the very thing."[28] A Zen person doesn't simply smell the flowers but *is* the flowers; doesn't simply discern the divinity in a waterfall but *becomes* the waterfall itself; doesn't see divinity in all things, but *is* all things. This is total exertion, total sincerity, and is becoming the thing itself.

Suzuki urges us not to think of nature as something separate to appreciate, but as ourselves. Most people do not know how to look at a flower, to comprehend what it really is, but apprehend things as though in a dream. They remain separated from the flower; an enormous gap exists that separates the viewer and the beheld. It is not just that we appreciate nature, or feel deeply its tranquility and exquisite beauty, or feel a deep kinship with it. Rather, we are actually one with it. Not even with it: we *are* it, we *are* nature itself. It is not simply that we have the same root source, or are of one single substance, but that if we allow ourselves to go beyond—or beneath—concepts, language, and thinking, to pure or direct experience as pre-reflective awareness, then we will actually be what we perceive. We will be golden-haired lions, fully engaged in the flux, the beauty, and the texture of the world, not at a distance, but directly *as* the flux, the beauty, and the texture. The Zen person loves nature by becoming nature. Things come forward, as Nishida says, and nature is us, and we are nature. This is Zen's unique contribution to the Japanese love of nature, and it could well serve as a basis for an ecological ethics. By encouraging, even demanding, that we become the other, we are forced to experience the other as the other, and not just as a phantasm of our imagination as like us in some ways. It is to enter into the essence, the spirit, the nature of the other as other. We don't make waterfalls giggle and gurgle: we roar in a torrential down-flooding, as does a great waterfall. We don't make the other "us," but we become the other. To practice Zen, then, would be to practice being-as-nature, to interfere minimally, to walk without leaving a foot print, and to sing with the cicadas and the birds, to run with the lion and the gazelle—and, no doubt, to exist with the virus and to divide with the cancer cell. From the human perspective, the world is not all glory and tranquility. From the perspective of nature itself, it just is what it is. Zen does not understand, nor does it explain away what we call "evil" in the world. It takes such things as being what they are. Rather than wishing for things to be other than they actually are, Zen begins with the understanding that things are as they are, and seeks to discover how to live in the midst of this as-it-isness.

Oh, but the cat! We still have to deal with the cutting of the cat in two. The lion kills to eat, the cat kills mice, and the Zen master may well have killed the cat. Imagine yourself a golden-haired lion, totally engaged and with nothing held back in reserve. You are totally, utterly, sincerely, and unreservedly in the moment, right-here-now. Your student does not understand, and seems to be making no exerted and sustained effort to understand. You have the cat, and you seek to mobilize the student, to wake him from his dream, to show him what it means to totally exert oneself. What would you do?[29]

And If the Cat Were Not a Cat?

In his remarkable and courageous book *Zen at War*, Sōtō Zen priest and scholar Brian Victoria concludes that it is imperative to try to get clear about how "a faith rooted in universal compassion, could have been transformed in modern Japan into a religion whose leaders, almost to a man, unconditionally pledged their support for Japanese militarism."[30] His chilling account reveals that many, if not most, of the most influential Zen masters, teachers, and scholars contributed to the literature that demanded total loyalty to the emperor, interpreted war as a holy act whose aim it was to make the world a better place, and taught that it was only in Japan that true Buddhism was alive and well due to effective Zen training in fearlessness, focus, and the fighting spirit. As notable a figure as D. T. Suzuki wrote of Zen as Bushido—the warrior code of the samurai swordsman—as being "no more nor less than that of Zen. The calmness and even joyfulness of heart at the moment of death which is conspicuously observable in the Japanese, the intrepidity which is generally shown by the Japanese soldiers in the face of an overwhelming enemy . . . all these come from the spirit of the Zen training."[31] Yet the ability to engage in an un-critical, hypnotic like double-talk is most surprising in that it comes from the enlightened and rational D. T. Suzuki. He wrote that the purpose of maintaining an army, encouraging the military arts, and constructing great ships and arms is "to develop more and more human knowledge and bring about the perfection of morality. . . . Therefore, if there is a lawless country which comes and obstructs our commerce, or tramples on our rights, this is something that would truly interrupt the progress of all humanity. In the name of religion our country could not submit to this."[32] Again, Suzuki boldfacedly argued that we must distinguish between "the sword that kills and the sword that gives life." He attempted to clarify and justify this distinction by observing that "the one that is used by a technician cannot go any further than killing," whereas "one who is compelled to lift the sword" in some supposedly righteous cause cannot be said to be involved in killing at all, "for it is really not he but the sword itself that does the killing. He had no desire to do harm to anybody, but the enemy appears and makes himself a victim. It is as though the sword performs automatically its function of justice, which is the function of mercy."[33] Surely this is spontaneousness at its amoral—or immoral—worst! So long as the ego-self is out of the way, anything is permitted. Here again, a strength has become a weakness, as spontaneity and selflessness are now enlisted in the carrying out of militaristic—and with the samurai, even mercenary—acts of killing in the name of whatever cause or master one is loyal to, even unto death. Suzuki noted that Buddhism generally and historically was clearly un-warlike. Yet nonetheless in Japan, as Brian Victoria paraphrases Suzuki, "Zen had 'passively sustained' Japan's warriors both morally and philosophically. They were sustained morally because 'Zen is a religion which teaches us not to look backward once the course is decided'."[34] It is well known that Zen became the spiritual ground of the samurai warriors; it is a surprise that the warrior-spirit became the legitimate active expression of Zen. It is a "fusion of horizons," a mutuality of influence with enormous ethical implications. Yet this is what emerged from much of the Zen experience of this century. Harada Daiun Sōgaku (1870–1961), whom Brian Victoria cites as having been "quite influential" in the West, wrote in a Zen magazine in 1939 that the activities of war are "the manifestation of the highest Wisdom [of enlightenment]. The unity of Zen and war of which I speak extends to the farthest reaches of the holy war [now under way]."[35] And again in 1944, when Japanese losses were mounting, Daiun wrote, "If you see the enemy you must kill him; you must destroy the false and establish the true—these are the cardinal points of Zen. It is said that if you kill someone it is fitting that you see his blood. . . . Isn't the purpose of the zazen we have done in the past to be of assistance in an emergency like this?"[36]

Yet how to decide the course itself? Does the cat die? I asked this of a senior Zen teacher, who reminded me that from the Zen perspective, destruction and construction occur at one and the same time, if an act is a truly Zen act. The act of killing the cat is a destructive act, and as an isolated act, it is wrong from a Buddhist perspective. At the same time—literally, at the same time, acausally speaking—that act served as a constructive force in the education of the monks, aided in dissolving a petty squabble at the all-too-human level, reminded all present of the persistence of dualistic thinking, and led Jōshū to place his sandal on his head as a lasting reminder to all in the Zen tradition that such a non-dualistic act is what Zen ought to be about. Such an act would have saved the cat, and in other morally perplexing instances, would have resulted in a resolution of a moral dilemma, somehow. Therefore, concluded the Zen teacher, the killing of the cat was both justified and a good thing.

Being less than convinced, I asked whether the answer would have been the same had the cat not been a cat, but a child. He responded that the situation was different. Indeed it was, but it was not then, nor is it now, at all clear whether that meant that such killing was somehow unacceptable, or exactly why.

Again, it is Suzuki who sheds light on this in an article written after the war, when he began to rethink Japan's role in the Second World War, and that of those Zen priests who had supported the war—somehow seemingly excluding himself from the criticism:

> With *satori* [enlightenment] alone, it is impossible [for Zen priests] to shoulder their responsibilities as leaders of society. Not only is it impossible, but it is conceited of them to imagine they could do so. . . . In *satori* there is a world of *satori*. However, by itself *satori* is unable to judge the right and wrong of war. With regard to disputes in the ordinary world, it is necessary to employ intellectual discrimination. . . . Furthermore, *satori* by itself cannot determine whether something like communism's economic system is good or bad.[37]

At the very least, this is an argument for some blending of rationality and enlightenment, or calculation and intuition in ethics—almost a blending of the best of East and West. If disputes in the "ordinary world" cannot be decided without the aid of rational decision making based on a weighing of the issues pro and con, then neither can the

killing of the cat be decided on the basis of the enlightenment experience alone. Indeed, it may be that a strength of Zen—and of Japan—
is, at one and the same time, Zen Buddhism's and Japan's greatest
weakness: the hubris of imagining that you know what is right and
wrong on the basis of having had a taste of enlightenment. Would it not
be more Zen-like to simply affirm that moral decisions are all too often
kōan-like? Moral situations all too often leave one unclear about what
is at stake, and unsure about what to do about it. Isn't that what Zen
teaches? Isn't it the genius of Zen that moral paths in life are often
obscured by ego, by blind patriotism, by karmic inheritances which
continue to blindside one in the very midst of attempts at self-cultivation?
The path is unending, ever new and renewed, thus leaving us ever in
the midst of a living kōan, an existential quandary from which no simple,
clear, or correct answer will emerge. We just do not know what to do,
often, and yet we must act in spite of the fog of ignorance. We can rely
on the precepts—on tradition—but that neither takes away the "stink"
of having to act on insufficient grounds, nor the burden of responsibility, karmic and otherwise, for acting as we inevitably do, one way or the
other.

    Whether one tries to justify war as an act of peace (I grew up in
the United States where I often stared in disbelief at a billboard at a
nearby Air Force base which depicted B-52 bombers and read "Peace Is
Our Profession," a kōan if ever there was one), as holy, or as approved
in scripture of one brand or another, it remains at best a lamentable
undertaking, and at worst utterly unjustifiable. Double-talk that pre-
tends to argue that "whether one kills or does not kill, the precept
forbidding killing [is preserved]" for "it is the precept forbidding killing that wields the sword. It is this precept that throws the bomb."[38]
Most religions have tried to justify war as holy, and Zen is no exception.
But whether it is Zen letting the precepts do the killing and bombing,
or Christianity and Judaism lending their support to the atomic bombing of Nagasaki and Hiroshima by blessing the planes, pilots, and bombs
as doing God's work, we are confronted by, at the very least, a kōan of
the most puzzling sort. With all the stress on compassion, love, human
heartedness, fellow-feeling, empathetic identification, and the various
precepts and commandments that prohibit killing, what continues to
go wrong given the ease with which patriotism, militarism, and the
glorying of war as a cure for present ills arise in our midst? It doesn't
seem to matter whether one has an ethics of duty, or compassion,
enlightenment, or love, war continues to happen, and it continues to
be justified.

One is tempted to conclude that those who claim to know the teaching of their great founders simply do not understand after all. Surely if one were to love, or if one had cleansed oneself of negative desires and emotions, then war would have to be lamented—at the very least—entered into with an intensity of regret and tumultuous soul searching. As to whether one should, reluctantly and with sorrowful heart engage in war—well, surely that remains a *kōan* with which each one of us must deal. What would you do?

6

The Fundamentals:
Modern Japanese Ethics

Japanese art, D. T. Suzuki observed, seeks to break free of human artificiality, in order to reach and to express "what lies behind" such surface forms.[1] Japanese ethics, like every other "art" in Japan, inevitably points beyond itself to an unfathomable depth, a deep profundity, an incredible mystery lying behind and beneath the surface of things. It is as with the fifteen rock outcroppings gathered into seven clusters, which appear to arise out of a vast and somehow indistinct sea of nothingness at the unforgettable Zen stone garden of Ryoanji. It is an emptiness which is, nonetheless, so chock-a-block full of potentiality, that formations and ripples in the stone particles constituting the sea seem to be there, in full form, out of a real necessity. That is what gives the garden its lasting greatness: everything is exactly where it had to be and as it had to be. There had to be fifteen arisings, in just seven groupings, connected to the emptiness out of which they arose by means of ripples of creative and powerful energy. Every grain of sand had to be just there, just now.

Notice, too, the unmistakable ecology of interconnection, of relationship, of Indra's spider-like net of codependent origination. The ripples connect the symbolic nothingness of the sand to the otherwise seemingly separate reality of the rock outcroppings. As such, they are, as ripples, neither thing nor no-thing, *neither* being nor nothingness, and, therefore, in true Zen fashion, are potentially both thing and no-thing, both being and nothingness. The logic is not that of either/or, but of both/and, and yet neither the one nor the other. It is all of this, and yet more, unspeakable, mysterious, profoundly out of reach and yet underfoot right here and now in this very instant. *Nirvāna* is *samsara,* and yet even *nirvāna* must be emptied, un-thingified, and grasped in the very midst of the everyday which is now deeply profound in its everydayness.

Precisely this formula is evident in the ethical writings of Watsuji Tetsurō, Japan's greatest interpreter and historian of Japanese ethics. What is distinctive about Japanese ethics is its marked emphasis on relationship; it is as though ethics was a wholesale application of the Buddhist theory of codependent origination, with decidedly Confucian specifics. An ethical person stands in the midst of the garden, as it were, intersecting with and creating ripples of social interconnection and community in ever-increasing complexity. It begins, for Watsuji, with the ancient but still vital Confucian cardinal relationships: "In ancient China, parent and child, lord and vassal, husband and wife, young and old, friend and friend, and so forth constitute 'the grand *rin* [relationships] of human beings.'"[2] Imagine, if you will, the ripple effect which *your* life has had, beginning with your close family relationships, and extending outwards in ever-increasing circles (of influence), to your school experiences, your early playmates and then teen associations, workplace encounters, friendships old and new, relationships with the many shopkeepers and clerks with whom you do business, dentists, doctors, taxi drivers, and even the authors whose books you have read, musicians whose music you have listened to, and media personnel whose offerings you have read, listened to, or watched. The list is long, but just consider how much has been left out. The ripple effect is staggeringly large and significant for each of us. When we focus upon the social impact that each of us may have on others, rather than on our isolation and privacy as individuals, both the responsibility for and the significance of most of our interactions is both formidable and striking. We are inextricably imbedded in community, in an expanse of relational ripples, and the importance and the mystery surrounding our interconnection is unmistakable; who knows what effect the simplest of gestures, the tamest of comments will have on another, and they on me. Community is serious business, and it is always and everywhere drenched in moral significance. Consider the importance of proper social form in Japan: the Japanese stress on using the right linguistic formulation for each person you encounter, which forces you to be mindful of their status, age, and social position in relation to you; tone of voice, body language, and an intangible cluster of attitudes that are expected and demanded. True, social form has lost much of its intended significance, and is often no more than ritual which is too demanding to be healthy, but the intention shines through nonetheless. One's social encounters count a great deal, always and regardless of the circumstances. The formal introduction in Japanese begins with "Hajime mashite . . . ," which loosely translates as "how do you do?," and ends with the hope that this first encounter will be favorably received by the other such that it will prove to be the foundation of a continuing and developing relationship in the future. It is not a casual "hello," but the beginning of a potential human encounter of significance, whose ripple effect may extend all the way from friendship, to influence, to assistance, and even to a major favor in the time ahead. What is on the surface is but a fraction of the mystery and the potential of a relationship, and one should never underestimate the simplest of encounters or gestures. Each center of conscious activity is a generator of influence potentially unlimited in scope. We must take care in what we do, say, and aspire to; we are almost never just private individuals, quietly doing as we wish, heedless of the effects we might be having on others, and unaware of the influence of others on us. Such an isolated individual is an abstraction, a strawman, more unreal even than a Robinson Crusoe.

Watsuji's intellectual journey took him from a rejection of Japanese social conformity together with an admiration for Western individualism, to a rejection of that particular brand of individualism and a rediscovery of the worth of community in Japanese culture and practice. Watsuji's objection to the ethics of individualism is that it loses touch with the vast network of interconnections that serves to make us what we are, namely individuals inescapably immersed in the space/time of a world, together with others. Steve Odin reminds us that Watsuji found the notion of the "betweenness of person and person" in the writings of Sōseki Natsume.[3] Sōseki, too, had earlier championed the cult of individualism, only to reject it in favor of a more traditional Japanese sense of community at about the same time that the younger Watsuji came to hold a similar view. The trouble with individualism, Sōseki concluded, was a traumatic sense of aloneness. "[T]he only solutions to this alienated existence of the isolated individual are seemingly madness, suicide, or faith in God, all three of which are rejected by Sōseki as individualistic alternatives to the problem."[4] The only path around the isolation of individualism was to somehow get beyond the hard shell of the ego, to break open to the countless possibilities of social interaction and interconnection. Community is to be found in the "betweenness" between people, the space in which people can interact with other people thereby eliminating the isolation rampant in Western thought and culture. But it was Watsuji who developed this idea, taking it back to its etymological roots, and to its ancient cultural foundations.

NINGEN

The title of Watsuji's study of Japanese ethics is *The Significance of Ethics as the Study of Human Being.* This last term in Japanese is *ningen*, which variously translates as "human being," "person," or "self." It is *ningen* that forms the focus of Watsuji's analysis of what is distinctive and original about ethics in Japan. It is composed of two characters, the first, *nin*, meaning "human being" or "person," and the second, *gen*, meaning "space" or "between," as in the betweenness between human beings. Watsuji makes much of this notion of "betweenness," and he uses the term *aidagara*, which refers to the space or place in which people are located, to make this "trace" ingredient in *ningen* even more explicit. In unpacking the significance of the *gen* in *ningen*, it is apparent that the concept of human person in Japan includes both the person or self as individual, and the self or person as inextricably and inescapably involved in community or group interaction. Thus, we are neither just individual, nor social beings, but both. Furthermore, there is a third component which is implicit, namely, that there is a place, a space between human beings in which they come to meet—it is a place of interactive potential, a space where community happens. *Ningen*, therefore, is a concept that contains three meaning-strands: as human being as individual, as human beings socially enmeshed in a vast network of relationships, and as the space between human beings in which these relationships occur.

Watsuji's student, and now an internationally known scholar, Yuasa Yasuo, writes of "betweenness" as consisting "of the various human relationships of our life-world. To put it another way, it is the network which provides humanity with a social meaning, for example, one's being an inhabitant of this or that town or a member of a certain business firm. To live as a person means . . . to exist in such betweenness."[5] Human being refers to a dual-structure or a dual-nature: we are individuals and we have individual personalities and unique histories, and yet, we are inextricably connected to many others, for we exist communally. We simply cannot be separated from social relationships except for the one-sided purposes of abstract thinking, for as individuals we use a common language, walk along common footpaths or travel along common roads, eat food grown and prepared by others, wear clothes made by others, and so on. We are private and public beings at one and the same time. We enter the world already within a network of relationships, expectations, and obligations, not unlike the network of roads, railways, and communication facilities that we share. We are, at one time or another, children and parents, cousins and friends, students and teachers, consumers and merchants, laborers and vacationers, patients in need of care and caregivers; we gossip and are the subject of gossip, offer praise and are occasionally praised by others. Betweenness refers specifically to the human relationships of our everyday world. The network of social relationships exists in this betweenness, and the Japanese live their lives within such a relational network. Yet the clarity and force of this awareness does not diminish the Japanese sense of individuality. One must see the two sides of the person as being in a constant state of tension (although this does not necessarily mean that the person is tense, psychologically speaking). We are social beings, and yet as such we are individuals, and we are individuals as beings in social relationship. What is distinctive about this way of looking at things is the Japanese sense of the appropriateness of the seemingly self-contradictory: we are social beings, and yet, we are individuals and not social beings; we are individuals, and yet, we are social beings and not individuals.

It was Nishida Kitarō (1870–1945) who formulated this notion of the "identity of self-contradiction," and it is another of the ideas that was "in the air" in Japan during the first half of this century. But the ready acceptance by the Japanese of as puzzling a notion as the identity of self-contradiction is not to be thought of as a concession to the illogical and a love of the obscure. Rather, what is being stressed is that some judgments of logical contradiction are at best penultimate judgments, which may point us in the direction of a more comprehensive and accurate understanding of our experience. A more profound understanding would reach below the surface level of contradiction and comprehend that opposites are necessarily opposites within some specified context. Take the example of a color. In order to be able to distinguish a color such as white from black, it is necessary that one has already grasped that white and black are colors located within a developed system of colors. White is located within a *system of colors;* and even though the distinction or contradiction of white and black is the primary judgment, it rests on what is, in fact, the real subject of the observation, namely the system of colors that makes distinction possible in the first place, and unifies all colors into a single system identity— a unity of opposites or an identity of self-contradiction. Thus, one must always ask, what is it that makes the distinction of opposites (in a given case) possible? And the answer must always be that the opposites are already closely related by some context or system in which they stand out as opposites.

THE ONE AND THE MANY

Watsuji calls to our attention the Japanese word *wakaru*, which means "to understand"; it is derived from *wakeru*, which means "to divide." In order to divide, to *wakeru*, one must already have presupposed something whole, that is to say, some system or unity which one now sets about to divide in some significant way. What would it mean to divide something that was not first a whole or unity of some sort? The distinction serves to reveal the original unity, as well as to mark a significant distinction within that unity. In Watsuji's words, "a statement separates and yet brings the original unity to awareness. What is divided is connected by means of is." And again, "the term 'is' is nothing more than an indication of the unity that has come to awareness by the disruption" of an original unity.[6] Equally succinctly, Nishida makes this point: "to think of one thing is to distinguish it from the other. In order for the distinction to be possible, it must originally have something in common with the other."[7] When one emphasizes the "common," or context or matrix of the distinction, one discovers the unity; when one emphasizes the distinction, the contradiction, one discerns the many, rather than the one. The one is self-contradictorily composed of the many, and the many are self-contradictorily one. The world and all that is in it can be viewed in two distinctly different ways, stereoscopically, as it were. The world of experience is not a unity of mere oneness, but of self-contradiction. The logical formulation for this is "A is A; and A is not-A; therefore, A is A." Note that there is a double negation in evidence here: an individual is an individual, and yet an individual is not individual unless one stands opposed to other individuals. That an individual stands opposed to others means that one is related to the others, that is to say, is a member of some group. In order that an individual may be an individual, it must negate its group features. Otherwise, it would be a member of something, and not a discrete individual. On the other hand, this negation must be negated as well, because the individual cannot be individual unless a member of some group or class from which it is being distinguished. Putting this in human terms, because an individual is a member of a group, one is both a member (as an individual) of a group and lost in the group.

Each of us is both one and many, both an individual as isolated, and inextricably interconnected with others in some community or other. As *ningen*, we negate our individuality to the extent that we are communally connected, and we negate our communality to the extent that we express our individuality. We are *both*, in *mutual* interactive negation: as well as being determined by the group, or community, we determine and shape the community as well. As such, we are living self-contradictions and therefore living identities of self-contradiction, or unities of opposites in mutual interactive negation. For Nishida, this emphasis on context is an emphasis on place, or *basho*. For Watsuji, the unity of self-contradiction arises in the betweenness between us. It is a logic of place as a matrix or as a network of relationships in which individuals face each other. The self-contradictory identity of the human being as individual and social in dynamic interaction is well articulated by Watsuji: "oneself and the other are absolutely separated from each other but, nevertheless, become one in communal existence. Individuals are basically different from society and yet dissolve themselves into society. *Ningen* denotes the unity of these contradictories. Unless we keep this dialectical structure in mind, we cannot understand the essence of *ningen*."[8]

It is little wonder, given this analysis, that the Japanese give more weight to their participation in society than do those of us in the West who are brought up on a heavy dose of individualism. Yet it is important to notice that, if Watsuji is right, the Japanese do not "honor" the group at the expense of individuality—or at least, they need not. The individual implies one's sense of connection with greater wholes—with communities—and one's participation in communities implies one's individuality. The experience of living in Japan makes one aware of just how important social relationships are, and how far back they extend in common, ordinary awareness. Even one's ancestors remain part of the remembered community. One lives in the midst of a network, a crossroads of interrelationships, and part of what it means to be a human being, in the best sense, is to keep this interconnection and mutuality of influence and support very much in mind. Not to be aware, not to care about one's relationships, is very un-Japanese. Nothing is more important than human relationships, and one brings shame upon all of one's groups of association—family, school, place of work, nation—if one forgets, or acts in antisocial ways. Recall the Shintō warning that it is possible to be less than human, to be animal-like in the worst possible sense, but that humanity demands an incessant striving to achieve the ideal, to be *kami*-like, to be connected to others, and even to nature. What we often mistake as an excessive group mentality,

or collectivism, is to the Japanese an integral part of being human. It can
be that one becomes swamped by the group, just as one can exaggerate
one's individuality at the expense of others to the point of becoming
antisocial. The ideal, however, is to be an individual in the world who is
thoroughly comfortable in the various communities through which one
is connected to others, to the past, to the divine, and to nature. Perhaps
more than anyone else, Watsuji has made this dual character of humanness unmistakably clear.

ETHICS

To be human is, then, to be in a rather wide array of relationships, and
ethics is concerned with those problems that arise between persons,
both as individuals, and as members of various societies. The Japanese
word for ethics is *rinri*, composed of *rin* and *ri*. *Rin* means "fellows,"
"company," or *nakama*, which refers to a system of relations guiding
human association, including some sense of the appropriate attitudes
to embody in one's relationships with others. *Ri* means "reason," or
"principle," and in particular in this context, the principles for the
rational ordering of human relationships. These are the principles
required for people to live in community in a friendly and nourishing
manner. It will come as no surprise that Watsuji himself, when specifying the sort of thing he has in mind when speaking of "principles" for
guiding human relationships, refers to Confucianism, which specified
the precise and appropriate relational interactions between "parent and
child, lord and vassal, husband and wife, young and old, friend and
friend, and so forth. . . ." Confucianism is the starting point for ethical
understanding in Japan. Watsuji concludes that the substance of ethics
is, therefore, "nothing else than the order or the way through which
the communal existence of human beings is rendered possible. In other
words, ethics consists of the laws of social existence."[9]

Japanese ethics, then, begins with those principles required for
principled interaction with others. *Aidagara*, or "betweenness," refers to
those relationships that connect us in the space or place between us,
and in which we now are able to interact with others properly. Yet
betweenness opens up far more than Confucian principled interaction.
For this space, or place of meeting, of encounter, is always already
subtly etched with the possibilities of genuine encounter, with expectation, good will, reverence, open-heartedness, fellow-feeling, sincerity,
and availability. It is here that the cluster of "virtues," or attitudinal

stances which have been collected in the earlier chapters of this study, come together. Take the word *kokoro* as a pointer here. *Kokoro* refers to both mind and heart. Here we encounter the first subtle or implicit attitudinal preparedness in the otherwise empty and unmarked betweenness; we meet here with both mind and heart unified. Not that the Japanese language indicates and insures that the Japanese are inevitably "together," unified and well adjusted. Rather, the suggestion here is that the language reveals a cultural trait, one which merges mind and body, reason and emotion, more often than not, thus making an encounter with a Japanese person more than a superficial, primarily intellectual, or purely calculated meeting. Furthermore, to say that one "has *kokoro*," is to say that such a person speaks and acts from the heart, that a sense of integrity and fellow-feeling wells up from the heart, and is expressed for no ulterior reason, with no hidden agenda and without mixed motives. It is a pure outpouring, an unblemished greeting, an honest and genuine welcoming, a sincere offer to help, or whatever. And while it need not be said that *kokoro* is something that every Japanese possesses, it is something that is valued, prized, recognized as the ideal, and perhaps even as a principle of authentic encounter in the betweenness. In other words, it is in the cultural "air," it *is* in the mix of things that people bring to their encounter with one another. It is a part of that greeting which recognizes that this, the first, is but a potential prelude to many more, so "please smile favorably upon me" in order to allow a relationship to develop—in the betweenness between us, both here and now and in the future.

If you think back to the chapter on Shintō, it should be evident just how many of the virtues and attitudes which were present there can now be read into the fabric of Japanese ethics. They are, all of them, etched on the unblemished space or place of encounter each and every time a relation begins, continues, or flourishes. It is that precious sense of being available, being open to the possibilities of something worthwhile in the making, that is so characteristically Japanese. There will never be another meeting exactly like this one, in this time, in this place, with this person, with these personal histories: cherish it, like the cherry blossoms which may be gone with the next breeze, the next storm. Make of it a haiku poem, a snapshot of the moment, captured for all time, and then let go in order to be ready for the next moment. One can begin to read into this betweenness so much that is distinctively Japanese, which makes relational interaction so precious and at the same time so fragile as to require that proper form, and even preparation, be in evidence in order to place no impediments in the way. Then and only then can the orderliness and harmony of the moment give way to a carefree spontaneity of interaction and expression. Only when the tension of not knowing what to do, what to think, or how to behave is dispelled can one engage fully in the relationship before one in the knowledge that all other matters have been taken care of appropriately. In Japan spontaneity comes at the end of discipline, not before it. Only then can one go beyond the form, or better, within the form, to express genuine creative uniqueness and individuality. It is only when the impediments to carrying out one's creative expression are out of the way that one can truly, and now spontaneously, dance one's heart out with the confidence that what it is one chooses to do, one will be able to do. In Japan trees are bent artificially so that they will eventually come to look as they would have looked in nature, under different circumstances. In Japanese gardens, old and partially submerged boats are "created," in order to give the garden a sense of antiquity, of the natural order of birth and decay, of imperfection which results in perfection because everything is naturally as it should be. Such worked-for "spontaneity" is not a spontaneity that just happens. It is the result of hard work, of sustained effort. It results from knowing the principles of beauty so well that one can actually re-create an effect that might only be found once in a thousand years in nature. Still, it is a principled knowing, the result of learning the discipline of gardening, which now allows one to spontaneously "know" exactly how to re-create such a scene. The master gardener does it with a spontaneity and a naturalness that is virtually unteachable to another. It can't be written out in a handful of principles, but must be handed on, if one is lucky, through an apprenticeship program which is more like that of Zen training. It is like working on a *kōan*, taking it in and finding some authentic way within oneself to break through, not by reason and written principles, but by "becoming" the *kōan*, becoming the garden, by entering into beauty directly. This seems to me to be a part of the betweenness, an openness to the possibilities, and an availability to the other, whether person or tree or rock, which yields an environment for genuine encounter of an I-thou sort. One is open to the other. Let the relationship begin.

TOWARDS NOTHINGNESS

The double negation referred to earlier whereby the individual is negated by the group aspect of self, and the group aspect is in turn negated by the individual aspect, is not to be taken as a complete negation that obliterates that which is negated. Rather, what is imperative is that the "identity," in the identity of self-contradiction, does not obliterate that which it unifies, nor does the disunity of distinction obliterate the unity. That which is negated is preserved, else there would be no true self-contradiction. By contrast, Hegel (or so many allege) moves to a synthesis in his analysis of dialectical interaction, apparently eliminating the thesis and the antithesis, or, to be more precise, blending them into a new synthesis. It is claimed that this blending does preserve the original elements, and in some sense it surely does. But it does not preserve them in the sense in which Watsuji and Nishida preserve them, which is without the creation of something new composed of the active ingredients of each. What is preserved is precisely the thesis as it is and the antithesis as it is, without transformation of any kind. What is added is the idea that the two together are needed to give a full(er) account of the experiential reality that is being described. What is "radically" empirical about this sort of analysis is that it is based on what is actually experienced, more or less in its immediacy, prior to and independent of various superimpositions of theory and epistemological anticipation. What is lost in the analytical attempt to break things into the smallest possible parts, even if only for purposes of contemplation or inspection, are the inescapable contradictions of common experience. The part simply is never experienced in separation from its context, and the context is simply never experienced apart from an awareness of a variety of those distinctions which are evident and possible. Thus, it is not that *ningen* becomes some third thing, which blends individuality and sociality, but rather that *ningen* is both the individual qua individual, and the social qua social, and moreover, that both of these are now taken to rest on a deeper ground, which itself is neither individual nor social, but is that greater context still out of which both the individual and the social arise; namely, *nothingness*, or that which is prior to all distinctions. Nothingness is that deep profundity, the indistinct, the indefinite, that which is beyond all characterization and without ordinary characteristics. It is the silence out of which sound arises, or against which sound is contrasted and in which sound becomes possible. It is the indistinct sand in the great rock gardens, the blank white rice paper of a simple *sumie* painting, and the unspoken which surrounds the briefest and simplest of seven-syllable *haiku* poems. Ethically speaking, it is the betweenness in which we meet, and to which we bring our cultural attitudes and expectations. The place or space is itself empty, and yet it makes possible all the delights, horrors, hopes, and failures of human interrelationship. It serves as the context in which both good and evil may arise, and, like

Heidegger's "clearing," is an opening for beauty, for truth, and for goodness, if we make of it the best possible. And like Heidegger's sense of truth, where all revealing is at the same time a concealing, and all concealing a revealing, so for Watsuji and Nishida, the place where good can appear is at one and the same time the very place where evil can appear. One must not be indifferent in one's choosing of good over evil, of beauty over ugliness, of truth over falsehood and ignorance, but it is also to be recognized that these contrasts arise from the same place of possibility. They are all a part of the same whole, the same infinite reservoir. No doubt this is why Nishida tells us that "the true absolute . . . must negate itself even to the extent of being Satan."[10] The absolute "sees itself even in the form of Satan," he adds. Nishida's position will be explicated shortly. For now, it is enough to suggest that he and Watsuji pack far more into notions such as place, space, silence, and potentiality than might be anticipated. What serves as the conceptual structure for this "more" results, I think, from their shared emphasis on the identity of self-contradiction.

Furthermore, for Watsuji there is another facet to be considered in dealing with the importance of "nothingness" in ethics. Centrally, it is the annihilation of the self, as the negation of negation which "constitutes the basis of every selfless morality since ancient times."[11] The losing of self is a returning to one's authenticity, to one's home ground. By contrast, a losing of self in Heidegger's negative sense, is an abandonment of self to mass consciousness, and, hence, is inauthenticity. Whether the individual faces becoming a victim of the masses or a victim of death itself, Watsuji asks how this focus on the individual is supposed to enable us to understand what is required of morality. Morality is not a concern of the individual alone, but one that of necessity involves at least one other. This is even true when considering one's own death.

The preoccupation with one's own death is by itself far less significant than a preoccupation with death that includes the implication of one's death for others, or for society at large. Hence, it is "only in the relationship between self and other that the preparedness for death gives full play to its genuine significance. As a spontaneous abandonment of the self, it paves the way for the nondual relation between the self and other and terminates in the activity of benevolence."[12] The ethics of benevolence—and notice the Buddhist influence here—is the development of the capacity to embrace others as oneself, or, more precisely, to forget one's self such that the distinction between the self and other does not arise in this non-dualistic awareness. One has now abandoned one's self, one's individuality, and become the authentic ground of the self and other as the realization of absolute totality. One has returned to one's home ground. Ethics is now a matter of spontaneous compassion, a spontaneous caring and concern for the whole. This is the birth of selfless morality, for which the only counterparts in the West seem to be the mystical traditions, and perhaps some forms of religiosity in which it is God who moves in us, and not we ourselves.

In attempting to summarize, morality is, for Watsuji, a coming back to authentic unity through an initial opposition between the self and other as the negation of betweenness, and then a re-establishing of that betweenness ideally culminating in a non-dualistic connection between the self and others that actually negates any trace of opposition. This, too, is the negation of negation, and it occurs in both time and space. It is not simply a matter of enlightenment as a private, individual experience, calling one to awareness of the interconnectedness of all things. Rather, it is a spatiotemporal series of interconnected actions, occurring in the betweenness between us, which leads us to an awareness of betweenness that ultimately eliminates the self and other, but of course, only from within a non-dualistic perspective. Dualistically comprehended, both the self and other are preserved. What is left is betweenness itself in which our human actions occur. In this sense, betweenness is nothingness, and nothingness is betweenness. Betweenness is the place where compassion arises and is acted out selflessly in the spatiotemporal theater of the world.

SINCERITY

Needless to say, there is a significant difference in the ideal of betweenness as nothingness just described, and the everydayness where most of us live, where we hope to gain some glimpse of a morality that effectively assists us in living our lives well. We need some guidance in enabling us to know what it means to be good or bad. Watsuji reflects extensively upon the importance of truth and trust as foundational for all positive and ethical human relationships. It is *makoto*, the virtue of "sincerity" which we met earlier as a crucial aspect of Shintōism, that serves as the root of truthfulness, honesty, and trustworthiness. To be sincere means that you will do what you say you will do, that you can be counted on to be as good as your word, and it connotes a recognition of one's intrinsic or innate spiritual purity that one strives to express in all of one's actions. *Makoto*, collectively understood, reveals a cultural attitude of mutual trust as an important aspect of what is always already etched in the betweenness.[13] Whether it is already there in the betweenness, or carried there by all those who meet there, is perhaps difficult to say. Yet it is as though it is a vital part of the very structure of meeting in the betweenness in Japanese culture. It is genuine piety, which results from having a sense of the divine in things, and in displaying real benevolence toward children and those whom one loves, a faithfulness toward friends, loyalty toward those to whom one owes or is expected to show loyalty, and love towards one's neighbors. Sincerity is the careful avoidance of error in word or deed and the fastidiousness required to keep one's soul unsullied by the grime of selfish desire, hatred, ill will, or materialism. It leads to *wa*, or group harmony. It implies solidarity, a solidarity of community feeling that manifests itself as peacefulness, good will, and happiness. Trust and truth are not intellectual demands made from a purely theoretical interest, therefore, but are to be found in the actions of human beings through and by which they are connected with one another. Even those who act in such a way as to seemingly reject truthfulness or trustworthiness in their relations with others—those who lie and cheat, break promises, and do physical harm to the persons and property of others—nevertheless rely on the expectation of others that they will act truthfully and in a loyal and trustworthy manner, in order to be able to carry out their nefarious deeds. The very fabric of social interaction of civilization, in any of its forms, is based on that network of trusting relationships and truth telling without which our lives together would be "nasty, brutish, and short." But there is no state of nature, as Thomas Hobbes may have argued, from which we emerge as individuals slowly making our way to a contractual society for the first time. There never was a time nor could there have been when we were not always already immersed in a network of social interconnections. And all such social interconnection is inescapably based on some sense of trustworthiness and the expectation that one will tell the truth. We are always already public, as well as private, social as well as individual, and the state of nature is but an abstraction that will simply not pass serious examination of our actual state with each other in the real world.

ETHICS AS CONTEXTUAL

Watsuji rejects all such "desert island" constructions as empty abstractions. Hobbes imagines a state of nature in which we are radically discrete individuals, a time before significant social interconnections have been established. And Kant employed a series of examples in an attempt to demonstrate his ethical maxim of action that whatever is morally acceptable must necessarily be self-consistent, at the least. For Watsuji, however, all ethical maxims are contextual. The consistency of an action is not just a matter of examining a maxim in sublime isolation from the interrelationships of an everyday life in a real society. To begin, Watsuji warns that even the notion of self-consistency is open to question, for in the East, the logic of the identity of self-contradiction actually resolves seeming inconsistencies by placing them in a broader context, as we have seen. We are both individual and social beings when we are understood as *ningen*. Moreover, even admonitions such as Kant's that suicide is always wrong are rejected by Watsuji on the grounds that whether or not suicide is in any way an acceptable form of behavior is not merely a matter of abstract principle, but is also heavily dependent on the norms and patterns of relationship already in place within a society. Even though he does not actually argue that suicide is sometimes correct, he does point out that, if it is morally wrong, "the real act of suicide is usually committed with an awareness of the bankruptcy of life, because suicide cannot be based on a principle. Accordingly, a suicide note is filled with excuses offered to one's family, friends, and sometimes, to the nation as a whole."[14] Thus, whether suicide is judged right or wrong is dependent on its relation to a network of social expectations, demands, concerns, and support from others. To try to decide the case by means of an abstract principle of some sort is to leave out most of the salient ingredients in the decision-making process. Similarly, his rejection of Kant's demonstration that a swindler acts wrongly—stealing cannot be taken to be a universal law because it is self-contradictory—is achieved by observing in a pointedly Japanese way that, before one succumbs to being a swindler, one's poverty "will be discussed among one's relatives and friends, and eventually various forms of assistance will be offered."[15] In other words, in traditional Japanese society, the many relational connections in the life of even the most down-and-out individual would likely have resulted in aid of some sort at a time of need. Someone on hard times did not need to steal or swindle, but could turn to those connections for assistance. They, in turn, may already have been cognizant of the difficulties of the situation, and most likely would have offered help. What is so striking about this rather pragmatic analysis is that it reveals a marked difference in cultural stance and expectation, for it is far less likely that friends and relatives would actually come to the aid of the down-and-out in a highly individualistic cultural context. It is not uncommon for the shelterless to die on the street in the cold of winter on the grounds that it is not anyone's responsibility, and increasingly not society's, to look after such people. In the Japanese context, traditionally at least, while there has been far less of a "social net" than has been available in developed Western countries, there has also been less need for it because of the acute sense of responsibility shouldered by friends, family, and members of the community at large. Furthermore, the relationship of lifetime employment has, to a significant degree, shifted the burden of responsibility from government to the corporate sector. In any case, one determines whether an action ought to be performed not by comparing the maxim of an action with a universal law, but in the context of one's social web of interconnectedness, the betweenness between us where we already exist as social beings. Social considerations alone cannot suffice to tell us how to act morally, neither can they be ignored in our attempt to decide what is right and what is wrong. In Japanese society there simply are other alternatives. And, even though such reflections are not enough to determine the rightness or wrongness of an action, they do make evident that the Japanese approach to moral decision making is not via abstract principles alone, but takes into account the social, contextual, and circumstantial elements in a particular instance, as well. Japanese contextualism is too ingrained for Kantian principled morality to seem at all adequate or accurate.

Instead, what is demanded is a system of social ethics grounded in a communal sense of the connectedness of one person with another. The state as a merely legal structure is not enough to express the demands of existence as human beings. To be truly ethical, there must be a sense of community and solidarity that arises from a sense of shared history and the interconnection of social and cultural activities expressed in the real space/time world. In other words, "the solidarity expressed legally falls short of expressing the way of *ningen*, if it is not backed up by the community of *sonzai*," that is, by a heartfelt awareness and appreciation of an intense web of human connectedness, stretching back into history, and reaching toward the future in the form of common goals and aspirations.[16] Betweenness is communality, and communality is a mutuality wherein each individual may affect every other individual and thereby affect the community; and the community, as a historical expression of the whole may affect each individual. This mutuality is an essential characteristic of the identity of self-contradiction. Things stand in contradictory opposition only in the sense that each pole of the opposition may affect the other in the betweenness between them. Their relationship is a *mutuality* of interconnection.

A striking example of the emphasis of community and interconnection can be found in the "corporate philosophy" of Ricoh Company, Ltd., makers of copiers, facsimile machines, and digital imaging systems. Its CEO, Hamada Hiroshi, is the author of several books on leadership. He writes that Ricoh is not "the kind of company where workers simply exchange their labour for a set wage," for in such a company "there is no need for a corporate culture or philosophy." Rather, "Japanese companies tend to develop strong group characteristics which vary according to the personality of each company. . . . [At Ricoh] I am concerned with creating an environment of consensus in which people can work harmoniously together."[17] Notice the emphasis on harmony and consensus, both central focuses of the Seventeen Article Constitution of Prince Shōtoku in 604 A.D., the remarkable Prince Regent who was most responsible for the early unification of Japan. The document is the first political document in Japanese history. Hamada explains that at the heart of his business philosophy is the concept of *oyakudachi*, which he prefers not to translate, but which means roughly "helping others," "being of mutual assistance," "doing what is useful for others," or "putting yourself in the other's shoes."[18] Echoing precisely Watsuji's own study (although no evidence of direct influence is given), Hamada, too, analyzes the notion of *ningen*, or human being. Noting that the term is composed of two characters, he writes, "the two characters literally mean 'person' and 'between.' I think that is beautifully thought out. We human beings live by forming groups, and these groups together make up society, which is based on the relations between one person and others."[19] He develops this into a philosophy of relationship, stating

> quite simply, all our interactions with other human beings are based on the amount of help or service that we provide for one another. In that sense we are bound whether we like it or not by a network of *oyakudachi*. As a manufacturer our products are only valuable to the extent that they help customers fulfil their needs. It's not enough to make a splendid design based only on the type of copier you happen to like or would like to make. Whether it qualifies as [good] work or not depends on whether it turns out to be useful to others. I want to think of ourselves as providing not copiers, but *oyakudachi*.[20]

The company is a network of human beings in mutual relationship, and so is "society itself . . . a network which connects human beings to one another from birth." This helping network must ever be in focus: "Everyone in the company is performing *oyakudachi* for someone, even if it's just for other members of the company. That's why I define work itself as 'conscious *oyakudachi* behaviour.' Unless you're performing for someone, you're not working." Hamada clarifies this position, and then extracts several benefits from conducting oneself in this way in the business world:

> When I suggest that Ricoh employees should find self-fulfilment by providing *oyakudachi* to others, I'm not suggesting a life of self-sacrifice. What I'm offering is a realistic way of living and thinking for business people: By living every day to the fullest, you will find purpose and happiness in your life. Zen Buddhism teaches that by throwing ourselves into a task with total concentration, we can totally forget ourselves and hence achieve enlightenment."[21]

The specific reference to Zen is helpful and to the point, yet it is also evident that a great deal of what is included in Hamada's position comes from a blend of Buddhism, Zen Buddhism, Confucian, and Shintō thought. Take the emphasis on group harmony, for instance.

The first of the "clauses" or articles in the Seventeen Article Constitution of Prince Shōtoku reads, "Harmony is to be valued, and an avoidance of wanton opposition to be honoured," and concludes by noting that "if those above [in station] are harmonious and those below [in station] are friendly, and there is concord in the discussion of business, right views of things spontaneously gain acceptance. Then what is there which cannot be accomplished?"[22] How easy it is to apply this instruction to contemporary business management without significant adjustment. Furthermore, how difficult it would be to apply Japanese business management practices to a Western context without significant cultural adjustment. We simply do not find in, or bring to, our sense of "betweenness" the same cultural legacy of relational networks and an interconnection which extends backwards to our earliest ancestors, culminating in a collective sense of a company, or a nation working in unison to achieve a shared goal with unflinching dedication and even passion. Little wonder that Hamada of Ricoh remarks that "since a company is by definition a group of people, you also need someone with the skills to encourage those people to work in unison."[23] These words could be echoed by a North American CEO, but they would rely on a quite different cultural legacy of individualism and an acceptance of self-interest as the primary goal of one's labor. The Japanese CEO conjures up a legacy of relational interconnectedness and a vital sense of the mutuality of responsibility which is actually quite rare in Western society. Hamada concludes that the philosophy of *oyakudachi* is concerned with "a person's sensitivity and heart . . . as much as their professional skills."[24] It is not just that one "does this for the group," as the simplistic reading suggests, but that, insofar as one is mindful of one's connections within the entire community, including one's fellows, one's customers, one's nation, and one's entire cultural heritage of sacrifice and dedication on the part of so many, known and unknown, from the past to the present, one must shoulder this great responsibility with all of one's heart, mind, and soul, for to do less would be to act shamefully, i.e., to do and be far less than could be reasonably expected of you in this cultural network of relationships and responsibilities. This long sentence does not at all represent a typical state of mindfulness for one who lives in a culture of individualism and self-interest, or limited family-interest.

The emphasis on group consensus is enshrined in article seventeen of the first Constitution: "decisions on important matters should not be made by one person alone. They should be discussed with many."[25] Less weighty matters can be decided by one in charge, or a few, but the consultative process, which is what lies behind consensus building, reflects the Japanese belief that the difference between right and wrong is far less clear, if achievable at all, than is thought. They tend to operate less from principle, as we have already noted, than from context, and part of the reason for this difference is a perspectivism which disallows easy access to either the truth or the morally right. Article Ten of the Constitution reads,

> Let us cease from wrath, and refrain from angry looks. Nor let us be resentful when others differ from us. For all men have hearts, and each heart has its own leanings. Their right is our wrong, and our right is their wrong. We are not unquestionably sages, nor are they unquestionably fools. Both of us are simply ordinary men. How can any one lay down a rule by which to distinguish right from wrong? For we are all, one with another, wise and foolish, like a ring which has no end.[26]

There is a humility, and a tolerance for differing perspectives which is built into the Japanese outlook. Undoubtedly this is why lawyers are traditionally sought out only when all other means have failed to resolve a dispute. It is better to reach a compromise—note the word—to insure that those involved in a dispute will be able to "save face," in the sense of there being no clear winner and loser in the dispute. That way, both parties will gain something from the resolution, and no one person will have it all his or her way. Oddly, from a Western perspective, this means that the "preferred" option is not likely to be achieved by either party. Each will likely accept a "consolation" option as the best possible mutually acceptable solution in this situation. The result is that all parties concerned will have chosen the winning option, and while getting less than would have been the case had their viewpoint simply won the day, there is far less chance that extreme anger, or an unwillingness to have anything to do with the decision, will be the result. A compromise position allows the parties to accept the compromise position as having something in it for them, and as being worthy of their continued loyalty and/or allegiance. Rather than feeling the alienation of "losing" the case, they have been listened to, and a compromise has been reached. Energies are now ready to be re-engaged in a common cause. Moreover, the openness to the possibility that other perspectives might have something to offer allows disparate or heretofore unknown viewpoints to be seriously entertained. One often hears of the Japanese as being involved in two or more religions at one and the same time. Perhaps there is a Shintō shrine in the home, and a Buddhist altar, and a Christian altar as well. Whereas we tend to think one or other of the traditions that are before us must be selected to the exclusion of others, and that not to be single-minded is to be both disloyal and fuzzy minded, the Japanese tend to think that it is only common sense to take what one can from as many sources as are before one. Japanese syncretism, the taking of something from each of several sources or traditions, is better understood against a backdrop of a perspectivism which is unwilling to declare any one vantage point as absolute, or the truth, or the morally correct. Life is far too complex for this, and those who must establish principles do so at the expense of lived experience, which is forever escaping the narrow confines of the specified principle, like an inner tube escaping from a tire first here, and then there. In any case, principle does nothing to create harmony when there is a disagreement. To tell another that you are on the side of the righteous is to pour oil on the fire, rather than to extinguish it. To maintain one's relationships, it is better, both now and in the future, to seek out some compromise position, or to gather information from many sources in an attempt to find a better solution or a better answer to a living perplexity which one has encountered. It is better, relationally speaking, to be willing to bend in order not to punish or humble the other, not only because it creates a more harmonious environment for all concerned, but also because "what goes around, comes around." That is to say, to create a livid enemy does not pay in the long run, if one can reasonably avoid it, for the enemy can usually find a way to pay you back at some point in time. In any case, the emphasis is on resolving differences, on avoiding disharmony and the destruction of relationships both now and in the future, rather than on deciding who is right, and who it is that has principle on one's side. From the Japanese perspective, a strictly principled person can become a very lonely and isolated person in a culture where relationships are centrally important.

THE IMPORTANCE OF THE FAMILY

At the core of the Japanese sensitivity to and high valuing of relationships is what Odin refers to as the "basis of traditional Japanese self and society," the family or household (called *ie* in Japanese). The individual is always already embedded in a family relational structure, and "in traditional Japanese household society the social context of one's family unit always takes priority over the individual, as seen by the fact that, as opposed to most Western societies, the larger whole precedes the part so that the family name comes first and the given name comes last."[26] Watsuji, too, takes the family as the central social structure in Japanese (and Chinese) society, and the term "house" is used to signify "the family as a whole. The latter is represented by the head of the house, but it is the family as a whole that gives the head of the house his authority; it is not the case that the house is brought into existence at the whim of the head." The family is a unity which is to be understood historically: "The family of the present shoulders the burden of this historical house and undertakes liability for its unity from past down into future. . . . The household member, then, is not merely parent or child, husband or wife; he is also a descendant of his ancestors and himself as ancestor to those that are to come."[27] In much of Japanese history, the individual who was morally aware would be willing to lay down his life for the "good name" of his house, or for his loved ones. This selflessness extended to the samurai who was willing to die out of loyalty to his lord, and the suicide pilots of the Second World War who put country over individual. Once again Watsuji discerns a duality of calm passion and a martial selflessness, of emotional intensity, yet without any sense of desperate clinging to life. Moreover, even before history itself, the founding *kami* of mythology were understood to be the ancestors of the house as a whole. "The people as a whole are nothing but one great and unified house, all stemming from an identical ancestor," and the Imperial House descends directly from these founding *kami,* and serves as the earthly home of these deities. Thus, "within the borders of this state as a whole, there should be the same unreserved and inseparable union that is achieved within the household. The virtue that is called filial piety from the aspect of the household becomes loyalty from the standpoint of the state. So filial piety and loyalty are essentially identical, the virtue prescribing the individual in accordance with the interests of the whole."[28]

The cluster of virtues that support the family are likely to be the same virtues, slightly adjusted, that support the corporation as well. They include, first and foremost, mutual trust, or *makoto*, a virtue claimed by Shintōists and Buddhists alike, and emphasized by Watsuji as being foundational for all worthwhile human interaction. Thus, even *wa* (harmony), according to Boye De Mente, "incorporates mutual trust between management and labour, unselfish cooperation between management and labour, harmonious relations among employees on all levels, unstinting loyalty to the company, mutual responsibility, job security, freedom from competitive pressure from other employees, and collective responsibility for both decisions and results."[29] What is being described is an attitudinal cluster, or a valuational cluster, i.e. a way of being in the world and in the workplace. It is a description of an environment more or less without conflict, or without unnecessary conflict, in an atmosphere of mutual trust, and mutual help, and mutual respect, and a willingness to cooperate and to show concern for the failures and difficulties experienced by others, and to join in their joy and successes. Of course, it will by now come as no surprise that not all institutions achieve anything like this high level of cooperation or mutual trust. Theory and reality are often at odds. Nevertheless, the attitudinal cluster described does serve as a norm, of which most Japanese are at least aware.

The Complexity of Climate

The attitudinal cluster extends beyond virtues, of course, to include other attitudinal stances-in-the-world. Watsuji theorized that these attitudes derived, in part at least, from the peculiar climate which exists in Japan. While at times he does seem to think like a cultural determinist, it seems more accurate to say that he attempted to show how much we are all influenced by our geographical, climatic, and cultural environment. These are all part of our inheritance, and the influence that they have on us is undeniable, although we retain the freedom to determine the degree of influence, and to reshape those same environmental influences.

In exploring the various climates of the world, Watsuji discerned that the idea of spatiality was less considered in the West, at least in modern times, than in the East. Not only does the West unduly emphasize individuality over our social interconnections as human beings, it also tends to neglect spatiality at the expense of temporality. This was most vividly seen, for Watsuji, in the works of Martin Heidegger. Odin summarizes this reaction as follows:

> [Watsuji enumerates] various archetypes of personhood which have been developed in the European and especially German history of philosophical anthropology running through such figures as Nietzsche, Kierkegaard, Dilthey, Scheler, and Heidegger, arguing that each of these archetypes represents an individualistic notion of self which abstracts individuals from social groups and attempts to grasp man as something independent or self existing. At one point in his *Ethics*, Watsuji argues that even Heidegger's notion of *Dasein* (Being-there) is ultimately an individualistic concept of man. His polemic here is that Heidegger overemphasizes the individuality of *Dasein* over the sociality of *Mitsein* (Being-with).[30]

It is precisely this stress on temporality that Watsuji believes kept Heidegger, and other Western thinkers from "developing an adequate conception of selfhood as the basis for an ethical system descriptive of persons in relation."[31] Watsuji's betweenness is primarily a spatial metaphor, although it is no less temporal for that. That is to say, whereas anything spatial is automatically assumed to be in time, things existing in time are not automatically assumed to exist in space. We don't (often) ask where thoughts or mathematical concepts are to be found, and especially we don't ask this of Platonic forms, to take a specific instance from the history of Western thought. The dual structure of person as *ningen* conveys both the individual and social aspects, and the temporal and spatial aspects. Watsuji enforces this conclusion through an analysis of the kind of existence which is human existence: human beings (*ningen*) exist (*sonzai*) in time and space, in relationship. *Sonzai* is a compound term consisting of two characters: *son*, which refers to time, and *zai*, which refers to space. The human person is inescapably a being in relationship, a social being in a world-matrix which is spatiotemporal. This is our environment, our "climate" of existence as Watsuji referred to it. But this "climate" is more complex still.

In his discussion of climate in *Climate and Culture*, Watsuji understood climate to be a geographical/cultural/social clustering of attitudes and expectations that relate to a specific region of the earth, populated by a particular people who share a great deal in common. Thus, it refers to the entire gestalt of a culture, a perspectival lens that is so much a part of growing up in that culture that one assumes that everyone sees the world in more or less the same way. It is Watsuji's belief that social interconnectedness, i.e. human beings in relationship, must be understood as a perceptual-structure which arises within the space/time existence of everyday life in Japan. Watsuji's major objection to the ethics of the individual, which he associates with virtually all Western thinkers to some degree, is that it loses touch completely with the vast network of interconnections that serves to make us what we are, as individuals inescapably immersed in the space/time world, together with others. Furthermore, without taking into consideration this network of social interconnections, ethics is impossible. Individual persons, if conceived of in isolation from their various social contexts, do not and cannot exist except as abstractions. Even a solitary writer writes for a possible audience, he tells us, although there may be no expectation that what is written will ever be published.[32] The writing is done as though others were looking over one's shoulder and in a language accessible to others, nonetheless. One does not write in a unique, private language, to insure that others will never be able to break the code. Writing is communication, if only potentially, and communication requires that there be at least one other, at least implicitly, to whom what is written may be communicated—perhaps's one's God, or one's dead mother or spouse. It is theoretically possible, all the same, to conjure up a reason for intentionally solitary coded writing—perhaps to remind oneself of one's own history, one's private autobiography that dealt with certain perverse and sordid sexual fantasies, for example. Even then, however, the purpose of the code is to hide something from others, specified or unspecified. Some consideration of others, as excluded by, or included in the secrecy of the code, is inevitable. One writes down such reflections and observations as being of possible interest to others at some point in time, or at least to preserve them for some vague reason which in all likelihood involves imagined or real "others."

One's sense of historical connectedness, which involves a lifelong showing of "respect" for one's ancestors, is an essential ingredient in one's own awareness of existence (*sonzai*) as a human being (*ningen*). We may choose not to bring to the surface of consciousness all of those influences that have come to us out of the historical and prehistorical past of our own coming to existence, but they will be present nonetheless. Our way of being in the world is an expression of countless people and countless actions in a particular "climate," which together have shaped us as we are. Respect for one's ancestors is an acceptance of this and an attempt to make our history our own, through a proper awareness of a communal solidarity that extends far beyond our birth and will extend far beyond our physical death. Culture and history continue to play out our actions and our influence long after we are gone. As such, we are already on our way to being the ancestors of generations to come. In Watsuji's words, "it is never inappropriate to grasp *ningen sonzai* as the unified structure of past, present, and future. To put this another way, the structural unity of *ningen sonzai* comes to the home ground in the present."[33] Each of us is, then, the intersection of past and future, in the present "now" of spatiotemporal existence.

For Watsuji, whereas it is easier to consider a human being as strictly individual when viewed temporally (i.e., through an introspective series that need not involve another, as with Descartes's *cogito*), it is much more difficult to do so when one thinks of an individual spatially. Spatially, we move in a common field, and that field is cultural in that it is crisscrossed by roads and paths and even by forms of communication such as messenger services, postal routes, newspapers, flyers, and broadcasts over great distances, in addition to ordinary polite conversation in homes, school, pubs or *sake*-shops, markets, shrines and temples, on public transportation, etc.

Climate, in the broad sense in which Watsuji intended it, "does not exist apart from history, nor history apart from climate." It is in climate that we apprehend ourselves as human beings: "The activity of man's self-apprehension, man, that is, in his dual character of individual and social being, is at the same time of a historical nature."[34] As said before, a human person is both a product of his or her environment, and a shaper of that very environment. We are determined by our climate, and yet our adaptation to it is a part not only of the history of the people of that climate, but alters the way that climate is perceived, accepted, and adapted by how we build our homes, dress our bodies, plan our work and play activities, construct our means of transportation and communication, educate our children, and celebrate who we are and where we are in art, music, and literature. Thus, it is our nature to be environmentally conditioned, and yet to condition our environment, just as we are individuals, and yet as such are at the same time members of many groups with many relationships with others and with our environment. To the extent that we are shapers of our environment, we are not environmentally conditioned. This is exactly what Nishida articulates in great detail in his notion of the identity of self-contradiction. We now turn to Nishida in our attempt to unravel the complexities of Japanese ethics.

7

An Ethics of Transformation:
Nishida, Yuasa, and Dōgen

Zen Buddhism is perhaps the least accessible of the various strands of influence that blend to produce a distinctively Japanese take on ethics. On the one hand, it appears to be thoroughly Buddhist in demanding that authentic and unwavering ethical practice is a precondition for enlightenment. On the other, Zen seems to reject the specific norms and the rigidity of ordinary morality. This apparent inconsistency generates partially from the fact that at one point the discussion takes place from the everyday vantage point of ordinary consciousness, while at another the perspective is that of enlightened consciousness, i.e., from the perspective of one who has "crossed over" to the other side of awareness. Everyday awareness yields an ethics that is legalistic, yet relativistic all the same; the latter an ethics that is spontaneous and without calculation, yet which in some sense is absolute in its validity and timeliness. However this tension plays itself out in detail, the transition from everyday consciousness to *satori* is a self-transformation which requires practice or cultivation. Whether the practice is Zen seated meditation (*zazen*) or walking meditation (*kinhin*), or a martial art such as *aikido*, *karate*, or *kendo*, the more subdued tea ceremony (*chado*), or painting or calligraphy, the aim is to still the ordinary mind in order to access what lies beneath it; the aim is to allow that which resides beneath the chatter of ordinary consciousness to surface in the quiet stillness of the moment.

149

While I will discuss the work of the contemporary Japanese philosopher Yuasa Yasuo to expand on the importance of practice or cultivation, it will be important first to say something about the nature of the transformation sought. The work of Nishida Kitarō (1870–1945) best lays the groundwork for an understanding of the nature and significance of that transformation in awareness which is termed "enlightenment." From there, it is hoped, it will be possible to think more cogently about the nature of the ethical as viewed from both "sides" of human awareness.

Most scholars agree that it is Nishida's exposure to and interest in Zen Buddhism that serves as the grounding for his philosophical journey, and for his central notion, "pure experience." In his first work, *An Inquiry Into the Good*, Nishida links religion and morality. We need to take seriously his unwavering insistence that morality has—indeed even that philosophy and science have—religion as a foundation, rather than the other way around, which tends to be the more fashionable way of viewing the matter. Zen Buddhist ethics is necessarily and inescapably religious ethics. Yet Nishida's sense of the "religious" is quite different from what we are more familiar with in the West. For starters, religion has little or nothing to do with what one believes. Rather, religion is, as Nishida steadfastly maintains, "an event of the soul."[1] This event is a matter of direct experience and is not an instance of deductive reasoning or of faith in some tradition. Nor is it a leap into the absurd. This event is an instance of "pure experience" (a term that Nishida borrowed from William James), the unpacking of which will lead us all the way to God, and beyond.

Yet even before the unpacking of "pure experience," Western assumptions make it difficult to follow Nishida. What evidence is there that pure experience is at all a coherent notion, let alone an achievable conscious event for ordinary mortals? Can one have an experience that is truly "pure" in Nishida's demanding sense of that adjectival qualifier? Nishida defines "pure experience" as "the state of experience just as it is without the least addition of deliberative discrimination."[2] Furthermore, Nishida wishes to claim for such experience that it offers us "facts just as they are," directly, and unmediated by our conceptual grid of understanding, our evaluative judgments, or our various contexts of meaning-granting and understanding. Pure experience is a state of immediate awareness prior to the distinction between subject and object: "when one directly experiences one's own state of consciousness, there is not yet a subject or an object, and knowing and its object are completely unified."[3] It is experience prior to the distinction of the various kinds of conscious abilities, i.e., knowing, feeling and willing, since these are all aspects of the subjective self which has not yet been differentiated. It is before meaning, and "is simply a present consciousness of facts, just as they are."[4] In one of his later essays, Nishida maintains that this ability to experience facts or things themselves is the distinctive genius of the Japanese people, and the key to the philosophical understanding of the type of knowing that is deemed most important in that cultural tradition. It is an ability based on a perspective that is comfortable with the idea of

> thoroughly negating the self and becoming the thing itself; becoming the thing itself to see; becoming the thing itself to act. To empty the self and see things, for the self to be immersed in things, 'no-mindedness' or effortless acceptance of the grace of Amida—these I believe are states we Japanese strongly yearn for. . . . The essence of the Japanese spirit must be to become one in things and in events. It is to become one at that primal point in which there is neither self nor others.[5]

This going to the things themselves means going beyond the subject/object dichotomy, to that which is "at the bottom of our selves, instead of considering the absolute to be in an infinite exterior."[6] It is an emptiness that, as pure awareness, can take the "shape" of whatever it beholds, without the usual imposition of purposes, fears, values, intentions, habits and prejudice which is involved in our ordinary way of making sense of our world and of our mediated experience. The point of Zen practice is to remove our conceptual, abstract glasses, and to be in a position to see things as they are, sans the glasses of the mind. Things, "reality," are to be found in pure experience, which is awareness prior to the addition of the distinctions of consciousness. Reality presents itself self-sufficiently, independently, as an activity. We might say that "things real" and this "realing" have the quality of unity about them. Nishida began *An Inquiry into the Good* by telling us that to experience is to know facts as they are, as they are directly given. Part of what is given in factuality is that I am myself present, as awareness. The scene and my presence are one and the same thing. The facts and the presence of the self are all one in the immediacy of experience. Reality, then, is to be found in the simple givens of life—seeing a flower, hearing a frog jump into the water, eating rice, touching another. And in these are to be found the true self, the deeper self which is beyond, or beneath the ordinary self, which permeates all things in a true knowing. It is then that one has a fundamental grasp of life, as Nishida expresses it. To have a grasp of life is to be immersed in the immediacy of pure experience where the later distinctions of empirical self, world, and abstract conceptualizations are not yet carved out of the unity of existence.

Of course, even though we hear the words, and perhaps even intellectually understand the concepts involved, and even though pure experience does take place in its original, non-dualistic form right before our eyes, we continue to see that experience in its "unoriginal" form, from the vantage point of the everyday dualistic self which has already processed experience in order to make it comprehensible. There is a discrepancy between what the self actually experiences and how the self interprets that experience. We hear the words, but we continue to see the world in the same old way. What makes Nishida's contribution unique is that he forces us to return from reasoning about experience, which characterizes the history of Western philosophy, to pure experience itself. What we are looking for is already underfoot, already within consciousness, but we continue to look past it in order to fabricate a world of distinctions. But what is it that we make distinctions within? What is there, in awareness, before distinctions are made?

In a way, it is precisely here that we encounter the great East/West split. The West maintains that there is simply nothing there, since all knowledge is knowledge "of" something. This is a mantra that we all recite, at least since Edmund Husserl, for the very act of consciousness unconditionally demands that there be a subject, which is aware of some object, in some mode of intending that distinction. For Nishida, however, there is a prior (epistemologically) whole which is the raw data for such cutting up into subject and object. This raw material is available to us all—already underfoot—if we will but quiet the active, rational, logical, analytical mind, and allow the deeper awareness beneath it to bubble up in the act of meditation. The cultures of the East are meditative cultures; the cultures of the West are analytically rational cultures. What Husserl says about rational analysis of experience is absolutely correct: all analyzed experience does contain precisely what he insists that they do contain. As to what was there before analysis, Husserl would speak for most Westerners in concluding that there is nothing there that we could possibly know about, and, hence, that it is pure speculation that there is anything there at all, prior to analysis. It is a post-Kantian question about what lies behind the phenomena of experience. The correct answer is that we have absolutely no idea whether there is a noumenal underlay, nor could we ever know it if there was. We have ordinary, everyday human experience to work with, and nothing more.

Nishida speaks for the East, however, in contending that there is another layer of experiential awareness beneath the everyday phenomena of which Husserl and Kant speak. There is pure experience which serves, in some sense at least, as the noumenal layer beneath the phenomenal experiential deposits which make up ordinary conscious awareness. In order to reach and come to comprehend the full range of human consciousness, it is necessary to break through the subjective self, and to reach the level of pure experience. Pure experience is always a self-unfolding as a unity. This deep self of pure experience cannot be objectified, spoken of directly, or perceived. It is a *basho*, a nothingness from which an objective self can be abstracted, but which presents itself as an awareness without one who is aware; a seamless awareness where knower and what is known are not yet distinguished. The deep self of pure experience is not a construction of consciousness, but a manifestation of that unity which lies at our depths. What is then to be plumbed is a consciousness which

> is never confined to the so-called individual, which is no more than one small system within consciousness. We usually take a microsystem with corporeal existence as its nucleus to be the center, but if we try to think of a larger system of consciousness as the axis, this macrosystem would be the self and its development the realization of the will of the self. It is something like this with serious devotees of religion or scholarship or art.[7]

Then it is that we would have deepened and widened the connections of the unifying power of pure experience with the unifying power of the universe itself. One passes beyond the frame of reference of the individual, to a self-awareness which becomes the broad and deep system of experience itself, prior to distinctions between self and various others. It is this move beyond the individual that leads Nishida to the religious, for what is now grasped is that "our true self is the very study of the universe. To know the true self is not only to be joined to the good of humanity in general, but also to melt into the stuff of the universe and to blend in with the divine will."[8]

Nishida's student and eventual successor at the University of Kyoto, Nishitani Keiji, writes that Nishida's understanding is that "to see things by becoming them is a standpoint that kills the ego completely to become the principle of the universe. It is a standpoint of pure experience at which he joins to the power that unifies all things. If we call it mind, it is not the mind of a mind-matter opposition but rather a mind that transcends them both, a mind like the mind of which it is said, 'the mind just as it is, is the Buddha.' "[9] Nishida's "intellectual intuition" is the grasping of life, of the unifying activity which is given in pure experience, and it signifies what could be termed a metaphysical and religious awakening, a being born-again, and what Dōgen refers to as the falling off of body and mind. It would be seen to be the fundamental intuition at the root of all religions, if religions would but return to their originary occasions or the experiences of their founders. And it is always, and at all times at the very root—albeit as an unnoticed background—of our own consciousness, and at the root of everything experienced. This is why we may be awakened by the splash of a frog on hitting the still surface of a pond, or the thunk of a bamboo pipe, now saturated with water, hitting the rock immediately below, or the heavy thwap sound of a falling ripe fruit hitting the metal roof of the dying master's hut. Everything is *kami*-infused, or God-filled, or a manifestation of absolute nothingness. Nothingness is underfoot—*nirvāna* is *samsara, samsara* is *nirvāna*. Everything in our experience opens a potential road before us which leads directly to the divine, to God, to nothingness, i.e., to a direct encounter with the unifying activity which is noumenal reality. It is only "given" in experience, and our language, concepts, and theories simply cannot deal with that undivided experience which is prior to all thing-ification—hence, which is no-thing. It is a mystical awareness of our oneness with the whole of things, although it is not mystical in the sense of being incapable of the sort of philosophical/rational analysis to which Nishida is able to subject it. It is pure experience which lies at the root of all religion and all morality, and which is a unity that includes self-awareness, which is a part of it from the start, although not yet separately distinguished. This is what it means to know facts just as they are. This raw "given" at the base of all knowing is reality, but "the gist of . . . [Nishida's] argument is that true reality is neither a phenomenon of consciousness nor a material phenomenon. . . . The distinction between mental and material phenomena in no way signifies that there are two kinds of reality. . . . In the distinction between the two, a single reality is viewed from two opposite sides."[10]

Furthermore, what is remarkable about the infinite unity which is experienced as an underlying activity is that, while unmistakably unified, nonetheless, it persistently develops through a constant moving from one infinite unity to another. It is termed "infinite," but this unity does not mean that experience comes to a standstill, and simply repeats itself. Rather, infinite unity implies at the same time infinite opposition and contradiction, and because of this opposition there is to be discerned an infinite development. This paradox of unity and yet opposition, constancy and yet developmental change, Nishida terms the identity of self-contradiction.[11] Thus, "In the establishment of reality, then, both a unity at the base of reality and mutual opposition or contradiction are necessary. . . . When these contradictions disappear, reality disappears as well. On a fundamental level, contradiction and unity are simply two views of one and the same thing. Because there is unity there is contradiction, and because there is contradiction there is unity."[12] What follows from this, metaphysically speaking, is a hint as to what ought to follow from the vantage point of enlightenment, ethically speaking. Opposition is a spontaneous self-unfolding or self-expression of unity; ethical activity arises spontaneously as a manifestation of who we have become, and not as a result of the memorization of externally imposed rules, or some sort of casuistic calculation. The real "reals" oppositionally, and the enlightened person "goods" spontaneously and effortlessly, as a direct expression of who he or she has become. But the details of this, and the notion of the "non-production" of evil, must await an examination of Dōgen's contribution to ethical understanding.

The one spontaneously self-unfolds, and becomes a many, and yet, remains one. When we operate from our depths, spontaneously unfolding in accordance with our true nature, we, too, effortlessly hit the moral mark out of the compassionate and wise sense of who we are. Recall that the enlightened, non-dual vantage point has taken us beyond subject and object, and beyond the taking of the individual as ultimate. Our sense of who we are has eradicated the boundaries between self and other, knower and known, and through some process of self-transformation, our desires have been purified of all selfish and evil tendencies. Little wonder that Nishida reflects upon the Buddha and Christ, whom he thought to have achieved the enlightened state of uniting with the one, the whole, by going to the bottom of self: "Those without a self—those who have extinguished the self—are the greatest."[13] Over and over again Nishida stresses the importance of abolishing the everyday, egoistic self. It is an abstract self, one that floats in the air even though it seems to us utterly concrete and real. It is not, however, given in experience. It is an abstraction, and it distances us from the reality of pure experience, and hence also from our true self. The true self lies at the base of this awareness, and, of course, is completely unobjectifiable. It is the observer which cannot be directly observed, the unifier, that which sees the objectified self from behind; it is the seer which is no seer, and it is a voice which has no voice. Ethically, it is a doer which acts without acting, as a spontaneous expression of who and what that person is, in his or her depths. This existential ground is not only the foundation of morality, but of religious under-standing as well. Religion, for Nishida, is a transformation of one's life, and that transformation consists of leaving the subjective self of ordi-nary experience behind, and becoming aware of the unity at one's depths, and the unity in nature which are one and the same. Nishitani says this unifying principle at work in immediate experience, and thus which is at the base of the self and nature, is "personal."[14] There is a tendency to fear or dismiss pantheistic interpretations of God and the world because such a rendering is thought to remove personality from things; at other times, we cling to personality in such a way as to sepa-rate ourselves from nature, and from the universe as a whole, keeping personality for ourselves, and rendering nature unresponsive, alien, or dense, as well as lifeless and without any trace of awareness. However, Nishida's meaning of "personality" is one that refers to something beyond the ordinary subjective self, to the true person behind or beneath, which only appears when the subjective self is forgotten, left behind. Then, this true unity simply appears, having been there all along, but covered over by the "chatter," and the dualistic assumptions of everyday existence. It is not an act of will to bring it into existence; we have to move beneath the surface noise, to the silence at our depths. This is the meaning of "realization," and it is no less personal. What has been realized is that there is an infinite unifying power at the ground of reality, and our own deep self is one with this power. To know reality is to know the self. The "personality" of this power is encompassed in the term "God." Yet, once again, Nishida does not mean by "God" what is more often than not meant by that term. God is the ground of reality, yet God is not something transcending reality, not something over and above the reality that is underfoot: "a God set up outside the universe as a creator or overseer of the universe cannot be deemed a true, absolutely infinite God." God is to be found within, with a "reversed eye," Nishida tells us, borrowing a phrase from Jakob Boehme.[15] One finds God by looking within, by reversing our glance from outward to inward. There, one finds the unifying reality in our own depths and this direct intuition confirms that our own depths, and the divine are one and the same, just as our own depths and the universe are kin. The unifying power of infinite reality is there, within. We join with this unifying activity of pure experience that embraces the universe when we realize our own pure experience. This is a mystical oneness that is without subject or object, with no distinction between knower and known, God and creature; the realizer is that which is realized. This is the "deep grasp of life" of which Nishida so often speaks. Yet this God is a no-thing, and as such is that which is at the base of all things. God, like the self, is beyond all objectification, beyond any sense of thing-ification, beyond description. God is directly experienced as an event in and of one's own soul.

It is Nishida's view that the religious desire is a desire to re-unite with God, to become one with our source, with the foundation of the universe. Yet Nishida's recognition of the importance of our attaining an awareness of our oneness with our original source, and with our own divine depths, certainly constitutes a mystical perspective. At the same time, he continues to warn against mysticism, perhaps because of its association with non-rational, and traditional Western theistic religious positions. He believes that religion can be analyzed philosophically; that a rational account of religion is both possible and essential. He also sees "oneness" as an experience to be had in one's soul, a recognition of one's always already being one with the source. And yet, as the unity of opposites demands, we are also separate and differentiated, individualistically distinct and free to seek a separate and unique destiny. He opposes most "Western mystical philosophy in that the true individual must be established from the absolute's own existential negation."[16] For Nishida, we are not separate from the absolute, and our individuality is but one aspect of who we are: we are also one with the divine, a self-manifestation of the absolute itself. Nonetheless, such a position seems a mystical one, albeit of a rational and intellectually demanding sort akin to that of Meister Eckhart. Of the many meanings of "mysticism,"—it is with the "mysterious," the "esoteric," or "occult" that he wishes no association. His own position is clearly stated in the following passage: "Religion is often called mystical. But when I speak of religion, I do not refer to a special kind of consciousness. . . . Were religion some special consciousness of privileged persons it would merely be the idle matter of idle men."[17] The unity sought is ordinary. It is underfoot, or within our own awareness at its depths. Nothing could be less esoteric or occult, nothing more ordinary. The oneness is right there, before our eyes so to speak, or at the base of our ordinary waking moments. Enlightened awareness is not a matter of being transported to another realm, nor is it some sort of union with that which is beyond. It is precisely this dualistic way of thinking, this continued use of "object logic" to which he objects. We are already self-contradictorily part of the many of existence, and yet one with the absolute. There is nothing esoteric about this. It is as common as leaves on a tree and mosquitoes. It is the seeing of this that is extraordinary in that few gain this perspective. It is not that we become one with the absolute through diligent practice and devotion, but that we have always been so. It is a mysticism which affirms that we are already what we seek. What is apparent to him is that the Oneness of existence differentiated, and thereby negated this utter unity in order to self-manifest as many. Nishida's analysis of why the one became many is central to his understanding of what it means to be human.

THE NEED TO DIFFERENTIATE

If we think of the development of the many forms that go to make up the universe of beings, we are, in a way, reflecting on the development of conscious awareness itself. Nishida tells us that "differentiation and development of consciousness is the other side of unity, and it is necessary for the establishment of consciousness. In fact, it constitutes a search for a greater unity, which is the alpha and omega of consciousness. Thus in this sense the religious demand is the demand for the unity of consciousness and, further, the demand for union with the universe."[18] It is almost as though Nishida is reiterating Husserl's dictum concerning the intentionality of consciousness: that all consciousness is consciousness of something. Ordinary, dualistic consciousness is thus perfectly characterized; to be conscious is to be conscious of something, and thereby one becomes aware of one's own subjectivity, as distinct from the object that one comes to know as well. This is not, of course, a description of pure experience, where the known and the knower become one in non-dualistic awareness. But there are two sorts of consciousness for Nishida, pure and ordinary, and thus it would not be wrong to say that the religious demand is actually twofold: it is a demand for union with the universe, ultimately; and it is a demand for separation or differentiation from the universe, in order for full consciousness to arise. Even for conscious union to occur, as pure experience, there must first be separation. One cannot seek this higher unity unless there is first the need occasioned by separation. Still, the unity which underlies this subject/object split is prior to that split epistemologically speaking, and is that kernel of awareness out of which that split is carved. It is carved, therefore, out of that which is previously without distinctions, which is unobjectifiable, which is without form, without voice, which is nothingness. In terms of pure experience, then, as a revelation of our own divine depths, we come to grasp the profound sense in which everything is interdependently divine. The fundamental nature of reality is spiritual, and is that out of which both the personal and impersonal, the animate and inanimate, the unconscious and the not obviously conscious must arise, and, in some sense must be both and neither of these paired contradictions.

Little wonder that the world of experience is a world of contradiction, while at the same time, this same world is a world of unity. This, I think, is the background to Nishida's emphasized foreground of the identity of self-contradiction as an account of what each of us actually experiences. The enlightened person comes to grasp both aspects of this stereoscopic panorama of existence; it is one, and yet it is many. It is non-dual, and yet it presents itself as dual as well. Moreover, all that comes to be differentiated from the original undifferentiatedness is a self-expression, or manifestation of this original unity. This is the universal spirit that functions at the base of consciousness. It is in this sense that faith is not something that you believe in, an intellectual deduction or commitment, but is based on direct experience, a going to the experience of living itself, an intuition, a direct givenness. If you choose to call it "God," as Nishida often does, this God is not a transcendent creator outside of the universe, for the universe is not a separate creation, but an emanation, or self-expression, or a manifestation: a natural, spontaneous, necessary manifestation of the primal unity. Furthermore, if we choose to refer to "this unifying power" as "personality, then God is the great personality at the base of the universe. . . . The universe is an expression of God's personality," an expression of the precise nature of this ultimate unifying power which underlies and gives expression to you, me, the trees, flowers, birds and rocks. They are "none other than God's self awareness."[19]

WHY THE ONE DIFFERENTIATES

This brings us to the precise argument Nishida sustains to explain why the original one became many. All phenomena in the entire universe are aspects of God's self-awareness. Following Augustine, he concludes that "in God there is accordingly no reflection, memory, or hope, and hence no special self-consciousness. Because everything is the self and there is nothing apart from the self, there is no consciousness of the self."[20] The self-consciousness of the ultimate necessitates the self-manifestation of the differentiated, and necessitates that at least some of the manifested exhibit free will, as separate personalities capable of reflecting back a myriad of perspectives, each unique and freely capable of innovation, development, and exploration. In his final essay, he writes that "each conscious act is an existential monad of the world's own self-reflection,"[21] a monadic view which reflects God back to God's

Self. The love of God, as primal foundation of reality, is an "infinite love for us," for all that is manifested. Nishida paraphrases the Christian mystic, Meister Eckhart, in concluding that "God's altruism is God's self-love. Just as we love our own hands and feet, God loves all things."[22] And it is but an extension of the logic to conclude that we, too, ought to comprehend and feel deeply that all that exists in our world is an extension of us in that all is kin to us and we to all else. We ought to care deeply about our environment, as about our own hands and feet. This, I think, is the basis of Buddhist compassion; the Buddha's realization was that all was interconnected, that all was divine, that each of us is but a manifestation of the divine in the form of our own Buddhanature within. Ethics on "the other side" is an ethics of empathetic identification, not just metaphorically, but literally. I am not only my brother's and sister's keeper; I am my brother and my sister. To be religious is to be on the path to enlightenment, and to be enlightened is to break beyond one's own small consciousness, and to realize that all is one great spirit, one great consciousness. This unity at the base of ourselves, and at the base of the cosmos, we cannot see or hear, for it can in no way become an object of knowledge. This demands an articulation of negation, that is, of God as, ultimately, pure nothingness. God and nothingness are, in this sense, two sides of the same coin. I take it that this is what Nishida means when he reminds us that "great people have spiritual experiences far deeper than those of average people."[23] They experience cosmically and compassionately.

This brings us to the Garden of Eden story, a story from the book of Genesis, which Nishida utilizes to compare and contrast his own position with that of much of Christianity. The Garden of Eden story is not about disobedience, or about the seductiveness of woman. It is about the "sin" of separation, of individuation, of estrangement, and of forgetting. The fall of Adam, Nishida concludes, "is nothing other than an expression of the existence of mankind as God's own negation."[24] It is an ongoing sin, one that repeats itself in each generation, and in each and every person, "moment by moment in our minds." The knowledge gained from eating the fruit, the knowledge of good and evil, is the knowledge that we are estranged, separate, individual, quite free, and alone in a dense universe. At the same time, "at the back of disintegration and reflection lies the possibility of a more profound unity."[25] Provocatively, Nishida's rendering of the story makes it clear that the expulsion from the Garden was not disobedience, but divine necessity. We had to leave the One, in order for there to be many; "individuality is an offshoot of divinity and each person's development completes God's development."[26] Not to have become an individual, exercising free will, would have been a "sin." Thus it is that evil itself is re-conceived. Evil is a necessary part of God's nature. "A creative God must possess negation within himself in order to express himself."[27] Not that God demands what we call evil, but that the root cause of evil is individual power, the free will to do as one chooses. This is why Nishida is able to say that "the absolute God must include absolute negation within himself, and must be the God who descends into ultimate evil." If God is the creative source and energy of all that is, then the evil in the universe must be a part of that energy which that "whole" set in motion. Therefore, "God is hidden even within the heart of the absolutely evil man."[28] If each of us were to be both free and individual, and yet realize our identity with the one, we would be supportive of the individuality and personality of others, rather than the opposite: we would exemplify the wisdom of compassion, the compassion of wisdom as understanding exactly how things are in this thoroughly divine universe. But leaving the Garden is a divine act, a divine necessity: Our relationship to God is that of part to whole. Here again we encounter a contradictory identity: we are independent consciousness, and yet we are fully part of the entirety of consciousness which is our identity with the divine. Just as the acknowledgment of the personality of another is love, so God's acknowledgment of our personality is divine love. Nishida writes, "love is the union of both personalities—that is, in love, two personalities, while independent and respecting each other, join together and constitute one personality. Viewed this way, God can envelop all personalities and acknowledge their independence because God is infinite love." Thus, there is nothing which is originally and fundamentally evil: "all things are fundamentally good," Nishida tells us.[29] Evil arises not from the heart or essence of God, "but from the contradictions and conflicts of the system of reality. If someone asks about the origin of these conflicts, we can answer that they are based on the differentiating activity of reality and are a necessary condition for the development of reality."[30] This view is remarkably, though not surprisingly, similar to that of the Shintō "rough and smooth" ultimate principle of creativity. In order for there to be development, the divine principle has to experiment, to wander out into the unknown, and in that very process mistakes happen, the unexpected occurs, and suffering and the seemingly evil arise. Looked at from one "side" of consciousness, what results is genuine evil; looked at from the other "side," what occurs is a manifestation of the divine wandering into the realm of creative possibility. In this sense, evil is "an essential element in the construction of the universe."[31] Nishida's summary of his position is worth quoting at length:

Because evil is not the activity of the unified advance of the universe, there is of course nothing in it that must be made into a goal. However, a tranquil, uneventful world with no sin and no dissatisfaction would be extremely mundane and shallow. Those who do not know sin cannot truly know the love of God, and those who have no dissatisfaction or anguish cannot comprehend the depths of spirituality. Sin, dissatisfaction, and anguish are necessary conditions for the spiritual advancement of humanity; a true person of religion does not see a divine contradiction in these experiences, but rather feels God's infinite grace. Such things as sin and anguish do not make the world incomplete; on the contrary, they make it rich and profound. If we were to rid the world of them, we would lose the way to spiritual growth and innumerable spiritual enterprises of great beauty would disappear from the world. If we assume the universe as a whole is established according to spiritual meaning, then there is no imperfection due to the presence of those things—on the contrary, we can know the reason for their necessity and indispensability. Sin is despicable, but there is nothing in the world as beautiful as a sin for which one has repented.[32]

By contrast, love is the ultimate in good action, for to love is to seek to unite with the object of one's love. Love and knowledge are fundamentally the same, for both are activities "in which the self unites with things."[33] To become one with things, Nishida asserts, is a yearning at the heart of what it means to be Japanese. To truly know and love, we now learn, is to be aware of one's identity with all things. Just as the Buddha's love extended to all living things, and possibly to all existing things, so human love extends to all human beings, to all living things, and beyond. Indeed, it is through love that we come to grasp ultimate reality, to know it. To know is to unite, and to unite is to love: in this sense, Nishida's epistemological position is a mystical one, one of knowledge through love. "Love," he tells us, "is the deepest knowledge of things. Analytical, inferential knowledge is a superficial knowledge, and it cannot grasp reality. We can reach reality only through love. Love is the culmination of knowledge." It should also follow that to truly know another person is to unite with that person in love, to reduce the gap between self and other to nothing, to meet the other in the betweenness between the two of you. To love is to know the other so well that one is able to "intuit the other's feelings."[34] One respects the other's personality, desires, aims, goals, aspirations, and feelings. One acts in such a way as to enhance the personality of the other, no doubt to the extent to which it does not harm others, with whom one also identifies. This is the root of compassion, and it is the root of good conduct. Such an identification would make it possible to break a rule, or deviate from the norm of expected and socially acceptable behavior, whenever it would seem necessary in order to preserve the worth of the personality of the other, and only to the extent to which such action would not harm others. Thus, it is not that enlightened Zen Buddhists flaunt the norms of society, or the teachings of Buddhism, but that there is a higher standard of behavior than either of these clusters of prescriptions. Consider the well-known story of two monks, sworn to avoid all contact with women as part of their lengthy renunciation of worldly temptations, who encounter a kimono-clad woman of significant beauty, who is unable to cross a swollen stream. The first monk, a moral literalist, avoids her, and refuses to listen to her pleas for help. The second monk carries her across the stream to dry land on the other side. The two continue on their way, but the first monk, now seething at the apparent immorality and weak resolve of the second monk, lashes out at him for his backsliding. The second monk, unperturbed, simply remarks that he had put the woman down miles back, while the first monk appears to be carrying her still, and therefore is evidently the one most affected by the act. The second monk, who saw through the rules to the compassion on the other side of the rules, was untouched by breaking his vow, because he did not break it for reasons of lust or personal satisfaction or gain, which, presumably, was what the vow was about in the first place. To have left the woman in distress, or conceivably in danger had she attempted the crossing alone, would have been a far greater evil. To act compassionately, to identify with the aims of the other, is at the heart of the meaning of acting well. To ignore another because of a formality is at least to miss the purpose of the original vow—to lead one to wisdom and compassion and not to lose out on an opportunity to selflessly express who it is that you are at your depths.

THE NATURE OF GOOD CONDUCT

Nishida defines the good as "that which satisfies the internal demands of the self." He elaborates that the greatest of these internal demands are those of personality, and, hence, to "actualize personality is for us the absolute good." These demands, i.e., those pertaining to the actualization of personality, are "an expression of the infinite unifying power at the base of reality," and at the base of the self.[35] The desire, and the aim, is to unite with this unifying power. Thus it is that "personality is the basis of all value," and from a transformed or enlightened personality derives all good conduct. All other values are valuable instrumentally, if at all, to the extent to which they enhance the demands of personality. "Wealth, honour, authority, health, skill, and academic knowledge are not in themselves good. When they run contrary to the demands of personality, they become evil." Good conduct, then, is conduct that serves to actualize personality, that is, that serves to achieve the unification of consciousness itself. It is conduct that arises from "the internal necessity of the self," or, in other words, it arises spontaneously as a self-expression of a significantly unified personality. Furthermore, and taking us back to the beginning full circle, "we can be aware of the demands of the whole personality only in the state of direct experience prior to deliberative discrimination," or as Nishida calls it, in a state of pure experience. Pure experience, therefore, is the foundation of good conduct, as it is of religion. Interestingly, almost as an afterthought, Nishida adds that "sincerity" is an additional condition which is necessary for good conduct to arise.[36] We have already seen that sincerity (*makoto*) was central to Watsuji's position, as it was to Shintō, Buddhist, and even Confucian ethics. It is not surprising, then, that Nishida should not only include it, but emphasize its importance. What is surprising, however, is that he does not attempt to show that it is an expected corollary of a personality which is grounded in pure experience. Sincerity, like personality, seems to be of intrinsic value.

Actually, his claim is that while personality is of absolute value, sincerity is good in itself, and while this marks a distinction between the two valuationally, it appears to leave them both instances of intrinsic value at the very least. Both are good in themselves, for their own sakes, while only the value of personality is absolute. At the same time, he seems to claim that sincerity is also of extrinsic value in that "to deceive another is to deceive oneself and to negate one's own personality."[37] The wording here is such as to imply that it is the negation of personality that makes deception wrong, and not the nature of deception itself. Nishida is less than clear in this analysis of the comparative value of personality and sincerity, and either one of two possible conclusions may be drawn. Either only personality is intrinsically valuable, which is why he terms it "absolute value," in which case sincerity is an extrinsic or instrumental value; or both are intrinsic, while one is intrinsic and absolute. In this latter case, "absolute" would carry the added weight of "ultimate," or "highest," or perhaps "unconditional," whereas in the

former case, sincerity is singled out as having something like "contributory" value, in that it is an essential quality of, and contributes to the
greater intrinsic worth of, the whole personality in this singular and
special way. If this were so, then sincerity would not actually be of
intrinsic value, but would appear to be because of its unique and essential status as a contributing part of a whole (personality) which itself is
of intrinsic value. A contributory value, then, is an apparent intrinsic
value which, however, is not actually intrinsically valuable itself, but
which is a part of a whole which is of intrinsic value.

Be that as it may, sincerity, as the union of knowing, feeling, and
willing, is the spontaneous expression of a person who has left, or
nearly left, consciousness of the self behind, as well as the calculating
intellect and self-conscious feeling, and who is now able to express "the
most solemn internal demands"[38] as a willing without willing. It is only
then that we leave behind expectation, and identify with the field of
awareness before us. This identification, or expression of love, is a
merging of subject and object, and "self and things forget each other,
and all that exists is the activity of the sole reality of the universe." One
is the other person, cares about his or her happiness and well-being,
and sees the world as "a reflection of the self" and the "self [as] a
reflection of the world."[39] Love, the union of self with other persons,
with nature, or with the absolute, is to manifest good conduct because
one's sense of kinship now extends to the limits of the universe. One
acts out of love, as selfless desire for union with all that is, which itself
is the selfless expression of the "personality" of God or totality. This
cosmic consciousness is a cosmic ecstasy, a realization that I am divine
as is everything else; "*tat twam asi* (That thou art)."[40]

FROM SELF TO NO-SELF

The actualization of one's unique individuality, of person, yields "supreme satisfaction to each person and makes each an indispensable
part of the evolution of the universe." The individual is concerned with
his or her well-being, but not with that alone: "Individualism and communalism are spoken of as if diametrically opposed to each other, but
I think that they coincide."[41] This position is no simple-minded assumption that what is in my interests will, more often than not, be in the
general interest of society. This is not a virtue of selfishness approach.
Rather, it is a view from the "other side," at the point where the consciousness of the individual and the entire cosmos actually coincide in

extent. Moreover, Nishida's emphasis on both the individual and the community echoes Watsuji's etymological analysis of *ningen* as expressing human nature as consisting of both individual and social connotations. The greatness of personality is to be measured by the social nature of one's inner demands and awareness capacity:

> Fundamentally, the center of the self is not limited to the interior of the individual: the self of a mother is found in her child, and the self of a loyal subject is found in the monarch. As one's personality becomes greater, the demands of the self become increasingly social.[42]

In his brief analysis of the fullest possible extent of our communal awareness, Nishida warns that it is not the nation which is the final expression of communal consciousness, although to date it "is the greatest expression of unified communal consciousness."[43] Nonetheless, a "genuine universalism" must emerge which, while not usurping the role of nations, must, nonetheless, unite them in a world vision, a social union of all humankind. No doubt this is to be achieved by a forgetting of self and other objects in a pure experiential realization of the oneness and worth of all people, nature, and beyond. Our own deepest desires and the truly good are here one and the same.

> . . . I think that our deepest demands and greatest goals unite automatically. While internally we discipline the self and attain to the true nature of the self, externally we give rise to love for our fellow humans and come to accord with the supremely good goal—good conduct that is perfect and true. From one angle, such perfect good conduct appears exceedingly difficult, but from a different angle, it is something anyone must be able to do. Morality is not a matter of seeking something apart from the self—it is simply the discovery of something within the self.[44]

The foundation of good conduct is also the realization and ultimate standard of good conduct: "Our true self is the ultimate reality of the universe, and if we know the true self we not only unite with the good of humankind in general but also fuse with the essence of the universe and unite with the will of God—and in this religion and morality are culminated." The road to this culmination is the realization of the real self always already beneath the "false self," and is the realization of the unifying power found in pure experience, and in the spontaneous expression of that power stemming from "the union of subject and object."[45] From this place of "no-mind," "no-self," no-thing are manifested truly selfless acts, acts which preserve and promote the expression of individuality, the awareness of universal kinship, as well as a loving ecstasy and compassionate concern for all that is. Here there is no need for moral rules, a codification of moral duties, or sanctions to promote the performing of good acts and the abstaining from evil. There is no greater motivation than the love of all, together with a selfless sincerity of purpose, e.g. the harmonization of the universe as divine expression. Still, the ideal is inevitably brought down to the earth of everyday experience due to the existence of real evil, incredibly selfish acts, and desires which lead directly to the harm and suffering of others, and to the potential destruction of the world itself. On "this side" of consciousness, the state of affairs is not nearly so rosy or promising. All the same, even on "this side," morality must be infused with at least a glimmer of that which lies beyond: ". . . there must be God's absolute love in the depths of the absolute moral ought. If not, the moral ought degenerates into something merely legalistic."[46] Even the goodness of ordinary acts must be driven by compassion, however dimly the grounds of that passion are comprehended, in order for them not to degenerate into empty husks, gestures intended to fulfil the letter of the law, but bereft of the very human heartedness which is the life blood of morality, of community, and of religiosity.

Nor is the situation likely to change very much on "this side" of enlightenment. Rules, laws, the police and the military do what little can be done to keep the moral dust down to liveable levels. This negative, even pessimistic, conclusion may well serve as a watershed recognition of a radically different perspective, East and West. If impure desires, selfishness, and a complete and utter ignorance of the divine in all things describes the human state in its most prolific form, then genuine evil and immoral acts will continue to be visited upon us. Something like this might well be Nishida's account of "original sin." Original sin is not a description of who we are, because of an ancient transgression that actually altered out human nature, but of who we have become in the world—estranged from the divine source within, teeming with impure desires, and selfishly focussed in a world from which one feels utterly alienated. Given such an account, it is little wonder that Japan in particular is so taken with existentialism. Existentialism's forte is its description of the human condition, of our sense of alienation from our own authenticity, from others, and from the world.

Worldly ethics, with all of its sanctions, cannot possibly hope for an earthly transformation, but only for local successes and sporadic improvements and victories. There is no clear indication that we are progressing or improving as a species, morally. Women have more rights and more justice than a century ago, but terrorism is increasing, and given the nonstop production of weapons of mass destruction, the net result may be a step backwards rather than a step forward. It is not that we should abort our attempts to achieve justice and the protection of basic rights, etc., for they are vitally important in the here and now. In fact, such attempts from "this side" of consciousness constitute the genius of the West in particular, and of moral systems the world over in general. That we have "progressed," however, is less clear. We have improved many areas of our individual and communal lives, to be sure, but violent crime rates are excessively high, land mines abound, biological warfare is on everyone's mind and continues to be heavily researched and manufactured the world over, and suitcase-size nuclear weapons are now available. Pollution is already endangering our health, species are being eliminated at an alarming rate, the vital rainforests are being cut and burned at a rate that is staggering and dangerous to our survival, our oceans and rivers are not reproducing fish stock, lakes are polluted and sterile, and our ground water is in danger. This is our existential situation. Some things are morally better, but overall radical evil could break out at any moment to overwhelm us. The streets and cities are not safe, and women have not been able to take back either the night, or even the daytime for that matter. Is there a morality in sight which will stabilize our current predicament, and lead us out of the moral wilderness to a promised land?

Nishida's understanding is a religious one: we must be radically transformed if we are to become truly moral. Moral goodness must come from within, and enforcing it from without yields only mixed results, at best. From the "other side" of consciousness, morality is an inner and effortlessly spontaneous expression of who one really is: a *basho* or place of awareness which takes all that is divine and of great worth. The impure desires and cravings have been tamed and brought under control by one or more of the methods of "cultivation," and so all desire to do evil has been eliminated. Love, the desire to know another intimately by becoming one with that other, is now one's primary motivation. As Dōgen will remind us, once one has forgotten one's own egoistic self, one can then become enlightened by all things. The entire universe is a vast panorama of divine expression, and, hence, of divine revelation (as well as self-revelation, therefore). To live in the world under the thrall of such a vision would thoroughly transform the way one would live, and walk, and talk in the world. It is important to apply Nishida's principle of the identity of self-contradiction to our own participation in, and our acting upon, the real world. We are determined by the world, and yet we ourselves determine the world. This important *mutuality* must not be lost sight of, for we are not victims, but creators. From the created to the creating (from *creatus* to *creans*), from the formed to the forming is how he describes our situation: we are created by our inheritance and our environment, and yet, we also are capable of re-shaping our environment and of altering our inheritance both for ourselves, and for our offspring. We are shaped, and we shape; are conditioned, and yet condition; are determined by our facticity, and yet are radically free to influence and re-create our world. Our existential situation allows us a spiral-like path of change: on the one hand, we are brought back to earth again and again by our factual circumstances, and on the other, we are able to take flight into the thin air of the possible, the creative, the better, and the ideal through the freedom to imagine another set of circumstances, and to so act as to bring these into existence. We are creators of our own destiny, as well as products of our age, biology, and culture. Nishida describes this dialectical spiral path as the path of history itself:

> . . . in the historical-social world subject and environment confront each other and form each other. This means that past and future oppose each other in the present, as unity of opposites, and move from the formed towards the forming. . . . The subject forms the environment. But the environment, though formed by the subject, is more than a part of the subject; it opposes and denies it. Our life is being poisoned by that which it has produced itself, and must die. In order to survive, the subject must, again and again, begin a new life. It must, as a species of the historical world of unity of opposites, become historically productive. It must become a spiritual forming force of the historical world.[47]

We are not just evolutionary results: we are also shapers and directors of the course of our own evolution, and of the evolution of all that surrounds us. We must come to see our role as one of active production, as offering an opportunity for action which will shape our world. Whatever action ensues is inescapably self-contradictory, for it reflects the given, while encompassing the creative and deviant: "But if we would act only according to the tradition, only in the way of the species, it would mean a mechanization of the Self, and the death of the species. We must be creative, from hour to hour."[48]

All of this represents a very different perspective on the world and our role in it. We are co-creators in the universe, co-creators with God, or nothingness. Recognition of our divine ancestry carries with it a formidable responsibility. Given that in the West, by and large, there is very little awareness of or credence given to there being an "other side" of consciousness at all, it is understandable that the conclusion is sometimes reached that there is little if anything to learn, ethically speaking, from the East. One of the most promising rejoinders comes from the scientific study of altered states of consciousness, including meditation, and the methods used in preparing for and achieving those states. What is provided is a contemporary and scientific account of the nature of the preparation required in order to open to the "other side," and the beginnings of an account of the psychology and physiology of the nature of that awareness. It is the work of Yuasa Yasuo that has distilled this research, and examined its significance for ethics and practice.

ON SELF-CULTIVATION

Yuasa has brought the issue of personal cultivation (*shugyo*) to the fore in the West because of its central role in the East's rendering of the mind-body relation. Eastern thinkers have long emphasized "the inseparability of mind and body." Central to self-cultivation is "the enhancement of the personality and the training of the spirit by means of the body."[49] This emphasis on the personality, together with a recognition of the existence of "spirit," is very much in line with Nishida's stress on the absolute value of personality, and the centrality of the recognition of a deeper self or "spirit" at our depths.

Yuasa calls attention to Watsuji's book, *The Practical Philosophy of Early Buddhism*, in which Watsuji analyzes the Buddha's non-metaphysical stance. As a result of which what is recommended is not theoretical speculation, "but, rather, the practice that eliminates delusions from one's own soul and detaches one from egoism."[50] Wisdom is not merely an intellectual matter, as Buddhism has long recognized, but demands preparation and purification of all aspects of our being, both body and mind. Realization comes to us only when we have taken the arduous journey from the ego state, to the state of no-ego or no-mind. The result is a blending of, rather than a separating of, cognition and practice. From the time of earliest Buddhism, an important aspect of personal cultivation has been the assiduous following of moral precepts.

Yuasa brings out well how different this preparatory practice is from the ordinary sense of moral prohibition and rule following:

> The precepts for the lay person are the famous Five Precepts: not to kill, steal, lie, commit adultery, or drink intoxicants. The Five Precepts, insofar as they are precepts, are accepted out of the believer's own resolve. Consequently, at least theoretically, they are not prohibitive imperatives of the 'Thou shalt not . . .' sort, but, rather, they express the positive resolution of the will, 'I will not . . .' In this respect, the precepts essentially differ from the Judeo-Christian moral commandments. To accept the precepts is to impose upon oneself constraints beyond the norms of ordinary life. In spite of the fact that the content of the Five Precepts seems to resemble closely the moral laws of our ordinary understanding, they theoretically involve something else— one's own choice of a way of life above and beyond the social norms under which ordinary people in society are constrained.[51]

Buddhism in Japan, however, was itself transformed by its cultural host. The Japanese placed considerably less emphasis on the precepts and ritual details of Indian or Chinese Buddhist thought, and instead took to heart the importance of meditation in this mix. Wisdom was reached by following the precepts, and by practicing meditation long and hard. There were several meditational practices available, but all sought this same personal cultivation, this same imposition on the body-mind of constraints far more strict than the obligations of ordinary, secular society. The purpose of such training was to enhance the personality, build character, and reveal the hidden depths both within and without. Yuasa insists that cultivation in the Buddhist tradition includes the controlling of desires—and, presumably, the eventual purification of desires by eliminating those that could generate evil action, as well as by meditative practice of one sort or other. In this way, there is both an "outward" and an "inward" practice, the former "oriented toward the external world" of communal existence, and the latter "inwardly directed practices" whose objective it is to transform the everyday body-mind as preparation for a rise in awareness of one's own "real" self which is, at the beginning of practice, not a part of our ordinary conscious awareness.[52] Ultimately, the goal or achievement of cultivative practice is the development of both wisdom and compassion, leading to the awareness of no-mindedness, a going beyond the ordinary mind or ego, which includes the awareness of the oneness and divinity which lies at the base of each of us.

Within the context of Japanese cultural tradition, Yuasa examines several of the "arts," each of which is also a cultivational way of focussing, clearing, purifying, and transforming the body-mind, thereby opening the possibility of realization. He includes ancient *waka* (thirty-one syllable) poetry, *Nō* drama, the tea ceremony, and the martial arts, including specifically *kendo* (the way of swordsmanship) and *judo*. It will be helpful here to follow Yuasa briefly in his analysis of the arts as cultivational techniques.

Perhaps the least likely cultivational practice, given the function of the poet in contemporary Western culture, is *waka*. Quoting from Jiwara Shunzei's (1114–1204) *Summary of Ancient Styles*, (which served as the first literary critical handbook of *waka*), it is obvious that the aim of spiritual transformation, specifically in a Japanese Buddhist context, is central. Yuasa walks us through the work of this early family of poets and literary critics:

> The beginning of this book refers to the "great cessation and discernment" (*makashikan*), a meditative cultivation method employed in the Tendai school. "Cessation" (*shi*) here means to arrest disordered or delusional functions; "discernment" (*kan*) means to observe the configuration of all *dharmas* (things) from a quiescent mental state. We see here that the act of composing *waka* was compared to religious cultivation. Obviously, since *waka* composition does not require physical training, we will be hard pressed to find passages in literary criticism referring to the body."[53]

He does find such passages, of course, and they clearly indicate a clear mind is required to compose *waka* poetry, that this necessitates assuming the correct bodily posture, for "one's bodily form directly expresses the mind. Striving for expression and entrance into a deeper aesthetic feeling, the poet resembles the cultivating monk, attempting to concentrate the mind and deepen the meditation and satori."[54] Later, Fujiwara Teika (1162–1241) wrote of his yearning to give expression to the "profound mystery" (*yugen*) at the heart of everything that exists.[55] This elusive depth is, of course, the same depth as that at the bottom of our self, but only by practice in stilling and purifying one's desires, by concentrating one's mind, and by abandoning any temptation to struggle to achieve such expression, can it be realized. One practices diligently and steadfastly until it happens, spontaneously and perhaps without warning. Abandoning one's egoic strivings and control, yet practicing steadfastly in the correct sitting posture, "with much training it will be composed naturally,"[56] and the desired result will have been achieved. This is another of the great paradoxes of Japanese cultural theory and practice: naturalness arises out of rigorous discipline and training. It is not something that is to be found apart from discipline, for that is mere rough-hewn existence, however innocent and cute, with little or none of the profound awareness that one later seeks present. As with the greatest dancers or musicians, spontaneity comes at the end of rigorous training, not at the beginning. At the beginning one has innocence and perhaps a lack of self-conscious performance, but not that profound creative expression within an art form that sits atop of that art's previous historical achievements, and then leaps beyond even these to a new expression and a distinctive style which does not ignore past greatness, but adds to it and transforms it. It comes from the core of the artist, the art, and the audience senses that this is an encounter with a decisive and transformational expression of that art's greatness.

The transformation of consciousness sought in meditation is a "higher" form of experience "which goes beyond the dualistic bifurcation operative in the field of our everyday experience."[57] This "higher" experience involved an awareness of the oneness of body-mind, i.e., a non-dualistic "pure experience" which lies beneath the apparent dualism of body and mind. Whether by "uninterrupted sitting in meditation," or "uninterrupted motion in meditation" (such as in walking meditation, or the martial arts, etc.), both body and mind are enlisted, as members of a "provisional dualism," in arriving at a non-dualistic oneness.[58] Yuasa contrasts this lofty aim of training to achieve a higher state of consciousness in which dualities disappear, especially the selfish ego, with Western sports training. The latter is primarily a training of the motor organs in enhancing "bodily technique which bears no relation whatsoever to the function of the mind, since a body-mind dualism is presupposed." In Japan, the ethical relevance of practice leading to a profound transformation of the person is a direct result of the Japanese insistence "that a certain kind of ethical, religious, or even an aesthetic purpose of perfecting the mind, i.e., personality or humaneness, must accompany the development of bodily skill."[59] Bodily exercise is mind-transformative, as well as body-transformative, and is always to be thought of as a meditational method.

The transformed state of awareness called "no-mindedness" is akin to Nishida's "acting intuition" (or action intuition). Action intuition is a state in which mind-body dualism is overcome, "and the body as an object is made completely subjective."[60] The body no longer resists the biddings of the mind, and there is a seamless body-mind intuition of what is the case right now before one, and an awareness of what needs to be done. The acting body now signifies and fully represents "the *mind just as it is*."[61] In this way, everyday acts are all of them instances of action intuition. That is to say, at their foundation lies pure experience out of which ordinary thoughts and action-responses are carved. So much calculation, deliberation, separation of mind from body and distancing from the things in our world environment has occurred, however, that we are no longer aware of the original unity and distant spontaneity present. Here, too, we are estranged from our origin, from our foundation, from our own authenticity or deep selves. We can recover the foundational and unseen background to our surface awareness of conceptualized and dichotomized existence, however. The pathway is through meditational practice which subjectivizes the body, unifies body-mind, and eventually reveals the spontaneity of no-mindedness. Then it is that the background will have become the foreground of awareness: indeed the only-ground from which to know is already to act, and to act for self is also to act for others. It is a state of wisdom-compassion-unity, where to know the good is the same as the doing of it, for now there is simultaneity, and there is no longer a distinction between knowing and doing, or between deciding what is the right thing to do and profoundly caring about doing it. The gap between *is* and *ought* is eliminated in that the "is" of knowledge and the "ought" of motivation or feeling are now one and the same, an identity of self-contradiction. Intuition is already action, and action is already the knowledge of how to act here and now. As with the swordsman artist, or the *waka* poet artist, the moral artist is so thoroughly practised in what is morally "good" that the demands of this situation right-here-now are intuitively seen and recognized, and a pathway leading to moral insight to help the other move towards self-transformation is acted upon without deliberation. Egoism is no longer a factor, nor are there impure desires to cloud the elements involved. Long moral and meditative practice, self-purification, and a deep love of the divine in all things have together resulted in a wise and compassionate nature whose deepest desire is to help others find this same seamless depth in themselves, in others, and in the world at large.

DŌGEN

If Nishida is Japan's greatest modern philosopher, then Dōgen (1200–1253) stands as the greatest classical Japanese philosopher. The founder of Sōtō Zen Buddhism, Dōgen was rescued from obscurity by Watsuji, who was the first modern thinker to recognize Dōgen's philosophical brilliance and importance. Time and again Dōgen reflects upon the standard teachings and scriptural passages, and interprets them in his remarkably unique way, shedding new light on, and revealing an unexpected depth to, the meaning of the familiar. This is due to his unremitting perspective from enlightenment, from the "other side" of awareness, rather than from the point of view of ordinary awareness. As a result, as Kasulis observes, "the discussion shifts from moral rectitude to authentication": from an ethical command or demand, to "a description of the ideal state of mind."[62] Authentication, the realization of one's Buddha-nature or deep self, is also, and at one and the same time, "an authentic selfhood *for others*—that is, its proper function is that of eliminating suffering and struggle in the world."[63] Enlightenment entails wisdom and compassion; they are not add ons. One's true self arises when the ego is forgotten, for then self and others are truly identified. To realize this deeper or true self it is necessary to practice, to self-cultivate, and, for Dōgen, to practice is to do *zazen*—to meditate. *Zazen* takes us beyond ordinary, ego-focused awareness to an awareness of our identity with all things: "To study the Way is to forget the self. To forget the self is to be enlightened by all things. To be enlightened by all things is to remove the barriers between one's self and others."[64] The ego is the primary barrier to be removed, and the "way" to do that is to meditate with constant, unremitting, and total effort. To so meditate is already to be enlightened, for there is no gap between practice and enlightenment. Enlightenment is not some far off goal, but is to be found in the very practice of meditation as fully engaged, total effort. And this practice with full effort entails, at the same time, the ethical practice of the traditional Buddhist precepts. As Yokoi writes, "novice monks must not enter the monkhood without having received the sixteen Bodhisattva precepts. In this sense, these precepts are the first gate through which monks must pass in their search for Zen."[65] Dōgen states this inescapable requirement in "Receiving the Precepts" (Jukai) with forceful clarity: ". . . if you wish to do *Zazen* and pursue Buddhism, you should first observe the precepts. How can you expect to become a Buddha or patriarch if you do not guard against faults and prevent yourself from doing wrong?"[66] The "highest Supreme Law" is first of all, to receive the precepts, and then to observe them. The first precept is "to do no evil," and the second is "to do good," yet these two simplistic sounding admonitions are transformed by Dōgen into an original and distinctive theory of moral action. Taken from classical Buddhist scripture, Dōgen's rendering of the original passage takes an unexpected turn: "do no evil" is taken to mean "the non-production of evil," and the thrust of this is to move us behind the surface distinction of good and evil, to a state of awareness which is prior to this very distinction.

It is a call to "pure experience," to a state of unified awareness prior to dualistic awareness. As well, this non-dual state of awareness would be a practiced state, and as such would bear the traces of self-cultivation and transformation. It would be an enlightened state of being. Utilizing Kasulis's skillful analysis of the passage from scripture in question, it becomes evident that Dōgen is exhorting his monks to view morality in a radically new way:

> ... terms like good and evil are interdependent concepts, they operate on the level of thinking, but nonproduction is prior to such categorizations. In this regard, to say "the nonproduction of evil" (*shoakumakusa*) is superfluous; "nonproduction" (*makusa*) is sufficient. Upon first hearing the phrase *"shoakumakusa,"* the novice takes it to be an exhortation to do no evil. In so doing, the disciple undertakes the Buddhist disciplines, but then, as the person is spiritually transformed, the words *state* the enlightenment of the disciple. That is, it is no longer an imperative; it is now a description of without-thinking. As Dōgen puts it, "the efficacy of one's cultivation is immediately presencing."[67]

Dōgen adds that even a pine tree in spring and a chrysanthemum in autumn "do not commit" (they non-produce). They do not do evil, or good, for they simply do not commit at all.[68] They non-produce just as they are. Fox emphasizes that the pine and the chrysanthemum are no longer to be seen as mere objects of nature, but each respectively "as another manifestation of that same ultimate which is the reality of both the command not to commit evil and the power to obey it."[69] The pine tree and the person are self-manifestations of the Absolute, the divine, and the non-production of evil is the direct result of this realization. There is no longer any desire to do evil, nor, for that matter, any to do good from this perspectival height. Good, evil, moral rules, ethical theory, laws, and constitutions are all beside the point. The vision of the universe as a manifestation of the oneness of God as a vast array of particularities issues forth a compassionate, protective, non-violent and cherishing way-of-being-in-the-world which is beyond good and evil. It is a vision from which one non-produces good and evil, but from which manifests compassion, and the sheer dedication to help in raising all others to this realizational height. It takes external ethics, and renders it a spontaneous and natural internal self-expression of who it is that we have become as transformed. The non-production of evil is the voice of the voiceless itself, of God, or the Absolute, or the Unborn, or the Buddha, or nothingness expressing its own nature as creator, sustainer, life-giver, cosmic explorer, and source of comfort and joy. As enlightened, one self-expresses as the divine. The realized "saint" is a true image of God, of the divine as self-manifested. We are the form of the formless, the voice of the voiceless, the self-expression of that which itself is expressionless. Fox's summary of this new scriptural hermeneutic is helpful:

> All this raises the trite sentence "Do not commit evil" to a new and surprising level of complexity and importance. It is not merely a rule, a Buddhist Boy Scout motto; it is the way that "that which eternally is" expresses its character, and therefore I must consider myself in some degree of alienation from Truth and Reality, bound in some measure to illusion, while it is ever a self-conscious struggle on my part to obey. "Do not commit evil" must become my subjectivity; it must not remain an externally imposed rule. When it is truly my subjectivity and my true self, then my self is no longer that separate, finite ego of which I once boasted, but is none other than the Unborn, the Absolute, the Eternal Truth. Dōgen resorts to a metaphor to illustrate the nature of the transformation we undergo in the process he is discussing. He says "Just as the Buddha hood-seed grows by favorable conditions, so the (very) favorableness of those conditions derives from the Buddha hood-seed." That is, the subjectivizing of the "Commit no evil" can be likened to the growth within us of the seed of true Buddha hood, and this seed, the favorable conditions for its growth, and the process of growth are all alike the Unborn. Among the "favorable conditions" for this growth of the Buddha-seed within us is, of course, the diligent practice of Dōgen's beloved *zazen*.[70]

The non-production of evil effortlessly results in the production of what we term "good." The non-production of either good or evil—just non-producing—results in the same effortless self-expression of the pine tree or the chrysanthemum: pure, divine expressions of compassion. To exist as a self-expression of the divine is to recognize the oneness, the interconnectedness of all that is as divine manifestation, and hence, is to be both wise in now knowing this to be so, and compassionate in one's selfless identification with all things. As such, one's knowing, feeling, and willing aspects are no longer separately identified, and hence one's integrated non-self knows this identificatory truth, cares about it profoundly, and wills it to persist and to assist in the self-discovery of these truths and compassionate feelings in each and every particle of the universe. This is the "desire" of the bodhisattva, to assist in the enlightenment of all beings. The ethical imperative has now become an imperative for enlightenment. The true goal of action is not goodness, but the spreading of the potential for transformation. And while almost always one's actions, as an enlightened being, will be deemed moral from the "outside" of enlightenment, nevertheless, at times what he does will be unexpected and unconventional enough to startle, and even to outrage. The legend of the Zen master who cut a living cat in two in order to bring a monk to enlightenment only underscores the point. To extract from this story that Zenists may kill cats if they so decide, or otherwise flaunt not only conventional morality, but even the morality of the Buddhist precepts themselves, is to miss the point of the story. The point is that there are times when extraordinary circumstances demand extraordinary interventions. In general, however, one ought not to kill living things. In our own modern world, we medically test drugs and medical procedures on animals in order to save human lives. Of course, the morality here is not clear. Should scientists so test? Ought industry to "use" so many animals in this way? Are technicians unnecessarily cruel in the testing that is demanded? How much of this testing is done for purely cosmetic, selfish, and trivial reasons? Yet it would not be difficult to envision a scenario where it was necessary to choose between saving a child or a pet, both having run in front of a speeding automobile; or between the life of a baboon and one's son awaiting a heart transplant.

When do we decide that this is an instance that justifies acting in disobedience to a moral rule or precept, such as not to kill? The answer is that there is no "answer." There is only spontaneous acting without acting, from the inside of self-transformation, which seizes on a specific instance as an opportunity to achieve transformative growth or well-being in another person. The decision must not be formulated as "it is appropriate to kill whenever . . . ," for that would negate the precept not to kill, and would further fail to recognize the uniqueness of the particular circumstances in this instance. Good and evil are "relative" in part because circumstances vary so widely from one case to another, one era to another, and one culture to another. Nor is the master to be free from criticism and even secular prosecution. At best, he or she will proclaim that a higher law was followed, but this begs the question as to what law it was, and how it is to be formulated for others to come to understand the decision. The sacrifice of the cat—if, in fact, it ever actually occurred—was a once and only event, and one that would certainly be condemned as a model by the perpetrator of the act. Nonetheless, the agent in question might well see this action as his or her finest hour as master, or teacher of transformation, for it might have brought about more realization-potential, both at the time and afterwards, than all of the other acts of a lifetime of teaching rolled into one. Fox sees this with clarity:

> . . . since what matters is that enlightenment should break out throughout the relative and empirical level and not that evil should be recompensed and punished, it follows that while we must operate at this empirical level, our obligation is not merely to do good in an amorphous fashion, but especially to do good which will provoke the awakening of our fellows. The need— especially but not exclusively for enlightenment—of our fellows is the root of our ethical behaviour, and therefore ethical theory may never be legalistic, reduced to a fixed program of rules and regulations, but must be contextual and flexible. . . . The Māhāyanist is commonly included to see the Hinayanist as bound by the letter of the law, while he himself is bound by *karunā*, compassion, which often means the transcending or suspension of the law.[71]

The good and evil distinction is not absolute, but relative. Rather than focussing on the external laws, Dōgen urges us to spare no effort in realizing our divinity within. The path of following the precepts, and of meditating with total effort in each and every moment, leads one to a self-transformation wherein every moment and every being is precious.

The precepts are to be learned, but the point of learning them is to unlearn them, to internalize them so fully, due to one's own enlightenment-transformation, that they, and meditation itself, simply come to express an "organic unfolding of a mode of conduct which was itself an expression of an enlightened nature."[72] The transformation is a transformation of the potential which one already is, to its actualization as recognition of our inextricable kinship with divinity. As Dōgen reminds us, "only Buddhas become Buddhas,"[73] for that is precisely what we have been all along.

DŌGEN ON THE "NOW"

One of the corollaries of enlightened living is that it transforms ordinary events and things which we encounter in the everyday world. By removing all valuational and moral judgments, one can then see events anew, in their "suchness," within each and every moment. By forgetting the self one also removes the grid of interpretation by means of which we have come to establish, and in turn to evaluate, our everyday world. When that grid is removed, things come to us, as Nishida saw, rather than our going to them with our habitual and presumptive analytical tools of understanding. It is in this sense that we can then be enlightened by all things. Francis Cook calls this "doing one thing at a time":

> ... this practice is simple, but it is difficult. The difficulty lies in not adding something extra to the events of our life. The practice I have been discussing might also be called the practice of the art of doing just one thing at a time. It is wonderful to learn to do one thing at a time. When we do formal *zazen,* we just sit; this means we do not add to the sitting any judgments such as how wonderful it is to do zazen, or how badly we are doing, or "When will I become a Buddha?" We just sit. When we wash the dishes, we just wash dishes, when we drive on the highway, we just drive. When pain comes, there is just pain, and when pleasure comes, there is just pleasure. There is nothing more to do than to learn to do one thing at a time. A Buddha is someone who is totally at one with his experience at every moment.[74]

It is to live each moment to the fullest, with total exertion or involvement in what one is doing that Dōgen is calling for. It is not that we are to be focally concerned with the goodness or badness of the things we do; there are only things to do, and the doing of these things constitutes our "living." It is how we encounter what we encounter that is vitally important, not what we encounter. So-called adversity, good fortune, health, sickness, accidents, hard work, sleep, eating, eliminating, are all just things to do. None of them are good or bad, they are just the events which together make up living. It is not that it no longer matters whether one performs evil or good actions, but that one now acts spontaneously, from one's deep nature. Since most, if not all negative impulses have by now been cleared away, one presumably acts from the center of one's compassionate awareness of the interconnection of all things. It is the same center from which the enlightened Buddha acted, out of compassion. The issue is no longer that of goodness or badness, but of the issuing forth of compassion from the depths of the self. Greet circumstances and conditions mindfully, deal with them, learn from them, and find in them the sheer magnificence of existence itself, that incredible mysteriousness which is so inexplicable, so fantastic, so wonderful in its many ways that even the most unaware of us catch occasional glimmers of this divinity underfoot. It is all beyond comprehension, of course. It comes as no surprise, therefore, that Dōgen would remind us that time does not fly away from us, but is ever present and complete in every moment. Spring does not become summer, but is completely and robustly spring; wood does not become ash when burned, but rather, wood "woods," ash "ashes," and fire flames and flickers. Each event is full as it is, and is to be appreciated just for what it is: a divine manifestation which exists as long as it exists fully, robustly, magnificently. Except for this existing-as-such, this presencing, all things are empty of any other substantiality or permanence, as Buddhists have always taught. Ashes "ash," and spring "springs" for a limited time. All is impermanent; ash gives way to soil, or a new plant, and spring gives way to summer. Existence is always conditional, and more often than not, relatively brief. All the more reason to glory in such existence, while it is here—before it has gone. To attend fully, to be really present to one's experiences is itself to practice, in a genuine and important sense. *Gujin*, or "total exertion" means to identify with what is at hand, to be single-mindedly present, and not to be thinking about one thing while doing another. As Cook writes, "when one thing is totally manifested or totally exerted, nothing else exists but that thing, for all of reality is focussed into that single circumstance."[75] It is we who are to transform the world by transforming ourselves, then, from which follows our acceptance of the flowing world. By immersing oneself in the river of pure experience, one catches the flow of being and nothingness, of growth and decay, of creation and destruction even before they have been distinguished, pulled out of the seamless flow by the analytical, dualistic mind. There is first the flow, the being-time of the what of reality. Even the Buddha, or God, or the Absolute is impermanent! Indeed the Buddha is impermanence, the very flow of being-time itself, the glorious mystery which, as a seamless one, is unknowable and unknown, but as many, is both knowable and known. And we, the knowers, are utterly unknowable and unknown, even to ourselves. Always hidden, never directly revealed as knowers knowing, but only as hardened objects, as knowers objectively known. We, too, are part of the mystery, the unknown knowings which know and act in and on a world which is us, and yet not us. That is the miracle of self-contradictory identity: it is what it is, and yet it is also something else, and this dual nature makes development, self-awareness, transformation, and enlightenment possible. Ashes are totally and utterly ashes, and yet ashes are also utterly divine, a self-expression of the Absolute. It is a recognition of a dualism, and of a non-dualism at one and the same time. What we have is a philosophical explication of a dualistic non-dualism, or a non-dualistic dualism. Through separation from the One, we can come to realize our own duality. Enlightenment recognizes the breach between God and humanity, God and nature, and thereby transforms it by recognizing it for what it is: a manifestation of the divine activity at the base of all things. The entire cosmos is now an Eden, not because there is no evil, but because evil and good and all other dualities have become the self-expression of the real. Things are as they are, and to be able to immerse oneself in them with total exertion, that is the true mystery and majesty of awareness: being robustly here, right now, with all of one's powers concentrated in the eternity of the moment. That is all there is, and it is magnificent.

Still, while the entire, throbbing, dynamic universe is an expression of the Absolute's self-manifestation, the independence of the "ten-thousand things" as differentiated yields a range of tendencies, including those which ordinary consciousness terms "evil," or "destructive," or "hateful." These, too, are divine expressions, although not divine intentions. Snakes eat frogs, lions kill live game, and people kill and torture people. This is not the work of a separate and evil cosmic force, according to Nishida. Rather, all of this, good and evil, occurs within the absolute-as-differentiated self-manifestation, and so is an aspect of the divine itself. It is a cost of the freedom of the differentiation and individuality which constitutes the many. Nevertheless, the deeper impulse, often unrecognized, is for a compassionate minimizing of harmfulness, and a maximizing of the impulse to preserve and protect. This is the root of compassion—it is a direct result of the recognition that all is One, yet human; individual, yet divinely interconnected. The world as manifested is not without suffering and pain, killing and dying, but compassionate understanding seeks to minimize these realities, not add to them, and to give succour in their midst. It is not that evil somehow disappears, but that it now comes to be seen as a necessity arising from the divinely creative act of self-expression as differentiation, and the arising of true freedom of will as "other." It is an aspect of the grand drama of cosmic unfolding and the self-expression of the *formless* as *formed*. This is not a world without what most of us would call "evil," but rather it is just the world that it is. There is no question of a perfect, or all-knowing, or all-seeing, or all-powerful God. This world is the world as creatively expressed by the Absolute, and we ourselves are a part of that self-expression. What we do in it is up to us; but if we listen to the whisper of our origin, our tendency in action will be towards compassion, preservation, dwelling, and an anticipation of eventual reunion with the source. It is an incredible journey of which we are in the midst.

Conclusion:
The Mutuality of Learning
in a Global Village

———

Watsuji's image of a crossroads where various pathways intersect has been magnified almost unimaginably by the image of the information highway. More and more we are electronically linked with one another across cultural, temporal, and even previously rigid linguistic boundaries. On a daily basis each of us in cyberspace interacts at the crossroads of information exchange, and it is perhaps now easier by some considerable measure for me to communicate with someone in Korea or Japan than it is to walk to my neighbor's home, or even to phone her. The long-term effects of this revolution are beyond my ability to gauge, but it is clear that the isolationism which so typified Japan for so much of its history is now but a faint memory in a culture that has become a central part of world culture. The global village is nearly a reality, and surely it will modify the uniqueness and differences within each culture due to exposure to quite different cultures. This has been happening for some time, but the pace is now accelerated incredibly. It would not seem too much of a jump to think that the same interactive effects will increasingly apply to ethics itself, both theory and practice. What I am envisioning is a mutuality of influence, a range of modification of the ethics of one culture by the ethics of other cultural traditions. This is not to suppose that we are heading towards one homogeneous ethical porridge where differences turn to mush, and a "lowest common denominator" sameness becomes the eventual result. Rather, I am supposing that significant and incommensurable cultural differences will remain, including ethical ones, but that cross-cultural

183

interaction and even dialogue as a result of increased exposure will result in significant changes to all of the cultural traditions involved.

The present study is, of course, incomplete. The already existing influence of the West on Japan is not a part of this study, nor is the warrior code of ethics of the samurai—*bushido*. Taoist influences are only indirectly discerned in Zen Buddhism, but have not been systematically gathered together for analysis. The various "practices" would also reveal an imbedded ethic—the martial arts, tea, haiku, sumie painting, calligraphy, flower arranging, swordmaking and training, landscape gardening—from which could be extracted a striking range of attitudes, ethical teachings, and communal interactive practices, encouragements, and prohibitions. Still, what has been included can provide a theoretical net of understanding which, while not able to catch all of the fish in the Japanese ethical sea, nonetheless may be able to provide some of what is needed to bring to the surface some of the larger ingredients in the mix.

Certainly a lack in this study is a sustained critical evaluation of the Japanese approach to ethics. I began with a critique of Danto's insight that the West has little or nothing to learn from the East ethically. I have tried to show how wrong he is, and yet, now that we are at the end of this journey, it is clearer than it was at the beginning that the apparent requirement of "enlightenment" makes much of what has been exposed out of reach of the vast masses of people in the West, and, for that matter in the East as well. Yet it is a Japanese methodological norm to establish the ethical and spiritual achiever as the standard, and not the average person. Yuasa remarks that in medicine, the West "uses for its standard the normal condition of the great majority of people, that is, *an unspecified, large number of cases.*" Contrasting this with the corresponding methodological assumption of the East, he writes, "Eastern medicine follows the principle of prescribing medication differently from patient to patient; even though the illnesses dealt with may seem identical, it is not uncommon for prescriptions to differ between patients. This is because Eastern medicine does not formulate an empirical law by generalizing as its standard the cases of an unspecified, large number of people." Then, in relating this to the meditative practices of self-development and personal transformation, he concludes that "the traditional Eastern pattern of thinking takes as its standard people who after a long period of training have acquired a higher capacity than the average person, rather than the average condition of most people."[1] When the average becomes the norm, as with the West's preoccupation with "what is the case with the vast majority of people," all deviation, whether below or above the line of the average majority, is considered "abnormal." Thus, we have the result that the most accomplished individuals in our society—the artists, athletes, saints, and intellectuals—are all considered abnormal, deviants. In the East, by contrast, the normal refers to what it is that we recover or reveal by removing the impurities, obstacles, and accretions which hide or cover our "normalcy." In a way, the deviants are the vast majority of people, who have hardly begun their journey to the realization of their own already existing depths. The tendency in Western science is, however, because of particular Western methodological assumptions, to view "both a genius and a madman" as being equally abnormal. Whereas the West might be said to have focussed on sickness as the ordinary state, the East has focussed "on the exceptional, elite experience."[2] Of course, there is not a right or a wrong here; the foregoing reflections simply serve to draw attention to the foreground variation in our attention and in our procedural methodologies. The East takes the "supernormal" as the norm, and the West takes the average as the norm, at least in medicine and psychotherapy. I would argue that the West tends to do so in ethics as well. We assume that most people are not anywhere close to enlightenment; and we are correct. We assume that most people need to be constrained by laws, rules, and the necessary enforcement; and we are correct. We assume that most people will not understand what is meant by developing a sense of the interconnectedness of things, or internalizing a sense of empathetic identification such that one lives a life of spontaneous compassion; and we are correct. The reality of the situation is that most people are average, with average concerns, average desires, and average horizons of understanding. And the real worry, over and above keeping the average in some sort of civilized check, concerns those who are below average, the criminal deviant, who needs to be kept in check through more powerful means still. It will do little good to protect society from such individuals with thoughts of self-transformation and interconnectedness. This might provide a larger perspective on what is taking place, and the result would be a calm unperterbedness, but it is hardly a prescription for moral improvement. What is required of the "average" person is that s/he be comfortably settled into a set of prescriptions and prohibitions, hopefully internalized so that proper behavior will be the result even when unsupervised. Furthermore, the emphasis on justice, fairness, and the subtleties of meta-ethics need to be explored and implemented in order for society, through its people and its institutions, to function in ways which provide, in general, maximum benefit and protection from harm in a context of justice and fairness.

The East is not without its laws, its courts, its police, and its willingness to use coercion when required. Yet the tradition of laws, rules, and enforcement appears to be different. The police box (*koban*) which is to be found in every small community, including the large number of sub-communities within large Japanese cities, has as its goal the development of community spirit. Children bring flowers to the local policeman in the spring and summer, and often bring treats for him to eat throughout the year. He knows the patterns of everyday behavior of most of his sub-community members, and is aware of who is ill, who is in childbirth, and which family is in mourning. He is a friend, one who is always there, willing to help, and whose job it is to look after the well-being of the community of individuals whom he has come to know in almost every case. It is not his job simply to enforce faceless laws in faceless ways. Indeed, there can never be enough policemen to insure that no criminal acts are performed. All that one can hope for is that people have internalized and identified with the moral code, and more importantly, identify with the moral spirit of the community, and see themselves engaged in a common enterprise of interconnectedness. Each and every *koban*-community is a crossroads, and it is in the betweenness of that community that quality of life is to be carved out and lived. Lying behind this communal sense is some vision of harmonious interaction, of fellow-feeling, of a common purpose without which the poor policeman would be hopelessly taxed and outflanked. There is some "healthy" vision of what it means to be a neighbor, a citizen, a Japanese. A major part of that vision is the assumption that everyone is well-meaning and intrinsically good in their depths, and that the enlightened achiever is representative of what we are all like in our healthy, normalized state. At our depths, with the impurities and distortions of civilization and other environmental influences removed, we are, in some real sense, by nature good. Of course, we are also evil, as Nishida saw, but this "evil" is not "original" in the same sense that "good" is original. Both God and Satan are aspects of the divine, of nothingness, but the goal of individualization, of separation from the pulsing creative force, is to carry this distance from the source with a fulsome awareness of our inseparability from and identity with the divine, with goodness. It is an identity of self-contradiction which is distinctively human. We are good, and we can become or manifest evil. We do need the local policeman. But we are, at the same time, self-manifestations or expressions of the divine activity itself. And in this lies our "original" goodness. To be individuated does not inevitably entail evil action. Once we experience directly our kinship with the divine—indeed our authentic God-hood—we inevitably treat others, and the world in which we find ourselves, differently. The "other" is not other, and is to be protected, preserved, and nourished whenever and wherever possible. It, too, is originally good, and the ordinary dualistic perspective on self/other, good/bad, and sacred/profane collapses. The universe is a majestic self-expression of divinity; everything is "lined" with nothingness.

Nishida makes use of an analogy borrowed from Nicholas of Cusa who imagined an infinite sphere on which every point is the center, because there is no circumference.[3] Nishida modifies this image, referring to a "self-contradictory sphere" which bears at least two directional indications. First, the centrifugal direction is a movement away from God, from the whole, which is represented by the center of the sphere. This direction is evil, for it is the movement of separation from God, of individuality as independent objective existence, of estrangement from the center or source of all things, including estrangement from one's own self-contradictory self. Second, the centripetal direction is the direction of goodness and is towards God. By drawing towards the center of the sphere, we discover the absolute subjectivity of the creative historical world, in contrast with the objectivity of the physical world. Recall, however, that the absolute is itself self-contradictory, and so both evil and good. God and Satan are but moments of, or directions in, the whole sphere, which itself is neither God nor Satan, and is therefore both. The sphere is, ultimately, absolute nothingness, and therefore it is, immanently, exactly what it is: godly and satanic. And as mirrors of nothingness, we, the places/*bashos* where nothingness expresses itself through conscious acts, must also be mirrors of God and Satan: "We, the centers of this bottomlessly contradictory world, are both satanic and divine. Hence my theology of the absolute present is neither theistic nor deistic—a theology neither of mere spirit nor of mere nature."[4] The direction of religiosity is centripetal, and it is characterized by the abandoning of self. Nishida makes clear which direction is the better by emphasizing that the spiritual movement "means to see our essential nature, to see the true self."[5] Estrangement is a partial, superficial understanding of our nature, cut off from its deeper core. Nothingness, as the centripetal direction, is not external to us, but is an event in our own soul, a re-discovery of one's own Buddha-nature. Movement towards the deeper layers of self, which culminates in the realization of bottomless self-contradictory identity as the place where absolute nothingness arises and becomes uniquely conscious of itself, is contrasted with movement away from our essential nature, which is increasingly evil (estranged) as it covers over its deeper nature. Delusion, the traditional cause of evil in Buddhist thought, occurs when we mistake the objective self for the real or deeper self. The logic of objects moves us in the wrong direction, whereas the logic of the identity of self-contradiction (paradox) moves us centripetally towards the absolute. Religious consciousness consists precisely in the realization of this contradictory identity of the true self and absolute nothingness. To see this is to have one's own experience of one's bottomlessness. Such an experience is self-transformative.

SOCIAL ETHICS

Neither Nishida nor Mahāyāna Buddhism generally provide a social ethics. This omission is a regrettable fact, but not a lamentable one. To focus on ethics as not fundamental, or as a penultimate stage through which one must pass on one's journey to enlightenment, seems both laudable and worthy of investigation. There would be reason for lament only if social ethics were rejected and abhorred in principle. Nishida does not take such a position, but instead attempts to infuse ethics with its originating impulse (fellow-feeling or love, a sense of the identity of all things, a sense of cosmic kinship), and then pushes beyond ethical structures to religiosity itself. That ethics does not receive sufficient attention along the way is a matter for regret. It does not distort Nishida's vision to pause and implant ethical theory into his perspective, however. Natural and spontaneous feeling must, after all, take on form, and while all form is partial, less rich, and to some extent distortive of the whole of which it is an expression, it is imperative that the form expressed be the highest and most spiritually grounded of which we are capable. And each succeeding generation has precisely the same responsibility anew. It is when the task is not shouldered anew, or when the old form is out of accord with the feelings and cultural embodiments of a new age, that the system handed on loses its grounding of vitality, and becomes an empty shell, a form without life or passion. It is then that a conscious re-examination of one's reflex actions, one's cultural habits, must be undertaken anew. To do so is to be engaged in the development of a new social-ethical dimension.

To speak of the Japanese generally, rather than Nishida specifically, there is more emphasis on the development of a feeling of community, or of fellow-feeling (human heartedness), than on the development of a written code of ethics. There is a hesitancy to generate crisp formulations, because to do so is to minimize the spontaneous outpouring of warmth and genuine caring, and to substitute for it a sort of paint-by-number code of behavior which one can follow without feeling. The word *kokoro*, which means both heart and mind, also has the connotation of a spontaneous arising of warmth and human heartedness towards another, with no ulterior purposes or hidden agendas. To "have" *kokoro* is to exude this unfettered and pure caring in a way that is transparent to those who can read character. I recall a rather ordinary example of this in my own Japanese experience. I was visiting Japan for the first time, and was being helped by a financially comfortable Japanese family whom I had met in Canada. They told me that they had spent a good part of the previous evening trying to decide what "gift" would be appropriate for me. They had thought of a variety of concerts, art objects, and so on, and then after much discussion opted for a shopping trip. They would make available a car, together with my host's wife and daughter as experienced and knowledgeable shoppers, for an entire day. Their reasoning was that what would be most difficult for me to achieve was to find the best quality goods, at a price I could afford, for my family and friends, in the shortest time. Thus, they gave of themselves to assist me in this way, even though to do so would be less "showy" than to present me with an expensive gift, or a lavish night out. They read me correctly as a family man, who wished to find Japanese "treasures" to bring home with me for family and friends. This is genuine human caring, without a hidden agenda or ulterior motive. It was not simply a matter of doing what is expected, or socially or morally required: it was an expression from the heart, an act of human heartedness or caring.

Shintō, too, it will be recalled, resisted a written ethical code. One learned how to live from one's upbringing, by observing what others did in society, and by visiting the shrines and attending the festivals. To formulate precisely what is required is to seek out a lowest common denominator of sorts, by specifying what is prohibited, rather than inspiring what is possible. In any case, what is focal is not what to do or not to do, but what one is to become. Feel the peacefulness which prevails at the shrine, and experience the mystery of divinity outside, and within yourself. Here, too, ethics is about self-transformation, not about obligations. It is to become aware of the *kami*-infusedness of the world, and of one's own *kami*-nature.

Buddhism, too, in Japan, was less a focus on the precepts, and more on the meditative practices of self-transformation. What Buddhism contributed was a clear recognition "that moral practice was regarded as a path to character formation, that is, it is comparable to the cultivation through which one can live a better life than the average person."[6] While Buddhism had a considerable influence on the Japanese, "no system of Buddhist moral law developed." Indeed, one of the most striking aspects of Buddhism is the fact that "it does not try to change the original, existing social norms and it does not embody a developed and organized system of moral laws capable of such change." The Buddhist *sīla*, or at least the minimal list of precepts serving as the norms for daily lay and monastic life (not to kill, steal, lie, drink, or

commit adultery), were understood, but the more complex compila-
tion of regulations "did not really take hold on Japanese soil."[7] On the
other hand, one of the meaning-layers of adherence to the precepts
and canons of ethical living (*kairitsu*) is meditation, and this aspect of
Buddhist practice and cultivation did catch on in Japan. In Zen in
particular, the practice of meditation almost completely overrode the
litany of precepts. For the Japanese, the point of meditation and morality was to further one along the path of self-transformation, towards
enlightenment.

As we have seen, however, both Shintō and Zen are particularly
problematic, because both traditions were drawn into the militarism and
right-wing nationalism of Japan. Shrine Shintō was allowed to be transformed into State Shintō, thereby serving as the foundation for imperialism
and claims of cultural and ethnic superiority. Practitioners of Zen Buddhism exhibited a nationalistic and militaristic complicity that is both
unexpected, and inexcusable. Zen masters, like anyone else, can make
mistakes, but that so many of them did, and with such passion, demands
that something more be said. Of course, it is not that the Christian world
was particularly notable in speaking out against the Nazis. Indeed, there
is a larger issue at stake here, and it concerns how it is that otherwise
good people, highly intelligent people, can do such stupid things, and
sometimes such evil things. Neither I nor anyone else can answer such
questions, but it might be worth hypothesizing that when the "heart" is
taken out of ethics, leaving only an unfeeling and uncaring husk, an
imbalanced result may occur. In Confucianism, to eliminate human
heartedness and the sense of shame leaves only rules and dust-dry rituals.
The bureaucrat, legendary in China—but to be found much closer to
home, as well—is one who is rule-bound and authority focussed. One
must do as is expected, regardless of the context and even the consequences, simply because that is the rule, and rules are to be followed. A
Shintōist who does not "experience" the serene divinity of the natural is
left with magic and superstitious rituals and procedures: visit the shrine
on New Year's Day, else you may have a course of bad luck. A Buddhist
who has no contact with, or for that matter interest in, the experience of
enlightenment, follows the Eightfold Path and the precepts with ritualistic unfailingness, even at the expense of causing suffering to others. Or,
even worse, uses enlightenment as an excuse for deviating (with an ease
that is alarming) from even the most fundamental ethical and spiritual
teaching of the Buddha. What makes them precepts and directions along
the path of righteousness is that they are not to be taken lightly, and are
certainly not to be ever abandoned with ease. But if the head without

feeling and compassion is "heartless," as we say, then the heart without wisdom is blind. It seems necessary in our living and acting to keep a "tension" between head and heart. To slacken off at either end of the tightrope of existential living is to make anything like morally successful passage impossible. To keep a tension between these two aspects of poles of human capacity presents us with another *kōan*: how does one fill one's head with heart, and how can one's heart be taught to be critically aware? Human beings must somehow keep the dialogue going between the critical mind and the compassionate heart. These represent the *yīn* and *yáng* of the soul, and the way of the soul is the keeping of some sort of balance between them. At times, an overdose of *yīn* or *yáng* will be required to re-establish the balance of mental, moral, and emotional health. The aim is to achieve a passionate, compassionate, and human-hearted rationality: to establish a person who is both critically aware, astute, and caring. The head and heart can act separately, or pull in opposite directions, but they need not. A well-integrated person, on this model, would more often than not reason heartfully, and feel wisely. Such a balance is both hard to achieve, and harder still to maintain at all times and under all circumstances. People make mistakes all along the way, and Zen masters are no exception. But we must learn from their mistakes, as well as from their successes. Their cold-hearted call to war was a mistake. It had passion, a fierce energy, but showed remarkably little compassion and a surprising lack of rational vision or critical balance. Zen had provided a spiritual grounding for the samurai warrior; now it was the warrior who overwhelmed Zen spirituality and taught the virtues of blind loyalty, single-mindedness even unto death, and utterly focussed fighting spirit. The tables were turned, and the teachers had become the students. The balance was lost, and the spiritual grounding of Buddhism was replaced by a technology of war and even an etiquette of the warrior. Even Zen masters make mistakes, yet sometimes the nature of the mistakes provides some indication of pre-existing tendencies or inherent weaknesses in a position. Given that a strength can become a central weakness, the Zen ability to focus, to dedicate energy, life, mind, and heart to one thing did lead to a powerful and worldly ability to fight without fear. In the meditation hall, such focus is laudatory, but in nationalistic politics or war it is one-sided, frightening, red-necked right wing-ism at its worst. Perhaps it is that they had lost sight of their own traditions, including the recognition that war itself is a *kōan* of the most impenetrable sort. Had the Zen masters and scholars agonized over what to do, eventually having to decide (as in *Sophie's Choice*), it would have been easier to comprehend afterwards what led to their wholehearted support of the war. To choose one way or the other, after incessant deliberation, profound anxiety, and the deepest of regrets would have shown that the *kōan* had not withered, but had remained in the forefront of mind and heart.

The ordinary, unenlightened person can catch an occasional glimpse of the ideals of a tradition, and accepts, in general, the teaching of its ethical and spiritual achievers. To accept is not, of course, necessarily to be able to live out or put into practice such teachings. To glimpse something of the ideal is quite different from having undergone significant self-transformation. Enlightenment, however, brings with it that transformation which enables one to stay the course, to practice what enlightened insight demands, to want what is required of one, and to enact the apparently difficult with a remarkable effortlessness and ease. The untransformed individual is not so unified, not so free of contradictory impulses, anger, hostility, greed, and ego. The ordinary person works very hard to be ethical, and at that misses the mark far too often. But the techniques of self-transformation are all instruments of potential enlightenment. As one self-perfects (self-normalizes), the motivation to do evil diminishes, and the ease with which one does what is good increases. As Plato noted long ago with respect to the harmonious person whose reason, emotions, and appetites work as one, to know the good is to do it, and what heretofore seemed to be a going against the grain of inclination and desire, is now an effortless and spontaneous expression of who it is that one has become. It is acting immorally that is to go against the grain of our true nature, and moral action is the spontaneous and natural reflex of the transformed person.

What is laid out, then, is a path, a way, and not a set of goals or commandments to obey. The path is endless, since self-transformation is endless, never fully accomplished, always in process (recall that "even the Buddha is improving," an expression one commonly encounters amongst Buddhists and Zen Buddhists). This is why ethics in the East is not to be encompassed by the closure of rules, regulations, laws, or judicial decision. All of these are "tentative" steps, perchings along the way of endless flight, and eventual soaring.[8] The path itself, however, is unbounded, extending indefinitely into the future of transformational growth. The path leads to the "other side" of awareness.

Pragmatically speaking, however, most of us live our ordinary lives on "this side" of ethics and awareness. Our concerns are more likely those of everyday survival, of needing to know that our families and friends are safe, and that there is an "impartial" system of justice at hand to insure the basics of civility and order. Lying on the pavement having just been robbed and mugged, it is of little satisfaction to recall that the mugger is a self-expression of God, and that his violent ego is not a true representation of who he really is. Perhaps this is the meeting place of East and West: the long-range vision of who it is that we could become is sustained by the traditions of the East; the immediate concerns of surviving, and of living justly and fairly, are addressed by the traditions of the West with their explicit moral codes, intensive systems of justice, and massive enforcement agencies and related facilities. Not that the East has none of the latter, or the West is totally lacking in visions of the former. It is a matter of degree, of emphasis. And this is precisely why there is both hope and advantage in not seeing this difference as an either/or situation. I think it is a mistake to think that the West has nothing to learn from the East. It would be equally wrong to conclude that the East can learn nothing of ethical significance from the West. But one does not have to become a Buddhist, or master the intricacies of Tibetan history and religious practice, in order to be able to gather advantage from the Buddhist vision of enlightenment. The strengths to be found on both "sides" of consciousness are not simply different visions; they are complementary. As one moves along the path to enlightenment, one holds the details of moral codes more lightly, while at the same time being increasingly saint-like in one's predictable goodness. At the very beginning of the journey, one adheres to the letter of the law, for that is the basis of civility, and rarely if at all does one think about self-transformation or the heights achieved by those who have gone before. Without a doubt, we desperately need a code of ethical behavior, a system of justice, and an apparatus for enforcement and mutual protection. Yet that is not all that we need. We also need a vision of what it is that the moral achievers in our societies have come to understand and to enact, and of a morality that is so completely internalized that the code is set aside, left behind like the raft that one used to cross a stream. When on the other shore, one leaves the raft behind, but one does not leave behind what it is that the raft accomplished. The raft of ethical demands got us to the "other side." We leave it behind in the sense that, when on the other side, we no longer need to be kept afloat by staying close to the raft at all times. Now that one is on the solid land of transformation, one goes beyond the raft, but not by rejecting it. Rather, one has internalized it, made it a part of one's history, one's journey, and one carries its influence along wherever one goes. The raft is not abandoned, but transcended in the sense that one is no longer confined by it, although one is intrinsically aware of its strengths and teachings. One doesn't forget a teacher who was an important influence in one's life. Neither does one simply set about to imitate that teacher in all respects, and to do everything possible to be exactly like that teacher. One goes beyond, while remaining appreciative of the influence, and then embarks on one's own journey towards creative expression and a fullness of living. If one is a virtuoso, one likely self-expresses by going beyond the tradition, and thereby one creates, or gives expression to something new. The teacher is not left behind, but the teacher is overcome.

FINAL REFLECTIONS

East and West are now inextricably enmeshed in a global web of communication which will inevitably change both. The wilful pilgrim from the West needs to unburden him or herself from the yoke of straining against the flow of nature. We have tried to "conquer" nature, and we are perhaps about to kill her altogether. It is time to release our wilfulness somewhat, and to learn to flow with nature, to treasure it rather than to conquer it, to preserve it rather than to mold it to our design. We must no longer see nature as "material at hand" for our use, as Heidegger warned we were doing increasingly, but must learn how to "dwell" in her midst, understanding that we are a part of that which we too often destroy. Of course, the East must increasingly develop a code of ethical behavior which is more in line with that of the West; the world stage no longer allows such issues as human rights to be removed from the full scrutiny of the media, and an unwillingness to acknowledge some common view of what is to be accepted as basic human rights will lead to economic and political ferment. A doctrine of rights cannot be imposed as separate from a vision of individual and cultural goals, however, indicating that here too we need to understand the underlying ethical and philosophical stance which generates differences in opinion about the legal and moral details of cultural practice.

This study has been an attempt to lay bare the underpinnings of the Japanese approach to ethics, in the hopes that it will make it easier for non-Japanese to make some sense of why they think and act as they do, and possibly allow for some degree of cross-fertilization to occur in our own thinking about ethics, living together, the care of the environment, and the relationship between ethics and spirituality. Yet it is only the beginning, at best the bringing side by side of two paths along which to walk. At most I have pointed out the paths, and it remains to be determined to what extent they will occasionally intersect, and when it is wise to switch to the other path for a time due to the poor repair or obsolescence of a stretch of one's own pathway. There is much to be learned from the way each of us walks along, and the directions we take.

Finally, it is perhaps worth noting that the Eastern emphasis on character development likely strikes chords of recognition in some Westerners. After all, Plato and Aristotle, and many of those who followed them, wrote of the virtues, and these were understood as vital aspects of good character. The Medieval period, too, placed great emphasis on the development of good character, and even walking a path which was itself an "imitation of Christ." The path was not a path to enlightenment, however, except perhaps for the Western mystics, nor was it a journey leading to the recovery of one's original divinity. Nevertheless, the West's recent re-visiting of the place of virtue and the development of character in ethical theory will likely serve as a vantage point from which to observe and appreciate what it is that these quite different paths might also have in common. Perhaps it is already a harbinger of the new winds which are blowing through philosophy and culture, both East and West. The work of Alisdair MacIntyre, Arne Naess, and Charles Taylor all point us towards a wider horizon of ethical understanding, and towards a renewed understanding that a broad-stroke metaphysics inevitably underlies such an ethics.

According to Taylor, modern and contemporary Western thought has so narrowed the focus of what is relevant to a consideration of morality, that it is extremely difficult to understand sympathetically our own cultural past, let alone the cultural past and present of cultures quite unlike our own. He writes, "Much contemporary moral philosophy, particularly but not only in the English-speaking world, has given such a narrow focus to morality that some of the crucial connections I want to draw here are incomprehensible in its terms."[9] What has been eliminated as unworthy of serious "objective" consideration is the more holistic cultural environment within which morality is but one factor, and without which it could not get its bearing. The sense of the valuable and the disvaluable, the good and the bad, the right and the wrong, the beautiful and the ugly are all generated by, and arise out of the cultural context within which such judgments are made. Even when we rebel against the norms of the "tradition," there is still a tradition against which we rebel, and without which rebellion would be impossible. We may reject certain of the norms of our tradition, but it is the existence of the traditional norms which makes our rebellion significant in the first place. As you may recall, Watsuji articulated this idea well. For Taylor, our attenuated sense of our cultural context is apparent in ethical theory: ". . . moral philosophy has tended to focus on what it is right to do rather than on what it is good to be, on defining the content of obligation rather than the nature of the good life; and it has no conceptual place left for a notion of the good as the object of our love or allegiance . . . as the privileged focus of attention or will."[10] The wider context or "framework" which Taylor explores is "a gamut of views a bit broader than what is normally described as the 'moral.' In addition to our notions and reaction on such issues as justice and the respect of other people's lives, well-being, and dignity, I want also to look at our sense of what underlies our own dignity, or questions about what makes our lives meaningful or fulfilling." Consideration of what makes life meaningful or fulfilling is encompassed by the somewhat vague term "spiritual," which nonetheless leads us to "the most urgent and powerful cluster of demands that we recognize as moral," and these include "the respect for the life, integrity, and well-being, even flourishing of others."[11] Moral intuitions are, on the one hand, more like instincts, and on the other, seem to involve claims about the nature and status of human beings. "From this second side, a moral reaction is an assent to, an affirmation of, a given ontology of the human."[12] In other words, claims and evidence make sense only against the background of some "whole story," or horizon of understanding, or cultural "climate" against which they are judged. What makes things even more complicated is that the moral ontology which serves as the background context of meaning and meaningfulness, value and disvalue, good and bad, etc., is usually implicit, and rarely explicit. As with Shintō, a great deal of our cultural perspective we take for granted, and if pressed to explicate our position, we are regularly left fumbling for words, wondering why the questioner doesn't simply see and feel what is so obvious to us. Therefore, "over wide areas, the background tends to remain unexplored. But beyond this, exploration may even be resisted. That is because there may be . . . a lack of fit between what people as it were officially and consciously believe, even pride themselves on believing, and what they need to make sense of some of their moral reactions, on the other."[13] Part of the reason why this form of "multiple personality" exists in the contemporary world is that it is easier to leave aside discussion and argument about the preferability of frameworks in a pluralistic age, and partly because it is embarrassing to discuss the "spiritual" background to our thinking and acting in an age of objective scientific methodology. There seems to be little that is either objective, scientific, or methodical about the "spiritual" or even the "cultural" climate within which we live and breathe, which may seem "so much froth, nonsense from a bygone age."[14] Recall Watsuji's exhaustive attempt to provide the *fudo* or climate by means of which Japanese ethical sensitivity may be accounted for and understood.

MacIntyre, too, maintains that I am what I am, like it or not, because of "a specific past that is present to some degree in my present.

I find myself part of a history and that is generally to say, whether I like it or not, whether I recognize it or not, one of the bearers of a tradition."[15] Our ethical practices always have histories, are always part of a tradition. Indeed, the modern emphasis on the individual has mislead us into thinking that we are independent and self-sufficient moral agents, whereas the truth is that we are "never able to seek the good or exercise the virtues only *qua* individual. . . . [W]e all approach our own circumstances as bearers of a particular social identity."[16] MacIntyre's solution is to return to the *virtues*, and to once more establish what it is that it means to be a virtuous human being, within a tradition, from this place and this time in this specific window of history. Aristotle, the early advocate and systematizer of an ethics of virtue, figures large in his account. For our purposes, it is enough to glean from MacIntyre's approach that he is rejecting an understanding of ethics that emphasizes the individual in glorious isolation, using reason alone to carve out the details of moral and valuational significance, as though culturally orphaned in aid of some misguided sense of objectivity. We are inescapably caught up in a tradition, in a history of ethical practice, and whatever refinements we wish to bring to the acts and arts of living must be understood against the richness of traditional history. I have tried to understand Japanese ethics against such a weaving of the intricacies of Japanese cultural history, but what is added here is that by revisiting our own cultural traditions in the West, we might well recover a collection of perspectives which are significantly closer to the Japanese approach than our own contemporary isolated and rationally objectivistic approach to the ethics of the individual. If nothing else, we would quickly discern that the virtues tradition in the West, and the traditions of Japan, all tend to emphasize the transformation and striving towards excellence of the person, rather than the ethical standing of actions themselves. Ethics concerns the good man or woman, not the right or wrong action alone. Danto is correct in saying that the ethics of the East for the most part rest on metaphysical positions that are markedly unlike those of the West. At the same time, to conclude that we have nothing to learn because of this difference simply does not follow. The stakes are raised, of course, for not only must we understand the ethics of the East, but their various metaphysical horizons of understanding as well. As a comparativist, it is difficult not to simply blurt out, "well, it's about time!" Perspectives which are seriously held and radically unlike our own are almost always significant challenges to our most basic assumptions and basic ways of looking at the world. If nothing else, such challenges force us to reconsider our least analyzed and most habitual axioms of understanding.

ECOLOGICAL ETHICS, EAST AND WEST

The Norwegian philosopher and ecologist Arne Naess has taken a position which displays great affinity to Buddhist ethics. For example, he says that he is "not much interested in ethics or morals. I'm interested in how we experience the world. . . . Ethics follows from how we experience the world. If you experience the world so and so then you don't kill. If you articulate your experience then it can be a philosophy or religion."[17] Naess, like many others in the school of Transpersonal or Deep Ecology, have been influenced by the psychologist Abraham Maslow, who emphasized the transformation of personality. One of the founders of the humanistic psychology movement, Maslow came to think that humanistic psychology was too narrow, atomistic, and particle-like in its sense of self. There were experiences that went beyond this, that transcended the narrow confines of the ordinary sense of self. Transcenders identify their own good with the good of the community of living things, existing things, and with the cosmos as a whole. Their sense of self is expansive, rather than narrow and egoic. This Maslow called a fourth psychology; transpersonal, transhuman, and centered in the cosmos rather than based on human needs and interest, and going beyond the now more limiting notion of self-actualization. Warwick Fox refers to this wider sense of self as a "field-like conception," wherein self-interest and other-interest or even cosmic-interest coincide. Fox elaborates with considerable impact:

> It is important to note that even if the moral demands of the normative-judgmental self are of the (unusual) kind that one *ought* to abandon exclusive identification with a narrow, atomistic, or particle-like sense of self and develop a wide, expansive, or field-like sense of self, the self that is being addressed the self that "ought" to do this—is still this particular self as distinct from other particular selves. Moral demands, in other words, *proceed* from the assumption of a narrow conception of self even when the *end* they aim for is the realization of an expansive sense of self. There is no way around this; it is inherent in the nature of moral demands. Moral demands necessarily emphasize a self that is capable of choice, a self that is a center of volitional activity, yet our sense of self can be far more expansive than that of being a center of volitional activity. For example, I can experience my volitional self as part of a larger sense of self that includes aspects of my own mind and body over which I do not experience myself as having particularly

much control (and toward which it therefore makes no sense to issue *moral* demands). In turn, I can also experience this larger, but still entirely personal, sense of self as part of a still more expansive, transpersonal sense of self that includes my family and friends, other animals, physical objects, the region in which I live, and so on. When this happens, I experience physical or symbolic violations of the integrity of these entities as violations of my self, and I am moved to defend these entities accordingly. However, to attempt to instill the realization of an expansive, transpersonal sense of self through moral demands is counter-productive since moral demands are directed to and thereby reinforce the primary reality of the narrow, atomistic, or particle-like volitional self.[18]

The expanded sense of self does not stem from moral activity, but moral activity arises from an expanded sense of self. Even the stringently and aggressively willful self that Danto recommends leads to a strengthening of the atomistic or particle-like self. It is not a matter of steadfast willing, but of the spontaneous moral unfolding of the caring, expanded, transpersonal self. Naess explains this well:

> Care flows naturally if the "self" is widened and deepened so that protection of free Nature is felt and conceived as protection of ourselves. . . . Just as we need not morals to make us breathe . . . [so] if your "self" in the wide sense embraces another being, you need no moral exhortation to show care. . . . You care for yourself without feeling any moral pressure to do it—provided you have not succumbed to a neurosis of some kind, developing self-destructive tendencies, or hating yourself.[19]

Fox points out that Naess's argument makes morality superfluous, and is in line with similar conclusions drawn by many whom we would classify as religious or spiritual in stance. To fix his point, he quotes Walt Anderson, from his book *Open Secrets: A Western Guide to Tibetan Buddhism*, where the distinction is made between exoteric religious traditions—i.e., those concerned with outer forms such as creeds, moral codes, etc.—and the esoteric traditions where personal growth and transformation are stressed. Anderson writes:

> In the esoteric traditions, codes of morality are less important [than in the exoteric traditions] for the simple reason that the ultimate purpose of the spiritual effort is to attain a level of

> personal development at which morality is natural. It is discovered within oneself, and external authority is no longer necessary or meaningful. This principle is not foreign to Western psychology. . . . The same point is made by Abraham Maslow in his studies of healthy, "self-actualizing" people, who, he says, have relatively little respect for the formal rules and regulations of the society but at the same time a strong sense of concern for others.[20]

The expanded self identifies with the greater whole, seeks to preserve it, cherishes it, is emotionally enraptured by it, and cares about its well-being. This caring, preserving sentiment naturally and spontaneously expresses itself in action—action-intuition—and so serves as the ground or foundation for all moral codification. It is akin to Nishida's pure experience which serves as the foundation for all distinctions which subsequently come to be made, including moral distinctions. Morality arises out of pure experience, out of that "grasp of life" which is always already there, prior to all moral calculation and prescription, but which moral calculation and prescription tries to pin down and communicate after the fact. At the level of pure experience, morality is natural, spontaneous, and that towards which one is always already inclined. Kant taught that we must not use our inclinations as a guide to moral action, and for ordinary consciousness he was correct. But those who are transpersonal, or are enlightened, moral prescription is always already internalized, a spontaneous expression of the field-like self, the *basho* beneath or behind the egoic self. At this level all that exists is worthwhile for its own sake (Naess's rendering of "intrinsic value"), and the Zen Buddhist self that is not a self, or Naess's transpersonal self, is now identified with the cosmic whole. The divine has become us, and we have become divine. The many is one, and the one is many. *Samsara* is *nirvāna,* and *nirvāna* is *samsara.*

It may be too much to render ecological consciousness as being the same as enlightened consciousness, but the affinities are clear. And the point of pointing out these similarities is to reinforce once more the insight that there is nothing in one cultural tradition that is not likely to be present in another, except that in the one it is the majoritarian position, and in the other the minoritarian position. The West has its footholds onto Eastern thought, and it is these footholds that make it possible for us to learn from the East, while at the same time modifying the traditions from the East in the light of our own achievements and cultural perspectives. If the West can bring itself to learn from the East, and the East from the West, then perhaps the globalism which Nishida strove so hard to communicate will become possible for the first time. Nishida wrote that "Japan is in the world, and therefore reverence for our particularity alone, for things Japanese, is not enough. True culture does not lie there. . . . Japanese culture must acquire a global character."[21] One can almost sense the fusion of horizons that occurred within the fertile mind of Nishida, who relentlessly sought some bridge between Eastern and Western cultures, some philosophic vantage point which would allow genuine dialogue across what was—and still is—perceived as a great divide: "I resonate with the depth and dignity of Eastern culture, but I cannot bring myself to forego my fondness for the wealth of Western culture that has meant such a great development of free humanness." Furthermore, "It is not a question of Eastern culture negating Western culture or vice-versa, nor of subsuming one into the other. It is a probing deeper than we have gone so far until both are bathed in a new light."[22] What he sought was a new theory, established on a deeper foundation than had heretofore been available, which would create a space within which East and West could come to understand and appreciate each other's perspective on the world. This seeking took the form of a struggle, and this struggle was both relentless and lifelong. Its essence is recorded by one of Nishida's successors at the University of Kyoto, Ueda Shizuteru:

> As is well known, for a period of nearly ten years, beginning in his twenties, Nishida gave himself heart and soul to the practice of Zen Meditation. At the time, as his diaries and letters attest, he was also devouring the classics of Western philosophy, from the ancient Greeks up to contemporary authors. In his own person the global world had become a reality and a painful split: on the one hand, a philosophy that originated in the West as a science of reflection, and even a high-flown reflection on reflection; on the other, the Eastern praxis of Zen, which implied an overcoming of reflection, a knowing of "non-knowing." The split was too deep and too broad to think of subsuming one into the other. But neither would Nishida forsake one for the other. Only the awareness that this was the world in which he had been "located" enabled him to accept the world split in his very person as a task to be overcome. It was as if he had given himself over to two worlds whose otherness split him down the middle but whose unity was already in the making. The split was itself his gateway to the "deeper foundations" of unity. Unlike *nihonjinron* theories of Japanese uniqueness, or even of comparative culture and thought, being bandied about

at the time, Nishida's intellectual efforts were rooted in his own self, and it was out of this self that all his philosophical work sprung.[23]

Whatever contradiction Nishida saw between East and West, he came to accommodate these as he did all other fundamental yet partially revealing and concealing contradictions; he included them both in an identity of self-contradiction. The self-contradictions are evident, and are the cause of whatever misunderstanding and lack of comprehension exists: but there is a deeper unity at their foundation, and this deeper foundation will form the basis for a new world culture of identity-with-diversity. Nishida wrote:

> [Eastern culture and Western culture] are divided, but in their foundation they are joined together and complement each other. Without discovering that deeper foundation, a world culture in which cultures East and West can unite is unthinkable.[24]

The foundation, as Nishida saw it, was pure experience, that rich manifold of experience out of which all distinctions are carved, all differences created, and all moral codes constructed. While there will be fusions of horizons, as culture encounters culture, the result will not be a homogeneous porridge in which all differences are lost, but, rather, a diversity of perspectives with common purposes, a common desire to understand and to preserve one another's achievements, and a common desire to know more, to live better, and to act with sincerity and integrity. What Nishida sought was a genuine mutuality, where each affects each, and yet the result is a strengthening of difference, not an elimination of it. The cultural gene pool must remain strong, robust, and rich enough to propel us into the next decades with vigor, creativity, a sense of common purpose, and a variety of perspectives on the problems and issues of our time. Ethics is but a formalized expression of such goodwill, such caring, and such preserving. Nishida and Heidegger would likely agree that such engagement would be among the highest and best senses of dwelling in the world.

Notes

FOREWORD

    1. The word translated here as "noble" is *kunshi* (君子; Chin., *jūnzǐ*) which is sometimes translated as "prince." "gentleman," or "morally superior person." In the Confucian scheme of personal development, *kunshi* is next to the ideal achievement of sagehood. Here it is translated as "noble man" in consideration of the context in which it appears. —TRANS.

    2. For example, in medieval Germany, the Catholic Church prohibited planting trees around individual churches for fear of attracting tree spirits.

    3. *Riki* philosophy (理気哲学; Chin., *lǐqì*) attempted to structure the cosmos in terms of two principles of *ri* (Chin., *lǐ*) and *ki.* (*qì*). *Ri* has an etymological origin in the experience of discerning a pattern in a stone or a grain of a wood. With this meaning as an experiential background it has come to mean an intelligible patternment of the cosmos, and as such it designates the transcendental, metaphysical order. On the other hand, *ki* originally refers to a steam arising from cooked rice, and has come to mean a psychophysical activity of the phenomenal order. Changes and transformations we observe in nature including the human being are understood in terms of *ki*–energy. Because it employs these two principles, this school of philosophy is sometimes referred to as embracing *riki* dualism. —TRANS.

    4. Jetavana was a monastery where the historical Buddha, along with his disciple Sudatta, preached his teaching. —TRANS.

    5. It literally means questions and answers. —TRANS.

    6. Take the example of Descartes's *ego-cogito*. When he formulated his position as *cogito ergo sum,* he must have assumed a reader in order for this statement to be meaningful. That is to say, only in the context in which a writer-reader relationship is assumed, can Descartes' assertion be meaningful. Otherwise,

Descartes' statement falls into solipsism. If, on the other hand, solipsism is upheld to be true, the death of an individual who upholds it cancels its truth. — TRANS.

7. In May of 1969, Mishima Yukio went to Tōkyō University to dialogue with members of Tōkyō University's "All Students Joint Struggle Committee" (*Zen kyō tō*), in the midst of the turmoil of the so-called "Campus Disputes" (*Gakuen Funsō*). The dialogue happened to be recorded on film.

INTRODUCTION: CONTRASTS AND IDEALS

1. Charles A. Moore, "Editor's Supplement: The Enigmatic Japanese Mind," in *The Japanese Mind: Essentials of Japanese Philosophy and Culture*, ed. Charles A. Moore (Honolulu: East-West Center Press, University of Hawaii, 1967), p. 296. Moore's full observation is worth repeating: "In comparison with other cultures, the aesthetic has been considered to be the essentially unique expression of spirituality in Japan, as is ethics in China, religion in India, and, possibly, reason in the West."

2. Sallie B. King, "Egalitarian Philosophies in Sexist Institutions: The Life of Satomi-san, Shinto Miko and Zen Buddhist Nun," *Journal of Feminist Studies in Religion*, 4 (Spring 1988): 8.

3. Ibid.

4. Ezra F. Vogel, *Japan as Number One: Lessons for America* (Cambridge, Mass.: Harvard University Press, 1979).

5. King, "Egalitarian Philosophies," p. 26.

6. Roger S. Gottleib, *A Spirituality of Resistance: Finding a Peaceful Heart and Protecting the Earth* (New York: The Crossroad Publishing Company, 1999), p. 27. Gottlieb writes that to "comply with religious rules is not enough. The general idea is often expressed by the notion that God asks us to engage in 'Tikkun Olan,' the 'repair of the world.' The cosmos, on this view, is unfinished and imperfect. God left its defects for us to remedy. If we fail to do so, our spiritual destinies are incomplete."

7. Arthur C. Danto, *Mysticism and Morality: Oriental Thought and Moral Philosophy* (New York: Columbia University Press, 1987), pp. xvi–xvii.

8. J. Z. Young, *Doubt and Certainty in Science: A Biologist's Reflections on the Brain* (Oxford: Oxford University Press, Galaxy Books, 1960), p. 106.

CHAPTER 1. THE "DO NOTHING" AND THE PILGRIM: TWO APPROACHES TO ETHICS

1. Sallie McFague, *Models of God: Theology for an Ecological, Nuclear Age* (Philadelphia: Fortress Press, 1987), p. 5.

2. Arthur C. Danto, *Mysticism and Morality: Oriental Thought and Moral Philosophy* (New York: Harper & Row, Publishers, 1972), p. vii.

3. Ibid., p. xiii.

4. Ibid., p. 17.

5. Ibid., p. 106.

6. Abe Masao, "Kenotic God and Dynamic Śūnyatā," in *The Emptying God: A Buddhist-Jewish-Christian Conversation*, ed. John B. Cobb, Jr., and Christopher Ives (Maryknoll, New York: Orbis Books, *Faith Meets Faith Series*, 1990), pp. 55–56. Indeed, Nishitani Keiji (in *Religion and Nothingness* [Berkeley: University of California Press, 1982], p. 251) writes of the Buddhist standpoint of *Śūnatā* (or emptiness) as an "orientation directly opposed to that of will. . . . The standpoint of *Śūnatā* is constituted only at a bottomless point . . . beyond all standpoints of any kind related to the will, through . . . absolute negation.

7. Danto, *Mysticism*, p. 81.

8. Ibid., p. 82.

9. Abe Masao, "The Problem of Evil in Christianity and Buddhism," in *Buddhist-Christian Dialogue: Mutual Renewal and Transformation*, ed. Paul O. Ingram and Frederick J. Streng (Honolulu: University of Hawaii Press, 1986), p. 145.

10. Ibid., p. 146.

11. Abe Masao, "Will, Sunyata, and History," in *The Religious Philosophy of Nishitani Keiji: Encounter with Emptiness,* ed. Taitetsu Unno (Berkeley: Asian Humanities Press, 1986), p. 287.

12. Ibid., p. 301.

13. Ibid., pp. 286–87.

14. Thomas Kasulis, *Zen Action/Zen Person* (Honolulu: The University Press of Hawaii, 1981), pp. 74–76.

15. Abe, "The Problem of Evil," p. 146.

16. Ibid., p. 154.

17. D. T. Suzuki, "Lectures on Zen Buddhism," in *Zen Buddhism and Psychoanalysis,* ed. D. T. Suzuki, Erich Fromm, and Richard De Martino (New York: Grove Press, Inc., 1960), p. 51.

18. Danto, *Mysticism*, p. 115.

19. Ibid., p. 118.

20. Ibid., pp. 118–19:

. . . I believe that generally the mechanism of the will is considered the enemy of ultimate happiness throughout the East. 'It might be better to flow away monotonously, like the river,' one of Charles Dickens' characters muses, 'and to compound for its insensibility to happiness with its insensibility to pain.' The sages would concur with this, except with regard to happiness, perhaps: they would urge that the happinesses Clenham has in mind are inextricably bound up with pains, and that there is an even and unbroken happiness of another order to be found by just this monotonous flowing away, of being at one with the stream.

21. Ibid., p. 119.

22. Ibid., p. 108.

23. Max Kaltenmark, *Lao Tzu and Taoism* (Stanford: Stanford University Press, 1969), p. 53.

24. Holmes Welch, *Taoism: The Parting of the Way* (Boston: Beacon Press, 1957), p. 20.

25. Ibid., p. 23.

26. Ibid., p. 33.

27. Kasulis, *Zen Action*, pp. 98–99.

28. David Loy, *Nonduality: A Study in Comparative Philosophy* (New Haven: Yale University Press, 1988), p. 297.

29. Ibid., pp. 130–31.

30. D. T. Suzuki, *Outlines of Mahāyāna Buddhism* (New York: Schocken Books, 1963), p. 54.

31. Ibid., pp. 53–54.

32. Ibid., p. 54.

33. Ibid., p. 47.

34. Loy, *Nonduality*, p. 284.

35. Abe Masao, "Religious Tolerance and Human Rights: A Buddhist Perspective," in *Religious Liberty and Human Rights in Nations and in Religions*, ed. Leonard Swidler (Philadelphia: Ecumenical Press, 1986), p. 204.

36. Danto, *Mysticism*, p. 108.

37. Benjamin I. Schwartz, *The World of Thought in Ancient China* (Cambridge: Harvard University Press, 1985), p. 207.

38. Loy, *Nonduality*, p. 106.

39. Toshihiko Izusu, *Sufism and Taoism: A Comparative Study of Key Philosophical Concepts* (Berkeley: University of California Press, 1983), p. 310.

40. Francis H. Cook, "The Jewel Net of Indra," in *Nature in Asian Traditions of Thought: Essays in Environmental Philosophy,* ed. J. Baird Callicott and Roger T. Ames (Albany: State University of New York Press, 1989), p. 213.

41. Ibid., p. 214.

42. Nakamura Hajime, "Interrelational Existence," *Philosophy East and West* 17, nos. 1–4 (1967): 112.

43. Loy, *Nonduality,* p. 298.

44. Ibid.

45. Robert E. Carter, *The Nothingness Beyond God: An Introduction to the Philosophy of Nishida Kitarō,* 1st edition, (New York: Paragon House, 1989), p. 104.

46. Nakamura Hajime, "The Basic Teachings of Buddhism," in *Buddhism in the Modern World,* ed. Heinrich Dumoulin and John C. Maraldo (New York: Collier Books, 1976), p. 29.

47. Ibid.

48. Nell Noddings, *Caring: A Feminine Approach to Ethics and Moral Education* (Berkeley: University of California Press, 1984), pp. 134, 194.

49. Danto, *Mysticism,* p. 115.

CHAPTER 2. THE SIGNIFICANCE OF SHINTŌISM FOR JAPANESE ETHICS

1. Robert J. J. Wargo, "Japanese Ethics: Beyond Good and Evil," *Intersect* 8, no. 8 (August 1992): 13.

2. Mark Teeuwen, "Western Understanding and Misunderstanding of Shintō—Progress of Studies on Shintō in the West and Some Remarks," in *International Symposium Commemorating the Founding of the International Shintō Foundation: Shintō—Its Universality* (Tokyo: International Shintō Foundation, July 1996), p. 79. Kuroda Toshio's essay, "Shintō in the History of Japanese Religion" tr. J. C. Dobbins and S. Gay, appeared in *The Journal of Japanese Studies,* 7, no. 1 (Winter 1981).

3. Ibid., p. 81.

4. Robert J. J. Wargo, "Japanese Ethics: Beyond Good and Evil," *Philosophy East and West* 40, no. 4 (October 1990): 499–500.

5. Jean Herbert, *Shintō: At the Fountain-head of Japan* (London: George Allen & Unwin Ltd., 1967), p. 59.

6. Wargo, *Intersect,* p. 14.

7. Stuart D. B. Picken, *Essentials of Shintō: An Analytical Guide to Principal Teachings* (Westport, Conn.: Greenwood Press, 1994), p. xxvi.

8. Ibid., p. xxvii. Picken writes,

> . . . Japanese religion exists much more at the subconscious level than does Western religion. The religious traditions of Japan, particularly Shintō, remain alive in habits of thought and behavior rather than in a formal way. People visit shrines at times like New Year and on special occasions within the cycle of life's events. There is less general discussion of religious ideas and a minimal history of religious controversy as compared to the West.

9. Ibid., p. xxviii.

10. Carmen Blacker, "Shintō and the Sacred Dimension of Nature," in *International Symposium: Shintō and Japanese Culture* (Tokyo: International Shintō Foundation June 1995), p. 2:

> State Shintō was a recent aberration of the beliefs that had peaceably existed in Japan for centuries, and animated Japanese culture, literature and folklore in a unique and natural manner. Its story rams home to us the salutary lesson of the terrifying way in which the powerful symbols of myth and religion can be manipulated, and how from the most unlikely beginnings they can be used, not only to weld together a new nation state, but also to create one in which a totalitarian fanaticism utterly alien to the real tradition of the culture can drive that nation to disaster.

11. Wargo, *Intersect*, p. 14. The reference to Confucianism and China is confirmed by Fung Yu-lan's *A Short History of Chinese Philosophy*, ed. Derke Bodde (New York: The Free Press, a Division of Macmillan Publishing Co., Inc., 1948), p. 1:

> Sometimes when the children were just beginning to learn the characters, they were given a sort of textbook to read. This was known as the *Three Characters Classic*, and was so called because each sentence in the book consisted of three characters arranged so that when recited they produced a rhythmic effect, and thus helped the children to memorize them more easily. This book was in reality a primer, and the very first statement in it is that "the nature of man is originally good."

Stuart Picken *(Essentials of Shintō*, p. 344) makes a similar claim for Shintō: "It is assumed that man is a biological descendant of the kami and that therefore human beings naturally know good from evil."

12. J. W. T. Mason, *The Meaning of Shintō: The Primaeval Foundation of Creative Spirit in Modern Japan* (Port Washington, N.Y.: Kennikat Press, Inc., 1967), p. 120.

13. Wargo, *Philosophy East and West*, pp. 504–05.

14. Kakichi Kadowaki, S. J., "Shintō and Christianity: Dialogue for the Twenty-first Century," *International Philosophical Quarterly* 33, no. 1 (March 1993): 72.

15. Ibid., p. 85.

16. Mason, *The Meaning of Shintō*, p. 61.

17. Quoted in Herbert, *Shintō*, p. 21. From Fujisawa Chikao, *Some Parapsychological Aspects of Shintō* (mimeographed).

18. Wargo, *Intersect*, p. 14.

19. *Basic terms of Shintō*, compiled by the Jinja-honcho, the Kokugakuin University and the Institute for Japanese Culture and Classics (Tokyo: 1958). Quoted in Herbert, *Shintō*, p. 59.

20. Herbert, *Shintō*, p. 59.

21. Ibid., p. 60.

22. Ibid.

23. Ibid.

24. Bansan Kumazawa, *Banzan Zenshū* (Tokyo: 1940 [3 vols.]). Quoted in Herbert, *Shintō*, p. 25.

25. Ibid., p. 60.

26. Herbert, *Shintō*, p. 67.

27. Mason, *The Meaning of Shintō*, pp. 111–12.

28. Ibid., pp. 61–62.

29. Ibid., p. 116.

30. Ibid., p. 117.

31. Ian Reader, *The Simple Guide to Shintō* (Folkestone, Kent, England: Global Books Ltd., 1998), p. 29.

32. Herbert, *Shintō*, p. 32.

33. Ibid., p. 32.

34. Hirai Naofusa, "The Principles of Pure Shintō," in *Proceedings of the Ninth International Congress for the History of Religion* (Tokyo: Maruzen, 1960, 16 pp.). Quoted in Herbert, *Shintō*, p.22.

35. Herbert, *Shintō*, p. 70.

36. Ibid.

37. Picken, *Essentials*, p. xxxii.

38. Mason, *The Meaning of Shintō*, p. 78:

When the primaeval subconscious intuition exerts its influence on man, either self-consciously or in terms of unanalysed responses, then the results are Shintō. But when self-consciousness goes its own way, heedless of the intuition of subjective reality, then the consequences must be called "not Shintō," in the sense that they are not reconcilable with life's inner knowledge of itself.

39. Herbert, *Shintō*, p. 32.

40. Watsuji Tetsurō, *Watsuji Tetsurō's* Rinrigaku: *Japanese Ethics*, tr. Yamamoto Seisaku and Robert E. Carter (Albany: State University of New York Press, 1996):

". . . *makoto* implies . . . that one is pure and without falsehood in one's attitude of mind as well as in one's words and deeds" (p. 273). Watsuji also defines *makoto* as "the path of Heaven," "sincerity," and truthfulness. He writes, " . . . human beings are obliged to fulfil the task of bringing deceitfulness to nought and of making truthfulness manifest" (pp. 273–74). Truthfulness and deceit are both based on trust, in the sense that "To deceive another person is a betrayal of trust. It cannot occur at a place where there is no trust. Seen in this light, we can say that truthfulness is decided in and through the human relation that consists in a relationship of trust. To speak truth exactly expresses this relationship" (pp. 274–75). *Makoto*, then, is an interactive attitude of mutual trust among human beings, on which all other human relationships are based.

41. Sallie B. King, "Egalitarian Philosophies in Sexist Institutions," *Journal of Feminist Studies in Religion* 4 (Spring 1988): 15. King adds,

One who is *makoto* or sincere is true to her or his total life situation: one is true to oneself by knowing one's true nature which is in a condition of absolute spiritual purity and by expressing that spiritual purity in all of one's actions. One is true to the *kami,* similarly, by living in the condition of spiritual purity which is identical to theirs. One is true to one's neighbors by doing what is right for them, again on the basis of one's spiritual purity. The concept of *makoto* thus expresses a sense of a continuum of spiritual purity which embraces both the *kami* and human being. All beings—myself, other persons, and the *kami*—are harmonized at the level of spiritual purity. Moreover, the power of *makoto* to transform the self and the world is virtually unlimited.

42. Herbert, *Shintō*, p. 71.

43. Ibid., p. 72.

44. Ibid., p. 73.

45. Ibid., p. 74.

46. Ibid., p. 76. Herbert's reference is to Hori Hidenari, *Shin-mei-kō* (*research into the names of kami*) (Tokyo: 1909), pp. 99ff., but since the statement is attributed to Nitobe, it is either an oral recollection, or it is from Nitobe Inazō's *Bushido: The Moral Ideals of Japan* (London: Heinemann, 1904).

47. Yanairu Tetsuo, "Special Characteristics of the Japanese *kami*—A Symbol for the Future," in *Shape of Religion in the Twenty-First Century—In Search of World Co-existence*. The Third International Symposium of the International Shintō Foundation (Tokyo: International Shintō Foundation, October 1997), p. 71.

48. Fujisawa Chikao, *Some Parapsychological Aspects of Shintō* (mimeographed). Quoted in Herbert, *Shintō*, p. 21.

49. Mason, *The Meaning of Shintō*, pp. 95–96.

50. Ibid., p. 104.

51. Herbert, *Shintō*, p. 75. Herbert observes that there is in Shintō a sense of duty "which I have never come across in any other religion, that of a duty to generations yet unborn." The Native American aboriginal peoples do have such a sense of duty, often expressed as an ethical imperative to imagine the consequences of a proposed action to seven generations into the future. Perhaps it is to be found elsewhere, as well.

52. Mason, *The Meaning of Shintō*, pp. 128–32.

53. Ibid., p. 130.

54. Ibid., p. 131.

55. Ibid., p. 132.

56. Nakamura Hajime, *Ways of Thinking of Eastern Peoples: India-China-Tibet-Japan*, tr. Philip Wiener (Honolulu: East-West Center Press, 1964), p. 351.

57. Ibid., p. 371.

58. Mason, *The Meaning of Shintō*, pp. 206–07.

59. Ibid., p. 213.

60. Sallie McFague has contributed three books to this discussion. In *Metaphorical Theology: Models of God in Religious Language* (Philadelphia: Fortress Press, 1982), she sets out the theoretical background for using such metaphors. In *Models of God: Theology for an Ecological, Nuclear Age* (Philadelphia: Fortress Press, 1987), she provides a detailed analysis and justification for the use of three new metaphors—or models as sustained metaphors—of God. In *The Body of God: An Ecological Theology* (Minneapolis: Fortress Press, 1993), she focuses directly upon the metaphor of the world as God's body in considerably more detail. Her most recent work, *Super, Natural Christians: How We Should Love Nature* (Minneapolis: Fortress Press, 1997), develops the theme of ecological concern as spirituality yet further.

61. McFague, *Metaphorical Theology*, p. 192: "God cannot be imagined in any one model, for the whole cosmos is God's 'body.'"

62. Mason, *The Meaning of Shintō*, p. 205.

63. David Edward Shaner, "The Japanese Experience of Nature," in *Nature in Asian Traditions of Thought,* ed. J. Baird Callicott and Roger T. Ames (Albany: State University of New York Press, 1989), p. 165. The phrase "seamless web of divine presence" is from Joseph M. Kitagawa, *Religion in Japanese History* (New York: Columbia University Press, 1966).

64. Nakamura, *Ways of Thinking*, pp. 350–72.

65. Picken, *Essentials*, p. xxxii.

66. Ibid., p. 346.

67. Mason, *The Meaning of Shintō*, p. 207.

68. Ibid., p. 208.

69. Shaner, "The Japanese Experience of Nature," p. 166. Shaner adds that "the land that would be considered optimal scenic real estate in most cites world-wide is preserved in a natural setting despite overcrowding and housing shortages. The needs of Japan's industrial complex have thus faced a head-on collision with the more ancient religio-aesthetic ideal centered in ecocentrism and personal 'nature' cultivation."

70. Blacker, "Shintō and the Sacred," p. 15.

71. Picken, *Essentials*, p. xxiv.

72. Blacker, "Shintō and the Sacred," p. 1.

73. Ono, Sokyo, *Shintō: The Kami Way* (Rutland & Tokyo: Charles E. Tuttle Company, 1962), p. 7.

74. Mason, *The Meaning of Shintō*, p. 210.

75. Ibid., p. 212.

76. Ibid., p. 214.

77. Ibid., pp. 215–16. "Kami Man not Two," writes Mason, "was written for the author by Rev. Ikashemaro Uda, Chief Executive and Assistant Chief Priest of the Grand Shrine of Ise."

78. Ibid., p. 219.

79. D. T. Suzuki, *Zen and Japanese Culture* (Princeton: Princeton University Press, Bollingen Series LXIV, 1973), p. 345.

80. Ibid., p. 346.

81. Ibid., p. 363.

82. Nakamura, *Ways of Thinking*, p. 350. The quotation is from *Fūkyō Hyakushu Kōsetsu* (Lecture on the "Wild Winds Eight-Hundred Fold"), in Katō Genchi, *Shintō no Shūkyō Hattatsushiteki Kenkyū (A Study in the Religious Development of Shintōism)*, p. 935.

CHAPTER 3. CONFUCIANISM AND JAPANESE ETHICS

1. Tu Wei-Ming, *Confucian Thought: Selfhood as Creative Transformation* (Albany: State University of New York Press, 1985), p. 8.

2. Ibid., p. 9. The quotation appears in the same book, p. 39.

3. Ibid., p. 8.

4. Ibid., p. 20.

5. Tu Wei-Ming, *Centrality and Commonality: An Essay on Confucian Religiousness; A Revised and Enlarged Edition of Centrality and Commonality—An Essay on Chung-yung* (Albany: State University of New York Press, 1989), p. 68. Tu adds that "Morality is not only means of preserving the community; it is also the very reason why the community is worth being organized in the first place" (p. 68). Human relationships are both central and foundational for Confucianism: "If the profound person seeks to manifest the ultimate meaning of ordinary human existence, he cannot afford to slight interpersonal relationships. To say that the way of the profound person has its simple beginnings in the lives of ordinary men and women implies that human-relatedness is, in fact, its point of departure" (p. 39).

6. Ibid.

7. Ibid., p. 83.

8. Ibid., pp. 9–10. Tu adds that, "In an ultimate sense, human beings, in order to manifest their humanity, must themselves fully participate in the creative process of the Cosmos."

9. Ibid., p. 53. Tu writes that the claim that a ruler who can administer his state with rites will have no further difficulties,

> is predicated on the assumption that only he who has fully harmonized his human relationships is capable of administering his state with rites. Since the harmonization of human relationships requires and entails a process of self-transformation, the proper administration of the state with rites further demands the rectification of the ruler's personal character (p. 53).

Therefore, a person of ritualistic precision will be effective if, and only if, he or she is already a person of true virtue, i.e., has already undergone the self-transformation necessary to become a sage, a person who is human hearted.

10. Donald J. Munro, *The Concept of Man in Early China* (Stanford, Calif.: Stanford University Press, 1969).

11. Wing-Tsit Chan, *A Source Book in Chinese Philosophy* (Princeton: Princeton University Press, 1963), pp. 65–66. Taken from *The Book of Mencius.*

12. Tu Wei-Ming, *Centrality and Commonality*, p. 86.

13. *Chung-yung* (*Doctrine of the Mean*), XX:8, in *The Confucian Classics*, tr. James Legge, 2nd ed., rev. (Oxford: Clarendon Press, 1893), vol. 1, p. 406.

14. Tu, *Centrality and Commonality*, p. 48.

15. Quoted in Tu, *Centrality and Commonality*, p. 71. The quotation is from *Chung-yung* (*The Doctrine of the Mean*), one of the Confucian "classics." XX: 18.

16. Ibid., p. 73. The reference is to *The Book of Mencius*, VIIA: 4, and is a modification of the D. C. Lau translation (D. C. Lau [tr.], *Mencius* [London: Penguin Classics, 1970], p. 182). Tu's translation of the passage reads: "There is no greater joy for me than to find, on self examination, that I am *true* to myself. Try your best to treat others as you would wish to be treated yourself, and you will find that this is the shortest way to humanity."

17. Tu, *Centrality and Commonality*, pp. 76–77.

18. Ibid., p. 79.

19. Ibid., p. 83.

20. Paul Reasoner, "Sincerity and Japanese Values," *Philosophy East and West*, 40, no. 4 (October, 1990): 476.

21. Ibid., p. 477.

22. Ibid., p. 477. From *The Doctrine of the Mean (Chung-yung)*, Wing-tsit Chan, *Source Book in Chinese Philosophy*, 1963), p. 108.

23. Ibid., p. 485.

24. David L. Hall and Roger T. Ames, *Thinking from the Han: Self, Truth, and Transcendence in Chinese and Western Culture* (Albany: State University of New York Press, 1998), pp. 42, 25.

25. Ibid., p. 26.

26. Ibid.

27. Ibid., p. 28.

28. Ibid., p. 32.

29. Aristotle, *Nichomachean Ethics*, 1109a 25–30; McKeon translation (Richard McKeon, *Introduction to Aristotle* [New York: The Modern Library, 1947]), p. 346.

30. Hall and Ames, *Thinking*, p. 38.

31. Ibid.

32. Ninomiya Genpei, "Ethical Backgrounds in Japan and Their Bearing upon the Rise of Social Consciousness of Japan," M.A. thesis, University of Chicago, 1927, p. 56.

33. Nakamura Hajime, *Ways of Thinking of Eastern Peoples: India-China-Tibet-Japan* (Honolulu: East-West Center Press, 1964), p. 401.

34. Warren W. Smith, Jr., *Confucianism in Modern Japan: A Study of Conservatism in Japanese Intellectual History*, 2nd ed. (Tokyo: The Hokuseido Press, 1973), pp. 8, 7, 9.

35. Ibid., p. 9.

36. Emperor Go-Kōmyō (1644–1654) commanded that the Sung Neo-Confucianism of Chu Hsi replace all other Confucian teachings, and forbad the use of Han and T'ang commentaries on the Confucian Classics.

37. Smith, *Confucianism in Modern Japan*, p. 11.

38. Ibid., pp. 15–16, from Simmons and Wigmore, "Land Tenure and Local Institutions," *Transactions of the Asiatic Society of Japan*, 1st series, XIX, pt. 1 (1891), p. 188.

39. Ibid., p. 158, from Ōkawa Shūmei, *Shintei Nippon nissen roppyakunen shi (The Two Thousand Six Hundred Year History of Japan)*, 21st ed., newly rev., (Tōkyō: Daiichi Shobō, 1940), pp. 22–23.

40. Ibid., p. 160.

41. Ibid., p. 161.

42. Ibid., pp. 160–61. Taken from Robert King Hall, *Shūshin: The Ethics of a Defeated Nation* (New York: Columbia University, 1949), p. 231.

43. Ibid., pp. 162–63. Various sources.

CHAPTER 4. BUDDHISM AND JAPANESE ETHICS

1. Thomas P. Kasulis, "Does East Asian Buddhism Have an Ethical System?" *Zen Buddhism Today* 8 (Annual Report of the Kyoto Zen Symposium) (October 1990): 48.

2. Gunapala Dharmasiri, *Fundamentals of Buddhist Ethics* (Antioch, Calif.: Golden Leaves Publishing Co., 1989), p. 8.

3. Ibid., p. 9.

4. Ibid.

5. Walpola Sri Rahula, *What the Buddha Taught*, rev. ed. (New York: Grove Weidenfeld, 1974), p. 17.

6. Dharmasiri, *Fundamentals*, pp. 8–9.

7. Ibid., p. 1 (italics mine).

8. Ibid., p. 14.

9. Damien Keown, *The Nature of Buddhist Ethics* (New York: St. Martin's Press, 1992), p. 19.

10. Ibid., p. 25.

11. Ibid., p. 26.

12. Ibid., p. 30.

13. Ibid., p. 43.

14. Ibid., p. 47.

15. Ibid., p. 48.

16. Ibid., p. 55.

17. The Confucian *jen* is an emphasis on feeling, on the "heart," rather than on reason alone. It is a rational passion, or a passionate reason. The Taoist *tz'u* is a mystical identification with the Tao as the source of all that is. It is a non-dualistic realization of the identity of all things. Tao, and everything else is kin. The Buddhist *karuna* is a compassionate embracing of, and an identification with all beings. U Thittila ("The Fundamental Principles of Theravāda Buddhism," in *The Path of the Buddha: Buddhism Interpreted by Buddhists*, edited by Kenneth W. Morgan [New York: The Ronald Press Company, 1956], pp. 94–95), argues that the Pali *mettā* is the more suitable Buddhist concept to describe what I am attempting to identify. *Mettā* is universal love, is more than mere good will in that it demands follow-through and action. He calls it an "active benevolence." And like the Taoist *tz'u*, "it attempts to break through all barriers separating one from another. . . . the true Buddhist exercises *metta*, universal love, toward every living being and identifies himself with all, making no distinction whatsoever with regard to caste, color, class, or sex."

18. Lawrence Kohlberg, *The Philosophy of Moral Development*, vol. 1 of *Essays on Moral Development* (San Francisco: Harper & Row, Publishers, 1981). Kohlberg cites H. Hartshorne and M. A. May, *Studies in the Nature of Character* (New York: Macmillan, 1928–30), remarking that

Hartshorne and May were dismayed to discover that they could locate no such stable personality trait as honesty in schoolchildren. A child who cheated on one occasion might or might not cheat on another: cheating was for the most part situationally determined. In a factor analysis, there was no clearly identifiable factor or correlation pattern that could be called honesty. Furthermore, 'honesty' measurements did not predict the later behavior. This contradicts the commonsense notion underlying the bag of virtues approach. It turns out that dictionary terms

for personality do not describe situationally general personality dispositions that are stable or predictive over development. (p. 79)

One person's definition of honesty may not be another's, and in any case,
not cheating or not stealing may be a contextually defined activity, rather than
principled behavior. Unless one understands that honesty is a principle which
extends to all behaviour, or has otherwise eliminated the desire for or causes of
dishonesty, there is simply no assurance that dishonesty will not break out once
more given different circumstances.

19. Rahula, *What the Buddha Taught*, p. 47.

20. Ibid., p. 48.

21. Keown, *The Nature of Buddhist Ethics*, p. 58.

22. Ibid., p. 59.

23. Ibid.

24. Ibid., p. 61.

25. Ibid. From *Encyclopedia of Buddhism*, "*Citta*," 169, 172.

26. Ibid., p. 62.

27. Ibid., pp. 62–63.

28. Ibid., p. 64.

29. Ibid., p. 66.

30. Dharmasiri, *Fundamentals*, p. 15.

31. Ibid.

32. Harvey B. Aronson, *Love and Sympathy in Theravāda Buddhism* (Delhi:
Motilal Banarsidas Publishers Private Limited, 1996), p. 3.

33. Dharmasiri, *Fundamentals*, p. 20.

34. Ibid., p. 21.

35. Ibid., p. 22.

36. Ibid., p. 114.

37. Keown, *The Nature of Buddhist Ethics*, p. 91; from Rhys Davies, *Pali Text
Society Dictionary*, entry entitled "*Nibbana.*"

38. Ibid., p. 92.

39. Ibid. The original reference to the "raft" is at *Majjhima Nikaya* vol. 1, p.
134 (Horner translation, Middle Length Sayings, vol. 1, p. 137) and repeated in
the *Vajracchedika- prajnaparamita* (*Diamond Sutra*), Conze edition, p. 32; Conze's
own translation in the same work, p. 61.

40. Ibid., p. 93. Keown refers to the 1986 *Buddhist Research Society* (Singapore) edition of Dharmasiri's *Fundamentals of Buddhist Ethics*, p. 186. On page 30 of the 1989 edition, which I have been using, Dharmasiri writes, "A realized person is said to have gone beyond morality."

41. Ibid., pp. 94–95. The "Ten Good Paths of Action include seven abstentions: from (1) taking life, (2) taking what has not been given, (3) sexual misconduct, (4) lying, (5) slanderous speech, (6) harsh speech, and (7) idle talk. The remaining three are (8) non-covetousness, (9) non- malevolence, and (10) right views.

42. Ibid., pp. 95, 103.

43. Ibid., p. 103. Referring to Buddhagosa, *Majjhima-Nikaya-Atthakatha* (ii. 307f).

44. Ibid., p. 55.

45. Ibid., p. 112.

46. Ibid., p. 113.

47. Ibid., pp. 221, 222.

48. Dharmasiri, *Fundamentals*, pp. 114, 115.

49. Ibid., p. 115.

50. Cited in Dharmasiri, *Fundamentals*, p. 119. From Nāgārjuna, *Mūla Mādhyamika Kārika*, chap. 25, 19.

51. Christine Feldman, "Nurturing Compassion," in *The Path of Compassion: Writings on Socially Engaged Buddhism,* ed. Fred Eppsteiner (Berkeley: A Buddhist Peace Fellowship Book, Parallax Press, 1988), p. 19.

52. Rahula, *What the Buddha Taught*, p. 46.

53. Dharmasiri, *Fundamentals*, p. 92.

54. Aronson, *Love and Sympathy*, p. 2.

55. Dharmasiri, *Fundamentals*, p. 89.

56. Aronson, *Love and Sympathy*, p. 11. "SA" is Aronson's abbreviation for a work by Buddhaghosa, *Sāratthappakāsinī: Buddhaghosa's Commentary on the* Samyutta Nikāya, ed. F. L. Woodwards (I, 1929; II, 1932; III, 1937).

57. Dharmasiri, *Fundamentals*, p. 91.

58. Cited in Keown, *The Nature of Buddhist Ethics*, p. 74. From *Majjhima Nikāya-Atthakathā*, 1.123.

59. Anagarika Dharmapala, *Return to Righteousness: A Collection of Speeches, Essays and Letters of the Anagarika Dharmapala*, ed. Ananda Guruge (Ceylon: The Government Press, 17 September 1965), p. 202.

60. Keown, *The Nature of Buddhist Ethics*, pp. 72–73.

61. Ibid., p. 74.

62. Ibid., pp. 74, 75.

63. Aronson, *Love and Sympathy*, p. 62.

64. Ibid., p. 69.

65. Ibid., p. 63.

66. Dharmasiri, *Fundamentals*, pp. 94, 95.

67. Ibid.

68. Ibid., p. 96. Quotation from Har Dayal, *Bodhisattva Doctrine in Buddhist Sanskrit Literature* (London: Kegan Paul, 1932), pp. 175–76.

69. See Robert Schinzinger's introduction to and translation of Nishida Kitarō's essay "The Unity of Oppositions," in *Intelligibility and the Philosophy of Nothingness* (Westport, Conn: Greenwood Press Publishers, 1976), pp. 163–241. My own explication of Nishida's "self-contradictory identity" appears as ch. 3 of *The Nothingness Beyond God: An Introduction to the Philosophy of Nishida Kitarō*, 2nd ed., (St. Paul, Minn.: Paragon House Publishers, 1997), pp. 58–80.

70. Dharmasiri, *Fundamentals*, p. 96.

71. Ibid.

72. Ibid.

73. Ibid., p. 97.

CHAPTER 5. ZEN BUDDHISM AND ETHICS

1. Abe Masao, *Zen and Comparative Studies*, ed. Steven Heine (Honolulu: University of Hawaii Press, 1997), p. 3.

2. Ibid., p. 9.

3. Ibid., p. 3.

4. Ibid., p. 25.

5. Christopher Ives, *Zen Awakening and Society* (Honolulu: University of Hawaii Press, 1992), p. 1.

6. James Whitehill, "Is There a Zen Ethic?," *Eastern Buddhist* (New Series) 20, no. 1 (Spring 1987): 9.

7. Ibid.: "Ch'an and Zen Buddhism have relied for centuries on general Buddhist and Confucian precepts, codes, virtues, and exemplars as the content of the moral life before and after spiritual liberation."

8. Roshi Philip Kapleau, *Zen: Dawn in the West* (New York: Anchor Books, 1980), p. 231.

9. T. R. Reid, *Confucius Lives Next Door: What Living in the East Teaches Us About Living in the West* (New York, Random House, Inc., 1999), pp. 23–24:

> But in statistical terms, these serious crimes are rare events, compared with what happens in the rest of the world. There are about 7.5 murders each year for every 100,000 Americans. England's murder rate is roughly 5.5 murders per 100,000 people. Germany has 4.3 per 100,000, France has 4.1. In Japan, the murder rate is below 1.0 per 100,000. . . . The most striking difference is in the rates of property crimes—arson, burglary, robbery, car theft, etc. According to the American criminologist David Bailey, the United States has about 140 times as many robberies per year as Japan does. In Tokyo, there are about 500 robberies per year—a little more than one per day. New York City has about 215 reported robberies every day. The reason people don't use car alarms in Japan—even though most cars are left out on the street at night—is that auto theft is not a problem there.

10. *Two Zen Classics:* Mumonkan *and* Hekiganroku, tr. with commentaries by Katsuki Sekida (New York: Weatherhill, 1977), p. 59.

11. Ibid., pp. 58–59.

12. Robert Aitken, *The Mind of Clover: Essays in Zen Buddhist Ethics* (San Francisco: North Point Press, 1984), p. 6.

13. Sekida, *Two Zen Classics*, p. 320.

14. Aitken, *The Mind of Clover*, p. 155. The statement appears in Aitken's book, but is attributed to Yamada Kōun Roshi.

15. Ibid., p. 156.

16. Kapleau, *Zen: Dawn in the West*, pp. 231–32.

17. In his work on the notion of truth, Heidegger provocatively observed that "truth" both reveals and conceals at one and the same time. He punningly noted that concealment (*lēthē*) was to be found at "the heart of alētheia," for just as *lēthē* forms the heart of the word used to express the negation of concealment (i.e., unconcealment or *alētheia*), so "truth" or revealedness (i.e., unconcealing) contains what appears to be its opposite, or "untruth." More precisely, rather than conceiving of concealment ("untruth") as the *opposite* of unconcealment ("truth"), it is rather the other of "truth," which is to say that it is to be found within "truth" itself. See Martin Heidegger, "The End of Philosophy and the Task of Thinking," in *Basic Writings*, ed. David Farrell Krell (New York: Harper and Row, Publishers, 1977), p. 390.

18. Christopher Ives, *Zen Awakening*, p. 35.

19. D. T. Suzuki, "Satori, or Acquiring a New Viewpoint," in *An Introduction to Zen Buddhism* (Kyoto: Eastern Buddhist Society, 1934). Also published for the Buddhist Society of London (London: Rider and Company, 1949). Quoted in Nancy Wilson Ross, *The World of Zen: An East-West Anthology* (New York: Vintage Books, 1960), p. 41.

20. A. D. Brear, "The Nature and Status of Moral Behavior in Zen Buddhist Tradition," *Philosophy East and West* 24, no. 4 (October 1974): 432.

21. Ibid., p. 434.

22. Ibid., p. 435. Brear quotes from Iino Norimoto, "Dōgen's Zen View of Interdependence," *Philosophy East and West* 12, no. 1 (April 1962): 52.

23. Although, as Professor Thomas Kirchner pointed out to me, in Buddhism the consumption of vegetables is not considered killing, as vegetables are not thought of as sentient beings.

24. Whitehill, "Is There a Zen Ethic?," p. 16.

25. Ives, *Zen Awakening*, p. 37:

Even today samu [work, practice] occupies a central place in Zen life. Monks or students cook meals, clean their quarters, rake gardens, sweep walks, construct monastery buildings and grow food and vegetables in the monastery's fields. Amongst other things, this emphasis on work as part of the Zen path breaks down distinctions between religious practice and 'productive' work.

26. D. T. Suzuki, *The Awakening of Zen*, p. 90.

27. D. T. Suzuki, *Zen and Japanese Culture* (Princeton, N.J.: Princeton University Press, Bollingen Series LXIV, 1959), p. 348.

28. Ibid., p. 349.

29. Sekida, *Two Zen Classics*, p. 61. "To understand Nansen's decree you must formulate one of your own. What is your decree? Zen stories are always to be taken as your own stories."

30. Brian (Daizen) A. Victoria, *Zen at War* (New York: Weatherhill, Inc., 1997), p. 193.

31. Ibid., p. 105. The passage cited is from D. T. Suzuki, "The Zen Sect of Buddhism," in the 1906 issue of the *Journal of the Pali Text Society*, p. 34.

32. Ibid., p. 109. The passage cited is from Suzuki, *Shin Shukyō Ron*, in *Suzuki Daisetsu Zenshū*, vol. 23, pp. 139–40.

33. Ibid., p. 110. The cited passage is from Suzuki, *Zen and Japanese Culture*, p. 145.

34. Ibid., p. 106. From Suzuki, *Zen and Japanese Culture*, p. 61.

35. Ibid., p. 137. Victoria found this passage in Ichikawa Hakugen, *Nihon Fashizumu ka no Shūkyō* (Tokyo: Enuesu Shuppankai, 1975), p. 197.

36. Ibid., p. 138. From *Nihon Fashizumu*, as above, p. 283.

37. Ibid., pp. 148–49. From Suzuki, "Zenkai Sasshin" (Renewal of the Zen World) in vol. 28, *Suzuki Daisetsu Zenshū*, p. 413.

38. Ibid., pp 35–36. The cited passage is by Sawaki Kōdō (1880–1965), a well-known modern Sōtō Zen master and scholar, from a 1942 magazine article for *Daihōrin*, entitled "On the True Meaning of the Zen Precepts." The longer passage, which Victoria translates and quotes, reads as follows:

> The Lotus Sutra states that "the Three Worlds [of desire, form, and form-lessness] are my existence and all sentient beings therein are my children." From this point of view, everything, including friend and foe, are my children. Superior officers are my existence as are their subordinates. The same can be said of both Japan and the world. Given this, it is just to punish those who disturb the public order. Whether one kills or does not kill, the precept forbidding killing [is preserved]. It is the precept forbidding killing that wields the sword. It is this precept that throws the bomb. It is for this reason that you must seek to study and practice this precept (pp. 35–36).

It need hardly be pointed out here that if all precepts may be observed in their breech, then a world of the kind which Dostoyevsky imagined, where everything is permitted, could arise. It is a way of justifying any and all activity, thereby destroying the very meaning of "ethics."

CHAPTER 6. THE FUNDAMENTALS: MODERN JAPANESE ETHICS

1. Daisetz T. Suzuki, *Zen and Japanese Culture* (Princeton, N. J.: Princeton University Press, Bollingen Series LXIV, 1959), p. 23.

2. Watsuji Tetsurō, *Watsuji Tetsurō's Rinrigaku*, tr. Yamamoto Seisaku and Robert E. Carter (Albany: State University of New York Press, 1996), p. 35.

3. Steve Odin, *The Social Self in Zen and American Pragmatism* (Albany: State University of New York Press, 1996), p. 52.

4. Ibid.

5. Yuasa Yasuo, *The Body: Toward an Eastern Mind-Body Theory*, ed. T. P. Kasulis, trs. Nagatomo Shigenori, and T. P. Kasulis (Albany: State University of New York Press, 1987), p. 37.

6. Watsuji, *Rinrigaku*, p. 35.

7. Nishida Kitarō, *Collected Works*, vol. 9, p. 73. Cited in Michiko Yusa, " 'Persona Originalis': 'Jinkaku' and 'Personne,' According to the Philosophies of Nishida Kitarō and Jacques Maritain," Ph.D dissertation, University of California at Santa Barbara, 1983, p. 58.

8. Watsuji, *Rinrigaku*, p. 15.

9. Ibid., p. 11.

10. Nishida Kitarō, *Last Writings: Nothingness and the Religious Worldview*, tr. David A. Dilworth (Honolulu: University of Hawaii Press, 1987), p. 100.

11. Watsuji, *Rinrigaku*, p. 225.

12. Ibid., p. 226.

13. Sallie B. King writes that it is *makoto* that links us to the *kami*, by way of *kokoro*:

> What links *makoto* in *kami* and human beings is *kokoro*. *Kokoro* is the seat of human emotion, intellection, and spirit; it is the human heart-mind, conceived by the Japanese as a single thing. A *kokoro* which is *makoto* unites human and *kami*. . . . The link between a sincere heart-mind and *kami* is direct since they are essentially one of a kind; there is no need of something extraneous, such as prayer, to establish a link.

("Egalitarian Philosophies in Sexist Institutions: The Life of Satomi-san, Shinto Miko and Zen Buddhist Nun," Journal of Feminist Studies in Religion 4 [Spring 1988]: 15).

14. Watsuji, *Rinrigaku,* p. 251.

15. Ibid., p. 252.

16. Ibid., p. 25.

17. Quoted in "Ricoh Family Values," by Simon Partner, *Impact* 21 (June 1997): 47.

18. Hiroshi Hamada, *Achieving "CS Number One: 'Oyakudachi,' "* tr. Simon Partner (Tokyo: Ricoh Company, Limited, 1995), p. v.

19. Ibid., p. 48.

20. Ibid., p. 49.

21. Quoted in "Ricoh Family Values," by Simon Partner, *Impact* 21(June 1997): 3.

22. Wm. Theodore De Bary, ed., *Sources of Japanese Tradition*, vol. 1, comp. Tsunoda Ryusaku, Wm. Theodore de Bary, and Donald Keene (New York: Columbia University Press, 1958), p. 48.

23. Partner, "Ricoh," p. 49.

24. Ibid.

25. Ibid., p. 50.

26. Odin, *The Social Self,* p. 62.

27. Watsuji Tetsurō, *Climate and Culture: A Philosophical Study,* tr. Geoffrey Bownas (The Hokuseido Press, Ministry of Education, Japan, 1961), p. 141.

28. Ibid., p. 148.

29. Boye De Mente, *Japanese Etiquette and Ethics in Business* (Lincolnwood [Chicago], Ill.: Passport Books, 1987), p. 3.

30. Odin, *The Social Self,* p. 53.

31. Ibid.

32. Watsuji, *Rinrigaku,* pp. 49–50.

33. Ibid., p. 190.

34. Watsuji, *Climate and Culture,* p. 8.

CHAPTER 7. AN ETHICS OF TRANSFORMATION: NISHIDA, YUASA, AND DŌGEN

1. Nishida Kitarō, *Last Writings: Nothingness and the Religious Worldview,* tr. David A. Dilworth (Honolulu: University of Hawaii Press, 1993), p. 47.

2. Nishida Kitarō, *An Inquiry into the Good,* tr. Abe Masao and Christopher Ives (New Haven and London: Yale University Press, 1987), p. 3. Originally written by Nishida Kitarō in Japanese under the title *Zen No Kenkyu* and published by Iwanami Shoten, Publishers, Tokyo, Japan.

3. Ibid., pp. 3–4.

4. Ibid., p. 4.

5. Wm. Theodore De Bary, ed., *Sources of Japanese Tradition,* vol. 2, comp. Ryusaku Tsunoda, Wm. Theodore De Bary, and Donald Keene (New York: Columbia University Press, 1958), p. 362.

6. Ibid., p. 364.

7. Nishitani Keiji, *Nishida Kitarō,* tr. Yamamoto Seisaku and James W. Heisig, (Berkeley: Nanzan Studies in Religion and Culture, University of California Press, 1991), p. 89. The passage here translated by Nishitani, appears in the Abe and Ives translation of Nishida's *Inquiry,* on p. 28.

8. Ibid., pp. 90–91; Nishida, *Inquiry,* p. 145.

9. Ibid. p. 91. Nishitani adds that "the mind that changes its perspective as it changes its location is the great free and unobstructed mind able to see things by becoming them" (p. 92).

10. Nishida, *Inquiry*, p. 44.

11. Ibid., pp. 63–64: "At the same time that reality is a unified whole, it must include opposition. If there is a real entity here, then there is necessarily another that opposes it. In such mutual opposition, the two entities are not totally independent realities, for they must be unified; they must be part of the development of one reality through differentiation."

Again, in an essay translated as "The Unity of Opposites" (Nishida Kitarō, in *Intelligibility and the Philosophy of Nothingness: Three Philosophical Essays*, tr. Robert Schinzinger [Westport, Conn.: Greenwood Press Publishers, 1973], p. 173), Nishida writes, "The world of reality is essentially the one as well as the many. . . . That is why I call the world of reality 'absolute contradictory self-identity' [or 'unity of opposites']."

See also chapter 3 ("Self-Contradictory Identity") of my book *The Nothingness Beyond God: An Introduction to the Philosophy of Nishida Kitarō*, 2nd ed. (St. Paul: Paragon House, 1998), pp. 59–80.

12. Nishida, *Inquiry*, p. 56.

13. Ibid., p. 77.

14. Nishitani, *Nishida Kitarō*, pp. 154–57.

15. Nishida, *Inquiry*, p. 81.

16. Nishida, *Last Writings*, p. 112.

17. Ibid., p. 115.

18. Nishida, *Inquiry*, pp. 151–52.

19. Ibid., pp. 161, 162.

20. Ibid., p. 163.

21. Nishida, *Last Writings*, p. 52.

22. Nishida, *Inquiry*, p. 164.

23. Ibid., p. 166.

24. Nishida, *Last Writings*, p. 97.

25. Nishida, *Inquiry*, p. 170.

26. Ibid., p. 171.

27. Nishida, *Last Writings*, p. 71.

28. Ibid., p. 75.

29. Nishida, *Inquiry*, p. 171.

30. Ibid.

31. Ibid.

32. Ibid., p. 172.

33. Ibid., p. 173.

34. Ibid., p. 175.

35. Ibid., p. 132.

36. Ibid., p. 133.

37. Ibid.

38. Ibid., p. 134.

39. Ibid., p. 135.

40. Ibid.

41. Ibid.

42. Ibid., p. 139.

43. Ibid., p. 141.

44. Ibid., pp. 144–45.

45. Ibid.

46. Nishida, *Last Writings*, p. 101.

47. Nishida, *Intelligibility*, pp. 184–85.

48. Ibid., p. 208.

49. Yuasa Yasuo, *The Body: Toward an Eastern Mind-Body Theory*, ed. T. P. Kasulis, tr. Nagatomo Shigenori and T. P. Kasulis (Albany: State University of New York Press, 1987), p. 85.

50. Ibid., p. 86.

51. Ibid., p. 88.

52. Ibid., p. 98.

53. Ibid., p. 100.

54. Ibid.

55. Ibid., p. 101.

56. Ibid.

57. David Edward Shaner, Nagatomo Shigenori, and Yuasa Yasuo, *Science and Comparative Philosophy: Introducing Yuasa Yasuo* (Leiden: E. J. Brill, 1989), p. 225:

> . . . the theoretical paradigm for mind-body theory in the philosophical traditions of the East is radically different from that of the West. In the Eastern tradition, the state of the 'oneness of the body-mind' has been regarded as the goal of practical training . . . we must first acknowledge, albeit *provisionally*, the distinction between the mind and the body which common sense dictates in the field of our everyday experience. In short, the mind-matter dichotomy has a restricted or limited validity as a *provisional paradigm* of cognition that can be applied to an understanding of human experience.

58. Ibid., p. 226.

59. Ibid., p. 228.

60. Yuasa Yasuo, *Body*, p. 108.

61. Ibid., p. 109.

62. T. P. Kasulis, *Zen Action/Zen Person* (Honolulu: University of Hawaii Press, 1981), p. 94.

63. Francis H. Cook, "Dōgen's View of Authentic Selfhood and Its Socio-ethical Implications," in *Dōgen Studies, Studies in East Asian Buddhism*, ed. William R. LaFleur, no. 2 (Honolulu: University of Hawaii Press, 1985), p. 141.

64. Discussed in Yokoi Yūhō, *Zen Master Dōgen: An Introduction with Selected Writings* (New York: Weatherhill, Inc., 1976), p. 39. From the "Manifestation of the Kōan" (Genjō Kōan) section of the *Shōbōgenzō*: see *Moon in a Dewdrop: Writings of Zen Master Dōgen*, ed. Tanahashi Kazuaki (San Francisco: North Point Press, 1985), p. 70: "To study the Buddha way is to study the self. To study the self is to forget the self. To forget the self is to be actualized by myriad things. When actualized by myriad things, your body and mind as well as the bodies and minds of others drop away. No trace of realization remains, and this no-trace continues endlessly."

65. Yokoi, *Zen Master Dōgen*, p. 39.

66. From section two of the *Shōbōgenzō*, "Receiving the Precepts," in Yokoi, *Zen Master Dōgen*, p. 84.

67. Kasulis, *Zen Action*, p. 95.

68. See *Master Dōgen's Shōbōgenzō* (book 1), trs. Nishijima Gudo and Chodo Cross (Woking, Surrey: Windbell Publications Ltd., 1994:

> When we investigate them like this, wrongs are realized as having become completely the same as *not committing*. Aided by this realization, we can penetrate the *not committing* of wrongs, and we can realize it decisively by sitting. Just at this moment—when reality is realized as the *not*

committing of wrongs at the beginning, middle, and end—wrongs do not arise from causes and conditions; they are nothing other than just *not committing*. Wrongs do not vanish due to causes and conditions; they are nothing other than just *not committing*. If wrongs are in balance, all dharmas are in balance. Those who recognize that wrongs arise from causes and conditions, but do not see that these causes and conditions and they themselves are [the reality of] *not committing*, are pitiful people. The seeds of buddhahood arise from conditions and, this being so, conditions arise from the seeds of buddhahood. It is not that wrongs do not exist; they are nothing other than *not committing*. Wrongs are not immaterial, they are not committing. Wrongs are not material; they are not committing. Wrongs are not "*not committing*;" they are nothing other than *not committing*. [Similarly,] for example, spring pines are neither nonexistence nor existence; they are *not committing*. An autumn chrysanthemum is neither existence nor nonexistence; it is not committing. (pp. 101–02)

69. Douglas A. Fox, "Zen and Ethics, Dōgen's Synthesis" *Philosophy East and West*, vol. 21, no. 1 (Jan. 1971): 37.

70. Ibid., p. 37.

71. Ibid., p. 39.

72. Francis Dojun Cook, *How to Raise an Ox: Zen Practice as Taught in Zen Master Dōgen's* Shōbōgenzō, *Including Ten Newly Translated Essays* (Los Angeles: Center Publications, 1978), p. 5.

73. Ibid., p. 6.

74. Ibid., p. 14.

75. Ibid., p. 55.

CONCLUSION: THE MUTUALITY OF LEARNING IN A GLOBAL VILLAGE

1. Yuasa Yasuo, *The Body, Self-Cultivation, and Ki-Energy*, tr. Nagatomo Shigenori and Monte S. Hull (Albany: State University of New York Press, 1993), p. 61.

2. Ibid., p. 62.

3. Nishida Kitarō, *Last Writings: Nothingness and the Relgious Worldview*, tr. David A. Dilworth (Honolulu: University of Hawaii Press, 1987), p. 76: "This is another aspect of Cusana's infinite sphere of God in which, because there is no circumference, every point is the center. The world of the absolute present is a bottomlessly contradictory sphere that reflects itself within itself."

4. Ibid.

5. Ibid., p. 77: "In Buddhism, this seeing means, not to see Buddha objectively outside, but to see into the bottomless depths of one's own soul."

6. Yuasa Yasuo, *The Body: Towards an Eastern Mind-Body Theory*, ed. T. P. Kasulis, tr. Nagatomo Shigenori and T. P. Kasulis (Albany: State University of New York Press, 1987), p. 92.

7. Ibid., p. 93.

8. William James, *The Principles of Psychology*, vol. 1 (New York: Dover Publications, Inc., 1950), p. 243.

9. Charles Taylor, *Sources of the Self: The Making of The Modern Identity* (Cambridge, Mass.: Harvard University Press, 1989), p. 9.

10. Ibid.

11. Ibid., p. 4.

12. Ibid., p. 5.

13. Ibid., p. 9.

14. Ibid., p. 5.

15. Alasdair MacIntyre, *After Virtue: A Study in Moral Theory* (Notre Dame, Ind.: University of Notre Dame Press, 1981), p. 206.

16. Ibid., p. 204.

17. Quoted in Warwick Fox, *Toward a Transpersonal Ecology: Developing New Foundations for Environtalism* (Albany: State University of New York Press, 1995), p. 219. Fox cites the source as "quoted in Bill Devall, 'Greenies: Observations on the Deep, Long-Range Ecology Movement in Australia' 1984, ms., p. 17."

18. Ibid., pp. 215, 217.

19. Naess, Arne. "Self-Realization: An Ecological Approach to Being in the World" (The Fourth Keith Roby Memorial Lecture in Community Science, Murdoch University, Western Australia, 12th March, 1986), pp. 39–40. Also published in *The Trumpeter* 4(3) (1987): 35–42.

20. Walt Anderson, *Open Secrets: A Western Guide to Tibetan Buddhism* (Harmondsworth, Middlesex: Penguin, 1980), p. 17; quoted in Fox, *Toward*, p. 218.

21. Ueda Shizuteru, "Nishida, Nationalism, and the War in Question," quoted in *Rude Awakenings: Zen, the Kyoto School, and the Question of Nationalism*, ed. James W. Heisig and John C. Maraldo (Honolulu: University of Hawaii Press, 1995), p. 100.

22. Ibid., pp. 101, 102.

23. Ibid., p. 103.

24. Ibid., p. 106.

Selected Bibliography

Abe Masao. "Kenotic God and Dynamic Śūnatā." In *The Emptying God: A Buddhist-Jewish-Christian Conversation,* edited by John B. Cobb, Jr., and Christopher Ives. *Faith Meets Faith Series.* Maryknoll, New York: Orbis Books, 1990.

———. "The Problem of Evil in Christianity and Buddhism." In *Buddhist-Christian Dialogue: Mutual Renewal and Transformation,* edited by Paul O. Ingram and Frederick J. Streng. Honolulu: University of Hawaii Press, 1986.

———. "The Problem of Self-Centeredness as the Root-source of Human Suffering." *Japanese Religions* 15, no. 4 (July 1989): 15–25.

———. "Religious Tolerance and Human Rights: A Buddhist Perspective." In *Religious Liberty and Human Rights in Nations and Religions,* edited by Leonard Swidler. Philadelphia: Ecumenical Press, 1986.

———. *A Study of Dōgen: His Philosophy and Religion,* edited by Steven Heine. Albany: State University of New York Press, 1992.

———. "Will, Śūnatā, and History." In *The Religious Philosophy of Nishitani Keiji: Encounter with Emptiness,* edited by Taitetsu Unno. Berkeley: Asian Humanities Press, 1986.

———. *Zen and Comparative Studies,* edited by Steven Heine. Honolulu: University of Hawa'i Press, 1997.

———. *Zen and Western Thought.* Edited by William R. LaFleur. Honolulu: University of Hawai'i Press, 1985.

Aitken, Robert. *The Mind of Clover: Essays in Zen Buddhist Ethics.* San Francisco: North Point Press, 1984.

———. *The Practice of Perfection: The Pāramitās from a Zen Buddhist Perspective.* New York: Pantheon Books, 1994.

———. "Right Livelihood for the Western Buddhist." In *Dharma Gaia: A Harvest of Essays in Buddhism and Ecology,* edited by Allan Hunt Badiner, 227–32. Berkeley: Parallax Press, 1990. Reprinted in *Primary Point* 7 (Summer 1990): 2.

———. "Gandhi, Dōgen, and Deep Ecology." In *Deep Ecology: Living As If Nature Mattered,* edited by Bill Devall and George Sessions, 232–35. Salt Lake City: Peregrine Smith Books, 1985. Reprinted in *The Path of Compassion: Writings on Socially Engaged Buddhism,* edited by Fred Eppsteiner, 86–92. Berkeley: Parallax Press, 1988.

Ames, Roger T., with W. Dissanayake and T. Kasulis, editors. *Self as Person in Asian Theory and Practice.* Albany: State University of New York Press, 1994.

Aronson, Harvey B. *Love and Sympathy in Theravāda Buddhism.* Delhi: Motilal Banarsidass Publishers Private Limited, 1996.

Batchelor, Stephen. "The Sands of the Ganges: Notes Towards a Buddhist Ecological Philosophy." In *Buddhism and Ecology,* edited by Martine Batchelor and Kerry Brown, 31–39. London and New York: Cassell, 1992.

Bellah, Robert N. "Japan's Cultural Identity: Some Reflections on the Work of Watsuji Tetsurō." *The Journal of Asian Studies* 24, no. 4 (1965): 573–94.

Blacker, Carmen. "Shintō and the Sacred Dimension of Nature." In *International Symposium: Shintō and Japanese Culture,* 9–15. Tokyo: International Shintō Foundation, June 1995.

Bocking, Brian. *A Popular Dictionary of Shintō.* Lincolnwood (Chicago), Ill.: NTC/ Contemporary Publishing Company, 1997.

Brear, A. D. "The Nature and Status of Moral Behavior in Zen Buddhist Tradition." *Philosophy East and West* 24, no. 4 (October 1974): 432.

Carter, Robert E. *Becoming Bamboo: Western and Eastern Explorations of the Meaning of Life.* Montreal: McGill-Queen's University Press, 1992.

———. "Comparative Value Theory: An Inquiry into the Notion of 'Intrinsic Value' in Contemporary Western and Japanese Philosophy." *Journal of Value Inquiry* 13, no. 1 (Spring 1979): 33–56.

———. *Dimensions of Moral Education.* Toronto: University of Toronto Press, 1987.

———. *The Nothingness Beyond God: An Introduction to the Philosophy of Nishida Kitarō.* 2nd ed. St. Paul, Minn.: Paragon House Publishers, 1997.

Chan, Wing-Tsit. *A Source Book in Chinese Philosophy.* Princeton: Princeton University Press, 1963.

Chapple, Christopher Key. *Nonviolence to Animals, Earth, and Self in Asian Traditions.* Albany: State University of New York Press, 1993.

Codiga, Doug. "Zen Practice and a Sense of Place." In *Dharma Gaia: A Harvest of Essays in Buddhism and Ecology,* edited by Allan Hunt Badiner, 106–11. Berkeley: Parallax Press, 1990.

Cook, Francis Dojun. *How to Raise an Ox: Zen Practice as Taught in Zen Master Dōgen's* Shōbōgenzō, *Including Ten Newly Translated Essays.* Los Angeles, Center Publications, 1978.

Cook, Francis H. "Dōgen's View of Authentic Selfhood and Its Socio-ethical Implications." In *Dōgen Studies, Studies in East Asian Buddhism,* edited by William R. LaFleur, vol. 2, 141. Honolulu: University of Hawai'i Press, 1985.

————. "The Jewel Net of Indra." In *Nature in Asian Traditions of Thought: Essays in Environmental Philosophy,* edited by J. Baird Callicott and Roger T. Ames. Albany: State University of New York Press, 1989.

Curtin, Deane. "Dōgen, Deep Ecology, and the Ecological Self." *Environmental Ethics* 16, no. 2 (Summer 1994): 195–213.

Danto, Arthur C. *Mysticism and Morality: Oriental Thought and Moral Philosophy.* New York: Harper and Row Publishers, 1987.

De Bary, Wm. Theodore, editor. Compiled by Tsunoda Tyusaku, Wm. Theodore De Bary, and Donald Keene. *Sources of Japanese Tradition,* vols. 1–2. New York: Columbia University Press, 1958.

De Mente, Boye. *Japanese Etiquette and Ethics in Business.* Lincolnwood (Chicago), Ill.: Passport Books, 1987.

De Silva, Padmasiri. "Buddhist Environmental Ethics." In *Dharma Gaia: A Harvest of Essays in Buddhism and Ecology,* edited by Allan Hunt Badiner, 14–19. Berkeley: Parallax Press, 1990.

————. "Environmental Ethics: A Buddhist Perspective." In *Buddhist Ethics and Modern Society,* edited by Charles Wei-hsun Fu and Sandra A. Wawrytko, 173–84. New York: Greenwood Press, 1991.

Dharmapala, Anagarika. *Return to Righteousness: A Collection of Speeches, Essays and Letters of the Anagarika Dharmapala,* edited by Ananda Guruge. Ceylon: The Government Press, 17 September 1965.

Dharmasiri, Gunapala. *Fundamentals of Buddhist Ethics.* Antioch, Calif.: Golden Leaves Publishing Co., 1989.

Duval, R. Shannon, and David Shaner. "Conservation Ethics and the Japanese Intellectual Tradition." *Conservation Ethics* 11 (Fall 1989): 197–214.

Earhart, H. Bryon. "The Ideal of Nature in Japanese Religion and Its Possible Significance for Environmental Concerns." *Contemporary Religions in Japan* 11, nos. 1–2 (March–June 1970): 1–25.

————. *Japanese Religion: Unity and Diversity.* Belmont: Calif.: Dickenson Publishing Company, 1969.

Eppsteiner, Fred, editor. *The Path of Compassion: Writings on Socially Engaged Buddhism.* Berkeley: Parallax Press, 1988.

Feldman, Christine. "Nurturing Compassion." In *The Path of Compassion: Writings on Socially Engaged Buddhism,* edited by Fred Eppsteiner. Berkeley: A Buddhist Peace Fellowship Book, Parallax Press, 1988.

Fox, Douglas A. "Zen and Ethics, Dōgen's Synthesis." *Philosophy East and West* 21, no. 1 (January 1971): 33–41.

Fox, Warwick. *Toward a Transpersonal Ecology: Developing New Foundations for Environmentalism.* Albany: State University of New York Press, 1995.

Fu, C. W. "Morality and Beyond: The Neo-Confucian Encounter with Mahāyāna Buddhism." *Philosophy East and West* 23 (July 1973).

Fu, Charles Wei-hsun, and Sandra A. Wawrytko, eds. "Buddhist Ethics and Modern Society: An International Symposium." In *Contributions to the Study of Religion Series* 31. New York: Greenwood Press, 1991.

Fung Yu-lan. *A Short History of Chinese Philosophy.* Edited by Derke Bodde. New York: The Free Press, a Division of Macmillan Publishing Co., Inc., 1948.

Gottleib, Roger S. *A Spirituality of Resistance: Finding a Peaceful Heart and Protecting the Earth.* New York: The Crossroad Publishing Company, 1999.

Grosnick, William Henry. "The Buddhahood of the Grasses and the Trees: Ecological Sensitivity or Scriptural Misunderstanding." In *An Ecology of the Spirit: Religious Reflection and Environmental Consciousness,* edited by Michael Barnes, 197–208. Lanham, Md.: University Press of America, 1994.

Gross, Rita. "Toward a Buddhist Environmental Ethic." *Journal of the American Academy of Religion* 65, no. 2 (Summer 1997): 333–53.

Hagen, Steve. *Buddhism Plain and Simple.* Rutland, Vt.: Charles E. Tuttle Co., Inc., 1997.

Hall, David L., and Roger T. Ames. *Thinking from the Han: Self, Truth, and Transcendence in Chinese and Western Culture.* Albany: State University of New York Press, 1998.

———— *Thinking Through Confucius.* Albany: State University of New York Press, 1987.

Hamada Hiroshi. *Achieving "CS Number One: 'Oyakudachi.' "* Translated by Simon Partner. Tokyo: Ricoh Company, Limited, 1995.

Hardacre, Helen. *Shintō and the State: 1868–1988.* Princeton: Princeton University Press, 1989.

Harris, Ian. "Buddhist Environmental Ethics and Detraditionalization: The Case of EcoBuddhism." *Religion* 25, no. 3 (July 1995): 199–211.

———. "Causation and 'Telos': The Problem of Buddhist Environmental Ethics." *Journal of Buddhist Ethics* 1 (1994): 46–59.

Hayward, Jeremy. "Ecology and the Experience of Sacredness." In *Dharma Gaia: A Harvest of Essays in Buddhism and Ecology,* edited by Allan Hunt Badiner, 64–74. Berkeley: Parallax Press, 1990.

Heidegger, Martin. "The End of Philosophy and the Task of Thinking." In *Basic Writings,* edited by David Farrell Krell. New York: Harper and Row, Publishers, 1977.

Heine, Steven. *Existential and Ontological Dimensions of Time of Heidegger and Dōgen.* Albany: State University of New York Press, 1985.

Herbert, Jean. *Shintō: At the Fountain-head of Japan.* London: George Allen and Unwin Ltd., 1967.

Hindery, Roderick. *Comparative Ethics in Hindu and Buddhist Traditions.* Delhi: Motilal Banarsidass, 1978.

Hirai Naofusa. "The Principles of Pure Shintō." *Proceedings of the Ninth International Congress for the History of Religion.* Tokyo: Maruzen, 1960.

Huh, Woo-Sung. "The Philosophy of History in the 'Later' Nishida: A Philosophic Turn." *Philosophy East and West* 40, no. 3 (July 1990): 343–74.

Hunt, Arnold D., Marie T. Crotty, and Robert B. Crotty. *Ethics of World Religions.* Revised edition. San Diego: Greenhaven Press, Inc., 1991.

Hurst, G. Cameron, III. "Death, Honor, and Loyalty: The Bushido Ideal." *Philosophy East and West: Special Issue: Understanding Japanese Values* 40, no. 4 (October 1990): 511–27.

Iino Norimoto. "Dōgen's Zen View of Interdependence." *Philosophy East and West* 12 (April 1962): 51–57.

Inada, Kenneth. "A Buddhist Response to the Nature of Human Rights." *Journal of Buddhist Ethics* 2 (1995): 55–66.

Izutsu Toshihiko. *Sufism and Taoism: A Comparative Study of Key Philosophical Concepts.* Berkeley: University of California Press, 1983.

———. *Toward a Philosophy of Zen Buddhism.* Tehran: Imperial Iranian Academy of Philosophy, 1977.

Ives, Christopher. *Zen Awakening and Society.* Honolulu: University of Hawai'i Press, 1992.

James, William. *Essays in Radical Empiricism.* Cambridge, Mass.: Harvard University Press, 1976.

————. *Pragmatism, and Four Essays from The Meaning of Truth.* Edited by R. B. Perry. New York: A Meridian Book, New American Library, 1955. First published in 1909.

————. *The Principles of Psychology,* vol. 1. New York: Dover Publications, Inc., 1950. First published in 1890.

Jayatilleke, K. A. *The Message of the Buddha.* Edited by Ninian Smart. London: George Allen and Unwin Ltd., 1975.

Jones, K. *The Social Face of Buddhism: An Approach to Political and Social Activism.* London: Wisdom Publications, 1989.

Kadowaki Kakichi, S. J. "Shintō and Christianity: Dialogue for the Twenty-first Century." *International Philosophical Quarterly* 33, no. 1 (March 1993): 70–89.

Kaltenmark, Max. *Lao Tzu and Taoism.* Stanford: Stanford University Press, 1969.

Kalupahana, David J. *Buddhist Philosophy: A Historical Analysis.* Honolulu: The University Press of Hawai'i, 1976.

————. "Toward a Middle Path of Survival." *Environmental Ethics* 8, no. 4 (Winter 1986): 371–80. Reprinted in *Nature in Asian Traditions of Thought: Essays in Environmental Philosophy.* Edited by J. Baird Callicott and Roger T. Ames, 247–56. Albany: State University of New York Press, 1989.

Kapleau, Roshi Philip. *Zen: Dawn in the West.* New York: Anchor Books, 1980.

Kasulis, Thomas. "Does East Asian Buddhism Have an Ethical System?" *Zen Buddhism Today* 8 (Annual Report of the Kyoto Zen Symposium) (October 1990): 48.

————. "Intimacy: A General Orientation in Japanese Religious Values." *Philosophy East and West: Special Issue: Understanding Japanese Values* 40 (October 1990): 433–49.

————. "The Kyoto School and the West: Review and Evaluation." *Eastern Buddhist* 15, no. 2 (1982): 125–44.

————. *Zen Action/Zen Person.* Honolulu: The University Press of Hawai'i, 1981.

Kawamura Ekio. "Ethics and Religion: From the Standpoint of Absolute Nothingness." *Zen Buddhism Today—Annual Report of the Kyoto Zen Symposium,* no. 8 (October 1990): 71–85.

Kaza, Stephanie. "Toward a Buddhist Environmental Ethic." *Buddhism at the Crossroads* 6, no. 4 (Fall 1990): 22–25.

Keown, Damien. "Are There 'Human Rights' in Buddhism?" *Journal of Buddhist Ethics* 2 (1995): 3–27.

————. *The Nature of Buddhist Ethics.* New York: St. Martin's Press, 1992.

Kim, Ha Tai. *Dōgen Kigen—Mystical Realist.* Tucson: University of Arizona Press, 1975.

King, Sallie B. "Egalitarian Philosophies in Sexist Institutions: The Life of Satomi-san, Shintō Miko and Zen Buddhist Nun." *Journal of Feminist Studies in Religion* 4 (Spring 1988): 7–26.

King, Winston L. "Buddhist Self-World Theory and Buddhist Ethics." *The Eastern Buddhist* 22 (Autumn 1989).

———. *In Hope of Nibbana: An Essay on Theravāda Buddhist Ethics.* LaSalle, Ill.: Open Court Publishing Company, 1964.

Kishimoto Hideo. "The Immediacy of Zen Experience and Its Cultural Background." *Philosophical Studies of Japan* 3 (1961): 25–32.

———. "Some Japanese Cultural Traits and Religions." In *The Japanese Mind: Essentials of Japanese Philosophy and Culture,* edited by Charles A. Moore, 110–21. Honolulu: East-West Center Press, University of Hawai'i, 1967.

Kiyohide, Krita. "Buddhism and Social Ethics—The Significance of Our Theme and a Few Propositions." *Zen Buddhism Today—Annual Report of the Kyoto Zen Symposium,* no. 8 (October 1990): 41–60.

Kohlberg, Lawrence. *The Philosophy of Moral Development.* Volume 1 of *Essays on Moral Development.* San Francisco: Harper and Row, Publishers, 1981.

LaFleur, William R., ed. *Dōgen Studies.* Honolulu: University of Hawai'i Press, Studies in East Asian Buddhism, no. 2, 1985.

Larson, Gerald James. "'Conceptual Resources' in South Asia for 'Environmental Ethics.'" In *Nature in Asian Traditions of Thought: Essays in Environmental Philosophy,* edited by J. Baird Callicott and Roger T. Ames, 267–77. Albany: State University of New York Press, 1989.

Legge, James, translator. *The Confucian Classics* 2nd edition, revised. Oxford: Clarendon Press, 1893.

Loy, David. "Mu and Its Implications." *Zen Buddhism Today—Annual Report of the Kyoto Zen Symposium,* no. 3 (September 1985): 108–24.

———. *Nonduality: A Study in Comparative Philosophy.* New Haven: Yale University Press, 1988.

MacIntyre, Alasdair. *After Virtue: A Study in Moral Theory.* Notre Dame, Ind.: University of Notre Dame Press, 1981.

Macy, Joanna. "Dependent Co-Arising: The Distinctiveness of Buddhist Ethics." *Journal of Religious Ethics* 7 (Spring 1979).

Magliola, Robert. *Derrida on the Mend.* West Lafayette, Ind.: Purdue University Press, 1984.

Mason, J. W. T. *The Meaning of Shintō: The Primaeval Foundation of Creative Spirit in Modern Japan.* Port Washington, N.Y.: Kennikat Press, Inc. 1967. First published in 1935.

McFague, Sallie. *The Body of God: An Ecological Theology.* Minneapolis: Fortress Press, 1993.

————. *Metaphorical Theology: Models of God in Religious Language.* Philadelphia: Fortress Press, 1982.

————. *Models of God: Theology for an Ecological, Nuclear Age.* Philadelphia: Fortress Press, 1987.

————. *Super, Natural Christians: How We Should Love Nature.* Minneapolis: Fortress Press, 1997.

McKeon, Richard. *Introduction to Aristotle.* New York: The Modern Library, 1947.

Mieth, Dietmar. "Meister Eckhart: A Mystical Alternative to Contemporary Ethics." *Zen Buddhism Today—Annual Report of the Kyoto Zen Symposium,* no. 8 (October 1990): 86–111.

Misra, G. S. P. *Development of Buddhist Ethics.* New Delhi: Nunshiram Manoharlal Publishers Pvt. Ltd., 1984.

Moore, Charles A., ed. *The Japanese Mind.* Honolulu: An East-West Center Book, The University Press of Hawaii, 1967.

Morgan, Kenneth W., ed. *The Path of the Buddha: Buddhism Interpreted by Buddhists.* New York: The Ronald Press Company, 1956.

Munro, Donald J. *The Concept of Man in Early China.* Stanford, Calif.: Stanford University Press, 1969.

Naess, Arne. "The Deep Ecological Movement: Some Philosophical Aspects." *Philosophical Inquiry* (1986): 10–31.

————. "Self-Realization: An Ecological Approach to Being in the World" (The Fourth Keith Roby Memorial Lecture in Community Science, Murdoch University, Western Australia, 12 March 1986). Also published in *The Trumpeter* 4(3) (1987): 35–42.

————. "Through Spinoza to Mahāyāna Buddhism or Through Mahāyāna Buddhism to Spinoza? In *Spinoza's Philosophy of Man: Proceedings of the Scandinavian Spinoza Symposium 1977,* edited by Jon Wetlesen, 135–58. Oslo: University of Oslo Press, 1978.

Nagatomo Shigenori. "Ki-Energy: Underpinning Religion and Ethics." *Zen Buddhism Today—Annual Report of the Kyoto Zen Symposium,* no. 8 (October 1990): 124–39.

Nakamura Hajime. "The Basic Teachings of Buddhism." In *Buddhism in the Modern World,* edited by Heinrich Dumoulin and John C. Maraldo. New York: Collier Books, 1976.

———. *Buddhism in Comparative Light.* New Delhi: Islam and the Modern Age Society, 1975.

———. "Interrelational Existence." *Philosophy East and West* 17, nos. 1–4 (1967): 112.

———. *Parallel Developments: A Comparative History of Ideas.* Tokyo and New York: Kodansha, 1975.

———. *Ways of Thinking of Eastern Peoples: India-China-Tibet-Japan,* translated by Philip Wiener. Honolulu: East-West Center Press, 1964.

Ninomiya Genpei. "Ethical Backgrounds in Japan and Their Bearing upon the Rise of Social Consciousness of Japan." M.A. Thesis, University of Chicago, 1927.

Nishida Kitarō. *Art and Morality.* Translated by D. A. Dilworth and V. H. Viglielmo. Honolulu: An East-West Center Book, University Press of Hawai'i, 1973.

———. *An Inquiry into the Good.* Translated by Abe Masao and Christopher Ives. New Haven and London: Yale University Press, 1987. Originally written by Nishida Kitarō in Japanese under the title *Zen No Kenkyu* and published by Iwanami Shoten, Publishers, Tokyo, Japan.

———. *Last Writings: Nothingness and the Religious Worldview.* Translated by David A. Dilworth. Honolulu: University of Hawai'i Press, 1987.

———. "The Problem of Japanese Culture" (excerpts). Translated by Abe Masao and R. DeMartino. In *Sources of Japanese Tradition,* vol. 2, edited by R. Tsunoda, W. T. deBary, and D. Keene, 350–65. New York: Columbia University Press, 1958.

———. "The Unity of Opposites." In *Intelligibility and the Philosophy of Nothingness: Three Philosophical Essays,* translated by Robert Schinzinger. Westport, Conn.: Greenwood Press Publishers, 1973.

Nishijima Gudo, and Chodo Cross, translators. *Master Dōgen's* Shōbōgenzō, book 1. Woking, Surrey: Windbell Publications Ltd., 1994.

Nishitani Keiji. *Nishida Kitarō.* Translated by Yamamoto Seisaku and James W. Heisig. Berkeley: Nanzan Studies in Religion and Culture, University of California Press, 1991.

———. *Religion and Nothingness.* Translated with an Introduction by Jan Van Bragt. Foreword by Winston L. King. Berkeley/Los Angeles/London: University of California Press, 1982.

Noda Matao. "East-West Synthesis in Nishida Kitarō." *Philosophy East and West* 4, no. 4 (April 1954–January 1955): 345–59.

Noddings, Nell. *Caring: A Feminine Approach to Ethics and Moral Education*. Berkeley: University of California Press, 1984.

Odin, Steve. *The Social Self in Zen and American Pragmatism*. Albany: State University of New York Press, 1996.

Ono Sokyo. *Shinto: The Kami Way*. Rutland, Vt./Tokyo: Charles E. Tuttle Co., Inc., 1962, 1995.

Palmer, Daniel. "Masao Abe, Zen Buddhism and Social Ethics." *Journal of Buddhist Ethics* 4, no. 19 (February 1997): 112–37.

Partner, Simon. "Ricoh Family Values." *Impact* 21 (June 1997).

Peerenboom, R. P. "The Religious Foundations of Nishida's Philosophy." *Asian Philosophy* 1, no. 2 (1991): 161–73.

Perspectives on Buddhist Ethics. Edited by Mahesh Tiwary. Delhi: Department of Buddhist Studies, 1989.

Picken, Stuart D. B. *Essentials of Shintō: An Analytical Guide to Principal Teachings*. Westport, Conn.: Greenwood Press, 1994.

———. *Shintō, Japan's Spiritual Roots*. Tokyo and New York: Kodansha International Ltd., 1980.

Piovesana, Gino. *Recent Japanese Philosophical Thought, 1862–1962: A Survey*. Tokyo: Sophia University Press, 1968.

Prebish, Charles S., ed. *Buddhist Ethics: A Cross-Cultural Approach*. Dubuque, Iowa: Kendall/Hunt Publishing Company, 1992.

Rahula, Walpola Sri. *What the Buddha Taught*. Revised edition. New York: Grove Weidenfeld, 1974.

Reader, Ian. *The Simple Guide to Shintō: The Religion of Japan*. Folkestone, Kent, England: Global Books Ltd., 1998.

Reasoner, Paul. "Individual and Social Morality in Japan and the United States: Rival Conceptions of the Self." *Philosophy East and West: Special Issue: Understanding Japanese Values* 40, no. 4 (October 1990): 489–97.

———. "Sincerity and Japanese Values." *Philosophy East and West: Special Issue: Understanding Japanese Values* 40, no. 4 (October 1990): 471–88.

Reid, T. R. *Confucius Lives Next Door: What Living in the East Teaches Us About Living in the West*. New York: Random House, Inc., 1999.

Rolston, Holmes, III. "Respect for Life: Can Zen Buddhism Help in Forming an Environmental Ethic?" *Zen Buddhism Today* 7 (September 1989): 11–30.

Rupp, G. "The Relationship Between Nirvāna and Samsāra: An Essay on the Evolution of Buddhist Ethics." *Philosophy East and West* 21 (January 1971).

Saddhatissa, H. *Buddhist Ethics: Essence of Buddhism.* London: George Allen and Unwin Ltd., 1970.

Naoki Sakai. "Return to the West/Return to the East: Watsuji Tetsurō's Anthropology and Discussions of Authenticity." *Boundary* 2, no. 3 (1991) 18: 157–89.

Sangharakshita. *The Ten Pillars of Buddhism.* Birmingham: Windhorse Publications, 1984.

Schmithausen, Lambert. "The Early Buddhist Tradition and Ecological Ethics." *Journal of Buddhist Ethics* 4 (1997): 1–42.

Schwartz, Benjamin I. *The World of Thought in Ancient China.* Cambridge, Mass.: Harvard University Press, 1985.

Sekida Katsuki. *Zen Training: Methods and Philosophy.* New York: Weatherhill, Inc., 1974.

Sensaki Nyogen, and Ruth Stout McCandless. *Buddhism and Zen.* New York: North Point Press, 1987.

Shaner, David Edward. "The Japanese Experience of Nature." In *Nature in Asian Traditions of Thought: Essays in Environmental Philosophy,* edited by J. Baird Callicott and Roger T. Ames, 163–82. Albany: State University of New York Press, 1989.

Shaner, David Edward, Nagatomo Shigenori, and Yuasa Yasuo. *Science and Comparative Philosophy: Introducing Yuasa Yasuo.* Leiden: E. J. Brill, 1989.

Shaner, David Edward, and R. Shannon Duval. "Conservation Ethics and the Japanese Intellectual Tradition." *Conservation Ethics* 11 (Fall 1989): 197–214.

Sizemore, Russell F., and Donald K. Swearer, eds. *Ethics, Wealth, and Salvation: A Study in Buddhist Social Ethics.* Columbia, S.C.: University of South Carolina Press, 1989.

Smith, Warren W., Jr. *Confucianism in Modern Japan: A Study of Conservation in Japanese Intellectual History.* 2nd ed. Tokyo: The Hokuseido Press, 1973.

Sponsel, Leslie E., and Poranee Natadecha-Sponsel. "The Relevance of Buddhism for the Development of an Environmental Ethic for the Conservation of Biodiversity." In *Ethics, Religion, and Biodiversity: Relations between Conservation and Cultural Values,* edited by Lawrence S. Hamilton with Helen F. Takecuchi, 75–97. Cambridge: White Horse Press, 1993.

Suzuki Daisetz T. *The Awakening of Zen,* edited by Christmas Humphreys. Boulder: Prajna Press, 1980.

———. "Eastern Ethical and Social Practice." In *Readings in Eastern Religious Thought,* edited by Allie M. Frazier, 156–76. Philadelphia: The Westminster Press, 1969.

———. *Essays in Zen Buddhism,* 3 vols. London: Rider & Company, 1953.

———. *Japanese Spirituality,* translated by Normal Waddell. Tokyo: Japan Society for the Promotion of Science, 1969.

———. *Outlines of Mahāyāna Buddhism.* New York: Shocken Books, 1963.

———. "Satori, or Acquiring a New Viewpoint." In *An Introduction to Zen Buddhism.* Kyoto: Eastern Buddhist Society, 1934. Also published for the Buddhist Society of London, London: Rider and Company, 1949.

———. *Zen and Japanese Culture.* Princeton: Princeton University Press, Bollingen Series LXIV, 1973.

Suzuki, D. T., Erich Fromm, and Richard De Martino. *Zen Buddhism and Psychoanalysis.* New York: Grove Press, Inc., 1960.

Tanahashi Kazuaki, editor. *Moon in a Dewdrop: Writings of Zen Master Dōgen.* San Francisco: North Point Press, 1985.

Taylor, Charles. *Sources of the Self: The Making of the Modern Identity.* Cambridge, Mass.: Harvard University Press, 1989.

Teeuwen, Mark. "Western Understanding and Misunderstanding of Shintō—Progress of Studies on Shintō in the West and Some Remarks." In *International Symposium Commemorating the Founding of the International Shintō Foundation: Shintō—Its Universality,* 76–82. Tokyo: International Shintō Foundation, July 1996.

Tu Wie-Ming. *Centrality and Commonality: An Essay on Confucian Religiousness: A Revised and Enlarged Edition of Centrality and Commonality—An Essay on Chungyung.* Albany: State University of New York Press, 1989.

———. *Confucian Thought: Selfhood as Creative Transformation.* Albany: State University of New York Press, 1985.

Tucker, Mary Evelyn, and Duncan Ryūken Williams, eds. *Buddhism and Ecology: The Interconnecting of Dharma and Deeds.* Cambridge, Mass.: Distributed by Harvard University Press for the Harvard Center for the Study of World Religions, 1997.

Two Zen Classics: Mumonkan and Hekiganroku. Translated with commentaries by Katsuki Sekida. New York: Weatherhill, Inc., 1977.

Ueda Shizuteru. "The Difficulty of Understanding Nishida's Philosophy." *Eastern Buddhist* 28, no. 2 (Autumn 1995): 175–82.

———. "Emptiness and Fullness: Śūnyatā in Mahāyāna Buddhism." *Eastern Buddhist* 15, no. 1 (Spring 1982): 9–37.

———. "Nishida, Nationalism, and the War in Question." In *Rude Awakenings: Zen, the Kyoto School, and the Question of Nationalism,* edited by James W. Heisig and John C. Moraldo. Honolulu: University of Hawai'i Press, 1995.

———. "Pure Experience, Self-Awareness, 'Basho.' " *Etudes Phenomenologicrues*. Bruxelles: Editions Ousia 18 (1993): 63–86.

Victoria, Brian (Daizen) A. *Zen at War*. New York: Weatherhill, Inc., 1997.

Vogel, Ezra F. *Japan as Number One: Lessons for America*. Cambridge: Mass.: Harvard University Press, 1979.

Wargo, Robert J. J. "Japanese Ethics: Beyond Good and Evil." *Philosophy East and West: Special Issue: Understanding Japanese Values* 40, no. 4 (October 1990): 499–509.

———. "Japanese Ethics: Beyond Good and Evil." *Intersect* 8, no. 8 (August 1992): 10–18.

Watsuji Tetsurō. *Climate and Culture: A Philosophical Study*. Translated by Geoffrey Bownas. Japan: The Hokuseido Press, Ministry of Education, 1961.

———. *Watsuji Tetsurō's* Rinrigaku: *Japanese Ethics*. Translated by Yamamoto Seisaku and Robert E. Carter. Albany: State University of New York Press, 1996.

Welch, Holmes. *Taoism: The Parting of the Way*. Boston: Beacon Press, 1957.

Whitehill, James. "Is There a Zen Ethic?" *Eastern Buddhist* (New Series), 20, no. 1 (Spring 1987): 9.

———. "Research Paper: Buddhist Ethics in Western Context: The 'Virtues' Approach." *Journal of Buddhist Ethics* 1 (1994): 1–22.

Wilson Ross, Nancy. *The World of Zen: An East-West Anthology*. New York: Vintage Books, 1960.

Yamamoto Yutaka. "A Morality Based on Trust: Some Reflections on Japanese Morality." *Philosophy East and West: Special Issue: Understanding Japanese Values* 40, no. 4 (October 1990): 251–69.

Yanairu Tetsuo. "Special Characteristics of the Japanese *kami*—A Symbol for the Future." *Third International Symposium of the International Shintō Foundation —Shape of Religion in the Twenty-first Century: In Search of World Co-existence*, 64–72. Tokyo: International Shintō Foundation, October 1997.

Yokoi Yūhō. *Zen Master Dōgen: An Introduction with Selected Writings*. New York: Weatherhill, Inc., 1976.

Young, J. Z. *Doubt and Certainty in Science: A Biologist's Reflections on the Brain*. Oxford: Oxford University Press, Galaxy Books, 1960.

Yuasa Yasuo. *The Body, Self-Cultivation, and Ki-Energy*. Translated by Shigenori Nagatomo and Monte S. Hull. Albany: State University of New York Press, 1993.

———. *The Body: Toward an Eastern Mind-Body Theory*. Edited by T. P. Kasulis, translated by Nagatomo Shigenori and T. P. Kasulis. Albany: State University of New York Press, 1987.

Yuichi Kajiyama. "Fundamentals of Buddhist Ethics." *Zen Buddhism Today— Annual Report of the Kyoto Zen Symposium,* no. 8 (October 1990): 61–69.

Yusa Michiko. "Nishida in Translation: Primary Sources in Western Languages." *Eastern Buddhist* 28, no. 2 (Autumn 1995): 297–302.

————. "*'Persona Originalis': 'Jinkaku'* and *'Personne,'* According to the Philosophies of Nishida Kitarō and Jacques Maritain," Ph.D. dissertation, University of California at Santa Barbara. Ann Arbor: University of Microfilms International, 1983.

————. "Reflections on Nishida Studies." *Eastern Buddhist* 28, no. 2 (Autumn 1995): 287–96.

Index

Abe Masao, 15–17, 99
Abidharma tradition, 85
abnormal: deviant, 184–85
absolute (the): as everyday world, 53; as flux, 104; beyond subject/ object, 151; expression, 182; God and negation, 160–61; in Satan, 134; -ly evil man, 161; manifestation, 157, 176; self-manifestation, 182; subjectivity of the historical world, 187; totality, 135; nothingness, 154, 187; value of personality, 170
acculturation, 22
action intuition; and the expression of caring, 200; state of, 173. *See also* intuition
agape, 48
ahimsā "non-injuring," 88
aidagara, "space where people are located," xxvii, 126, 130. *See also* betweenness; Watsuji
aikido, 3, 149
Aitken, Roshi Robert, 107
akaki "cheerfulness of heart," 48
alter/shrine, 142
Amaterasu, 52
anatman "no-self," 23
anattā "non-substantiality," 78
Anderson, Walt, 199

anicca "impermanence," 78
anthropocentrism, 87
anukampā "sympathy," 87
Apollo, xxiii
arahant "disciple," 92
Aristotle, xx–xxvii, 195; as systematiser of ethics, 197
Aronson, Harvey B., 87, 93, 217n 32
art, 123, 171; as cultivational techniques, 172; as transformational expression, 173; ballet, 64; calligraphy, 3, 149, 184; *haiku,* 184; *judo,* 172; *karate,* 149; *kendo,* 3, 149, 172; landscape gardening, 184; living, 197; of doing one thing at a time, 180; martial arts, 51, 149, 172, 184; music, 64; *Nō* drama, 172; Ryōanji, 123; scholarship, 153; *sumie* painting, 184; sword making and training, 184; tea ceremony, 149, 172, 184; *waka,* 172, 174
assimilation, 13
attitude: cluster, 144. *See also* value
Augustine, 159
awareness: as given, 151; compassionate, 180; communal, 166; enlightened, 157; God's self, 159; mystical, 154; non-dual, 115; pre-reflective, 116; self, 153; the

245

awareness *(continued)*
   "other side," 192; transformed
   state: no-mindness, 173–74. *See also*
   enlightenment; self

basho, xxix; deep self, 153; field-like
   self, 200; place, 129; place of
   awareness, 168; place where
   nothingness expresses itself as
   "we," 187
behaviour: normal/abnormal, 184–
   85; right action vs commandments,
   83–84
being in the world: as way, 7; as way
   of life, 35, 146, 176; being and
   nothingness, 181; Buddha's way,
   116; cluster of attitudes, 46;
   dwelling, 25; Far Eastern version, 3
betweenness, xxvi–xxviii; as openness
   similar to Heideggerian "clearing,"
   154; as spatial metaphor, 144;
   between us, 131; bringing to, 140;
   compared to *basho*, 129; is communality, 138, 186; negation and
   re-establishment, 135. *See also*
   spatial; Watsuji
Blacker, Carmen, 59
Bodhidharma, xxv; introduction of
   Buddhism to China, 99
bodhisattva, 112; as ultimate ethical
   ideal, 92–93; "desire" to assist in
   enlightenment, 178; ethical life,
   90; path, 95; precepts, 175; the
   perfections, 95–97
Boehme, Jakob, 156
Book of Changes (The), xiii–xxviii. *See
   also Tao Te Ching*
Brear, A.D., 111
Buddha: and benevolence, 91; and
   dharma, 99–100; and Christ 155;
   and mind 153–54; as compassionate being, 45, 180; enlightenment,
   104; three "Metaphysical" Truths,
   77–79; Four Noble Truths, 109–10;
   middle way and Eightfold Path,

79, 81–82, 90, 190; mind, 113–14;
   nature, 175, 187; nature of
   teachings, 115; non-metaphysical
   stance, 170; Shakayamuni, 107;
   teachings, 80, 82, 109–10, 114,
   190; becoming, 113
Buddhism, 36, 53–54; amorality, 15;
   and *śūnyatā* 17–18; and war, 118;
   and wisdom, 170; becomes Zen, 6–
   7; Buddhist temples, 2–3; centrality
   of human-heartedness, 33; Ch'an,
   6–7, 37, 99; ethical foundations,
   77, 92; form of conversion, 37;
   Hīnayāna, 178–79; influence in
   Japan, 44, 189–90; Japan as
   Buddhist country, xiv; Japanese
   adoption, 3–4; Mahāyāna/Theravādin,
   92–93; paradox, 99; separated
   from Shintōism, xvii; Shintōism,
   xxiii; teaching, 23, 100; virtues, 94
Buddhism (Mahāyanā), 2, 89, 94–95,
   99, 178–79, 185–88; and *dharma*,
   99; and ethics 89; and perfections
   11–12; and Satomi Myōdō, 2; and
   social ethics, 187–88
Buddhism (Zen), 37, 139–40, 192;
   and acceptance, 104–05; and
   Buddhism, 99; and enlightenment,
   109–11; and interrelation, 33; and
   Japanese culture, 62, 103; and
   Nishida, 149–50; and Satomi-san,
   4; and spiritual grounding for
   samurai, 180–81; and sympathy,
   94–95; as this-worldly, 96–97; at
   war, 117, 190–92; *bushido*, 117,
   183–84; ethics, 101–02, 107–08,
   115, 150, 164 (*see also* Buddhist
   ethics); enlightenment, 162; in
   Japan, 171, 189–90; *kōan*, 100,
   101–02, 105–06, 132–33; practice,
   151, 171 (*see also* meditation;
   practice); person, 115–17; real
   nature, 103–04; Rinzai, 108–10;
   Sōtō Zen, 102–03, 108–10, 174;
   theory, 101

Buddhist thought, 139–40, asceticism, 80; as naturalistic, 85–86, 100; Chinese ritual, 171; compatibility with Shintō, 63, 76, 77; ethics, 79–80, 84–85, 106, 197–98; evil, 187–88; ideal, 104, 114; perspective, 119; precepts 175

Buddhist: compassion, 160; ground of, 86; ideal *ahimsā*, 88; impermanence, 181; influence, 134–35; *karunā*, 82–83; *kairitsu*, 189–90; morality, 81–82, 94; practice, 189–90; self and other, 87; *sīla*, 189 90 (*see also anukampā*); Ten Good Paths of Action, 82, 90–91

bushido "warrior code," 183–84; *bushi*, xx–xxi; *bushi* Confucianism xxi. *See also* Buddhism (Zen)

caitta "mental states," 84–85

calculative: acts, 21; dualistic calculating mind, 32–33; reasoning, 16–17, 26–27, 30, 48

causality: universal, 112

chih "cleverness," 68

Chinese thought, 171; Ch'an, 96; contemporary, 5; cosmos, 65; in Japan, 75–76; self-consciousness, 71

Christianity, 184, 190; and capitalism, xxx; and Jung, xxvii; at war, 120–21; Christ, 155–56; Garden of Eden, 160; Judeo-Christian tradition, 82–83; Puritan, xxx; sin of, 160; Ten Commandments, 82–83, 109–10, 112. *See also* God

Chuang Tzu: "chaotification," 27, 67

citta "mind," 84–85

civilization, 11–12; mark of, 25; past, 11–12

climate, 147. *See also* environment; Watsuji

communal: awareness, 165–66; existence, 126–27, 130, 171; good, 190; interactive practices, 184, 186; solidarity, 146–47

communality: is mutuality, 138

communication: global, 194

community, 126–27; connectedness, 128–29; imbeddedness, 124–26; spirit, 185–86

comparative philosophy, 115; goal, 14

compassion: and cosmic ethics, 112–13; and ethical conduct, 92; and sympathy, 93; and teachings of Buddha, 109–10; and the sanctioning of war, 120–21; and universal obligations, 68–69; and will, 25–26; as being-the-world, 176–77; as foundation, 33; as natural Way, 30; as true wisdom, 88–89, 160–61; Buddhist, 160; from the standpoint of *śūnyatā*, 16–18; root, 162, 182; spontaneous arising, 27; state of awareness, 16–17, 180–81; unthinking, 16–17

compassionate: acts, 81, 163; concern, 80; identification, 16–17, 84–85; heart/critical mind, 190–91

concealing/revealing, 134. *See also* Heidegger

conduct: good, 162, 164–67

Confucian thought: as communal harmony; as social ideal, 71–73, 124; compatibility with Shintō 63; culture/tradition, 103; ethics, 164; in Japan, 76; sagehood, 65–66, 70; self, 65, 71–72; sincerity, 69–70, will (*zhi*), 72–73

Confucianism, xviii–xxviii; and centrality of human-heartedness, 33, 190; and Watsuji, 130; ethical core in Japan, 101; Chinese, 77; in Japan, 3–4, 37, 44, 65; introduction into Japan, 77; Taoist break from, 27; Neo-, 3–4, 74–75, 101

Confucius, 26–27, 45

conscious: abilities, 151

consciousness, 154, 158; communal, 165–66; dualistic-pure and

consciousness *(continued)*
    ordinary, 158; human, 152–53; of
    transition to *satori*, 149–50;
    ordinary/enlightened, 149–50;
    present, 151; two sides, 193
Cook, Francis, 28, 179–81
cosmic: consciousness, 165–66, 182;
    cosmic-interconnectedness, 68–69,
    112–14; ethics, 112–13
cosmos, 111, 198–99; absolute, 104–
    05 (*see also* universe); as Eden 182
creation: immanent, 104–05
cultivation: and control of desire,
    168–69; and Eastern traditions, 35;
    as Buddhist ideal, 104; of compas-
    sion, 94; in the Buddhist tradition,
    171; meditation, 58, 149–50; self,
    65–66, 68, 102–03, 107, 112–13,
    119–20; of ethical life, 88–89;
    shugyo, 170. *See also* meditation;
    enlightenment
cultural: assumptions, 12–13; climate,
    196; differences, 12–13, 183–84;
    foundations, 125–26; insight, 53–
    54; Japanese consciousness, 33, 37;
    legacy, 140–41; primal anticipa-
    tion, 54; traditions 5–6, 12–14
culture, 1–2; Buddhist, Confucian
    traditions, 183–84; corporate,
    138–39; cross, 8; deep, 4; East
    and West, 200–01; Eastern, 48–49;
    Japanese, 57–58, 65, 77, 103, 135–
    36; meditative, 152–53; of indi-
    vidualism, 140–41; resource, 61;
    shame, 48–49; Western, 36, 103,
    125– 26
cyberspace: electronic linkages, 183–
    84; ethics, 183–84

dāna "charity," 94–95
Daimōn, xiii
Danto, Arthur, 184; and *wu wei*, 24;
    atomistic view, 32–33; error, 19–20;
    moral philosophy, 16; *Mysticism
    and Morality*, 12–13; on Eastern

ethics, 6–7, 197–98; on the will,
    13–14, 199; on Western ethics, 27
Daoism. *See* Taoism
Dasein/Mitsein, 145
Davids, Rhys, 89
death, 134
demythologized universe, 59
dependent origination (interdepen-
    dent): co-dependent
    interconnectedness, 86; Indra's
    Net, 123–24; *Mahāyāna* doctrine,
    28–29
Descartes, xxvi, 42, 146–47, 203n 6
De Mente, Boye, 144
dharma, 84–86, 9, 109–10, 115–16;
    direct passing, 100
Dharmapala, Anagarika, 93
Dharmasiri, Gunapala: existence and
    debt, 87; extinction, 91–92; on
    Buddhist asceticism, 80; on the
    three metaphysical truths, 78; Raft
    Parable, 89; sense of reverence for
    all life, 88; vow of bodhisattva, 92
dhyana, 15
direct: experience, 88–89, 150;
    intuition, 156; pure, 150. *See also*
    pure experience
divine: (the), 156; activity, 182, 186;
    Ara-Mitama/Nigi-Mitama rough/
    divine spirits, 42–43, 52–53; as us,
    43; beauty, 55–56; creative act of
    self-expression, 182; directly
    underfoot, 180–81; energy, 49–51;
    everything is, 158–59; expression,
    168–69; God and Satan, 186;
    interconnectedness, 59; manifesta-
    tion, 96–97, 104, 177, 180–81;
    mysterious, 75; non-dual wonder
    of, 107, 182; origin 109–10;
    sincerity, 68–69; soul, 41–42; spirit,
    40–41, 42, 48, 55, 68–69; self and
    other, 46–47; toward and away
    from, 186; ultimate, 115–16;
    universality, 54; universe, 104–05
Doctrine of the Mean, 68–70

Dōgen: and ego, 168–69; and mind, 154; and moral action, 190; and non-production of evil, 176–77, 227n 38; and practice/enlightenment, 102–03, 108–09; and precepts, 175; and time, 180–81; classical philosopher, 174; good and evil, 178–79, 180–81; transformation and *zazen*, 179–80
dosa "aversion," 86
dualism: of mind and body, 19; non-dualism, 181
dukkha "suffering," 78
dwelling: and Heidegger, 194; in the world, 182, 202; in the world ecologically, 25–26

East Asian thought: ethics, 35, 192; character development, 194–95; influence of West, 200–01; inseparability of mind and body, 170; medicine, 184; metaphysical horizons, 197–98; self, 65; sincerity/cheerfulness, 35, 68; spiritual and secular, 35; the East, 185–86
East/West, xxii, xxvii; and Danto, 6–7; as contradictory identities, 201–02; blending, 119–20; change, 194–95; culture, 5–6; East vs West, 5; ethical difference, 82–83, 113–14; experience, 151–52; global communication, 194; globalism, 200–01; ideals, 111–14; meeting place, 192; moral agency, 109–10; perspective, 167
Eckhart, Meister, 157, 159
ecological, 5–6, 58; consciousness/conscience, 56–59, 200; cultural environment, 52; ethics, 116–17; environment 49–50; in Shintō, 55–56; living, 25; reformation, 61
ecology: and Shintō, xvi; deep or transpersonal, 197–98; interconnection, 123
Eliot, Charles, 62

emptiness, 104–05, 123
energy: divine, 108–09; field like, 87
enlightenment: *satori* xxix; and Buddhism, 114; and *nirvāna*, 96–97; and *satori*, 112–13; and Zen, 100; as cultivation of ethical life, 88–89; as practice, 175; as transformation, 149–50, 191–92; direct, 101–02; enlightened person, 158–59; experience, 101, 104, 107–09; imperative for, 178; morality as foundation of, 94; nature, 160; path to, 94–95, 160, 193; recognition of God, humanity and nature, 182; requirement of, 184; supreme, 95; transmission, 109–10; wisdom, 80
environment, 159; climate, 145; holistic cultural, 195–96; interconnectedness with, 58, 61
environmental: influences, 144–45
epistemological: anticipation, 133
epistemology, xix; Shintō, 62; Zen, 62
eternal, 104–05. *See also* absolute; cosmos; form; nothingness
eternity: of the moment, 182
ethical: achiever, 184; activity, 154–55; awareness, 88; behaviour, 84–85, 194; conduct, 91; imperative, 38–39, 178; living, 89; practice, 149–50, 197; maxims, 136–37; standard East/West, 184; system, 112; teachings, 101–02, 184; theory, 195–96
ethics, xi, 15; and nature, 61; and virtue, 82; Buddhist, 84–85; cross cultural understanding, 6–7; eastern, xii; good and evil, xii; ground of, 109–10; in Japan, 33, 77; in Zen, 99; imbedded, 184; is about, 189–90, 197–98; Japanese, 124, 125–26, 129–30, 149–50; of benevolence, 134; of identification, 160; of individualism, 125; of

ethics *(continued)*
    spontaneous compassion, 134–35;
    of the individual, 146; root, 178–
    79; *sīla*, 90–91; social, 101, 187–88;
    worldly, 168. *See also* compassion;
    ecological
evil, xii, 163; and Japanese culture,
    103; and Shintō, 52, 56–57; and
    willingness, 23; as individual
    power, 160–61; cosmic force, 182;
    desire to do, 112–13, 176–77;
    dualistic state of consciousness,
    26–27; is delusion, 29–30, 104–05;
    not original, 186; non-production,
    175–77, 228n 68; real/genuine,
    167; Taoism/Buddhism, 24
evolution, 18
existence: as debt, 87; is empty, 111
Existential: ism, 167; impermanence,
    181; situation, 168–69
experience: enlightenment, 106;
    originary, 106, 112–14; pure, 106,
    116–17, 150. *See also* enlighten-
    ment; meditation; direct

family, 143. *See also* loyalty
Feldman, Christina, 91–92
feudal: isolationism, 63
filial piety, 143–44
Five Relationships, 74
form: lessness, 109–10. *See also*
    universe; cosmos; nothingness;
    eternity
foundational renovation, 12–13
Fox, Douglas, 176–79
Fox, Warwick, 198–99
fudo "climate," 197
Fujiwara Teika, 172–73
fusion of horizons: mutuality of
    influence, 118; ethics, 13–14;
    East/West, 80, 200–02

Gadamer, Hans-Georg, 12–13
Gandhi, Mahatma, 45
genuine; human caring, 189–90
gestalt: culture, 145

God: absolute law, 167; and evil,
    104–05, 176–77; and Jesus, 45;
    and Nishida, 156–57; and pure
    experience, 150; and Satan, 186–
    87; and western mysticism, 134–
    35; as personality, 158–59; as
    reality, 159; away from, 187; body,
    55–56; creative expression of, 182;
    divine love, 160–61; divine spirit,
    45; everything is manifestation,
    109–10; faith in, 125–26; filled,
    154; God is dead, 103; God-hood,
    186; God vs Satan, 56–57, 186;
    ground of reality, 156; pantheistic
    interpretation, 155–56; salvation
    and sin, 48–49; self-awareness, 159;
    self-expression, 192; Ten Com-
    mandments, 109–10; word of,
    112–13
good and evil, xii; Abe, 16; Carter,
    30; and pure experience, 175–76;
    and Taoism, 24; and Shintō, 39;
    and *śūnyatā*, 19; arising in
    betweenness, 133; as directions in
    nothingness, 187; as neither, 104–
    05; as relative, 178, 180–81; as self-
    expression of the real, 182; as
    valuational perspective, 104;
    beyond, 89, 103, 111, 115, 176–77;
    distinction, 178–79; evil is delu-
    sion, 29–30; good and bad, 85–86;
    goodness, 4–41, 84–85; fundamen-
    tal, 160–61; supreme good, 16. *See
    also* evil
good; as foundationally transforma-
    tive, 107–08
Gotama, 79–80. *See also* Buddha
guijin "total exertion," 181

haiku, xxiv, 51, 131–33
Hall, David L. and Ames, Roger T.,
    71
Hamada Hiroshi, 138–41
Harada Daiun Sōgaku, 118–19
harai "divine interconnectedness,"
    44–45, 47

harmonious: environment, 143
harmony, 57–58, 131–32, 142
Hearn, Lafcadio, xv
Hegel, George Wilhelm Friedrich, 132–33
Heidegger, Martin, xxviii; and nature, 5–6; and dwelling, 194, 202 (*see also* dwelling; Watsuji); clearing, 133; homeground, 134; on language, 12–13; revealing/concealing, 107–08, 220n 17; spatiality, 144–45
Herbert, Jean, 37–38, 41–42, 44–45
Hiroshima, 120–21
hisng "good," 67
historical: connectedness, 146
hito "human being," 41–42
Hobbes, Thomas, 136–37
homeground, 14, 134–35
homeostasis, 46–47; homogeneous, 59; homogeneous ethics, 183–84
hsin "heart," 21, 25
Hsun Tzu, 67
Hua-yen, 28
human heartedness, 18, 33, 188–89; *jen, tz'u, kokoro, karunā mettā*, 25–26; compassion, 33 human: rights, 194
humanistic: psychology, 197–98
Husserl, Edmund, 152–53, 158

"I": the non-substantive self, 86; without boundary, 86
ideal (the), 167; Buddhist, 104; Confucian, 65–66, 71–72; cultural, 103; enlightened state, 16–17; exemplary human being, 72–73, 82, 101; of betweenness, 134–35; Japanese, 71; *michi* as path of, 44–46; mind/heart, 16; moral, 68, 72–73; state of mind, 175; striving for, 129–30; world, 84
ideals: of tradition, 191–92
identity: contradictory, 160–61; empathetic, 185; of self-contradiction, 127–29, 132–33, 138, 154–55,

158–59, 174, 181, 186, 201–02; principle of, 168–69; social, 197; with all things, 177; with the one, 160–61. *See also* unity of opposites; Self; pure/immediate experience
Iishi Shrine, 59
immanent, 104–05
immediate: experience, 155–56; immediacy of pure experience, 151–52. *See also* pure; experience
impermanent: even Buddha, God and the Absolute are, 181; existence, 181
Indian: thought, 171
individual (the), 65, 133; communal lives, 168; ethics, 146; relatedness, 65–66; transformation, 65, 80
individualism and communalism, 165–66; cult of, 125–26; culture of, 140–41; isolation, 125–26; modern emphasis, 197; western, 125, 129–30
individuality, 131–32, 160–61, 165–66
ineffable, 113–14. *See also* nothingness
infinite: reality, 156; unity and opposition, 154–55; unifying power, 156, 163
inheritance, 7; creation of and altering of through the environment, 168–69; Japanese, 1–3; perspectives, 12
intellectual, 77; intuition, 65–66, 153; unifying activity, 153
interconnectedness: self, 185–86; social/community, 124, 146. *See also* Buddhist/Confucian/ Japanese thought
interconnection, 185
intuition; action, 173–74; direct, 156; direct awareness, 29–30; intuitively active, 16–17. *See also* action intuition
itsu-kushi-bi "benevolence," 48
Izanagi, 52–53
Izutsu Toshihiko, 27, 206n 39

James, William, 150
Japanese: adaptation, 64; business,
   140–41; contexualism, 138;
   cultural consciousness, 33; culture
   and religion, 57–58; ethics, 124,
   130–31, 147, 184, 194–95, 197 (*see
   also* ethics); genius, 151; individuality, 127; isolationism, 183–84;
   love of nature, 116–17; mind, 35;
   perspectivism, 141–43; social
   conformity, 125; society, 138;
   syncretism, 142; tradition, 38–39,
   63, 171–72; uniqueness, 201–02
Japanese thought: Chu Hsi, 74–75;
   Confucianism, 73–74, 107;
   communal harmony as social
   ideal, 71, 72–73; sincerity, 70. *See
   also* Confucian
jen "human-heartedness," 65–66, 72–
   73, 82–83, 216n 17
Jesus, 45–46, 92
Jewel Net of Indra, 28
jinkaku "psyche," xii; enlighened
   personality, xxix
Jiwara Shunzei, 171–72
Jōshū, 106, 119
Jung, Carl, xxvii
jukai "receiving the precepts," 175–76

kairitsu "ethical living," 189–90
Kakichi Kadowaku, 40–41
kami, xiv, 58, 61; and Buddha xxiii;
   animistic and pantheistic, 55–56;
   as formless, xv; cults, 6–7, 37, 62;
   communal relationships, 37–38;
   kami/God, 40–41; heavenly/great,
   44–46, 55; infused, 154, 189–90;
   mythology, 143–44; nature, 42, 49–
   50, 57–58, 189–90; worship of, xvii
kannagara-no-michi "the way of the
   kami," 44
kansha "spirit of thankfulness," 48
Kant, Immanuel, xxviii–xxix, 26–27,
   135–37, 200; comparison to
   Buddha, 88; post-, 152–53
Kantian: morality, 138

Kao Tzu, 67
Kapleau, Philip, 101–102, 107
karma 13–14, 103, 112; karmic
   inheritance, 104–05, 119–20
karunā "compassion," 94, 178–79
Kasulis, Thomas P., 25, 175–76
Katsuki Sekida, 105–06
kenshin "to offer one's person," 48
Keown, Damien: and *dharmas,* 84–
   86; and the Buddhist moral life,
   94; and the Raft Parable, 89–91;
   on Buddhist ethics, 81
ki, xx
King, Sallie B., 2–3, 48
King, Winston, 84–85
King of Kalinga, 95
Kitagawa, Joseph, 57–58
knowledge, 152–53
kōan, 132–33, 190–92. *See also*
   Buddhism (Zen); paradox
koban "police box," 185–86
Kohlberg, Lawrence, 83
kokoro "mind and heart" 21, 44–45,
   130–31, 188–90; human-hearted,
   22, 223n 13
KsāntiPāramitā "Perfection of
   Patience," 96

Lao Tzu xiii, 25, 68; unlearning of
   rules, 102–03, spontaneous
   "natural" flow, 102–03
Lévi-Strauss, Claude, xv
li, 27; ritualism, 66–67; filial piety,
   68–69
lobha "emotional attachments," 86
logic, 159; of either/or, both/and,
   123; identity of self-contradiction,
   136–37, 187–88; objects, 187–88
love, 162, 164–65, 168–69. *See also*
   compassion
Loy, David, 22–23, 26–27
loyalty: genuine piety, 135–36, 143–44

MacIntyre, Alastair, 194–95, 197
makashikan "great cessation and
   discernment," 171–72.

makoto: as genuine piety, 48, 143–44; as metaphysical principle, 70; intrinsic value, 164; in most Oriental philosophies, 47, 69–70, 135–36, 210n 40, 210n 41, 223n 13

Marxist, xxi, xxii

Maslow, Abraham, 197–99, 200

Mason, J.W.T.: on ecology in Shintō, 55–57, 58–59; on humankind, 39; primal cultural anticipation 54; rough and gentle spirits, 42–43, 53–54; Shintō and evil, 52

McFague, Sallie, 55–57

Mead, George Herbert, 71

meditation, xxviii, 80; and Dōgen, 108–09; and harmony, 105–06; and precepts, 103; and the transformation of consciousness, 174; and wisdom, 171; Five Perceptions, 96–97; ideal sites, 80–81, 96–97; practice, 108–09; *zazen/kinhin,* 149–50, 173, 175; Zen, 200–01

meditative: practices, 174, 184, 189–90

Meiji period, xxi, 37; Meiji Shrine, xxi; Meiji Emperor, xvi; government, xxii; restoration, 64

Mencius, 24, 66; Four Beginnings, 67

metaphysics, 87; insight, 88–89; Shintō, 62; three truths, 77; Zen, 62

mettā "love," 26, 82, 94, 216n 17

michi, "sacred energy of cosmos," 44–47

microcosm/macrocosm, 65–66

militarism, 190

Mishima Yukio, 29, 204n 7

misogi shuh "purification under a waterfall," 57–58

moha "ignorance," 78, 80

Mohammed, 45–46

Moore, James A., Jr., 2

moral actions: law, 111, 166–67, 192; agent, 109–10; and spirituality in Buddhism, 77; artist, 174; behaviour, 137; demands, 198–99; education, 52; evaluations, 40; forces, 187; goodness, 168; guidance, 113–14; ideal, 68; imperative, 16–17; categorical, 88; improvement, 185–86; institutions, 196; life, 107; morality, 19–20, 79–80; ontology, 196; ought, 167; prescription, 200; rules, 93, 176–78; situations, 43; spirit of community, 185–86; standpoint in Zen, 101; systems, 168; morality, 134, 166–67; as superfluous, 199; beyond, 101–02; for Watsuji, 134–35; foundation, 155–56; natural and spontaneous, 200; of Buddhist precepts, 178; out of pure experience, 200; perfection, 117

Motoori Norinaga, 49–50; *mono no aware,* 50

muditā "sympathetic joy," 94

Munro, Donald, 66

musubi "spirit of birth," 42–43

mutual: identity 28–39, 57–58; interaction, 86; interactive negation, 128–29; interconnectedness, 87. *See also* dependent

mutuality, 168–69; influence, 183–84; interconnectedness, 138–39

mystical: perspective, 157

Nachi Falls, 54

Naess, Arne, 194–95, 197–99; on intrinsic value 199–200

Nāgārjuna, 191–92

Nagasaki, 120–21

nakama "system of relations guiding human association," 130

Nakamura Hajime, 28–29, 31, 53–54, 57–58, 73

Nansen or Nan-ch'uan, 105–06

natural, 46; affection/sympathy, 93; and spontaneous self-expression, 176–77, 187–88; and spontaneous morality, 200; flow of Tao, 102–03;

natural *(continued)*
world, 115. *See also* pure experience

nature, 40, 49–50, 155–56, 164–65; as free, 199; as material at hand, 194; deep, 180–81, 187–88; essential, 106; as *kami*, 55–57; original, 100; state of, 136–37; true, 111; universal spirit, 54–55; wonder, 60

negation: of negation, 134

nibbāna "*nirvāna*," 90–91

Nicholas of Cusa, 186, 228n 3

Nietzsche, Friedrich Wilhelm, 103

nihonjinron, 201–02. *See also* Ueda

nikon, 108–09

ningen "human being": and community, 128–29, 138; and Hamada, 138–39; and Watsuji, 125–27,165–66; both individual and social, 133, 136–37; in time and space, 145; historical connectedness, 146–47

nirodha "extinction," 91–92

nirvāna, xxii, 89; as a purely ethical state, 90–91; as ideal personality, xxix; "Golden Rule," 22–23, 80–81; *summum bonum* of Buddhist ethics, 88–89

Nishida Kitarō, xxviii–xxix, 30, 174; and enlightenment, 149–50, 159; and Francis Cook, 179–80; and nature, 115–16; basho, 128–29; compassion, 162; consciousness, 157–59; epistemology, 162; free will, 160; fusion of horizons, 200–02; Garden of Eden, 159; God/Absolute, 155–56, 158–60; good conduct, 163; ethics as originating impulse, 187–88; identity as synthesis, 132–33; identity of self-contradiction, 127–28, 147; immediacy of pure experience, 151–52; intellectual/ action intuition, 153, 200; *kokoro*, 188–89; morality 155–56, 164–67; *ningen*,

165–66; on good and evil, 186; paradox of unity, 154–55; personality, 170; pure experience, 150–67; radical understanding of religion, 168; the absolute in the form of Satan, 134; the philosopher, 95; unifying activity, 153, 163

Nishitani Keiji, 153, 155–56

Nitobe Inazō, 48–49

Noddings, Nell, 31–32

nothingness: absolute, 68–69, 154; and divine and God, 154; and individual and social, 133; and *nirvāna*, 80; as *basho*, 152–53; as betweenness, 134–35; as centripetal, 187; as divine, 186; as higher unity, 158–59; formlessness, 109–10 in ethics, 134; of *nirvāna*, 96–97; "radical emptiness," 17–18; symbolic, 123. *See also* absolute; divine; eternity; interconnectedness

Odin, Steve, 125–26, 143; on spatiality, 144–45

Ōkawa Shūmei, 74–75

Okinoshima: island of, xvii

Okuninushi, 52–53

Old Testament (The), xii, xxvii

Omagatsumi "Great Evil Doer," 52–53

Omiwa Shrine, xvii, 58

oneness, 158

Ono Sokyo, 59

Orient and Oriental thought, 12–13, 16; attitude, 19–20; mind, 26–27

original: divinity, 194–95; goodness, 186; originary experience, 106; purity, 61; sin, 167; unity, 128, 158–59; undifferentiatedness, 158–59

originating: impulse, 187–88

origination: co-dependent origination, 123–24. *See also* dependent *oyakudachi*. *See* Hamada

paññā "wisdom," 79–80, 90–91
Parable of the Raft, 89
paradox, 187–88; *kōan,* 107; Japanese culture, 172–73; unity, 154–55; Zen, 112–13
pāramitā "perfection," 94–95; practice of, 94–95
pavatti "devotion," 94
perfection, 107–108; perfections, 94–97
personality: God's, 159, 165–66; enlightened, 164; of absolute intrinsic value, 164, 170
perspectivism: Japanese, 141
phenomenal: absolute, 53–55, 57–58; noumenal, 152–53
Picken, Stuart, 37–39, 44–45, 56–58
Plato, xvi, xxvi, 92, 192, 194–95; forms, 145
Pound, Roscoe, 5
practice, 97, 171–72, 175; meditational, 174; spontaneous, 172–73. *See also* enlightenment
precepts: Four Noble Truths and Eightfold Path, 109–10, 12; and self-cultivation, 119–20; as ritual, 190; five, 170; learning, 179–80; practice, 175; not moral commandments, 107. *See also* Buddha; Buddhism; Confucianism
primordial: identification, 102–03
Prince Shōtoku, 64, 138–40
principle: identity of self-contradiction, 168–69
profound: person, 69–70
protection: of society, 185–86
psyche, xii, xxix
psychology: humanistic, 197–98
pure experience: and morality, 200, 202; as foundation of good conduct, 164; as immediate awareness, 150, 152–54, 156; as non-immersion in, 181; experiential realization, 166–67; Nishida's, 150; nothingness, 160. *See also* James, William
p'u "uncarved block," 25

Reader, Ian, 44
reality: is spiritual, 158–59; noumenal, 154; permanent, 104; pure experience, 155–56; realism, 105–06; true, 154; ultimate, 115–16, 162, 166–67
Reasoner, Paul, 69–70
religion: and morality, 150; for Nishida, 155–56
religious: consciousness, 187–88; demand, 158–59; ethics, 150; to be, 160; exoteric traditions, 199. *See also* ethics
religiosity: is centripetal, 187
riki philosophy, xix, 203n 3
rinri "ethics," 130
ritual: Confucian practice, 71–72, death, 77; pagan or primitive rituals, western view, 59
Ryōanji, xxiv, 123–124

salvation, 80
samsara and *nirvāna,* 13–14, 16, 19, 53–54, 91–92, 154, 200; immanent/transcendent, 68–69; emptying, 123
samurai, 143–44, 183–84
satori, xxix, 108–09, 112–13, 119. *See also* enlightenment
Schwartz, Benjamin, 25–26
Schweitzer, Albert, 109–10
self-consciousness: cultivation and transformation, 175–76; of ultimate, 159. *See also* cultivation
self: as narrow and atomistic, 199; awareness, 153; autonomy, 71–72; contradictory identity, 181; sphere of, 187; expanded, 200; negation, 151; no-mindedness, 151; other-centeredness, 16–17; path, 190; selfless compassion, 16–17; selfless self-centeredness, 16–17, 23; transformation, 192; *tz'u,* 68; Zen Buddhist, 200. *See also* identity; transformation
Shaner, David, 56–57

Shintō, xiv–xviii, 135–36, 139–40; and Blacker, 59; and Buddhism, xviii; and Confucianism, 73; and ecology, 61–62; and humanity, 129–30; and Mason, 52; and Nakamura Hajime, 53–54; and Satomi-san, 2, 4; as source for Japanese ethics, 36, 131; and Zen ethics, 115; centrality of human-heartedness, 33; communality, 65; ethical living of lives, 101, 189–90, 196; ethics, 164; festivals and tree metaphor, 37–38; is the center, 46–47; *kami*-cults, 6–7; metaphysics, 38–39, 77; monism, 56–57, 62; nature is divine, 49–50; religion, 37; rough and smooth, 161; soul *tama*, 41–42; shrines, 2–3, 60; Shrine/State, 190; State and Ancient, 36, 39, 54

shoakumakusa "non-production of evil," 175–76

Shrine of the Falling Waterfall. *See* Nachi Falls

shugyo "personal cultivation," 170

sīla "morality," 79–81, 90–91

sīlaPāramitā "Perfection of Precepts," 95

sincerity: absolute/intrinsic or extrinsic, 163–65; and integrity, 202; *ch'eng*, 69–70; intrinsic value, 164. *See also makoto*; East Asian thought; divine

Smith, Warren W., Jr., 74–76

social, 133; ethics, 187–88; forms, 125; identity, 197; interconnectedness, 124, 136–37; relationships, 127; web of interconnectedness as between-ness, 138

Socrates, xiii

Socratic humility, 7

sonzai "human existence," 138, 145, 146–47

Sōseki Natsume, 125–26

spatial: betweenness, 125–27

spiritual: achiever, 184; background, 196; knowledge, 106; monism, 58; that which leads to the moral, 196; transmission, 171–72

spontaneity: as amoral, 118; Buddha's, 91; freedom, 30; impulse, 84–85; in discipline, 131–32; new, 43; original, 30; practice in community ritual, 71–73; rigorous practice, 172–73; thinking, 22–23; universal, 19–21, 27, 48

spontaneous, 140–41, 154–55; abandonment, 134; action, 102–03, 140–41, 178, 180–81; compassion, 90–91, 113–14, 134–35, 185; human-heartedness, 188–89; practice, 172–73. *See also* spontaneous expression

spontaneous expression: and Plato, 192; and Suzuki, 115; as self-expression, 164; of God and the universe, 166–67; of person, 155–56, 164–65; will without willing, 94–95

St. Anselm, 42

subject/object, 151

suicide, 137, 143–44

sumie, 51

summum bonum, 88–89

śūnyatā , 15, 16–19

Susano-no-Mikoto, 52–53

Suseri-bime: Susano's daughter, 52–53

sūtras, 100

suttas, 81; *Karanīya Mettā-Sutta*, 88

Suzuki D.T., xxviii; and Japanese cultural life, 61–62; and *satori*, 108–09; on art, 123; on nature, 114–16; on the Golden Rule, 22–23; during the war, 116–19; will in Zen, 18

tamashi "spirit bestowed by the *kami*," 41–42

Tao Te Ching, 19–20, 68, 101–03. See also *Book of Changes*

Taoism: amoral, 15; and Danto, 19–20, 32–33; and ethical influences, 27; and evil, 25; and non-violence, 24; and Shintō, 36–37; as a religious influence on Shintō, 44; break from Confucian rigidity, 103; classical Taoism, 54; heavenly Way, 13–14; Indian Buddhism, 77; in Zen 6–7; influences, xiii, xix; methods, xxvii–xxviii; philosophical origin, xii

Taoism: critic of Confucianism, 22–23; self cultivation, 102–03; *tz'u,* 82–83

Tathāgata, 81

Taylor, Charles, 194–96

tea ceremony, 2–3, 51, 149–50. *See also* art

Teeuvenn, Mark, 37

Tokugawa officials, 74–75

traditional: history, 197. *See also* culture

transcendence, 17–18; of ethical values, 89; moral, 194; nirvānic, 96; transcendental, 91–92

transformation, 132–33, 164; growth, 178; of consciousness in meditation, 172–73; of potentiality, 179–80; is endless, 192; self-, 155–56, 185–86, 191–92; state of no-mindness, 173–74; techniques, 192

transpersonal: deep ecology, 197–98; self, 200

tsutsushimi "reverence," 48

Tu Wei-Ming, 65

tvaritam "generosity," 95

t'zu, 26, 82, 216n 17

U Thittila, 216n 17

Ueda Shizuteru, 200–01

ultimate/formless, 104–05; reality of universe, 166–67

United States, xii, xvii, xxix–xxx

unity of opposites, 32–33, 128, 157; in mutual interactive negation, 128–29; unifying activity, 153–54,

156, 158–59. *See also* identity: of self-contradiction; intellectual: intuition

unity: higher, 158–59; infinite, 154; paradox, 154–55

universal: law, 138; love, 92

universe, 104–05, 153, 156, 186; co-creators, 169–70. *See also* cosmos; eternity

upekkhā "equanimity," 94

uyamau "showing proper respect," 48

vacuum, 27

valuational cluster, 144–45

value, 164; intrinsic in being, 87; perspective, 104–05; valuational awareness, 104

vedanā "feeling," 91

Victoria, Brian, 117–18

vikalpa "bifurcation of experience," 22

vipallāsa "false values," 91

vīrya "vigour," 96

Vogel, Ezra, 3–4

voice: of the voiceless, 176–77. *See also* nothingness; absolute

wa "group harmony," 48, 135–36, 143–44

waka "thirty-one syllable poetry," 171–73

wakaru "to understand," 128

wakeru "to divide," 128

Walpola, Rahula, 78, 83, 91–92

Wáng Yángmíng, xxiii, xxix

war, 120–21

Wargo, Robert J.J., 36, 37–39

Watsuji Tetsurō, 165–66; and Dōgen, 175; and Hobbes, 136–37; and *mahoto,* 17, 161, *wakuru,* 128; and Yuasa, 170; betweenness, 125–30, 145, 146–47; crossroads, 183–86; cultural climate, 196; Japanese ethics, 124–26; on the family, 143; on the individual and the social, 136–37; Nishida and synthesis,

Watsuji Tetsurō *(continued)* 132–33; nothingness in ethics, 134; rejection of traditional norms, 195–96; sincerity, truth, and trust, 135–37; *wa*, 144–45

Watsuji Tetsurō on Japanese culture, xiv; *Climate and Culture,* xvi; Robert Bellah, xviii; *aidagara,* xxvi–xxviii; on relationships, xxi–xxii

Way: of Heaven, 69–70. *See also* Buddhist thought

Welch, Holmes, 20

Weltanschauung, 36

western thought, 35, 125–26, 145; contemporary moral, 195–96; God "The Father," 44; influence of East, 200–02; mystical traditions, 134–35, 157; *nirvāna,* 91–92; philosophy, 201–01; religion, 37–38, 56–57; self, 71; selfhood, 145; spatiality, 144–45

western: the West, 169–70, 185; analytical/rational, 152–53; assumptions, 150, 185; business, 140–41; countries, 137; individualism, 125; influences, 183–84; perspectivism, 141; pessimism, 53–54; philosophy: history of, 151–52; psychology, 200; religion, 150; science, 185; society, 140–41, 143; sports training, 173; *waka* "least likely," 171–72

Whitehill, James, 101, 112–13

will, 5, 19–20; aggressive will, 18, 199; Confucian (*zhi*), 72–73;

emancipated, 15; free, 15; freedom, 182; free will and evil, 160–61; human, 15; in dualistic states, 22–23; itself, 16–17; *kami* 44–45, 48; nature of, 14; of God, 166–67; primal, 19; self, 153; without willing, 94–95; Zen, 18

wisdom, 88–89, 91–92, 170; of compassion and unity, 174; of compassion, 160–61, 171–72; enlightenment, 118; reached in the practice of meditation, 171. *See also paññā*

world: nexus, 16–17; contemporary, 196; in flux, 78; modern procedures, 178

wu wei, xii, 19–20, 24, 68; laws of aggression, 21

Yamada Kōun Roshi, 107

Yamaori Tetsuo, 49–50

Yasaka Shrine, xxii, 52–53

yīn/yáng; xvi; of soul, 190–91

Yokoi Yūhō, 175

Young, J.Z., 8–9

Yuasa Yasuo, 126–27, 149–50, 170–73

yugen "profound mystery," 172–73

Zarathustra, 103

zazen "seated meditation," 175–76, 179–80. *See also* meditation

Zen Buddhism, xxiii–xxvi, 99–121. *See also* Buddhism (Zen)

Made in the USA
Lexington, KY
01 March 2012